God Is Undead

ALSO AVAILABLE FROM BLOOMSBURY

Atheism and Agnosticism, Peter A. Huff
Lacan, Miguel de Beistegui
Christian Atheism, Slavoj Žižek

God Is Undead

Psychoanalysis for Unbelievers

**Lorenzo Chiesa and
Adrian Johnston**

BLOOMSBURY ACADEMIC
LONDON • NEW YORK • OXFORD • NEW DELHI • SYDNEY

BLOOMSBURY ACADEMIC
Bloomsbury Publishing Inc, 1385 Broadway, New York, NY 10018, USA
Bloomsbury Publishing Plc, 50 Bedford Square, London, WC1B 3DP, UK
Bloomsbury Publishing Ireland, 29 Earlsfort Terrace, Dublin 2, D02 AY28, Ireland

BLOOMSBURY, BLOOMSBURY ACADEMIC and the Diana logo are trademarks of Bloomsbury Publishing Plc

First published in Great Britain 2025

Copyright © Lorenzo Chiesa and Adrian Johnston, 2025

Lorenzo Chiesa and Adrian Johnston have asserted their right under the Copyright, Designs and Patents Act, 1988, to be identified as Authors of this work.

For legal purposes the Acknowledgements on p. vii constitute an extension of this copyright page.

Cover design: Ben Anslow

All rights reserved. No part of this publication may be: i) reproduced or transmitted in any form, electronic or mechanical, including photocopying, recording or by means of any information storage or retrieval system without prior permission in writing from the publishers; or ii) used or reproduced in any way for the training, development or operation of artificial intelligence (AI) technologies, including generative AI technologies. The rights holders expressly reserve this publication from the text and data mining exception as per Article 4(3) of the Digital Single Market Directive (EU) 2019/790.

Bloomsbury Publishing Plc does not have any control over, or responsibility for, any third-party websites referred to or in this book. All internet addresses given in this book were correct at the time of going to press. The author and publisher regret any inconvenience caused if addresses have changed or sites have ceased to exist, but can accept no responsibility for any such changes.

A catalogue record for this book is available from the British Library.

A catalog record for this book is available from the Library of Congress.

ISBN: HB: 978-1-3505-1604-5
PB: 978-1-3505-1605-2
ePDF: 978-1-3505-1606-9
eBook: 978-1-3505-1607-6

Typeset by Deanta Global Publishing Services Chennai India
Printed and bound in Great Britain

For product safety related questions contact productsafety@bloomsbury.com.

To find out more about our authors and books visit www.bloomsbury.com and sign up for our newsletters.

Contents

Acknowledgements vii

Introduction: Not ending with the end of the end of religion 1

Lorenzo Chiesa

Divine ignorance: Jacques Lacan and Christian atheism 21

Adrian Johnston

Psychoanalysis and agnostic atheism 111

Lorenzo Chiesa

Conclusion: The modest absolute: Or, why I am not an agnostic (or even an agnostic atheist) 189

Adrian Johnston

Notes 215
Bibliography 276
Index 294

Acknowledgements

Among many comrades and friends, both colleagues and students, who have enriched this book by means of mostly locked-down dialogue in adverse circumstances, I would like to particularly thank Gioele P. Cima, Matthew Collins, Moritz Herrmann, Dominiek Hoens, Paul Livingston, Frank Ruda, the participants of the 'New Leading Thinkers' course organized by Chris Fynsk at the European Graduate School (especially Katherine Everitt and Paris Lavidis), the participants of the 'Lacan and Truth: The Unfuckable Partner' workshop organized by Moritz Herrmann and Jan Weise at the Goethe University in Frankfurt, the participants of the 'Lacan in Scotland' seminar organized by Amanda Diserholt and Calum Neill, and the participants of the 'Newcastle Festival of Philosophy' organized by the Newcastle Philosophy Society.

A special thanks goes to Slavoj Žižek, whose faithful belief in the present book made its publication possible against an underhanded inquisitorial attempt to silence it.

Needless to say, Adrian Johnston opens this list of acknowledgements as *Unglaubensgenosse* zero. Last but first ('but not least' is not enough), Danka Štefan closes it, for still bearing with me during countless research nights, weekends and holidays, and for obsessively testing together some far-out ideas.

Lorenzo Chiesa

I would like to begin by thanking those institutions and organizations that hosted presentations by me of portions of *God Is Undead*. These include the Departments of Philosophy at DePaul University, the New School for Social Research, the University of New Mexico, and Villanova University; the Department of Psychology at Duquesne University; the Department of Psychosocial and Psychoanalytic Studies at the University of Essex; the Institute of Philosophy of the Scientific Research Centre of the Slovenian Academy of Sciences and Arts, Ljubljana, Slovenia; and the Mahindra Humanities Center at Harvard University. The participants and audiences at these speaking engagements provided me with invaluable questions, comments and feedback on various ideas contained in this book.

Also, two relatively short excerpts from an earlier draft of my half of the main body of *God Is Undead* appeared in the journals *Filozofski Vestnik* and *Problemi*.

These are 'Lacan and Monotheism: Not Your Father's Atheism, Not Your Atheism's Father', *Problemi International* (ed. Simon Hajdini), vol. 3, no. 3, 2019, pp. 109–41; and 'Working-Through Christianity: Lacan and Atheism', *Filozofski Vestnik*, vol. 40, no. 1, 2020, pp. 109–38. I would like to thank the editors for allowing modified versions of these texts to be included here.

I am deeply grateful to Slavoj Žižek in particular for his enthusiasm for and support of this book project, both intellectually and practically. Additionally, while working on *God Is Undead*, I benefited greatly from a number of conversations about Lacan and religion with one of my good friends, namely, Rick Boothby. Finally, without my beloved partner Kathryn Wichelns, neither this book nor my life overall would be what they are; she means everything and more to me.

Adrian Johnston

Introduction

Not ending with the end of the end of religion

Lorenzo Chiesa

1

Undeniably, over the last three decades, there has been a wide-ranging resurgence of critical interest in religion, motivated by an equally indisputable return of things religious to the centre stage of current affairs and globalized geopolitics. The ensuing debates have coalesced into two general atheistic tendencies that compete with one another for intellectual hegemony but are, to different degrees, increasingly proving sterile in the face of a mounting wave of belligerent theism. The first, sustained by a distinctly Anglo-American hubris, limits itself to a flat, quasi-tautological and politically liberal-conservative denunciation of delusional irrationality, which remains totally oblivious to the lessons imparted by the dialectic of the Enlightenment. The second carries out a more sophisticated and, at face value, cosmopolitan appropriation of theological categories into a nominally lay and progressive agenda, which nonetheless still underestimates the impasses of secularization it otherwise acknowledges.

For the former tendency, 'faith is belief in spite of, even perhaps because of, lack of evidence' and thus 'very, very dangerous'.[1] However, as soon as this broad stance moderates its paternalistic invectives and attempts to adopt a constructive tone, it paradoxically, and somewhat grotesquely, finds it very difficult to abide by the constraints it itself imposes on reason: 'Atheism is [. . .] extremely simple to define: it is the *belief*', without evidence, 'that there is no God or gods'.[2] According to the latter tendency, we should instead welcome a religious – and, more often than not, pointedly Christian – legacy that would atheistically be worth fighting for. As made evident by the slogan 'Christian atheism', whether understood in psychoanalytic, messianic, pro-universalistic or anti-Imperial ways, such a position in turn immediately gives rise to similar oxymorons, which denote in a symptomatic manner how the incorporation of a legacy does not necessarily entail the overcoming of what it originated from. Working-through is strangely being put aside. The fact that, as already sensed by Alexandre Kojève in the 1930s, religious atheism comes close to our 'concrete actuality' is not matched with an adequate theoretical elaboration.[3]

In this rather stagnant scenario, we need to take notice of a third atheistic tendency, one that has become popular only within specialistic philosophical circles yet seems far more promising. This tendency follows the second, even in generational terms, in rejecting the first tendency's vacuous and counterproductive marking of religion with the stamp of stupidity. But it also develops and problematizes the orientation of its mentors. Simply put, in order to oppose religion, it now engages in theological investigations that are no longer merely, or mostly, *analogical*. It respectfully confronts religion on its least unsolid grounds. In addition to that, and without solution of continuity, it assumes the conundrum derived from a historicized treatment of the religious legacy – can an *atheistic* relaunching of this legacy really differ from the *theistic* failure of irreligious modernity? – and shifts the focus of the discussion to a more structural and *ontological* level. Moreover, in doing so, it explicitly or implicitly reignites the question of agnosticism as entwined with that of atheism.

One should here single out, with some subsequent provisos, the work of Quentin Meillassoux and, to a lesser extent, that of Martin Hägglund. In *Radical Atheism*, an original interpretation of Derrida that moves well beyond his theories, Hägglund demonstrates how the line allegedly dividing a Christian *atheistic* from a *Christian* atheistic reading of deconstruction turns out to be untenable upon close scrutiny.[4] He succeeds in this task precisely by positioning his discourse in the field of an ambitious interrogation of 'the condition for everything that can be'.[5] For Hägglund, if being, in a strict sense, depends on being mortal, then to not be mortal, as nothing but a name for the divine, means not simply that God is dead but also, more strongly, that God is death.[6] Hence, as programmatically stated in the first paragraph of *Radical Atheism*, 'traditional atheism' as a whole (whether it openly flirts with religion or not) clings to theism in that 'mortal being is still conceived as a lack of being' – or evidence, we may add – 'that we desire to transcend'[7] – so as to attain the evidence of the lack of evidence. Contrary to this, Hägglund promotes the immanence of our infinite finitude as imposed by the so-called ultra-transcendental, yet not transcendent, status of time.

Along contiguous methodological lines, in *After Finitude* and *Divine Inexistence*, Meillassoux challenges normally accepted depictions of atheism and ventures into deeper and deeper onto-theological regions. In the process, he manages to conceptualize an eccentric, extreme and, in his view, positive implication of a consistent unfolding of the tensions inherent to Christian atheism. Meillassoux unhesitatingly advances that current atheism 'is reduced to a mere belief, and hence to a religion',[8] in the sense that – complicating Hägglund's point – it ends up approving 'the religious partition between immanence and transcendence: for atheism consists in being satisfied with the unsatisfying territory that religion cedes to it'.[9] Philosophy should thereby not bequeath God to priests. Philosophy should instead occupy a position that is neither religious nor obtusely atheistic. Or better, it should be devoted to a novel form of atheism (which Meillassoux refrains from calling by its name), revolving around a notion of divine *inexistence* that does not rule out the *possibility* of 'a God still to come'[10] – or not to come, in what would persist as an enduring virtuality. In short, decidedly moving beyond and against Hägglund here, yet also amplifying his emphasis on im-mortality, according to Meillassoux, the only extraordinary next step obtainable in the absolute necessity of contingency of a conclusively acausal and super-chaotic universe that can as such be grasped by human thought would be the *immanent* resurrection of the dead in a just world. Although neither we nor any inexistent external agent can *cause* this advent, it is our ethical duty to hope for 'the re-emergence of thought in accordance with the reign of a rigorously egalitarian justice among thinking individuals',[11] to hope for it *without* having faith in it, since the world of justice can be *not* produced. Accordingly, awaiting such an advent requires carrying out in the present acts of justice that can *condition* it, insofar as in their absence 'we would be dealing only with a blind recommencement imposed anonymously on humanity'.[12]

However much this last line of argument may sound bizarre, provocative and counterintuitive – it certainly deserves all these qualifications – and however major and entrenched are our theoretical reservations to its presuppositions,[13] the present book as well as our respective previous writings on religion, as supportive of a reconfigured atheism, are to be located in the same speculative constellation of Meillassoux's and Hägglund's. Up to a point, *God Is Undead* shares their questions and appreciates their urgency. But it also tries to provide different answers to them through Freudian and Lacanian psychoanalysis, whereas Lacan's significant contributions to reformulating an atheistic outlook are understated if not grossly misunderstood by Hägglund and Meillassoux. For Hägglund, Lacan would put forward an ontology of lack and a concomitant desire for 'atemporal fullness';[14] for Meillassoux, his notion of the real would persist in submitting being to the subject and therefore manifest its incapacity to tackle an event, or advent, in properly ontological terms.[15]

In overall agreement with Hägglund and Meillassoux, yet availing ourselves of Freud's and especially Lacan's protracted, though vigilant, dialogue with religion, both Adrian and I profoundly contest religious atheism, independently of whether it stresses one or the other of its components, and of whether it boasts psychanalytic credentials or vituperates them. At the same time, from this basis, we assess with neither contradiction nor disdain the incontrovertible atheistic seeds of the Christian tradition, which includes modern science. As already indicated by the title of the book, we are thus even more suspicious of, tacit or vocal, advocates of a weak atheism that, in presuming to having it done with God once and for all, does not contemplate its relapse into theism. By delving into the structural reasons of such a relapse, we equally embrace an unmistakably ontological approach. This is the case not only with regard to what Meillassoux would still label a subject-centred consideration of how the superseding of the conscious belief in God as an ultimate substance leaves intact the existence of an unconscious and irradicable – for it is our species-specific transcendental – God *hypothesis*, whose gap (not-One) and continuous symbolic oscillations (not-One/One/not-One etc.) soon reacquire an imaginary essence (One) as a subject-supposed-to-know – a first way in which God is unconscious. It is also and primarily the case in relation to a direct inquiry into how the immanent and contingent genesis of this transcendental not-One, its real if you wish, which is not to be conflated with a mere lack, cannot definitively attest to the inexistence of the divine. In a second way, God *might* here be unconscious in the guise of his own utter ignorance, of a God that does not believe in God, as Lacan has it, or, in my own jargon, of a *self-deceiving* God.

At least for what concerns me in particular, it is precisely thanks to the adoption of this *meta-critical* vantage point and the final albeit exclusively practical suspension of the self-deceiving God – or better, thanks to cutting the Gordian knot of the epistemological undecidability between either not-oneness is, and God is not, or the not-One is One is not-One is One and so on, in favour of the former – that Meillassoux's accusation that psychoanalytic thought confines itself to the correlate of subject and world and Hägglund's reproach that it essentializes lack can atheistically be turned on their head. After all, both authors can be shown to be unwittingly rehabilitating theism. Given that they pay prominent attention to avoiding this predicament, they could be taken as emblematic proponents of what we could refer to as *strong* weak atheism.

Against Meillassoux, his assumption, in *After Finitude*, of the absolute necessity of contingency, of hyper-chaos, cannot but evoke a transcendent *deceiving* God who deceives us but not himself, namely, a God who guarantees there is no God.[16] When conceived of as *absolutely* necessary, contingency idealistically closes onto itself. It is only because of *non*-absolute contingency, contingency allowing for the contingent emergence of human necessity (or logic as incomplete), that Meillassoux can *correlationally* posit the absolute *necessity* of contingency.

Meillassoux's plain addition, in *Divine Inexistence*, of an allegedly immanent and therefore anti-religious 'philosophical divine'[17] through contingent resurrection – whereby 'the God of the philosophers is no longer on the side of the chaos of nature, but on that of the rebirth of humans in an order worthy of their condition'[18] – does not change much the rules of the game. For instance, and moving quickly, if the absolute necessity of contingency is preserved, and it is, why should resurrection not simply be temporary, or intermittent, as a result of a deceiving God's perennial throw of dice, which can transiently even correspond to the 'divine'? Would this not be the ultimate cheat?

Most importantly, Meillassoux fails to recognize how, without compromising his own presuppositions, the absolute necessity of *contingency* (*not*-One) might perfectly coincide with the absolute contingency of *necessity* (not-One *equals* One) and that it is only this *possible* coincidence, the *self*-deceiving God, that enables us to think the absolute – if there is One – in an immanent manner. In other words, Meillassoux cogitates about 'worlds beyond science' that, due to their relative instability, become 'too chaotic' for scientific theories yet remain 'conceivable without "incoherence"' and further convincingly contends that, outside of a probabilistic context, 'a world that does not obey to any law has no reason to be chaotic rather than ordered'.[19] But why is he here not prepared to take the next step and postulate the eventuality of a world *at once* absolutely unstable *and* stable, stable as unstable (not-One = One) and unstable as stable (One = not-One), where inconsistency *is* consistency and vice versa?

In this book, and more generally in my work of the last decade, I wager that such a world can and should be conceived as the only coherent alternative to a godless world. Conceiving such a world does not only maintain room for the contingent emergence of human necessity, since the self-deceiving God would be indifferent to it, but also and by the same token liquidate the deceiving God as a last resort for metaphysical reassurance – which inevitably resurfaces whenever we straightforwardly assert the godless world and keeps on looming on the horizon of Meillassoux's most advanced pronouncements. The self-deceiving God does not really uphold any transcendence, for its transcending of incompleteness (not-One = *One*) is nothing but its incomplete immanence (One = *not-One*).

As for Hägglund, in *God Is Undead*, we can literally not just endorse his association of God with death and, as it transpires from his more recent works, his quietist eulogy of the mortality of 'this life'.[20] On the one hand, Hägglund justifiably insists on the fact that the 'idea of secular life as empty and meaningless is itself a religious notion'.[21] Yet, on the other, this is programmatically countered with a dubious call for 'secular faith' as being 'devoted to a life that will end', where devotion fundamentally means spending our time caring about others.[22] While, at face value, there is hardly anything objectionable in these – grand and no-nonsense alike – resolutions, we should still philosophically question whether their exaltation of infinite finitude would relinquish implicitly religious premises.

Adrian has already demonstrated how inasmuch as, according to Hägglund, finitude 'is the ultimate and unsurpassable horizon of everything for us as the psychical beings that we are', his consequent temporal logic of difference (or *différance*) both misses that which phenomenologically resists differential representation (the Lacanian real) and meta-psychologically proposes itself as an overarching worldview.[23] To this I would simply add that, on a meta-psychological level, any *reification* of difference, as always anthropocentric, necessarily brings about the reinstallation of transcendence. The replacement of the Kantian transcendental with a Derridean ultra-transcendental only pushes the threshold of the transcendent (God) one notch further. In brief, if, as Hägglund lucidly infers from his phenomenology, '*the thing itself is* [spatio-temporal] *différance*',[24] then, as he instead does not admit, that thing is in the end differential only by differing from something else, namely, the identity of the *T*hing it *lacks*.

A cogent but partial way out of the deadlock of transcendence caused by positing *différance* as independent of 'language or experience or any other delimited region of being'[25] – in opposition to understanding our phenomenological difference as in-*different* from other potentially in-*different* regions of indifferent being, an option I hereby champion – would be to unashamedly identify *différance* as chaosmotic *D*ifference with a divine *P*rocess, as Deleuze arguably does in some of his writings.[26] Although Deleuze filters this nuanced conjunction through a disproportionally pro-immanence vocabulary, he here comes relatively close to the final proclamation and celebration of the self-deceiving God, which, again, I solely see as a mandatory speculative passage that needs to be practically discarded.[27]

2

Adrian and I have been exchanging our thoughts for almost fifteen years. A common acquaintance's initial prediction that, as 'young-Lacanians', he would soon become my 'nemesis', and I his, has been invalidated by a longstanding series of extremely productive research collaborations as well as, if not especially, unabating informal correspondence. In addition to being a superb philosophical interlocutor, first and foremost, Adrian is a friend, with whom I share a lot. Moving from the biographical to the intellectual along a continuous line, the two of us were raised as Catholics and felt early on that one cannot easily unsubscribe from such a baptism. Still, our theoretical orientation has persistently been materialist and realist, and thereby arguably irreligious. We are both firmly convinced that a renewed materialism and realism must pass through psychoanalysis as far more than an anti-philosophy. Politically, this makes us Freudo-Marxists. We are thus profoundly indebted to the work of Slavoj Žižek. We nonetheless dissent from some sweeping, albeit foundational, ontological aspects of his project, which possibly make him too at home with religion.

Having said this, Adrian's 'transcendental materialism' does part ways with my 'meta-critical realism', or para-ontology, and, in the present book, this is reflected in our respective addressing of the question of atheism. I must confess that jointly writing a volume where we so frequently speak in unison has made it difficult for me to pin down our divergencies, regardless of previous and quite systematic attempts at doing so. I will leave it to readers to establish their precise magnitude – or irrelevance – and content myself with a few remarks.

At times, it seems to me that our dissensions are mostly terminological. Specifically, in the current context, when Adrian understands staunch atheism as a 'long, arduous process' involving a 'recurring distance-taking from theistic structures' that can only be secured as 'an intermittent meta-level occurrence',[28] this seems to me extremely proximate to what I call *agnostic* atheism as strong *atheism*. At other times, and probably more often, I am of the view that, in spite and because of such a proximity, there lingers an unbridgeable gap between our positions. For example, why should Adrian's admittedly 'meta-level' atheistic process then be downgraded to the critical idea that 'God is created through being spoken about'[29] rather than also include the meta-critical evocation *and* suspension of the self-deceiving God, as something more than a Kantian transcendental illusion? In other words, without recourse to the self-deceiving God, how can the meta-level Adrian advocates as necessary for atheism not replicate on its own level the linguistic creation of a transcendent God? Scrupulously following Lacan, Adrian summons in passing the possibility of a 'barred' God,[30] yet he does not ratify it as part of the solution to the replication he himself might succumb to.

Drawing on the broader ontological framework of our respective projects, and in response to some inflated accounts of our disagreements, I think that what separates them revolves around neither my alleged 'science-phobia' nor his supposed subjective idealism, if not solipsism.[31] These are quite poor oversimplifications of the matter at stake, as already witnessed by the unwanted similarity of such allegations. In the past – perhaps sounding more polemical than I intended to be – I indeed argued (in a footnote[32]) that, at times, Adrian may give the impression of conceding too much to the neurosciences, in the sense of excessively stressing the biological component of psychoanalysis in view of making it more palatable to certain anti-psychoanalytic circles. In his harsh reply – perhaps lending himself to subsequent misrepresentations of my work as anti-naturalist – Adrian accused me of, unconscious and quasi-clinical, 'sentimental [. . .] resistance' to (neuro-)biology as well as of operating on the basis of a flawed methodology that a priori 'pick[s] winners' – namely, psychoanalysis.[33] Although it is always gratifying to be labelled an ultra-orthodox in a field, the Lacanian one, where creative orthodoxy almost invariably leads to reactive excommunication, I am happy to say we have in the meantime, in our conversations, acknowledged that this (sentimental) line of discussion was simply blowing divisions out of proportion and thus counterproductive. By way of further exculpation, let me just recall that, over the years, I have myself insisted on how a psychoanalysis-oriented materialist and realist philosophy cannot do without science, often praising Adrian precisely for breaking ground in this direction. Here, I will not rehash my stance ad nauseam.

After all – and this is instead crucial – the two of us concur that the right platform for thinking philosophically the relation between psychoanalysis and science can already be found in what Freud set out, hesitantly, in his seminal 'The Question of a Weltanschauung', which moreover has vast repercussions on the very question of atheism. Is psychoanalysis a world-vision that 'solves all the problems of our existence uniformly on the basis of one overriding hypothesis, which, accordingly, leaves no question unanswered and in which everything that interests us finds its fixed place'?[34] Absolutely not; otherwise it would be a religion. Is psychoanalysis then a branch of the scientific Weltanschauung? Yes, but only inasmuch as science is itself not really a Weltanschauung, 'for it is not all-comprehensive [. . .] too incomplete and makes no claim to being self-contained'.[35] But, importantly and against Freud, this claim to self-containment should also not be 'relegated to the future'[36] or, as I will detail in my contribution below, tacitly made present in the negative form of a *Weltanschauung* for which there is no Weltanschauung; otherwise science would itself become a religion. Taking advantage of my own purported *Widerstand* to science, I would go as far as positing that psychoanalysis as a branch of science first and foremost acts as an internal *resistance* to these 'scientific' outcomes, which are today more tangible than ever.

With respect to the trickier question of idealism – as profoundly embedded in that of the relation between psychoanalysis and science, as well as the latter's pitfalls – I am fully aware that what Adrian pursues with his transcendental materialism, which by his own admission aims at nothing less than a new and Marx-inflected German idealism, is not a trivial anthropocentrism, masked by a veneer of dialectics, but rather, in Frank Ruda's felicitous formula, an idealism *without idealism*. Yet I also think that, in his overall project, Adrian somehow remains exposed to the dangers of a *Weltanschauung* for which there is no Weltanschauung. Put differently, and quickly, I am not persuaded by the path he chooses to investigate the – apparently conclusive – not-oneness of being and the contingent emergence of the anthropic-subjective oscillation not-One/One out of it. Hoping that this will propel an even more meticulous and mutually beneficial refinement of our positions, and amicably teasing him, I dare to suggest that there seems to persist some *not-enough-without*-idealism in his idealism without idealism.

To sum up and simplify my arguments from *The Not-Two*,[37] Adrian:

a. Criticizes any crypto-idealistic attempt at surreptitiously injecting the not-oneness of being with a proto-subjective vector that would *always-already*, albeit not teleologically, anticipate and sustain the advent of the subject.

b. Considers the not-oneness of being as in-itself *not*-One (or 'barred'), independently of the advent of the subject, but *thereby* projects a subjective vector onto the not-oneness of being.

c. Implies a God/One guaranteeing that all is not-One, while, beyond Meillassoux and Hägglund, sensing this deadlock.

Since Adrian and I are totally on the same page with regard to the first point, and I derive the third from the second, his counterarguments comprehensibly focus on the latter, namely, in his own jargon, on the issue of a 'self-*denaturalizing* natural real'.[38] According to him, in my reading of transcendental materialism, I would basically mistake 'what is an epistemological thesis about a concept – the thesis that a materialist reconceptualization of denaturalized subjectivity as fully immanent to natural substance requires a radical reconceptualization of the latter – for an ontological thesis about *Natur an sich*'.[39] Yet, if this is the case, what is Adrian's ontological thesis about *Natur an sich*? Either we are here facing a question not to be asked, but then it would be difficult to grasp how transcendental materialism evades the boundaries of a 'classical Kantian-style epistemology that refrains from directly speculating on the nature of metaphysical substance' (to quote a reproach a supporter of Adrian makes to Ray Brassier and me).[40] Or the epistemological thesis he puts forward has also a direct ontological dimension, nature is as such denaturalized or 'self-conflictual' in his view, but then, I suspect, my challenge still stands. After all, Adrian speaks of 'clashes and collisions within and between the strata of nature's inanimate dimensions' as 'drastically different from the differential relations between [. . .] signifiers', the dimension of the subject.[41] Is this not an ontological statement about being's being in-itself *not*-One?

On a closely related front, Adrian nonetheless finds my assertion that signifying differentiality *is and is not* a break with nature to be 'kicking down an open door',[42] by which I suppose he means that, retrospectively, with human hindsight *only*, non-human nature can be regarded as foreshadowing human structures. This is, indeed, a truly open door, if there ever was a dialectical door. Against all evidence, he strangely deems I forget about it. Yet this is not the closed door I have been intending to open. Let me try to do it otherwise: Is Adrian's door actually not both locked (given his previous statement about drastically different pre-human clashes and collisions) and, at the same time, off its hinges (given his – not fully assumed – assumption of a differential nature *an sich*)? In a properly dialectical materialist fashion, would it not be more congruous and fruitful to inspect the way in which signifying differentiality is and is not a break with nature even and especially in the sense that insofar as it *is* a break with nature it still is *not* a break with it?

At this stage, I need to touch on my notion of in-difference, which Adrian tends to ignore in his rebuttals and instead plays a most significant role in what I have been developing over the last decade, including the present book – as it is entwined with agnostic atheism and the self-deceiving God. To cut a long story short, and running the risk of seeming naïve (or of passing again for a backer of 'frictionless ideational spinnings in speculative voids'[43]), on the one hand, human difference has never really emerged. Human difference is indifference as *we* live and think of it. Even the modest statement for which we have never superseded the 'age of bacteria' (Stephen Jay Gould),[44] because the signifying differentiality I am employing right here and right now to write these sentences functions as nothing more than an optimized receptacle for – allegedly protodifferential – bacteria, or viruses, or the chemical bonds that compose them, on closer inspection rests on an immodestly anthropocentric and unfounded overstatement. On the other hand, and concomitantly, although human difference *is* (a break with undifferentiated non-human nature), for our differential being is no illusion but real, this still amounts to in-*difference*. In this context, and for the sake of a truly materialist and realist agenda, I must say that I find the very idea of 'a self-denaturalising natural real' perplexing if not misleading. As indifference, the natural real is not at all self-denaturalizing itself. It boringly is what it is. And as in-*difference*, the natural real is self-denaturalizing itself through us, while it is not, for it also remains *in*-different to human difference. For me, this does not in the least refute the fact that 'the substances of the natural Real are affected and altered by the subjects of the more-than-natural Symbolic'.[45] Of course, they are. Natural indifference is differentiated through human difference – otherwise, science could not have effects on nature. Yet, again, this differentiation also persists as sheer indifference, here and now. For me, the bottom line is not dividing between parts of the natural real that are transformed by the symbolic and parts that are not,[46] but emphasizing that the natural real *is and is not* transformed by the symbolic at the same time.

As Moritz Herrmann summarizes with a perspicuous outspokenness that, I suspect, I sometimes lack (because of the imperative of deploying a strict and novel philosophical vocabulary for the sake of internal coherence), for me, the basic 'question does not revolve around the evident *empirical* effects of our symbolic differentiality but around the *ontological* status of this very differentiality'[47] *as* natural indifference. Moreover, methodologically, while an exploration of the fact that there is no sexual relationship, as the ground of symbolic differentiality, comes first – which is what psychoanalysis is all about – what follows should not so much be a genealogical investigation of how or why this has happened – which inevitably leads to the impasse of attempting to demonstrate anthropogenesis – but a full, and empirical on another level, assumption that the natural real *is* indifference also in an everyday sense. In the simplest terms, it does not care about our human-all-too-human predicament. Vulgarly, but appropriately here, it does not give a fuck *about fuck*. This does not only apply to the absence of the sexual relationship but, a fortiori, to every fuckupedness the latter unchains, including the prospect of maximal anthroentropic indifferentiation (*anthropie*) by means of ecological, viral, nuclear and so on Armageddon.

Perhaps, in a nutshell, my main outstanding and brutally ingenuous question for Adrian is: *Are* the 'clashes and collisions' he speaks about such in nature *an sich*, that is, independently of human in-differential nature – a position which, in sum, resembles Žižek's understanding of the pre-subjective but proto-subjective 'out-of-jointedness' of nature as 'movement'[48] – or are they *such* only through in-differentiation, whereby they also concurrently subsist as meta-*static* indifference? If the former is the case, then transcendental materialism gestures towards Difference as an ontological a priori, or better, towards not-oneness *as* a differential *not*-One. In turn, transcendental materialism thus insinuates some variant of the ultimate One, which seems to hover between that implied by Hägglund, the One with respect to which Difference (the linguistic oscillation not-One/One taken as a cosmic principle) is differential, and that implied by Meillassoux, the deceiving One that guarantees the absolute necessity of indifferent not-oneness (for Meillassoux, the contingency of the world 'gives itself to us as *indifferent*, in being what it is, to whether it is given or not'[49]).

As I was saying earlier, I think it is difficult to put one's finger on these, unconfirmed but likely, ontological disagreements in the present book. They tend to be dissimulated by the robust alliance Adrian and I have forged against a host of common enemies – hypocritical theists, closet atheists, relative atheists, conservative atheists, mystical materialists, extreme metaphysicians, Lutheran Freudians, Jesuit Lacanians, Christian *père-verts* and psychoanalytically inclined orthodox 'radicals', to mention just a few – as well as the fact that our interpretations of Lacan continuously intersect. This is all the more so since here Adrian hints at the Lacanian 'barred God'.[50] From my perspective, the latter notion is not synonymous with that of the 'barred real' on which he extensively dwelt in the past but, on the contrary, an only initially implausible remedy for its dilemma. In short, while the barred real, or 'weak nature',[51] leads to the antinomy of a not-oneness that in being *not*-One structurally evokes a transcendence, the barred God (or self-deceiving God, in my parlance), who as barred remains *God* but who as *God* is nothing but barred (not-One = One = not-One etcetera), immanently exhibits this transcendence as a real possibility that as such can be disposed of. Conclusively, *either* indifferent not-oneness is, *or* the self-deceiving God is. This most rational alternative remains rationally undecidable, and thus speculatively agnostic. *But*, first, the either/or prevents us from surreptitiously yet directly positing the *One* (not-One). And, second, it allows us to *practically* act as if there were no God, for if there were One, he would only deceive us by first and foremost deceiving himself. With this passage, we move from strong agnosticism to agnostic *atheism* as *strong* atheism.

Perhaps, in his present contribution, Adrian perpetuates a discourse on not-oneness as *not*-One, taking it for granted or at least not spelling it out, precisely where this is most expectable and hence barely visible, right under our otherwise consensual noses, namely, in not considering the agnostic moment I have just described as paramount for a viable atheism that 'does not contradict [itself] all of the time'.[52] If this were the case, then what at first looks like as an innocuous specification – practical strong atheism issues from epistemological strong *agnosticism* – would actually already contain the kernel of our general ontological *differend*. For Adrian, in spite of it being a process, atheism stands alone on its own feet. For me, the fact that 'the true formula of atheism' is 'God is unconscious'[53] problematizes the very credibility of any form of non-agnostic atheism.

On close inspection, this is echoed on an exegetical level. For Adrian, 'Jacques Lacan looks like an atheist. He talks like an atheist. But, do not be fooled: he really is an atheist'.[54] For me, trying to reply to a pun I am not at ease with, 'Jacques Lacan often does *not* look like an atheist. He often does *not* talk like an atheist. But, do not be fooled: he really is an atheist *only because he often does not look or talk like an atheist*'. Similarly, for Adrian, 'divine ignorance'[55] in Lacan is, after all, little more than a strategically rhetorical figure of speech – ad litteram. For me, in the guise of self-deception, it alludes on the contrary to the (for us) coherent possibility of an ontological figure of God that is thus captured not simply in his attribute but in his inconsistent essence.

If all this were the case, then our respective readings of Freud in an anti-religious context and of the role of the psychoanalytic clinic in the search for an atheistic praxis, which I reckon might straightaway strike the reader as incompatible, would also be illuminated. With regard to Freud, Adrian contends that he 'establishes himself as one of the most virulently and uncompromisingly atheistic thinkers in history' and therefore 'contrast[ing] between Freud's and Lacan's fashion of relating to religion' is by and large 'exaggerated, even false' – although he subsequently retracts this in part.[56] I am instead of the view that, as the later Lacan himself has it, 'Freud retains in fact, if not in intention [. . .] what he designates as being the most essential in religion'.[57] In my own jargon, foreshadowing what I will unfold in my contribution below by complicating Lacan's assessment, at his best, Freud promotes a ('scientific') *Weltanschauung* for which there is no Weltanschauung, a weak atheism whereby the not-One is the world in itself and for itself and there is *absolutely* no God. At his worst, he espouses an (equally 'scientific') weak agnosticism whereby the not-One is the world *for us*, and we must not venture into metaphysics. As Adorno, a hardcore Freudian in many respects, presciently put it already in the 1940s, the 'neutralisation of religion seems to have led to just the opposite of what the enlightener Freud anticipated',[58] and, I would add, this is also due to Freud's own botched neutralization of religion. As Ruda nicely chimed in upon reading the sections of the present book I devote to Freud, regarding religion, the discoverer of the unconscious seems to have forgotten he had an unconscious too.[59]

Concerning the psychoanalytic clinic and its concrete input into 'how to make a real atheist',[60] Adrian reveals considerable optimism. Here, he seems himself to be 'picking winners' in advance – curiously but understandably to the detriment of the 'naturalistic atheism of the scientific Weltanschauung appealed to by Freud'.[61] For Adrian, thanks to psychoanalytic treatment, not-all human beings are unconscious theists. 'True' atheism can be achieved through the dissolution of the transference and the transitory disbelief in any subject supposed to know. This transitory disbelief nonetheless instils a 'lasting, persistent vigilance in analysands'.[62] At bottom, the end of the treatment would thus enable '(dis) belief "in the second degree", namely, a second-order dis-believing in first-order beliefs (with obdurate religious/theistic *sinthomes* perhaps being instances of the latter)'.[63] In other words, and leaving aside my difficulty in assimilating how a thus characterized atheism would be 'real' or 'true', Adrian acknowledges that, however much an analysis is successfully completed, these persistent *sinthomes* – the *One* (not-One) – keep on installing themselves as more subtle and perverse – albeit also allegedly 'more liveable'? – versions-of-the-Father (One).[64] Still, in his opinion, analysis could possibly overcome *père-version* tout-court through a new kind of signifiers that would not be tied to the unbarred Other but to the barred Other. Such a move would resonate with a – no better specified – messianic atheism.[65]

Although I do not develop this point at length in what follows, as things stand, I am far more doubtful about the anti-religious future of psychoanalysis as a practice. In line with the later and especially latest Lacan, religion has perhaps already defeated psychoanalysis. This does not simply mean that, as claimed in *The Triumph of Religion*, a text I will delve into, psychoanalytic discourse might have been, already in 1973, just a 'little flash' of truth between two religious worlds,[66] but also that, as laconically stated in Lacan's very last Seminar, in its everyday interpretative exercise, psychoanalysis 'irresistibly tends' towards religion.[67] In line with Elvio Fachinelli, a dissident Freudian and Lacanian psychoanalyst, psychoanalysis has time and again proved that, above all after Lacan and despite his warnings and the final hara-kiri of his School,[68] it can no longer be presented as the 'investigative dialogue which is probably the most significant innovation introduced into Western discourse after the "noble sophistry" of Protagoras and Socrates' and which, at first, thus smoothly translated itself into a lived experience of 'unexpected surprise'.[69] Psychoanalysis has by now 'closed in' on itself and proliferates only through a 'sharp forest of' – technical and political – 'defences'.[70] I would go even further than Fachinelli and intimate that, with very few exceptions, this has ended up aligning current psychoanalysis with today's hegemonic discourse and practice of victimization – independently of whether the victim is the subject of psychoanalysis or psychoanalysis itself.

More to the point, in terms of Adrian's unflinching albeit laborious optimism, we should ask: Does tying – however qualitatively – new signifiers to the barred Other, which he reads as applicable to the effectiveness of a more thoroughly atheistic treatment-to-come, not simply repropose the theoretical impasse of not-oneness as *not*-One? Is the problem at stake not precisely the fact that we *cannot but tie* (old or new) signifiers (the oscillation not-One/One) to the bar, or even that the bar itself is a proto-signifier (or unary trait), and that *this* necessarily gives way to an unbarred Other? Does the resourcefulness of *Christianity* not lie precisely in an open endorsement and monumental exploitation of this simple logical movement?[71] When we, in Lacanian circles, flaunt the signifier 'new signifier'[72] as a panacea – which, *mea culpa*, I myself did in the past[73] – are we envisaging an in-depth refashioning of our linguistically transcendental condition? If so, how could we ever transcendentally think, and a fortiori practice, a substitute transcendental? If not, insentiently conniving with traditional religions and technologically advanced, yet retrograde, post-humanisms, are we instead plotting the decapitation of the transcendental? Would the latter not come close to what Lacan understands as supreme 'evil'?[74] And are questions like these not evidently far removed from the immediate clinical field? On the other hand, would a full assumption of all the above not, less unrealistically, as a first step, entail an ample clinical reconsideration of *paranoia* under the light of the (self-)deceiving God and, I dare say, a universalization of it as a *more* structurally human condition, with potentially *liberating* consequences (against Deleuze and Guattari's scolding of it as fascistic)?[75] Would this not extend what Lacan already accomplished, beyond Freud, on the level of neurosis and perversion as 'normal'?

3

The (self-)deceiving God argument is not yet another rabbit I am pulling out of the reputedly unfalsifiable psychoanalytic hat. In various guises, more or less explicitly, it instead crops up as a tenacious, albeit marginal and unexplored, undercurrent in psychoanalysis, even before Lacan. And, of course, with Descartes, it lies at the origins of modern philosophy and science.[76]

Throughout his genealogy of religion as an infantile disorder of civilization, which was, in his view, inevitable for the development of human knowledge and even advantageous to it, Freud often returns to the question of the 'Evil Spirit' and increasingly refines it.[77] In *Totem and Taboo* (1913), he confines 'demonic powers' to an animistic stage that still confuses malignant and benevolent beings in the taboo object, which would be overcome by religion in the strict sense.[78] Bizarrely, he feels obliged to clarify that demons can nonetheless not be treated as '"earliest" things' since, obviously, they are creations of the human mind – and 'it would be another matter if demons really existed'.[79]

In *The Future of an Illusion* (1927), Freud adds that such creations tend historically to coalesce around a transcendent 'evil Will', which he has now no problem in understanding as the 'first step' in the 'humanization of nature', since such Will is made accountable for our helplessness and mortality and therefore amounts to a primal species-specific defence.[80]

His reasoning becomes more complex in *Civilisation and Its Discontents* (1930) and 'The Question of a Weltanschauung' (1933). Not only is there a 'vestige' of the Evil Spirit in every religious system, but this has been retained most essentially in both Christianity as the religion of 'His all-goodness' and what irreligiously yet animistically lies 'behind religion'.[81] Just as primitive people animated the world with overall hostile demons, so Christians cannot but justify wickedness through the Devil 'as an excuse for God' (the former would thus play the same role as 'the Jew does in the world of the Aryan ideal') and 'the philosophy of today' cannot but still believe that 'the real events in the world take the course which our [fundamentally demonic] thinking seeks to impose on them'.[82]

In a 'A Seventeenth-Century Demonological Neurosis' (1923), a greatly underestimated text, Freud further insists on the mutual dependence and reversibility of God and the Devil. As equally based on the external projection of an ambivalent – phylogenetic and ontogenetic – relation to the really existing father, the two should be regarded as fundamentally 'identical'.[83] On the one hand, this means that Divine Powers can at times be taken as sheer manifestations of the Devil tout-court.[84] On the other hand, and for the same reason, under certain conditions, the Devil himself can serve as a comforting 'father-substitute'.[85]

However, Freud stops here. He, quite surprisingly, concedes that demonology's psychic accounts of possession are more convincing than the attempts of '"exact" science' at explaining them somatically.[86] But, after all, psychoanalysis would conclusively prove that demons are only 'bad and reprehensible wishes [. . .] that have been repudiated and repressed'.[87] All that psychoanalysis needs to do is to eliminate their projection into the external world and consider them as arisen in the patient's internal life.

Moreover, to the best of my knowledge, Freud does not ever openly associate his considerations on the Evil Spirit with the specific epistemological question of deceit. In a well-known 1929 letter, he tackles Descartes's dreams (as related by Baillet via Leroy), tritely confirms Descartes's own interpretation of the wind in one of them as the evil genius (*animus*) who was trying to seduce him, but fails to dwell on the significant fact that the philosopher – half-awake or continuing to decipher his dream while again asleep, he tells us – then displaces the question of the evil genius onto the phrase '*Est et non*' (It is and is not) as, Descartes thinks, directly relevant to 'Truth and Falsehood in human knowledge'.[88]

In spite of its untenable – uber-animistic – reliance on the existence of an 'archetypal unconscious structure'[89] or, better, an all-encompassing unconscious Meaning awaiting to be rediscovered, in this context, it is unexpectedly more instructive to mention Jung's 1954 'On the Psychology of the Trickster Figure'. Here, the Freudian motif of the Evil Spirit is considered through a historical, anthropological and psychoanalytic approach as both deceitful and deceived. Even leaving aside Jung's musings, the Winnebago mythology on which he comments proves extremely telling with respect to what I am pursuing in this book. The trickster is 'the Foolish One'.[90] Freudian ambivalence becomes fully internal to the trickster itself – for instance, the trickster is such only by making its right arm fight its left. Not only that: there are no discrete One and not-One poles in the trickster – it falls and disappears in its own excrement and manages to get out of it only with great difficulty. This is the case to the point that it can be named a 'Foolish One' only 'by their calling me thus'.[91] Most importantly, its stratagems aimed at deception cannot be distinguished from self-deception – the trickster pretends to take care of children and eats them, yet it then ends up eating its own intestines without realizing it. As Radin puts it, in duping others, the trickster actually 'is always duped himself',[92] and we should add, as already implied by the example above, its being duped depends on its own actions (it also dispatches its penis, which is kept in a box, to secretly have intercourse with the chief's daughter, but it drops to the bottom of a lake; when the detached penis finally lodges in her, an old woman pulls it out and 'spoil[s] all the pleasure'[93]).

Jung himself highlights how the trickster is eventually always cheated and makes a number of other observations. Its deceptions' turning into self-deceptions depend on the fact that the trickster is 'unconscious of [it]self'; because of that, it 'is not really evil' even when it carries out the most atrocious deeds; its 'extraordinary clumsiness and lack of instinct' rather mythically encapsulate the predicament of dis-adapted human nature as such; by developing a 'higher level' of consciousness, modern man has forgotten the trickster, which still somehow survived in mediaeval customs; at most, it is today only present either in pathological instances of double personality, or when one (non-pathologically) 'feels [oneself] at the mercy of annoying "accidents" [. . .] with apparently malicious intent', or also – more interestingly, as this seems to problematize the naive teleology of Jung's argument – in the 'monkey tricks' of contemporary demagogic politics.[94]

All in all, like for Freud, for Jung, the trickster (or Evil Spirit) amounts to a primitive psychological projection that psychoanalysis can unmask and do away with. My perhaps reckless take in what follows is instead that, unlike Freud and Jung, and precisely due to his materialistic understanding of the unconscious, Lacan sketches his own version of the trickster, the self-deceiving God, on which I then elaborate in my own terms, as a real *ontological* possibility paradoxically capable of paving an atheistic way out of resiliently animistic thought. He does so especially by means of an original rereading of Descartes's evil genius.

In brief, first, Descartes's evocation and repression of the deceiving God founds modernity and modern science in particular. As stated in Seminar II – in the same year of the publication of Jung's article on the trickster – the axiomatic 'idea that God is no deceiver', which is 'precisely what we don't know', is itself a 'simple trick', not contemplated by 'classical theory', at which Einstein himself still 'got stuck'.[95] Second, Descartes's repression of the deceiving God relies on the invocation of a *non*-deceiving God who, on close inspection, as we shall see, is already proximate to a *self*-deceiving God. Third, scientific modernity perpetuates the repression of the deceiving God to a point of self-implosion, whereby its weak atheism is tantamount to a *Weltanschauung* for which there is no Weltanschauung, which necessitates the deceiving God. Fourth, thanks to a psychoanalysis-oriented and thoroughly revised first philosophy, we can exit the structural implication of the deceiving God by thinking the self-deceiving God as a rationally undecidable possibility through strong agnosticism and then practically suspend it through agnostic atheism.

Agnostic, and *as such* strong, atheism thus emerges as an answer to weak agnosticism and weak atheism. In order to help readers to follow the evolution of my arguments, let me provide some approximate definitions. I call *weak agnosticism* the position that posits the possibility of an ultimate One but does not investigate it as a priori impenetrable to reason. I call *weak atheism* the position that posits the impossibility of an ultimate One but does not investigate it as allegedly already demonstrated by reason and thus implicitly posits the One (not-One). I call *strong agnosticism* the position that problematizes weak atheism, posits the possibility of an ultimate One, rationally investigates it and finally qualifies it as One = not-One = One = not-One etcetera. I call *agnostic or strong atheism* the position that ir-rationally decides for a *practical* atheism of the not-One on the basis of the rational undecidability of strong agnosticism.

The particulars of the genealogical passages I mentioned above, and, at their outset, of Descartes's radical break with previous religious ontologies, will conceivably become apparent herein. In response to Dominiek Hoens, who very kindly read the manuscript in detail, I hope these initial definitions, rephrased and specified in the main body of the book, at least tentatively elucidate my 'ultimate step' with regard to the *logical* sequence '[implicit/scientific deceiving God], Descartes's deceiving God, Lacan/Chiesa's self-deceiving God',[96] which he found slightly elusive despite appreciating the cogency of the sequence.

As for one of Hoens's other – very incisive and tricky – related requests for clarification, I am aware of the fact that the question as to why the self-deceiving God should be posited precisely as *self-deceiving* rather than simply as *non-knowledgeable* remains to be further articulated. In the latter case, the undecidability of strong agnosticism would consist of the alternative between either God is not or God is stupid. Referring to my heterodox interpretation of Descartes's doctrine of eternal truths, which I push beyond Lacan, Hoens contends that 'God could both create and be unaware of an eternal truth, *without* deceiving Himself [. . .] Self-deception should also include a contradictory [. . .] knowledge'.[97]

It seems to me that I already provide some preliminary answers in this respect. Drawing on Descartes's unprecedented separation of truth from knowledge, which turns truth into 'God's own business'[98] (all this will be explained step by step), what we embryonically, and arguably against his intentions, find in Descartes's attempt to *obviate* the impasse of the *deceiving* God, if forced in a certain direction, is an identification of truth with the negation of the law of contradiction. The self-deceiving God is such on the level of truth. Here, lack of knowledge becomes in the end irrelevant, a secondary and humanly contingent attribute. The One and the not-One, or better, the One that is not-One and the not-One that is One, without solution of continuity, are both true. Such is the truth, unacknowledged by Descartes, of his doctrine of eternal truths, which, for Descartes, can nonetheless accommodate a circle whose radii are unequal and a mountain without valleys as easily as a circle whose radii are equal and a mountain with valleys[99] – although, for him, eternal truths are still, somehow, *God's* truths. This inconsistency, or better, consistent inconsistency and inconsistent consistency, *is* divine self-deception. Locating such being on the level of any theory of knowledge or epistemological enquiry, which I surmise is what Hoens proposes, would instead only *call* the self-deceiving God 'the Foolish One'.[100]

As insightfully observed by Paul Livingston,[101] another fascinating issue yet to be tackled in this framework is the positioning of Spinoza's *Deus sive natura* both against Descartes's quasi self-deceiving God and with respect to the accounts I provide below of paganism (the not-One *as immanent One*), mysticism (the not-One *as the transcendent-in-immanence One*) and, far more briefly, although it was a constant matter of interest for Lacan, Chen and Zen Buddhism (the One *as the immanent-in-transcendence not-One*).

In what begins to look like a sort of pre-emptive *auto-da-fé*, punctuated by the apostate's stubbornly dissenting voice, I also want to warn readers that there is certainly much more to be unpacked in the anti-Pascalian wager with which I suspend the self-deceiving God – let us practically act as if there were no self-deceiving God. For the time being, this wager stands as the end of my itinerary, but only as a signpost of work to be carried out in the future, including on Lacan's evaluation of Pascal.[102] It is also a practical conclusion I share with Adrian, although we arrive at it from different paths (again, in my view, for Adrian, the *not*-One is but we cannot really say it without evoking the One; for me, *either* not-oneness is *or* the not-One is One is not-One etcetera, independently of what we can and cannot say). Equally, it draws attention to our diametrical opposition to Meillassoux's concrete and hyper-diabolical prescription for which, in view of immanent resurrection, 'it is necessary to believe in God because he does not exist'.[103] In the present contribution, I do, however, offer some hints at how the anti-Pascalian wager is to be ethically and politically played out against suicidally opting for the self-deceiving God, which is what capitalism does as a discourse of indifferentiating totalization and totalizing indifferentiation.

One final word about the title of the book. Adrian and I have long debated its suitability to what we expose. I must say I still have my doubts. It is both direct, in-your-face, and highly suggestive, and may thus attract wider interest (not least because of its intuitive anti-Nietzschean connotations), which we would very much welcome. Still, I feel compelled to neatly disassociate the undeadness at stake from any kind of allegedly im-mortal drive or repetition that would insist beyond life and death. The latter has by now become a fashionable yet profoundly misleading trope in Lacanian discourse. It leads us back to the ontological assumption of some sort of proto-subjective vector inherent to not-oneness as such. Or, worse, it returns us to an unconcealed divine: 'There is room in human life for the "undead" (or transcendent) energies of the real.'[104] In a certain biopolitical literature, loosely influenced by psychoanalysis, the undead has also vitalistically, that is, religiously, been saluted as a 'life as pure potentiality' and 'our authentic political-ethical thinking and action'.[105]

Let me be absolutely clear. For me, the undead God here in question is *less* than a living-dead. Evidently, from a very limited and historical perspective, we can refer to it as such, in the sense that in pseudo-secularized late-modernity, God survives his own death and prospers as a relic. This was already Nietzsche's point: 'There is no "God" anymore [. . .] *and yet everything goes on as before.*'[106] But, ontologically, a zombie remains far too alive for my line of argument. As I pointed out elsewhere, in a non-theological discussion, perhaps it might instead be helpful to thematize the opposite figure of the *dead-living*, of the always-already terminal inclusion of any form of living homeostasis in metastatic indifference.[107] Against the background of indifferent not-oneness, in terms of signifying differentiality – namely, on a critical level – the undead God would, therefore, however ineluctably, be revived only as the *anti-*zombie. In agreement with Badiou, it is a God who is both always 'already dead, or dead from the beginning' *and* 'live[s] only in the death of the letter'.[108] Mutatis mutandis, the anti-zombie could perhaps also be applied to the meta-critical eventuality of the self-deceiving God as an intrinsically barred God. Or, in all likelihood, at this stage, in these speculative lands, it would be more beneficial to entomb any life-related image.

PS: For the sake of clarity and intellectual honesty, the reader should also know that I wrote this Introduction after reading Adrian's main contribution to this volume. Adrian wrote his Conclusion after reading my main contribution. But we are here not responding to the Introduction and the Conclusion, the content of which we ignored at the time of writing. They are such in *God Is Undead* only as the punctuation of an ongoing dialogue. Adrian's Conclusion could thus also be read as a provisional Introduction and, vice versa, my Introduction as a provisional Conclusion. Our common aim remains not to end with the end of the end of religion.

Divine ignorance: Jacques Lacan and Christian atheism

Adrian Johnston

1. How to make a real atheist: The analysis of Lacan

Jacques Lacan looks like an atheist. He talks like an atheist. But, do not be fooled: He really is an atheist.

Having to argue that Lacan is indeed atheistic might seem rather strange. Despite Lacan's background as a Jesuit-educated French Catholic, his biography reveals someone who, with a little help from Baruch Spinoza, very early on broke for good with the religious ethos of his childhood.[1] Anyone even minimally familiar with facts about his adult character and behaviors would have trouble maintaining with a straight face that he led the life and embodied the values of a devout Christian. Moreover, Lacan devoted his entire career to teaching and practicing psychoanalysis. He truly was, as he insisted, a tireless champion of Sigmund Freud, another 'godless Jew' (along with Spinoza and Karl Marx).

Yet, other details about Lacan tempt the faithful. These include his taste for custom-tailored dress shirts with clerical-style collars, his Benedictine monk brother Marc François (dubbed by Paul Roazen 'Lacan's first disciple'[2]) and his overtures to the Vatican and visits to Rome.[3] Lacan's discourse is littered with references to Christian texts and traditions. Some of his key terms and images (*le Nom-du-Père*, the trinitarian Borromean knot, etc.) are taken directly from this religious legacy. He even designates his female followers as 'the nuns of the Father' (*les nonnes du Père*).[4]

But, likely the most important feature of Lacan's version of psychoanalysis attracting the theologically minded is what appears to be a pronounced difference between him and Freud apropos their evident attitudes to religion. Freud's staunch commitments to the ideals of the Enlightenment and the *Weltanschauung* of the modern natural sciences render him implacably hostile to religiosity *tout court*.[5]

In works such as 'Obsessive Actions and Religious Practices' (1907), *Totem and Taboo* (1913) and *The Future of an Illusion* (1927), Freud establishes himself as one of the most virulently and uncompromisingly atheistic thinkers in history.

By seeming contrast, Lacan not only refrains from Freud's more bluntly combative style of anti-religiosity – he often comes across as somewhat sympathetic towards the religious materials he references. Lacan's careful invocations of the Bible, Saint Paul, Augustine, the Christian mystics and so on give the impression of an analytic theoretician who, despite his avowed fidelity to Freud, does not share with the founder of psychoanalysis a fierce animosity to all things religious. Similarly, the difference in manner between how Freud and Lacan each engage with religions leads some to suspect that the latter never really left behind the Catholicism surrounding him during his upbringing. As the title of a 2015 study by Jean-Louis Sous expresses this suspicion, *Pas très catholique, Lacan?*[6] Others go even further, trying to lay claim to Lacan as an analytic theologian rendering Freudianism and Christianity fully compatible with one another. The Jesuit priest-turned-analyst Louis Beirnaert pins on Lacan his hopes for a rapprochement between psychoanalysis and faith.[7]

I can begin arguing against these various doubts about and denials of Lacan's atheism by pointing out the exaggerated, even false, contrast between Freud's and Lacan's fashions of relating to religions. Freud, despite his clear, unwavering atheism, nonetheless carries out sophisticated examinations of Christianity and Judaism especially. Indeed, his last major work is 1939's *Moses and Monotheism*, a project that consumed him for much of the 1930s. There is no substantial difference between Freud and Lacan in terms of one dismissing and the other attending to religious subjects.

Furthermore, Lacan repeatedly reminds his audiences of his own irreligiosity. In *Seminar VII* (*The Ethics of Psychoanalysis* [1959–60]), during a discussion of Saint Paul's Epistle to the Romans, he observes, 'We analysts . . . do not have to believe in these religious truths in any way . . . in order to be interested in what is articulated in its own terms in religious experience'.[8] During a two-part lecture in Brussels summarizing much of his then-current seventh seminar, Lacan avers, 'the least that one can say is that I do not profess any confessional belonging'.[9] In this same lecture, he speaks of 'earth' (*la terre*) and 'heaven' (*le ciel*) as 'empty of God' (*vides de Dieu*).[10] Likewise, in the contemporaneous 1960 *écrit* 'The Subversion of the Subject and the Dialectic of Desire in the Freudian Unconscious', Lacan declares, 'We need not answer for any ultimate truth, and certainly not for or against any particular religion'.[11] One does not have to believe in religion to take it seriously. And, even if one denies the reality of other worlds, one cannot deny the all-too-real cultural and socio-historical presence of religions in this world. Jean-Daniel Causse, in his 2018 study, *Lacan et le christianisme*, contends that Lacan is interested specifically in the secularizable form, rather than the doctrinal content, of 'religious experience'.[12]

Sous, at one point in his above-mentioned book, asserts that, 'Lacan always left in suspense the answer to the question of knowing if the analyst should make a profession of atheism or not'.[13] As I just indicated, and as I will proceed to substantiate further, Sous's assertion here is highly contestable. But, even if one grants it, Lacan's alleged hesitancy about professions of irreligiosity arguably concerns the analyst-*qua*-practitioner, rather than the analyst-*qua*-theoretician. The analytic clinician should, with few if any exceptions, refrain from confessions of his/her beliefs (or lack thereof) to analysands. However, the analytic thinker addressing persons other than analysands on the couch is another matter altogether. Lacan, in his role as theorist and teacher of analysis, showed no hesitations about openly professing his atheism to various others.

In the inaugural session (1 December 1965) of the thirteenth seminar (*The Object of Psychoanalysis* [1965–6]), published separately in the *Écrits* as 'Science and Truth', Lacan maintains that the truths of religions always amount to posited final causes.[14] Religion is centred around significance-sustaining teleologies, meaning-giving purposes. By contrast, both modern science and psychoanalysis as conditioned by such science immerse humanity in what is ultimately a meaningless material Real devoid of design, plan or direction. Hence, analytic truths are, in essence, irreligious[15] (at least for Lacan's anti-hermeneutical rendition of analysis as oriented towards 'the materiality of the signifier', instead of the meaningfulness of signs).

Also in 'Science and Truth', Lacan pointedly repudiates religifications of analysis. He states, 'As for religion, it should rather serve us as a model not to be followed, instituting as it does a social hierarchy in which the tradition of a certain relation to truth as cause is preserved'.[16] He immediately adds, 'Simulation of the Catholic Church, reproduced whenever the relation to truth as cause reaches the social realm, is particularly grotesque in a certain Psychoanalytic International, owing to the condition it imposes upon communication'.[17] Religion generally, and Catholicism especially, with its truths as final causes, is said by Lacan to pose a great threat to and have deleterious effects upon the integrity of psychoanalysis. Considering Lacan's disdain for the International Psychoanalytic Association (i.e. 'a certain Psychoanalytic International'), made intensely bitter by his 1963 self-described 'excommunication' from the Church of the IPA, his association of it with Catholicism speaks powerfully against attributing to him any desire to somehow or other Catholicize psychoanalysis (in a roughly contemporaneous text, he asserts that a truly Freudian 'Church' would be one 'without faith or law'[18]). Close to the time of 'Science and Truth', in 1967, Lacan characterizes analysis, both metapsychological and clinical, as involving the 'most complete as possible laicization' of a 'practice without idea of elevation'.[19] Relatedly, in the 1974 interview 'The Triumph of Religion' given in Rome, he vehemently repudiates any superficial association between the Catholic ritual of confession and the clinical practice of analysis.[20]

At one point in the *écrit* 'The Youth of Gide, or the Letter and Desire' (1958), Lacan suggests that 'the psychoanalyst in our times has taken the place of God', coming to be viewed as 'omnipotent', by being the addressee of persons' religious needs.[21] Quite obviously, this suggestion anticipates Lacan's subsequent identification of the 'subject supposed to know' as the essential centre of gravity of all transference phenomena. Unsurprisingly, Lacan goes on to depict God as the *Ur*-instantiation of the structural role of *le sujet supposé savoir*.[22] He consequently maintains that the figure of the analyst, in becoming the pivotal incarnation of the subject supposed to know thanks to analysands' transference neuroses, is positioned as occupying the 'place of God-the-Father . . . that which I have designated as the Name-of-the-Father'.[23] Lacan likewise depicts transference as inherently involving 'idealism' and 'theology'.[24]

For Freudian psychoanalysis, transferences are ubiquitous in human life off as well as on the analytic couch. Hence, the position/function of *le sujet supposé savoir* sustains omnipresent idealist and theological dimensions across vast swathes of humanity, including most of those who take themselves to be non-believers. From a Lacanian perspective, many people can and do believe in the subject supposed to know while not believing in any of the deities on offer from culturally recognized religions. Subjects supposed to know substituting for God include not only clergy and analysts but also, for example, parents, doctors, scientists, politicians, professors, gurus, institutions, traditions and experts and authorities of myriad stripes.

According to Lacan, so long as one transferentially invests in anyone as representing an unbarred big Other (in Lacan's mathemes, S(A)) possessing some sort of absolute knowledge about the ultimate meaning of existence, one remains a theist. Thus, 'God is unconscious' for many self-proclaimed atheists. By itself, 'God is dead' leaves in place and intact *le sujet supposé savoir*[25] (Jacques-Alain Miller speaks of the death of God as failing to kill 'the power of the signifier "one"', namely, Lacan's 'master signifier' [S_1])[26]. In *Seminar XVI* (*From an Other to the other* [1968–9]), Lacan observes that most supposed atheists, while disavowing God, still believe in some sort of 'Supreme Being' (*l'Être suprême*), an ontological foundation of significance, lawfulness and/or order.[27] As such, these believers are not really atheists. Just about everyone remains religious, even if only unconsciously.[28]

Also in the sixteenth seminar, Lacan at one point declares, 'A true atheism, the only one which would merit the name, is that which would result from the putting in question of the subject supposed to know'.[29] He echoes this a year later in the seventeenth seminar (*The Other Side of Psychoanalysis* [1969–70]), when he states, 'The pinnacle (*pointe*) of psychoanalysis is well and truly atheism'.[30] Even Father Beinaert concedes that at least a momentary loss of faith is integral to the analytic experience.[31] Lacan furnishes a lengthier explanation of all this in *Seminar X* (*Anxiety* [1962–3])[32]:

Within what I might call the heated circles of analysis, those in which the impulse of one first inspiration (*le mouvement d'une inspiration première*) still lives on, a question has been raised as to whether the analyst ought to be an atheist or not, and whether the subject, at the end of analysis, can consider his analysis over if he still believes in God . . . regardless of what an obsessional bears out in his words, if he hasn't been divested of his obsessional structure, you can be sure that, as an obsessional, he believes in God. I mean that he believes in the God that everyone, or nearly everyone, in our cultural sphere (*tout le monde, ou presque, chez nous, dans notre aire culturelle*) abides by, this means the God in whom everyone believes without believing (*croit sans y croire*), namely, the universal eye that watches down on all our actions.[33]

Lacan soon adds, 'This is the true dimension of atheism. The atheist would be (*serait*) he who has succeeded (*aurait réussi*) in doing away with the fantasy of the Almighty (*Tout-Puissant*)'.[34] He signals that this line of questioning apropos the atheism (or lack thereof) of analyst and analysand is to be taken seriously. He does so by attributing it to those who remain, like him, moved and impassioned (i.e. 'heated') by Freud's original influence (i.e. *'le mouvement d'une inspiration première'*). Indeed, Lacan likely intends these remarks to be taken as friendly supplements to Freud's 'Obsessive Actions and Religious Practices', a text in which the founder of psychoanalysis characterizes obsessional 'neurosis as an individual religiosity and religion as a universal obsessional neurosis' (*die Neurose als eine individuelle Religiosität, die Religion als eine universelle Zwangsneurose*).[35]

As Lacan indicates, 'nearly everyone' (*tout le monde, ou presque*), if only unconsciously (as 'believing without believing'), has faith in God as omniscient (i.e. the all-seeing 'universal eye' as the fantasized locus of absolute-*qua*-infinite knowledge) and omnipotent (i.e. 'the fantasy of the Almighty [*Tout-Puissant*]'). However, the qualification 'nearly' (*presque*) is not to be overlooked here. On the one hand, theism, in the broader Lacanian sense as a belief in any instantiation whatsoever of the subject supposed to know, is virtually omnipresent and stubbornly persistent. As Lacan puts it in 'The Triumph of Religion', religion is 'tireless' (*increvable*).[36] That same year (1974), Lacan, in another interview, points to religiosity's contemporary revivals and describes religion as a 'devouring monster'.[37] As a Freudian would put it, transference (investment in a subject supposed to know à *la* Lacan) is ubiquitous and recurrent.[38] *Le sujet supposé savoir*, this fantasmatic unbarred Other of thoroughly total knowledge, indeed is a relentless, all-consuming spectre.

But, on the other hand, not all are theists. Or, at least, not everyone is doomed to what would be a universal, eternal and invincible religiosity. In the material quoted from the tenth seminar above, Lacan does not say that uprooting an obsessional's neurotic 'structure' is by itself automatically sufficient for transforming him/her into a true atheist. When speaking of true atheism, he does so conjugating in the conditional tense (*serait, aurait réussi*). Yet, in 1975, and dovetailing with claims I already quoted from the sixteenth and seventeenth seminars, Lacan muses, 'Perhaps analysis is capable of making a true atheist'.[39] How so, exactly?

The simplest and shortest preliminary answer is readily arrived at by doing as Lacan does and returning to Freud. On Freud's conception of analysis, the formation in the analysand of a 'transference neurosis' is crucial to the therapeutic process.[40] Furthermore, the 'dissolving' (*Auflösung*) of the transference is a major criterion for the successful termination of what could count as a satisfactorily completed analysis.[41] For Lacan, the Freudian dissolution of the transference (neurosis) is equivalent to a (transitory) disruption of the function of *le sujet supposé savoir* in the structure of the analysand's subjectivity.[42] Therefore, as seen, Lacan goes so far as to equate a thoroughly analysed subject with someone who has, at least for a time, acceded to what would count as real, true atheism *qua* disbelief in any and every subject supposed to know.

François Balmès and Sidi Askofaré both highlight the specificity of Lacanian analytic atheism as disbelief in *le sujet supposé savoir tout court*, not just loss of faith in a religious God or gods.[43] Askofaré and Sous appropriately warn that the working-through of all fantasies of the Almighty (i.e. all configurations of the subject supposed to know) is a long, arduous process coextensive with the labor of analysis itself, namely, a hard-won achievement.[44] Causse adds to this that 'psychoanalysis leads the subject to becoming an atheist' by enabling him/her to disinvest from neurotic symptoms that themselves are tantamount to Other-sustaining (self-)sacrifices.[45] Causse's addition fittingly suggests that neurotics become truly atheistic when analysis enables them to cease consciously and unconsciously making themselves suffer in the name of shielding certain significant Others in their life histories from ignorance and/or impotence. If and when the apparition of a flawless *Tout-Puissant* is exorcised, the analysand is free to stop martyring him/herself in vain to preserve the illusory existence of this phantasm.

In a 1972 seminar session, Lacan coins one of his many neologisms: '*incorreligionnible*'.[46] That is to say, the religious are incorrigible in their religiosity. This neologism resonates with Lacan's above-cited remarks about religion's invincibility in 1974's 'The Triumph of Religion'. This prompts one to ask: Is radical analytic atheism a sustainable stance according to Lacan? Both Askofaré and Causse contend that it is not. For Askofaré, whereas religiosity is a curable symptom for Freud, it is an incurable *sinthome* for Lacan.[47] Causse says the same thing specifically in terms of the function of *le Nom-du-Père*.[48] Furthermore, for Causse, insofar as the structural place of the subject supposed to know cannot be entirely eliminated – in other words, transferences continue to arise for post-analytic subjects too – there is no sustainable atheism in the aftermath of even the most thorough analytic process.[49]

Apropos the alleged unsustainability of radical analytic atheism, I would caution against making the perfect the enemy of the good. As with the ego, so too with theism for Lacan: The related eclipses of the ego and theism during the concluding moments of the analytic process must be experienced and endured by the analysand for a complete analysis, although this is a fleeting event of passage rather than entrance into a thereafter persisting state of being. Identifications, transferences, defenses and the like inevitably will reemerge on the hither side of the end of analysis. But, in Lacan's view, there is enormous value in the speaking subject passing through, if only momentarily, disappearances of ego-level identities and subjects supposed to know. Such traversals make a difference in relation to whatever post-analytic selfhoods and theisms (re)congeal for the analysand.

Another aspect of Lacan's substitution of 'God is unconscious' for 'God is dead' as 'the true formula of atheism'[50] is crucial to appreciate at this juncture. The unconscious never disappears anytime during or after analysis; the analytic process does not result in a liquidation of the unconscious. Likewise, the spontaneous theism of conscious and unconscious transferential investments in subjects supposed to know does not vanish forever either.

So, analysis can and should instill a measure of lasting, persistent vigilance in analysands. Lacanian atheism thus amounts not to a permanently assumed and unchangingly occupied position. Rather, it involves a recurring distance-taking from theistic structures and phenomena. Such disbelief is an intermittent meta-level occurrence, instead of a constant and unfaltering first-order stance.[51] Its salutary disruptions are no less worthwhile for all that.

In the seventh seminar, Lacan stresses that, 'desire . . . is always desire in the second degree, desire of desire'.[52] The same might be said of belief. If so, Lacan's atheism perhaps is (dis)belief 'in the second degree', namely, a second-order (dis)believing in first-order beliefs (with obdurate religious/theistic *sinthomes* perhaps being instances of the latter).[53] As I will highlight below, Lacan places himself in the same post-Hegelian lineage epitomized by Ludwig Feuerbach, among others. In a Feuerbachian-style inversion, Lacanian atheism is an ascension by a second-order subject over the first-order (resurrected) God, rather than an ascension of this God over the subject.

2. Not your father's atheism: Surpassing the scientistic *Weltanschauung* (through religion)

Lacan's analytic atheism amounts to non-belief in the very position of the subject supposed to know. And, insofar as *le sujet supposé savoir* represents for Lacan an unbarred big Other, the Lacanian atheist holds to the barring of any such Other. Therefore, this atheism's emblem is nothing other than Lacan's matheme of the signifier of the barred Other, S(A).[54]

Yet, can more be said, particularly without excessive reliance on Lacanian technical jargon, about the features that distinguish properly analytic atheism from non-analytic (i.e. garden-variety) atheism? Lacan indeed is convinced that there is a drastic distinction here.[55] But, in what does it consist?

Lacan, during his 1971–2 seminar on *The Knowledge of the Psychoanalyst*, dismissively depicts ordinary, commonplace atheism as mere 'drowsiness' (*somnolence*).[56] Such disbelief allegedly would be due to a mere thoughtlessness about the issues and concerns animating religious belief systems. It definitely would not be due to a focused, conscientious thinking through of theological concepts. This explains Lacan's provocative remarks to the effect that only theologians can be true atheists.[57] Yet, I would note that one need not be a card-carrying professional theologian to qualify as a Lacanian 'theologian' *qua* someone who has seriously worked through theological ideas. That noted, even if, for Lacan, religious answers to certain questions are not to be accepted, the questions themselves are still important to ask.

In addition to drowsy atheism as intellectually indefensible in its thoughtlessness, there is the naturalistic atheism of the scientific *Weltanschauung* appealed to by Freud. Lacan dismisses this variety of atheism, too. He does so because, by his lights, it is not really atheistic. As Lacan observes in *Seminar XII* (*Crucial Problems for Psychoanalysis* [1964–5]), these sorts of 'atheistic arguments . . . are often much more theist than the others'.[58]

In fact, modernity's empirical, experimental sciences of nature, from their very inception onwards, arguably rely upon something along the lines of the Cartesian–Einsteinian God guaranteeing the knowability of reality by not being a game-playing trickster.[59] Likewise, by at least presupposing an omnipotent and absolute knowledge of a unified, at-one-with-itself physical Real, the natural sciences remain theistic in the sense of continuing to be invested in a version of the subject supposed to know.[60] Moreover, Lacan, however fairly or not, accuses the scientific worldview of subscribing to a pseudo-secular theodicy. He charges that 'scientific discourse is finalist',[61] namely, teleological *qua* oriented by final causes. Specifically, this Lacan sees Freud's favored *Weltanschauung*, including as it does certain perspectives on the implications of Darwinian evolutionary theory, as wedded to a grand-scale teleology and metaphysical hierarchy valorizing human consciousness as the crown jewel of all creation, the ultimate *telos* of the entire history of nature.[62] In a similar vein, Lacan derisively associates naturalism with an organicist harmonization of micro- and macro-spheres of existence and a related Jungian-type religiosity anathema to any true Freudian.[63]

There also are Lacan's arguments, spelled out in 'The Triumph of Religion' and directed against Freud, upending the Enlightenment progress narrative about the victory of science over religion. In 1974, Lacan contends that the advances of the sciences, instead of compelling a withering away of religions, provoke intensifications of religiosity, spiritualism, idealism and the like. This is so because, as the material universe is scientifically rendered ever more foreign and indifferent to human experience, intentions, significances and so on,[64] humans seek compensatory refuge in the religious. Such refuge provides a seemingly secure little boat of oriented meaning on science's sea of senselessness. Science (re)vivifies and sustains, rather than corrodes and destroys, religion – hence religion's invincibility despite, or rather because of, science.[65]

In the écrit 'In Memory of Ernest Jones: On His Theory of Symbolism' (1959/60), Lacan speculates about the 'elimination' of God from the natural sciences.[66] Lacan's repeated observations about the theism subsisting within these ostensibly secular, if not atheistic, disciplines implicitly call for efforts to detheologize them fully.[67] He prompts one to wonder: What would the sciences be like without presupposing or positing any variant whatsoever of God? Could there be a new scientific Weltanschauung that is really, instead of speciously, atheistic?

Relatedly, whereas Freud considers his atheism and scientism to be of a piece, Lacan indicates that Freud's Godlessness is undercut by his fidelity to what he takes to be the scientific worldview. Adherents of this view are those Lacan has in mind when, in Seminar XVII, he provocatively maintains that 'materialists are the only authentic believers'.[68] Lacan gives to this a further counterintuitive twist: Not only is the scientific Weltanschauung embraced by Freud theistic – Christian theology furnishes key resources for a genuinely atheistic materialism.

Lacan's privileged 'Exhibit A' for this assertion is the theological conception of creation ex nihilo.[69] The idea here is that, despite its religious provenance, only this conception allows for thinking the existence of things without a God or a God-like substance as their origin. It permits replacing the Other-as-creator with a void. As I will show later, Lacan's general thesis about the utility of theology for atheism and materialism should be seen as indicative of his membership in a lineage of figures arguing for an 'atheism in Christianity', a lineage including G. W. F. Hegel, Feuerbach, Marx, G. K. Chesterton, Ernst Bloch and Slavoj Žižek. I will return to this placement of Lacan subsequently.

For now, it preliminarily must be asked: How is (Christian) theology atheistic? What does Lacan mean when he says things such as 'atheism is tenable/bearable (soutenable) only to clerics?'[70] I already have mentioned one response to this line of questioning, a response that can be summarized now in the form of a syllogism: One, true atheism can be arrived at only via the arduous working-through of religious concepts; two, anyone who arduously works through religious concepts is a 'theologian' in the sense of a thinker who thinks about theological matters; therefore, true atheists are also theologians. This argument dovetails with Seminar XI's 'God is unconscious'. A conscious atheism arrived at without the costly effort of critically scrutinizing theological ideas and arguments will remain haunted by unscrutinized remainders of religiosity (i.e. God as unconscious).

However, there are two more senses to Lacan's paradoxical equation of theology with atheism. One of these arguably harks back to Blaise Pascal's reactions specifically to René Descartes and generally to philosophical attempts at rationally proving God's existence.[71] In 'The Subversion of the Subject', Lacan speaks in passing of 'the proofs of the existence of God with which the centuries have killed him'.[72] From a Pascalian perspective, philosophers and rational(ist) theologians debase God by turning Him into merely one entity among others to be judged before the tribunal of human (all-too-human) rationality. God is made subservient to reason in a hubristic, blasphemous inversion of the proper order of things. Rendering the divine the object of a *logos* is to betray this divinity. Making God's existence depend upon reason's proofs is to nullify His very being (as the just-quoted Lacan indicates). This entails that not only philosophy but also any and every rational theology is inherently antithetical to *theós* itself. Rational theology is deicide.

Another sense in which theology is atheistic according to Lacan surfaces in the twentieth seminar (*Encore* [1972–3]). He states there:

> God (*Dieu*) is the locus where, if you will allow me this wordplay, the *dieu* – the *dieur* – the *dire*, is produced. With a trifling change, the *dire* constitutes *Dieu* (*le dire ça fait Dieu*). And as long as things are said, the God hypothesis will persist (*l'hypothèse Dieu sera là*).[73]

Lacan immediately remarks, 'That is why, in the end, only theologians can be truly atheistic, namely, those who speak of God (*ceux qui, de Dieu, en parlent*)'.[74] He then proceeds to assert:

> There is no other way to be an atheist, except to hide one's head in one's arms in the name of I know not what fear, as if this God had ever manifested any kind of presence whatsoever. Nevertheless, it is impossible to say anything without immediately making Him subsist in the form of the Other.[75]

Lacan, consistent with other pronouncements of his I already referenced earlier, maintains a broad definition of 'theologians' as 'those who speak of God' (*ceux qui, de Dieu, en parlent*). Linked to this speaking (*parler*), he coins here another neologism: '*dieur*', a combination of '*dire*' (saying) and '*Dieu*' (God). This neologism emphasizes that '*le dire ça fait Dieu*', that God is created through being spoken about (whether by theologians or others).[76]

Lacan's claims at this moment during *Seminar XX* cannot but call to mind the Feuerbach for whom the secret of theology is anthropology[77] (although, of course,

Lacan does not endorse a Feuerbachian anthropology with its humanism). Indeed, two sessions later in the twentieth seminar after introducing 'the God hypothesis', Lacan indicates that this manner of linking the divine to the socio-symbolic big Other 'was a way, I can't say of laicizing, but of exorcising the good old God'.[78] When he proclaims that *'le dire ça fait Dieu'*, it sounds as though he is deliberately echoing the young Marx when the latter declares that 'The foundation of irreligious criticism is: *Man makes religion*, religion does not make man'.[79] Restated in Lacan's terms, analytic atheism affirms that the speaking subject makes God through its saying (*dire*), rather than God making the speaking subject through His Word; in the beginning was not God's Word but, instead, that of the *parlêtre*. Again, the neologism *'dieur'* is designed to condense and convey this thesis. Although Lacan makes no references to Feuerbach by name that I know of, he seems to entertain some very Feuerbachian ideas (as will be seen, he rightly credits Hegel as the forefather of such atheistic insights). I soon will treat in much more detail Lacan's relationship to Hegel, Marx and Feuerbach.

For the time being, I wish to draw attention to a tension within these just-quoted statements from the twentieth seminar, a tension that marks one of Lacan's divergences from Feuerbach and a certain Marx. On the one hand, Lacan underscores his own thoroughgoing atheism when suggesting that God has never 'manifested any kind of presence whatsoever'. This God is feared only by those drowsy, thoughtless atheists who, in their half-hearted disbelief still haunted by (unconscious) theism, are vulnerable to reconversion by such sophistical priestly cons as Pascal's wager.

Yet, on the other hand, this same Lacan, in his resignation to 'the triumph of religion', maintains that 'the God hypothesis will persist' (*l'hypothèse Dieu sera là*).[80] There is a socio-symbolic structural place (i.e. a 'locus') where the inevitable God-effect of *dieur* comes to be. Any and every instance of speaking/saying (*parler/dire*) conjures up the divine, at least in the form of a hypothesized (and hypostatized) *grand Autre* ('it is impossible to say anything without immediately making Him subsist in the form of the Other'). What does it mean for an atheist such as Lacan to concede these points apropos theistic phenomena?

The Symbolic, in Lacan's register theory, is a condition of possibility for speaking subjectivity. And, as just seen, this register also inevitably secretes 'the God hypothesis' through any and every speaking/saying as involving *dieur*. Therefore, it would not be much of a stretch to connect Lacan's account of divine Otherness in the twentieth seminar with Immanuel Kant's doctrine of transcendental illusion (*transzendentalen Schein*) in the *Critique of Pure Reason*.[81]

Kant carefully distinguishes between a phenomenon being 'defective' (*mangelhaft*) and its being 'deceptive' (*trüglich*).[82] Once Kantian critique has identified a transcendental illusion as illusory, the illusion ceases to risk being deceptive to the critic, but still continues to be defective. As a flawed and initially misleading experience, the illusion continues to be experienced. This is because, as transcendental, it is generated and sustained by the subject's own possibility conditions. It thus is transcendental as well as illusory.

Nonetheless, through Kant's comparisons of transcendental illusions with those optical illusions viewers learn to judge as deceptive (such as distortions of objects' sizes and shapes due to the effects of refractions of light rays), he indicates that subjects can be taught through critique to treat transcendental illusions similarly to how they do such optical illusions.[83] At the same time, Kant urges eternal vigilance:

> there is a natural and unavoidable dialectic of pure reason, not one in which a bungler might be entangled through lack of acquaintance, or one that some sophist has artfully invented in order to confuse rational people, but one that irremediably attaches to human reason, so that even after we have exposed the mirage it will still not cease to lead our reason on with false hopes, continually propelling it into momentary aberrations that always need to be removed.[84]

Lacan's 'God is unconscious', as 'the true formula of atheism', likewise counsels being perpetually on guard against the inexorable phantom of *l'hypothèse Dieu*. This hypothetical God arises on the basis of the register of the Symbolic as itself a possibility condition for both the speaking subject and the unconscious-structured-like-a-language. Hence, Lacan's God hypothesis would appear very much to qualify as a case of transcendental illusion *à la* Kant. As such, Lacan in no way compromises his atheism in conceding the inescapability and necessity of the God illusion, just as Kant in no way compromises his critical epistemology in conceding to 'pure reason' that its dogmatic transgressions are encouraged by transcendental illusions.

However, Lacan goes beyond the conscious-centric horizon of Kantian critical epistemology. As a Freudian psychoanalyst, the unconscious is central to Lacan's perspectives as regards various issues, theosophical ones included. Even if a transcendental illusion is corrected and compensated for consciously, this illusion *qua* defect may continue to deceive unconsciously.

Again, if God (or the God hypothesis) is a transcendental illusion, 'God is unconscious' signals that a mere adjustment of one's conscious cognitive attitude to and judgements about the illusory divine is not necessarily enough. Additional working-through of cognitive-ideational, emotional-affective and motivational-libidinal investments in God at unconscious levels too is absolutely requisite. Lacan further complicates this labour by, through his concept of *le sujet supposé savoir*, revealing the multitude of pseudo-secular or speciously atheistic incarnations of the divine. The God hypothesis/effect persists unconsciously in part through manifesting itself in the guises of things other than the monotheistic God, in forms that do not appear to be theological in any received sense.

Furthermore, Lacan can and should be construed as subscribing to a post-Kantian line of thought laid down by both Hegel and Marx. With Hegel's 'concrete universality' and Marx's 'real abstractions', both Hegelianism and Marxism contend that the notion of the concrete apart from the abstract is itself the height of abstraction.[85] Similarly, as Lacan emphasizes against the May 1968 slogan 'structures don't march in the streets', his structures have legs; rather than being lifeless abstractions, they walk about.[86] For Hegel, Marx and Lacan alike, even if the concepts of monotheisms are illusory conceptual-symbolic constructs, they nonetheless are far from being merely epiphenomenal. Lacan's God hypothesis, if it is a Kantian-style transcendental illusion, is also, although illusory, nonetheless a very real abstraction with the most palpable of consequences. No tenable atheism can or should deny this.

3. A refined irreverence: Lacan and the Hegelian legacy

As with so many other aspects of Hegel's philosophy, his stance regarding religion has remained a matter of fierce dispute for the past two centuries up through the present. Hegel has been portrayed as a Protestant theologian, an insidious atheist and everything in between. Although Bruno Bauer's 1841 rendition of Hegel as vehemently atheistic is hyperbolic,[87] I at least agree with the Left Hegelians that Hegelianism is, at a minimum, in tension with orthodox Protestantism specifically and theism generally.

To be more precise, I would argue that Hegel is the forefather of Feuerbach's philosophy of religion.[88] Feuerbach's 22 November 1828 letter to Hegel indicates that the eventual author of 1841's *The Essence of Christianity* recognizes this himself.[89] And evidence suggests that Hegel left this letter unanswered out of political and professional cautiousness, due more than anything else to fears of the practical consequences of being associated with atheism.[90] However, neither Hegel nor Feuerbach is an atheist in the sense of simple dismissers of all things religious as unworthy of consideration, appropriation or subl(im)ation.

The debates about Hegel's religiosity or lack thereof initially erupt in German-speaking intellectual circles during the 1830s and 1840s. With this original context's repressive and reactionary political atmosphere, questions about the Hegelian philosophy of religion cloak, and are motivated by, the issue of what politics follows from Hegel's thought. It is no coincidence that the distinction between Right and Left Hegelians aligns with that between those who affirm Hegel's Protestantism and irreligiosity, respectively.

Relatedly, one finds in Hegel's political philosophy some of the clearest statements of his philosophy of religion. Of course, perhaps the most (in)famous instance of this Hegelian linkage between the political and the religious is the declaration from 1821's *Elements of the Philosophy of Right,* according to which 'The state consists in the march of God in the world (*es ist der Gang Gottes in der Welt, daß der Staat ist*)'.[91] Starting with critics such as Rudolf Haym,[92] those eager to tar and feather the mature Berlin-era Hegel as a rationalizing apologist for the Protestant conservatism of Friedrich Wilhelm the Third's Prussia latch onto this statement as evidence for their accusations.

Yet, one ought to ask: By saying that 'The state consists in the march of God in the world', is Hegel divinizing the state (as many critics allege) or politicizing God? If the latter, does such politicization leave intact the religious, theological dimensions of the divine? Or, instead, does this politicization bring about a secularization and de-divinization of the very notion of God? I would suggest that the textual evidence indicates Hegel intends, so to speak, to bring Heaven down to earth in a secularizing, de-divinizing manner.[93]

From 1798's 'The Spirit of Christianity and Its Fate' through 1831's 'The Relationship of Religion to the State', Hegel consistently indicates that the God of (mono)theism arises from, and is an expression of, human beings and their this-worldly communities. As he bluntly asserts in his 1805/6 *Philosophy of Spirit,* 'divine nature is none other than human nature' (*die göttliche Natur ist nicht eine andere als die menschliche*).[94] This proto-Feuerbachian thesis runs like a red thread through the entire span of his intellectual itinerary. 'The Spirit of Christianity and Its Fate' contains a line that would fit well within the pages of Feuerbach's *The Essence of Christianity* – 'faith in the divine grows out of the divinity of the believer's own nature; only a modification of the Godhead can know the Godhead'.[95] As Feuerbach would put this, 'That whose object is the highest being is itself the highest being'.[96]

Then, from the early 1800s through 1831, Hegel regularly claims that the absolute spirit of monotheism's deity is nothing other than an idealized, picture-thinking way of forms of human 'ethical life' (*Sittlichkeit*) representing themselves to themselves. In 1802's *System of Ethical Life,* God is identified by Hegel with *Sittlichkeit*.[97] He writes of 'the divinity of the people', 'the God of the people' as 'an ideal way of intuiting' ethical life itself.[98] Approximately a year later, in the *First Philosophy of Spirit*, Hegel proposes that 'in the organization of a *people* the absolute nature of spirit comes into its rights'.[99] That is to say, the fullest actualization of God is not as the fiction (albeit as a real abstraction[100]) of a supernatural transcendent authority projected into an imagined supernatural Beyond. Rather, this actualization occurs as the reality of an immanent configuration of communal existence in the earthly *hic et nunc*. Feuerbach similarly connects politics and religion, people and God.[101]

Likewise, the later Hegel of the Berlin period, in resonance with a post-Hegelian refrain about Christianity being the religion of atheism, indicates that Protestantism especially is the religion of secularism. He sees the socio-political secularization of the divine as genuine progress.[102] This same Hegel pointedly asserts that 'there is nothing higher or more sacred', religion included, than the secular state, with its 'Morality and Justice'.[103] For him, sublated religion-as-secular-politics is more valuable and advanced than mere, unsublated religion-as-religion. All of this is affirmed even in Hegel's contemporaneous *Lectures on the Philosophy of Religion*.[104] And, just before his death, in 1831's 'The Relationship of Religion to the State', he argues that, insofar as the essence of religion is humanity's *'free spirit'*, religion's maximal realization is to transubstantiate itself into the structures of the secular state.[105]

Admittedly, Hegel is far from a straightforward, unqualified, no-frills atheist. Yet, as the preceding shows, he is no believer in the actual doctrines of religion-*qua*-religion either. What is more, his privileging of Christianity generally and Protestantism specifically does not signal philosophical endorsement of their theological contents in their literal guises. Like Feuerbach, Christianity for Hegel is, as it were, 'the one true religion' because it comes closest to admitting that anthropology is the secret behind all theology. Furthermore, Hegel's privileging of Protestantism in particular is due to it being the religion most invested in its own secularization[106] (something also underscored by Feuerbach[107]).

Feuerbach too, despite his reputation, is no crude atheist. His irreligiosity is not that of, for instance, eighteenth-century French materialists such as Baron d'Holbach (nor that of more recent examples of d'Holbach's brand of atheism, such as Richard Dawkins). To cut a long story short, Feuerbach's atheism *qua* secular humanism is a Hegelian *Aufhebung* of (Protestant) Christianity, not an outright negation of theism.

The closing sentence of the introduction to *The Essence of Christianity* announces, 'What yesterday was still religion is no longer such to-day; and what to-day is atheism, tomorrow will be religion'.[108] A year later, in 'Preliminary Theses on the Reform of Philosophy', Feuerbach preaches at greater length:

> The Christian religion has linked the name of man with the name of God in the one name 'God-man.' It has, in other words, raised the name of man to an attribute of the highest being (*höchsten Wesens*). The new philosophy has, in keeping with the truth, turned this attribute into substance, the predicate into the subject. The new philosophy is *the idea realized* (*die* realisierte Idee) – *the truth* of Christianity. But precisely because it contains within itself the *essence* of Christianity, it abandons the *name* of Christianity. Christianity has expressed the truth only *in contradiction to the truth*. The pure and unadulterated truth without contradiction is a *new truth* – a *new, autonomous deed* of mankind.[109]

Today's atheism is destined to become tomorrow's new religion as the '*realized . . . truth* of Christianity'. That is to say, Christianity, as theologized anthropology, will be dialectically inverted into anthropomorphized theology, namely, the new religion of secular humanism. The old religion misattributed the virtues of natural, this-worldly humanity to a supernatural, otherworldly God. Feuerbach's 'new philosophy' will be transformed into the new religion once human beings start self-consciously celebrating and venerating their virtues as their own (and not those of a superhuman deity). Unlike certain sorts of atheists, Feuerbach does not forecast or advocate the disappearance of the experiences of awe, reverence, wonder and the like historically associated with religions. He sublates (*als Aufhebung*) Christianity, rather than simply negating it externally and without remainder.[110]

Lacan locates his Freudian analytic atheism in a line of descent tracing back to a Feuerbachian-*avant-la-lettre* Hegel.[111] He is most explicit about this in *Seminar VII*. This seminar contains some of Lacan's discussions of the notion of the death of God. Speaking of this, Lacan notes, 'there is a certain atheistic message in Christianity itself, and I am not the first to have mentioned it. Hegel said that the destruction of the gods would be brought about (*se complète la destruction des dieux*) by Christianity'.[112] A couple of sessions later in the seventh seminar, Lacan equates atheism itself with Christianity's barring of the big Other, along with this Other's 'Law', through staging the death of God Himself on the Cross.[113] This Christianity, with its dialectics oscillating between religion/theism and irreligion/atheism,[114] is identified by Lacan here as 'the first weighty historical example of the German notion of *Aufhebung* (*premier example historique où prenne son poids le terme allemand d'*Aufhebung)'.[115]

On a prior occasion, I have dealt critically with an instance, in *Seminar IV* (*The Object Relation* [1956–7]), where Lacan approvingly invokes the conception of the Holy Spirit.[116] I would observe in passing that some of Lacan's more pro-Christian moments, such as in the fourth seminar, occur when he is most proximate to Kant's critical transcendental idealism (i.e. the Kant who 'had to deny knowledge in order to make room for faith'[117]– a Kant Lacan later pointedly repudiates in, for instance, 'The Triumph of Religion'[118]). When Lacan does not enforce a Kantian-style epistemological limit partitioning reality from the Real, he is less prone to allow for theological-type speculations about the Real-beyond-reality.

That said, Lacan's only other sustained reference to the Christian conception of the Holy Spirit, apart from the one to be found in *Seminar IV*, can be interpreted as reflective of his adhesion to the post-Hegelian atheism-in-Christianity tradition. In the fifteenth seminar (*The Psychoanalytic Act* [1967–8]), Lacan remarks, 'The Holy Spirit is a notion infinitely less stupid (*bête*) than that of the subject supposed to know'.[119] As seen, *le sujet supposé savoir* is, in Lacan's analytic framework, the core structural place and absolutely essential function of any and every theism. So long as one believes in some form of the subject supposed to know, one is not a true atheist. Hence, the Lacan of *Seminar XV*, in playing off *le Saint-Esprit* against this heavenly super-Subject, implies that one can (and should) have the Holy Spirit without God or His pseudo-secular surrogates. And with the Holy Spirit as the human community left behind after the disappearance of God-the-Father and death of Christ-the-Son, Lacan's favouring of the horizontal immanence of *le Saint-Esprit* over the vertical transcendence of any divine *sujet supposé savoir* clearly is in line with the Hegelian tradition of Christian atheism.[120]

Moreover, the fifteenth seminar's reference to the Holy Spirit indicates that this *Geist*, as at odds with the subject supposed to know, is anything but omniscient. In other words, the this-worldly socio-symbolic order is barred, riven by ignorance and devoid of final answers and unifying certainties. Elsewhere, Lacan attributes this lack of omniscience not only to *le Saint-Esprit* but even to God Himself. In short, he bars God too.

On several occasions in the 1960s and 1970s, Lacan raises the question of whether God believes in God.[121] Eventually, during the 21 May 1974 session of *Seminar XXI* (*The Non-Dupes Err* [1973–4]), Lacan finally answers this query: God does not believe in God.[122] In this same seminar session, he immediately spells out the implications of this answer.

To begin with, this Lacan of the twenty-first seminar equates 'God does not believe in God' with 'There is something (of the) unconscious' (*Y a d'l'inconscient*).[123] How should this equation be understood? On Lacan's assessment, as highlighted, the essence of God resides in the structural function of *le sujet supposé savoir*. Furthermore, the kind of knowledge attributed through supposition to God (or any other transferentially invested subject supposed to know) is the reflexive, self-transparent variety of philosophical and theological traditions. From such familiar traditional perspectives, knowledge is inherently auto-reflexive and self-conscious.

When one knows, one knows that one knows. When one thinks, one thinks that one thinks. Additionally, when one believes, one believes that one believes.

On a Lacanian assessment, what is really revolutionary about Freud's self-styled 'Copernican revolution' is his positing of the unconscious as irreflexive mentation. One is gripped by the unconscious in knowing without knowing that one knows, thinking without thinking that one thinks and believing without believing that one believes. Lacan's denial that God believes in God, with its associations to the irreflexivity characteristic of the Freudian unconscious, is another version of 'God is unconscious' (i.e. the Lacanian 'true formula of atheism').

But, the unconscious definitely is not God nor a substitute for Him. There is no analyst, priest, parent, etc. anywhere to be found who knowingly could provide the decisive final word about the singular, coherent unconscious truth of one's being. Furthermore, there is no such truth to be found even within and by the subject of the unconscious itself. Admittedly, in the analytic relationship, knowledge of the unconscious resides on the side of the analysand rather than the analyst *qua* subject supposed to know (but not actually knowing, since this knowledge is a transferential supposition of the analysand to be worked through by him/her). Yet, this does not mean that the analysand is or could ever become *le sujet supposé savoir* in relation to his/her own unconscious and its knowledge.

There are two reasons why the analysand, despite being the lone locus of knowledge of his/her unconscious, cannot be the subject supposed to know in lieu of the analyst or anyone else. First, no matter how much analysis a person undergoes, regardless of how well-analysed someone is, he/she always still will have an unconscious. No amount of analysis ever results in a complete elimination of the unconscious, in a becoming-fully-transparent-to-oneself. Analysts do not and cannot produce absolute self-consciousnesses, even through lengthy didactic analyses.

However, leaving things at this first reason risks leaving intact the impression that although the powers to make conscious are limited, some form of complete, self-consistent and meaningful unconscious knowledge remains beyond these limits. Although I cannot consciously know it (even after years and years of analysis), maybe there still is a unique governing truth of my being. Perhaps my own unconscious is the subject supposed to know. Perhaps 'God is unconscious' means my unconscious is God (or God-like) as the hidden omniscient and omnipotent power that makes me who I am and fatefully pulls the strings of my life history.

The preceding motivates and leads to Lacan's second reason as to why even the analysand's unconscious cannot qualify as measuring up to the role outlined by the position of *le sujet supposé savoir*. The first reason, as just explained, is that conscious efforts cannot ever make all of the unconscious known to (self-)consciousness. The second reason is, so to speak, that there is no 'all' (*pas tout*) of unconscious knowledge to be known, not even in principle.

The unconscious is not its own subject supposed to know. It is not a whole aware and in command of itself. No one is in charge of you, not even your unconscious. While the unconscious involves knowledges, it is not a synthesized and synthesizing knower. There is no divine homunculus in heaven, on earth or between your ears. Not only does the analyst not hold a secret set of keys to your unconscious – your unconscious has no such keys either. And, it does not even have corresponding locks to these non-existent keys, since there is no one-of-a-kind treasure chest of mysteries waiting to be unlocked. Just as God does not believe in God, so too should you not believe in your supposed (unconscious) self. There is nothing there worthy of faith or veneration.

This second reason, having to do with the not-all-ness of unconscious knowledge, is emphasized by Lacan at the same moment in *Seminar XXI* when he denies that God believes in God. After equating this denial with an affirmation of the existence of the unconscious, he proceeds to claim that 'The knowledge of the unconscious is totally the opposite of instinct' (*Le savoir de l'inconscient est tout le contraire de l'instinct*).[124] Lacan immediately clarifies that, by 'instinct', he intends to evoke the vision of a natural harmony.[125] Instinct would be, for him, knowledge in the Real as a materially innate *savoir-faire* provided by nature and guaranteeing synchronization between organism and environment. Indeed, a few months earlier during the twenty-first seminar, Lacan describes the instinctual as 'a supposed natural knowledge' (*un savoir supposé naturel*).[126]

This description of the instinctual, through its resonance with *le sujet supposé savoir*, signals that the concept of instinct brings with it an idea of a Nature-with-a-capital-N, an all-knowing and benevolent creator. This Nature as unbarred big Other obviously is a mere substitute for God, just another permutation of the subject supposed to know. It is the expression of the unprocessed theism persisting within speciously secular or atheistic naturalisms. Self-styled scientific atheists, including ones who are members of the analytic community, are nondupes who err (as per the title of *Seminar XXI, Les non-dupes errent*).

Hence, falsely naturalizing the Freudian unconscious along these lines, wrongly identifying it with (repressed) instincts (rather than drives [*Triebe*]), brings about an illusory deification of it as an incarnation of a fantasized God-like Nature, *un Dieu comme ça* (a God as id). Authentic analytic atheism entails, among other things, that the unconscious itself cannot be made into another deity or divine avatar through appeals to a still-theistic version of the category of the natural. 'God is unconscious' means that there is no God, no unbarred big Other, as a locus of self-transparent omniscience – not even in/as the unconscious itself imagined as a profound nature or knowledge exceeding any and all consciousness.

Likewise, if the satisfactory conclusion of an analysis involves the dissolution of transference as, for Lacan, the fall of the subject supposed to know, then the analysand comes to settle for 'some unconscious' (*à la* 'Y a d'l'inconscient'). He/she accepts what there is of bits and pieces of unconsciousness as revealed by and within the inconsistencies and tensions of analysed consciousness. This acceptance of these still-valuable scraps puts an end to awaiting a final Revelation-to-end-all-revelations from the unconscious as an expected ultimate exclamation point or punchline bringing to a neat close the labor of the analytic process. The analysand ceases anticipating such a last judgement from his/her unconscious as well as from the analyst as its presumed anointed representative. He/she somehow comes to appreciate that there is no transcendent, ineffable Other of the immanent, effable Other, no deep truth underlying and uniting the tangled knots of unconscious truths that do surface (*à la* Lacan's denials of there being an Other of the Other and a truth about the truth[127]). There is no other shoe yet to drop.

This theme of the interrelated self-opacities of both God and the unconscious arguably traces back to an earlier period of Lacan's teaching. I am thinking particularly of a comment Lacan makes in *Seminar III* (*The Psychoses* [1955–6]). He remarks there, 'Our own atheism is . . . linked to this always elusive aspect of the *I* of the other (*ce côté toujours se dérobant du* je *de l'autre*)'.[128] Considering this context and period of Lacan's teaching, 'this always elusive aspect of the *I* of the other' should be interpreted as designating neither the Imaginary little-o-other *qua* inter-subjective alter-ego nor the Symbolic big Other *qua* trans-subjective socio-linguistic order. Instead, it designates Real Otherness, namely, the impenetrable opacity of alterity inaccessible not only to the subject relating to this Other but also to this Other itself.[129] The atheistic upshot of such alterity Lacan has in mind in the third seminar is the same as with his later 'God does not believe in God': The Other, whether as God, parent, analyst, one's own unconscious or whoever and whatever else, is not a subject of absolute (self-)knowledge but is, rather, irreflexive, blind and enigmatic to itself.

Just a few years after *Seminar III*, in the seventh seminar, 'this always elusive aspect of the *I* of the other' becomes the Real Otherness of the Freudian *Nebenmensch als Ding* (neighbor as Thing [*das Ding*]).[130] In Balmès's view, Lacan's Christian-atheistic God is a version of this Thing.[131] Balmès muses that 'One could . . . say that *das Ding* is a divine name in the times of the death of God'.[132]

But one has to be careful apropos Balmès's suggestion here. Linking God with the Thing risks implying that Lacan somehow or other reduces Christianity to the dark, threatening deity of the Old Testament and/or to a repressed matriarchal basis (given the equation of *das Ding* with the mother as Real Other in *Seminar VII*). To avoid this risk, one must appreciate that any connection between the Christian God and the Freudian Thing would signify again that *Dieu est inconscient*. Put differently, even the New Testament God is the name for a barred, irreflexive and de-divinized lack. Nonetheless, this void interpellates those 'left behind', namely, persons who unite together around this absence (i.e. the Holy Spirit as a this-worldly human community).

Seemingly despite all of the preceding, Lacan (in)famously declares in 1974's 'The Triumph of Religion' that 'The true religion is the Roman one. . . . There is *one* true religion and that is the Christian religion'.[133] As Lorenzo Chiesa and Alberto Toscano observe, this can be taken to state that Christianity is the 'least false' of all religions.[134] By way of friendly supplement, I would add to this that, insofar as Lacan explicitly situates himself in a post-Hegelian atheism-in-Christianity current, Christianity's 'truth' resides in what it self-subvertingly reveals unknowingly and inadvertently. On this reading, what makes Christianity truer than other religions is that it stands on the threshold of bringing about an immanent sublation of all religiosity/theism. As Causse correctly notes, Lacan's identification of Christianity as 'the one true religion' is not to be taken as praise of it.[135]

Indeed, *Seminar XX* provides strong evidence that Lacan's acknowledgement of Christianity's truth is a backhanded compliment. Therein, Lacan considers this acknowledgement to be bad news for Christianity *qua* religion – 'That it is the true religion (*la vraie religion*), as it claims (*comme il prétend*), is not an excessive claim (*prétention*), all the more so in that, when the true (*le vrai*) is examined closely, it's the worst (*pire*) that can be said about it'.[136] Later, during the same seminar session (8 May 1973), he maintains, 'Christians – well, it's the same with psychoanalysts – abhor (*ont horreur*) what was revealed to them. And they are right'.[137]

What is this abhorrent truth? What is this repulsive, scandalous 'x' revealed to both Christians and psychoanalysts? I believe that a hint is to be found in Lacan's 1963 *écrit* 'Kant with Sade' when he claims, 'Christianity has assuredly taught men to pay little attention to God's jouissance'.[138] The horrifying worst that both Christianity and psychoanalysis brush up against has something to do with *jouissance*. But what, exactly, is this divine enjoyment? And what does it have to do with the ostensible truth of Christianity as well as the radical atheism of psychoanalysis?

4. Not your atheism's father: From a Feuerbachian Freud to a Marxian Lacan

Freud's reflections on religion readily can be situated in a Feuerbachian lineage too.[139] Simply put, just as Feuerbach reduces theology to anthropology, so too does Freud reduce the God of Judeo-Christian monotheism to the father of the Oedipus complex. Both thinkers bring heaven down to earth by making the latter the truth of the former.

But as Marx's fourth thesis on Feuerbach maintains, 'once the earthly family is discovered to be the secret of the holy family, the former must then itself be destroyed in theory and in practice'.[140] Although, as I have shown, Lacan situates himself in the Christian-atheist current of a proto-Feuerbachian Hegel, Lacan's actual position is closer to that of Marx. What holds for Marx *vis-à-vis* Feuerbach's atheism holds for Lacan *vis-à-vis* Freud's atheism too. To be more precise, Lacan comes to see Freud as analysing the monotheistic God into the Oedipal father without, in turn, going through to the end with a critical analysis of the latter. Like Marx's Feuerbach, Lacan's Freud leaves too much to 'the earthly family' he uncovers as secretly underlying 'the holy family'.

Of course, the move of tethering the divinity of Judeo-Christian monotheism to the paternal figure of the Oedipal family drama is absolutely central to Freud's entire atheistic analytic assessment of religion.[141] And, Lacan, in, for instance, *Seminar XII*, indeed credits this Freud with further radicalizing atheism.[142] Interestingly, Balmès and Miller present diverging renditions of Lacan's stance with respect to this Freud. On Balmès's construal, Lacan seeks to invert Freud's analysis of God into father, instead explaining the paternal function as determined by a theological socio-symbolic constellation; God explains father, rather than *vice versa*.[143] By contrast, Miller's reconstruction has Lacan dissatisfied with Freud for failing to dissipate fantasies about fathers after so thoroughly dissipating fantasies about gods.[144] Evidence from the twelfth seminar and elsewhere favors Miller on this point.

In 'The Subversion of the Subject', Lacan himself pointedly cautions that 'We would be mistaken if we thought that the Freudian Oedipus myth puts an end to theology'.[145] If there is something religious (i.e. mythical and/or theological) about Freud's Oedipus complex,[146] then the apparent atheism of his grounding of the religious in the familial is merely apparent. But, in what way(s) is the Oedipal *à la* Freud still bound up with religiosity?

The four sessions of *Seminar XVII* grouped together by Miller under the fitting title 'Beyond the Oedipus Complex' contain Lacan's most developed explanations of the mythical/theological residues clinging to Freud's reflections on the family. Therein, Lacan identifies the Oedipus complex as 'Freud's dream'.[147] As he notes in good analytic fashion, 'Like any dream it needs to be interpreted'.[148]

Lacan similarly depicts Freud's Oedipus as a 'myth'.[149] During this same stretch of the seventeenth seminar, he comments, 'One can bullshit (*déconner*) a lot over myths, because it is precisely the field of bullshitting. And bullshitting, as I have always said, is truth (*la vérité*). They are identical'.[150] Perhaps the fiction in Lacan's 'the truth has the structure of fiction'[151] can be bullshit (*déconnage*) too. More precisely, and as also a 'dream', the Freudian Oedipus complex offers a manifest text (with its myths, fictions and bullshit) that, when interpreted properly, discloses latent thoughts (as this dream's truths).[152] Or, in phrasing borrowed from Marx, this complex of Freud's wraps a 'rational kernel' within a 'mystical shell'. For Lacan, the mystical shell of Oedipus is anything but atheistic. Yet, Oedipus's rational kernel, which it shares with Judeo-Christian monotheism, allows for an immanent critique of both the Oedipal as per Freud and the monotheistic. There is something in both the Oedipus complex and monotheism more than these formations themselves, an extimate 'x' that can explode these formations from within their own confines. But what is this 'x' according to Lacan?

At the end of the 18 February 1970 seminar session, Lacan begins answering this question. His remarks on this occasion deserve quoting at length:

> this recourse to the myth of Oedipus is really quite sensational. It is worth making the effort to elaborate this. And I was thinking of getting you today to appreciate what is outrageous in the fact that Freud, for example, in the last of the *New Introductory Lectures on Psychoanalysis*, should think he had cut the question of the rejection of religion off from any acceptable horizon, should think that psychoanalysis has played a decisive role in this, and should believe that it was the end of the matter when he has told us that the support of religion is nothing other than this father whom the child

has recourse to in its childhood, and who he knows is all loving (*il est tout amour*), that he anticipates, forestalls what may manifest itself within him as malaise.[153]

Lacan continues:

> Isn't this an odd thing when one knows how things in fact are with the father's function? To be sure, this is not the only point at which Freud presents us with a paradox, namely, the idea of referring this function to some kind of *jouissance* of all the women (*quelle jouissance originelle de toutes les femmes*), when it is a well-known fact that a father barely suffices for one of them, and even then – he mustn't boast about it. A father has, with the master – I speak of the master as we know him, as he functions – only the most distant of relationships since, in short, at least in the society Freud was familiar with, it is he who works for everybody. He has responsibility for the 'famil' . . . Isn't that sufficiently strange to suggest to us that after all what Freud retains in fact, if not in intention, is very precisely what he designates as being the most essential in religion, namely, the idea of an all-loving father (*un père tout-amour*)? . . . the father is love, the first thing to be loved in this world is the father. Strange vestige (*survivance*). Freud believes this will make religion evaporate, whereas it is really the very substance of it that he preserves with this strangely composed myth of the father.[154]

He then proceeds to reflect further on the Freudian father of *Totem and Taboo* (i.e. the *Urvater* of the primal horde):

> it all ends with the idea of the murder, namely that the original father is the one whom the sons have killed, after which it is through the love of this dead father that a certain order unfolds. In all its enormous contradictions, in its baroqueness and its superfluousness, doesn't this seem to be nothing but a defense against these truths (*vérités*) that the abundance of all these myths clearly spells out, well before Freud diminishes these truths in opting for the myth of Oedipus? What is there to conceal? That, as soon as the father enters the field of the master's discourse where we are in the process of orientating ourselves, he is, from the origins, castrated.[155]

In the following two sessions of *Seminar XVII* (11 March and 18 March 1970), Lacan reiterates these points. He again stresses the fictive character of the primal father of *Totem and Taboo* ('not the slightest trace has ever been seen of the father of the human horde').[156] He reemphasizes that 'he who enjoys all the women is inconceivable to imagine', with fathers, as speaking beings, being symbolically castrated *qua* cut off from any presumed full, absolute *jouissance*.[157]

All of this calls for some careful unpacking. To begin with, Lacan appeals to certain common-sensical intuitions. For him, if one bothers even to glance for a moment at flesh-and-blood fathers, what one sees is anything but the Freudian *Urvater* ('We have seen orangutans', but not a human version of this sort of alpha male[158]). Empirical embodiments of the paternal function are miserable schmucks just like all other speaking beings, rather than ferociously potent monopolizers of a total and complete Enjoyment-with-a-capital-E. Each father barely knows what to do with one woman, let alone, like the fantasmatic primal father, all women ('a father barely suffices for one of them'). At least in recent memory, the ostensible *pater familias* is anything but an omnipotent lord (as Lacan declares already in 1938, modernity has come to be marked by the 'social decline of the paternal imago'[159]). If anything, the modern father is everyone else's servant, frenetically dancing attendance on family members as well as bosses, clients, colleagues, etc. ('it is he who works for everybody'). In an inversion the Hegel of the *Phenomenology of Spirit* would appreciate, the supposed paternal master is, in reality, a slave[160] (with Lacan, as regards the master's discourse, also repeatedly referring to this same Hegel[161]).

In the above-quoted material from the sessions of the seventeenth seminar assembled by Miller under the heading 'Beyond the Oedipus Complex', Lacan invokes 'the discourse of the master' as per his theory of the four discourses (those of master, university, hysteric and analyst) central to *Seminar XVII*. The 'master' of the master's discourse is anything but the all-powerful paternal figure of Freud's myth of the primal horde. As Lacan says in the preceding, 'as soon as the father enters the field of the master's discourse . . . he is, from the origins, castrated'. How so? What precisely does this mean?

The later Lacan of the early 1970s defines a 'discourse' (*discours*) in his sense as a 'social link' (*lien social*) between speaking beings (*parlêtres*).[162] That is to say, a Lacanian discourse is a specific socio-symbolic structure configuring the positions of subjects caught up in its matrices of mediation. And, the discourse of the master is the 'elementary cell' of all the discourses. This is because, for Lacan, the master's discourse represents the initial, zero-level position of any and every subject as a speaking being. The other discourses (of the university, hysteric and analyst) are subsequent permutations of this first form of socio-symbolic bond.[163] The discourse of the master is the initial result of the symbolic castration that brings the *parlêtre* as such into existence.[164]

Thus, when Lacan says, 'as soon as the father enters the field of the master's discourse . . . he is, from the origins, castrated', he is saying that the paternal figure, as a speaking being subjected to language and everything bound up with it, is symbolically castrated like all subjects. He is no exception to this castration. Hence, he too has no access to any purported complete, undiluted *jouissance*, whether of 'all women' or of anything else.[165] Freud's *Urvater* is pure fantasy.

This absence of limitless enjoyment is what the 'myth of Oedipus . . . is there to conceal'.

Apropos the fiction of the primal horde in *Totem and Taboo*, Lacan, in *Seminar XVII*, also draws attention to the murder of the primal father by the band of brothers. In Freud's story, the *Urvater*, the enjoyer of *toutes les femmes*, ends up dead. Deploying a Lévi-Straussian structuralist approach to this story as a myth, Lacan reads the diachronic sequence in which the primal father goes from domineering *jouisseur* to vanquished corpse as indicative of a synchronic identity between unlimited enjoyment and death.[166] For him, the dead father signifies 'the Law' bringing about desire (*désir*) through marking the prohibition/impossibility of absolute *jouissance*.[167]

As Lacan observes, 'no one knows, no living being in any case, what death is . . . death is properly speaking unknowable (*inconnaissable*)'.[168] Therefore, *Totem and Taboo*, interpreted as a myth *à la* Claude Lévi-Strauss, indicates that infinite *jouissance* too is 'unknowable' for human beings.[169] This indeed is the conclusion Lacan reaches:

> The fact that the dead father is *jouissance* presents itself to us as the sign of the impossible itself. And in this way we rediscover here the terms that are those I define as fixing the category of the real, insofar as, in what I articulate, it is radically distinguished from the symbolic and the imaginary – the real is the impossible. Not in the name of a simple obstacle we hit our heads up against, but in the name of the logical obstacle of what, in the symbolic, declares itself to be impossible. This is where the real emerges from (*C'est de là que le réel surgit*).[170]

For Lacan, the myth of the primal horde with its *Urvater* is the true version of Freud's Sophocles-inspired Oedipus complex.[171] Its core truth is that, as Lacan puts it (in the seventeenth seminar and elsewhere) in a twist on a famous line from Fyodor Dostoyevsky, 'If God is dead, then nothing is permitted'[172] (with this Lacanian line being, in part, a paraphrase of Freud's comment in *Totem and Taboo* that 'The dead father became stronger than the living one had been . . . What had up to then been prevented by his actual existence was thenceforward prohibited by the sons themselves'[173]). Specifically, the murdered *Urvater* as a dead God – for Freud, the primal father is the prototype of the divine father[174] – signifies that no flawlessly total *jouissance* is attainable and livable.[175] As Lacan states in the just-quoted passage, such enjoyment is Real *qua* impossible.

Moreover, the preceding block quotation subtly resonates with Lacan's earlier-glossed remarks about the God hypothesis in *Seminar XX*. This passage from *Seminar XVII* can be interpreted as suggesting that the fantasy of the impossible figure of the primal father *qua* all-powerful total enjoyer is a version of this hypothesized divinity. The Lacan of the twentieth seminar, as seen, argues that *l'hypothèse Dieu* arises out of the symbolic order; so long as there are speaking beings subjected to this order, there will be some version of this hypothetical construct.

Similarly, the Lacan of the seventeenth seminar contends that 'the dead father' of non-existent *jouissance* (i.e. the Freudian *Urvater* as the prototype of all gods) is a mythical manifestation of an impossible Real immanent to the Symbolic.[176] The Real of inaccessible enjoyment 'emerges' (*surgit*) out of, is secreted by, a register within which this enjoyment is nullified by signifier-inflicted barring. So long as there is symbolic castration, humanity will remain haunted by the fantasmatic specter of something along the lines of the primal father – whether as *Urvater*, God, the at-least-one (*au-moins-un*) of the *hommoinsun/hommoinzin* who is magically exempt from *jouissance*-barring symbolic castration ($\exists x \sim \Phi x$),[177] etc. This version of the God hypothesis will not be exorcised quickly and easily.

Also in the same set of sessions of *Seminar XVII*, Lacan draws attention to two oddities featuring in Freud's reductions of the God of religions to the father of both the primal horde and the Oedipus complex. What makes these two features so odd is that they fly in the face of various other aspects of the Freudian framework; they involve Freud coming into conflict with some of his own commitments. The first of these is Freud's insistence on the historical, factual reality of the tall tale of the primal horde and its killing of the *Urvater*. Lacan says of Freud that 'he clings strongly to what actually happened, this blessed story of the murder of the father of the horde, this Darwinian buffoonery'[178] and that 'Freud holds that this was real. He clings to it. He wrote the entire *Totem and Taboo* in order to say it – it necessarily happened, and it's where everything began'.[179]

Indeed, Freud spends the final paragraphs of *Totem and Taboo* weighing whether or not to treat the narrative of the murder of the primal father as a 'wishful *phantasy*' (*Wunschphantasie*).[180] Starting with Freud's 21 September 1897 letter to Wilhelm Fliess, he maintains that repressed fantasies can be just as causally efficacious in the psyche as experienced events impressed upon the mind by 'the real world'.[181] In other words, for Freud, psychical reality can be as significant and influential as external reality.

In the concluding moments of *Totem and Taboo*, Freud revisits these considerations about fantasy.[182] Their relevance for the question of whether the murder of the primal father was an actual historical occurrence or a fantasmatic construction projected back into pre-history is made even more appropriate by Freud's long-standing Haeckelian tendency to draw parallels between phylogeny and ontogeny. This tendency leads Freud on a number of occasions to equate 'primitives' and neurotics.[183] Hence, if neurotics can be traumatized by repressed fantasies acting as if they were episodic memories, why not conjecture that the same holds for the proximate descendants of the primal horde? Considering that the scene of the killing of the *Urvater* is a highly speculative anthropological hypothesis on Freud's part, why not incline towards viewing this scene as a causally efficacious fantasy?

But Freud abruptly brings *Totem and Taboo* to a close with an adamant insistence on the extra-psychical reality of the primal father's murder by the band of brothers. In this instance, he pointedly rejects his own habit of establishing equivalences between 'primitives' and neurotics. Although the latter might be affected as much or more by thinking (as intending, fantasizing, etc.) apart from acting, 'primitive men actually *did* what all the evidence shows they intended to do'[184] (note Freud's italicization of 'did'). The last line of *Totem and Taboo* is a quotation from Johann Wolfgang von Goethe's *Faust*: 'in the beginning was the Deed' (*Im Anfang war die Tat*).[185] In a metapsychological paper, not discovered until 1983, dealing with phylogenetic matters, Freud reaffirms that this 'triumph over the father . . . was realized'.[186] That is to say, the deed of killing the *Urvater* really did transpire as a matter of cold, hard historical fact. Lacan thinks Freud doth protest too much here – and does so even against his own theoretical insights as regards the (in)distinction between psychical and external realities.

As seen, Lacan, in *Seminar XVII*, additionally underscores Freud's striking insistence that the father who lies at the basis of monotheistic religions is full of nothing but love. By Lacan's lights, this is a 'strange vestige (*survivance*)'. More precisely, this is a *survivance* of theism within Freud. Reducing God to the paternal figure is anything but irreligious if this figure himself still is deified as 'an all-loving father (*un père tout-amour*)'. Hence, Lacan judges the Freudian mythical father as a far-from-atheistic construct.

What heightens the strangeness of this vestige of religiosity in Freud is that much of the rest of what he has to say about fathers in his corpus paints a picture of them as hardly pure love. The relationship to the paternal figure of the Oedipus complex often involves aggression, envy, fear, hatred, jealousy, rivalry and the like. Strong currents of negative affects pervade the rapport with the Oedipal father. This makes Freud's equation of father with love in his treatments of religion all the odder.

A few years later, Lacan presses home his critique of Freud as preserving rather than destroying monotheism. In the twentieth seminar, he alleges:

Freud saves the Father once again. In that respect he imitates Jesus Christ. Modestly, no doubt, since he doesn't pull out all the stops. But he contributes thereto, playing his little part as a good Jew who was not entirely up-to-date.[187]

Freud props up the father figure on the eve of a 'social decline of the paternal *imago*' with which he is 'not entirely up-to-date'. In so doing, Freud ends up implicitly placing himself in the same position as Christ (as I will underscore below, this position occupied by Christ and Freud alike is a properly perverse one as per the Lacanian rendition of perversion). This remains a long way from atheism indeed.

Freud's myth of the *Urvater*, this exceptional *tout jouisseur* ($\exists x \sim \Phi x$), saves fathers by occluding their unexceptional castration ($\forall x \Phi x$).[188] As Miller, following Lacan, observes, both Christianity and Freud confront but recoil from the paternal figure's lack of potency and his embodiment of the impossibility of (full) *jouissance*.[189] Thus, Lacanian atheism entails affirming the non-existence not only of the subject supposed to know but also of the subject supposed to enjoy[190] (or, to combine these two, the subject supposed to know how to enjoy). This non-existence is the abhorrent truth at the core of both Christianity and psychoanalysis.

Again, Freud, like Feuerbach, demythologizes the holy family by grounding it in the earthly family without demythologizing the latter in turn. Like Marx *vis-à-vis* Feuerbach, Lacan *vis-à-vis* Freud takes this further step of critically analysing the earthly family itself. Moreover, whereas Feuerbach's God is a projection of humanity's strengths and virtues, Lacanianism diagnoses this projection as defensively masking the opposite, namely, humanity's weaknesses and vices. Whether as the primal father or the divinities of monotheisms, this figure is an Other-Subject whose omniscience and omnipotence are the representative reversals, the symptomatic inversions, of human beings' ignorance and feebleness.

Additionally, as some of Žižek's remarks indicate, Feuerbach merely transfers the status of subject supposed to know and/or enjoy from a supernatural heavenly God to a natural earthly human species (*Gattung*). For Feuerbach's not-truly-atheistic 'atheism', the big Other really does exist, albeit as the praiseworthy features of this-worldly humanity's *Gattungswesen* (species-being), rather than as an otherworldly deity.[191] By contrast, for Lacan's genuinely consequent atheism, *le grand Autre n'existe pas*, not as God, humanity, father or anything and anyone else.

As I have highlighted already, Lacan delights in counterintuitively associating monotheistic theology with atheism while simultaneously associating naturalistic materialism with theism. This reversal is especially applicable in the case of Freud's ostensibly atheistic rooting of monotheism in the figure of the *Urvater*. As with Feuerbachian anthropology, too much theology persists within Freudian anthropology.

If anything, *Totem and Taboo*'s myth of the primal horde is a much less atheistic scenario than that of the Christian crucifixion. In the latter, the transcendence of God-the-Father vanishes (if only apparently and momentarily), with Christ-the-Son losing faith and dying on the cross. François Regnault, in his 1985 study *Dieu est inconscient*, emphasizes the Christian God's status as 'jealous, not-all, incarnated, etc.'[192] By contrast, Freud's primal father is virtually omnipotent, all-enjoying, uninhibited and mythically dream-like.

As Chesterton remarks, 'Christianity is the only religion on earth that has felt that omnipotence made God incomplete'.[193] Perhaps Bloch is justified in proposing that the immanent critique of religion via Christian atheism is more potent and effective than its external critique through plain old garden-variety atheism.[194] The evidence examined by me thus far seems to suggest that Lacan might agree with this fellow post-Hegelian.

5. After Christian atheism?: Analysis between determinate and absolute negations

Chesterton, in his 1908 book *Orthodoxy*, furnishes a powerful rendition of Christianity as the religion of atheism. He focuses on the scene in which the crucified Jesus laments aloud, 'Father, why hast Thou forsaken me?' Taking Jesus as Christ *qua* God-become-human, Chesterton comments that 'in that terrific tale of the Passion there is a distinct emotional suggestion that the author of all things (in some unthinkable way) went not only through agony, but through doubt'.[195] He goes on to explain:

> God . . . passed in some superhuman manner through our human horror of pessimism. When the world shook and the sun was wiped out of heaven, it was not at the crucifixion, but at the cry from the cross: the cry which confessed that God was forsaken of God.[196]

Chesterton then urges:

> let the atheists themselves choose a god. They will find only one divinity who ever uttered their isolation; only one religion in which God seemed for an instant to be an atheist.[197]

Of course, atheists as proper atheists would opt to not 'choose a god' in the first place. That aside, Chesterton's gloss on the crucifixion is echoed approvingly by both Bloch[198] and Žižek.[199] This depiction in *Orthodoxy* of the final moments of the dying Christ is meant to absorb atheism into Christianity so as better to preserve the latter. Chesterton injects the germs of atheism into Christianity precisely so as to inoculate this theism. In his hands, Christian atheism is *Christian* atheism.

But, what about the likes of Lacan, Bloch and Žižek? Marc De Kesel, in a Lacanian assessment of monotheistic religion, says of a psychoanalytic critical approach to theism that 'such criticism should continue to reflect on its monotheistic background'.[200] For how long ought this to continue? Should this reflection be terminable or interminable? If terminable, what are the criteria for finally letting drop the 'monotheistic background?' If interminable, how would this criticism not lose its critical sting in condemning (analytic) atheism forever to genuflect towards its Christian ancestors?

These questions give rise to others. Does a (self-)barred Christianity, as an atheistic theism (as per the post-Hegelian line adhered to by Lacan), eventually make possible an atheism freed from having to continue kneeling before its religious progenitor? Can *Christian* atheism, as the atheism in Christianity, become Christian *atheism* as an atheism beyond or after Christianity? Is atheism condemned to remaining eternally, in Hegelian terms, a determinate negation of Christianity – and, hence, permanently dependent or parasitic upon what it negates? Can one move from sublating (*als Aufhebung*) religion to finally outright negating it? Is Judeo-Christian monotheism the disposable ladder of a thoroughly historical possibility condition for atheism? Or is it an indispensable logical necessity for making possible all future atheisms?

Given my interests in the present context, I will focus on Lacan's answers (or, at least, hints towards answers) to these questions. I believe he confronts these thorny problems more explicitly and directly than many of the other advocates of atheism-in-Christianity, including Hegel, Feuerbach and Bloch. And, unlike Chesterton, Lacan in no way is invested in sophistically exploiting atheistic sentiments in the service of Christian orthodoxy. Moreover, insofar as Žižek and De Kesel both rely heavily on Lacanian theory, looking at Lacan's wrestlings with Christian atheism and its enigmas promises to shed light on their perspectives too.

During the sixteenth seminar, Lacan contends that subjectivity itself is made possible by the barred status of the big Other – with this barring epitomized by, among other things, the unprovable, unknowable existence of God.[201] In relation to the concerns I just raised, it must be asked: Does confronting the atheistic truth that 'the big Other does not exist' (*le grand Autre n'existe pas*) always and unavoidably require passage through monotheism's immanent-critical negation of a transcendent divine Father? *Seminar XXIII* (*The Sinthome* [1975–6]) seems to propose that a viable atheism engages with theism (a proposal Causse imputes to Lacan[202]):

> Presupposing the Name-of-the-Father, which is certainly God, is how psychoanalysis, when it succeeds, proves that the Name-of-the-Father can just as well be bypassed. One can just as well bypass it, on the condition that one make use of it.[203]

On the one hand, the later Lacan on this occasion reaffirms the atheistic *telos* of the analytic experience itself. A 'successful' analysis 'bypasses' (or, at a minimum, makes explicit the option of bypassing) anything along the lines of the

Judeo-Christian paternal divinity. On the other hand, such bypassing still must pass through (or 'make use of') *Dieu comme le Nom-du-Père*. Why? And what does this mean?

Does the precondition of analysis somehow or other utilizing 'God' entail that, for Lacan, the clinical process must traverse a form of monotheism? Is working through Judeo-Christianity specifically an integral part of the Lacanian analytic process? I would argue against reaching such conclusions on the basis of moments like the one quoted above from the twenty-third seminar. On what do I base myself in arguing thusly?

As I underscored earlier, Lacan operates with an analytically broadened conception of theism. On this conception, God, instead of being limited to what goes by that name in established, received religions, is equivalent to the structural function of the subject supposed to know. If this is the essence of the *theós*, then it can appear in any number of guises: not only God but also parent, analyst, leader, expert, nature, society, etc. According to the later Lacan particularly, this God as the Name-of-the-Father would be any 'master signifier', any S_1,[204] designating the place of a *sujet supposé savoir* (and/or *sujet supposé jouir*).

One must connect the immediately preceding with two other claims. First, for Lacan, the subject supposed to know generates transference. Second, for both Freud and Lacan, working through the transference is essential labour in the analytic experience. Therefore, with Lacan's equivalence between theism and investment in *le sujet supposé savoir*, working through the transference could be redescribed as passing through or 'making use of' *Dieu comme le Nom-du-Père*.

Transference doth make believers of us all. Thus, with the dissolution of transference being a criterion for analytic termination, atheistic unbelief indeed is the 'pinnacle of psychoanalysis' (as Lacan puts it in *Seminar XVII*). Such disbelief goes much further than what ordinarily counts as atheism, withdrawing not only from God but also from all instances of the subject supposed to know.

Yet, Lacan's paraphrase of Dostoyevsky, according to which 'if God is dead, then nothing is permitted', seems to convey the sense that permanent radical atheism is undesirable as per the strict Lacanian definition of *désir*. De Kesel claims that, for Lacan, religion enjoys the virtue of sustaining desire.[205] If so, does Lacan's version of analysis really seek to do away with theism, religiosity and the like?

Similarly, the Lacanian alteration of the line from Dostoyevsky's *The Brothers Karamazov* can be taken as insinuating an ambivalent stance *vis-à-vis* core aspects of Friedrich Nietzsche's philosophy. On the positive side of this ambivalence, Lacan looks as though he agrees with Nietzsche that 'untruth' can be desirable, that falsehoods, fantasies, fictions, illusions, etc. can be life affirming.[206] On the negative side, Lacan, unlike the vehemently anti-Christian

Nietzsche,[207] appears to flirt with the idea that Judeo-Christian monotheism is precisely such a desirable untruth, a life-affirming lie.

Correlatively, Lacan repeatedly indicates that Nietzsche's anti-Christianity falls prey to the libertine delusional belief according to which if God is dead, then everything indeed is permitted.[208] In fact, in 1950's 'A Theoretical Introduction to the Functions of Psychoanalysis in Criminology', Lacan, when referencing *The Brothers Karamazov*, invokes the 'modern man . . . who dreams of the nihilistic suicide of Dostoevsky's hero or forces himself to blow up Nietzsche's inflatable superman (*la baudruche nietzschéenne*)'[209] (thereby hinting that the Nietzschean happy pagan lord of antiquity is nothing more than a very recent fabrication of modernity). Likewise, in the seventh seminar, he responds to Nietzsche, among others, with the proclamation 'Great Pan is dead'.[210] This arguably is a retort to Nietzsche's declaration of the death of the Judeo-Christian God, a declaration the Lacan of *Seminar XI* describes as Nietzsche's 'own myth' akin to that of Freud's myth of the death of the father.[211]

Lacan's 'Great Pan' is to be associated with Nietzsche's romanticization of antiquity's 'master morality' and its pagan hedonism. The Nietzschean Great Pan and *Übermensch*, on Lacan's judgement, both are permutations of Freud's always-already dead *Urvater*. On a Lacanian interpretation, this deceased father himself represents, *contra* Nietzschean libertinism, the fact that uninhibited, uncastrated Dionysian enjoyment is not to be found anywhere, including in the pre-Christian world of ancient Greece (something Lacan indicates against Nietzsche in the nineteenth seminar [. . . *ou pire*][212]).

Maybe the preceding apropos Nietzsche is another implication of Lacan's 'God is unconscious': The libidinal economy of the unconscious, centred on *désir* with its fundamental fantasies involving *objet petit a*, is sustained by the Law of God as the dead father and/or Name-of-the-Father. If this God dies, then the entire economy He supports collapses (i.e. 'nothing is permitted'). In *Télévision*, Lacan, speaking of matters Oedipal, remarks, 'Even if the memories of familial suppression weren't true, they would have to be invented, and that is certainly done'.[213] Paraphrasing this remark, one might say that, by Lacan's lights, if God is dead, then, at least for libidinal reasons, he would have to be resurrected – and that has certainly been done.

Nonetheless, as I already stressed, Lacan is a staunch atheist and identifies his proposition 'God is unconscious' as 'the true formula of atheism'. Under the shadow of the immediately preceding, it now would look as though Lacan's atheism is a particularly perverse sort. What I will proceed to argue is that the later Lacan places the post-Hegelian thesis of atheism-in-Christianity in relation to his very precise psychoanalytic conception of perversion as a diagnostic category.

At least as early as the tenth seminar, Lacan begins portraying perversion as involving placing oneself at the service of a certain version of the big Other. Specifically, as he says in *Seminar X*, 'the perverse subject . . . offers himself loyally to the Other's jouissance'.[214] Subsequent years of *le Séminaire* echo this characterization of the pervert.[215] Perverse subjectivity devotes itself, through its conformist transgressions, to keeping up appearances to the effect that there really exists somewhere a locus of absolute knowledge, enjoyment and/or authority. In the sixteenth seminar, Lacan identifies his matheme for the signifier of the unbarred Other, S(A), as the veritable 'key' to perversion.[216]

Seminar XVI also links perversion to monotheism in general and Christianity in particular. Through this linkage, Lacan is not just making the point that speciously atheistic libertines and superficially blasphemous hedonists (or a Nietzsche for whom God is dead rather than simply non-existent) need the divine big Other as an implicit or explicit point of reference lending their pseudo-transgressive actings-out an aura of titillating defiance. He additionally maintains that this monotheism's God-the-Father, Christ-the-Son and community of believers (i.e. the Holy Spirit) all are figures of perversion themselves.

In Lacan's Freudian eyes, all parties to Christianity's Trinity are at least as perverted as the anti-Christian provocateurs whose cheap thrills rely upon permanent impotent rebellion against this theistic triumvirate. God is grounded in the fantasmatic figure of the *Urvater*, the obscene paternal *jouisseur* whose excessive enjoyment tries to blot out his own barred, castrated status. Christ sacrifices himself so as to not only save humanity but also cover and compensate for the supposed transcendent Father's ignorance, impotence, evil and/or other imperfections. The Holy Spirit, especially as the social institutionalizations of organized religion, often involves repressing those moments within Judeo-Christianity when it comes perilously close to atheistic realizations within its own contents and confines. Lacan emphasizes the especially intense perversity of the strictest literalists of paternal monotheism.[217] And, in *Seminar XXI*, he directly associates Christianity with perversion[218] (likewise, the sub-title of Žižek's 2003 book *The Puppet and the Dwarf* is *The Perverse Core of Christianity*).

In the sixteenth seminar, Lacan observes that 'the pervert is he who consecrates himself to plugging the hole (*boucher le trou*) in the Other . . . he is, up to a certain point, on the side of the Other's existence. He is a defender of the faith'.[219] This observation is reiterated several sessions later.[220] Also in *Seminar XVI*, Lacan asserts of the perverse subject that 'He gives to God His veritable plenitude'.[221] Similarly, in the twenty-third seminar, he describes the pervert as a 'redeemer' (*rédempteur*).[222]

Given the preceding, the figure of Jesus Christ counts as a Lacanian perverse subject. He explicitly functions within Christianity as the redeemer *par excellence*. On Lacan's account, Christ-the-Son's primary redemption, as perverse, is of the big Other (i.e. God-the-Father).[223] His life and, particularly, His death are meant to restore the lawful reign of S(A). By extension, all those Christian believers (i.e. 'defenders of the faith', the earthly community of the Holy Spirit) who seek to emulate Christ come to operate as little redeemers, as copycat perverts.

The paradoxical status of Christianity as the religion of atheism, a status Lacan joins everyone from Hegel to Žižek in assigning to this monotheism, is integral to what makes it perverse in the strictest of senses by Lacan's reckoning. The Lacanian pervert plays a double game. On the one hand, he/she registers, at least unconsciously, the signifier of the barred Other, S(A̸), namely, indications that there is no locus of omniscience, omnipotence, perfection and the like. On the other hand, the pervert repeatedly sets about, in reaction to this registration of S(A̸), trying in one or more ways to plaster over the cracks in *le grand Autre* (i.e. 'plugging the hole in the Other').

As the religion of atheism, Christianity simultaneously both reveals that '*le grand Autre n'existe pas*' ('Father, why hast Thou forsaken me?', etc.) and conceals this revelation through various means (denying God's death, deifying/fetishizing Jesus as Christ-the-God and so on). Octave Mannoni, one of Lacan's analytic followers, famously depicts the fetishist, the paradigmatic perverse subject, as living according to the logic of '*je sais bien, mais quand même*' (I know full well, but nonetheless).[224] Christianity, including the *Christian* atheism of the likes of Chesterton, indeed plays the double game of 'I know full well that God is dead, but nonetheless'.

However, Lacan insinuates in multiple fashions that even the most thoroughly analysed person, on the other side of concluding an exhaustive (and exhausting) analysis, cannot but lapse into this same double game of '*je sais bien, mais quand même*' – albeit perhaps now with a little more occasional self-conscious awareness of doing so. In Lacan's view, analysis does not rid the analysand of his/her unconscious or, for that matter, his/her ego either (and the latter despite Lacan's lifelong, vehement critiques of ego psychology). Passage through a concluding experience of 'subjective destitution', in which ego-level identifications as well as points of reference such as big Others and subjects supposed to know vacillate or vanish altogether, indeed is an essential, punctuating moment of the Lacanian analytic process.

Nevertheless, Lacan does not consider it possible or desirable to dwell permanently in such an analysis-terminating destitute state. He sees it as both appropriate and inevitable that egos, big Others, subjects supposed to know and the like will reconstitute themselves for the analysand in the aftermath of his/her analysis. Hopefully, the versions of these reconstituted in the wake of and in response to analysis will be better, more livable versions for the analysand. But in their unavoidability, persistence and resilience, they arguably are *sinthomes* rather than mere symptoms.

For reasons I have delineated at length above, the structural *sinthomes* of *le grand Autre* and *le sujet supposé savoir* bring with them (mono)theism as a *sinthome* too. Another of Lacan's neologisms, one he coins starting in *Seminar XXII* (*R.S.I.* [1974–5]), is connected to what I have just been discussing: '*père-version*' as associating perversion with paternity.[225] As Lacan puts it the following year in the twenty-third seminar, *père-version* is perversion as the 'version towards the father'.[226]

I view it as no accident that Lacan introduces this particular neologism in a seminar (the twenty-second) whose title, *R.S.I.*, is intended, in its original French pronunciation, to evoke the word '*hérésie*' (heresy). In *Seminar XXIII*, Lacan indeed heretically depicts Christianity as entailing sadomasochistic *père-version*.[227] Christ and Christians *père-versly* serve a God who, according to Freudian psychoanalysis, is modelled on a *père-vers* (obscene, brutal, etc.) primal father.[228] These servants/redeemers seek to prop up and render consistent this *père-vers* Other, as Himself really barred, as S($\cancel{A}$).

In the twenty-second seminar, while discussing Freud's theory of religion and God as *père-vers*, Lacan reminds his audience of just how monotonously repetitive and rigidly unimaginative perverts are.[229] Perversions exhibit pronounced mechanical, stereotyped characteristics, as anyone familiar with the Marquis de Sade's writings, pornography website categories and taxonomies or various types of fetishisms readily can attest. Instead of being thrillingly subversive and mind-bendingly transgressive, perversions are, in fact, profoundly boring formulaic spectacles ultimately laboring to sustain the authority of some form of *grand Autre*.[230] Just as Freud famously compares the rituals of obsessional neurotics to religious practices, so too does Lacan compare perverse practices to theistic rites.

Similarly, in *Seminar XXIII*, Lacan complains aloud that psychoanalysis has not invented, at least not yet, 'a new perversion'.[231] In light of this lack of inventiveness, he proclaims analysis to be 'a fruitless practice' (*quelle infécondité dans cette pratique*).[232] Analysis itself originates in part with Freud's identification of the inherently perverse nature of human sexuality starting in 1905's groundbreaking *Three Essays on the Theory of Sexuality*. As Lacan indicates, despite this, neither the theory nor the practice of analysis has (yet) prompted the genesis of novel, previously unseen perverse phenomena. Although Freud's self-styled Copernican revolution revolutionizes thinking about sexuality, it does not seem, on Lacan's assessment, to revolutionize sexuality itself.

Lacan's 1976 complaint about the analytic failure to invent a new perversion directly applies also to his contemporaneous reflections on the *père-version* of monotheisms. It is no coincidence that the God hypothesis, *dieur*, God not believing in God, the critique of the Freudian Oedipus complex and *Urvater*, the *sinthome* and *père-version* all surface during the same period of Lacan's teachings. The Lacan of this later era additionally evinces pessimism at times about analysts, analysands and humanity as a whole, so as to sustain livable lives of desire, coming up with anything other and better than the old gods or these gods' thinly veiled substitutes and disguises. These would be lives that are livable through at least something being permitted to desire.

Again, if God is dead – this God comes in the myriad fantasmatic guises of the omniscient and omnipotent subject supposed to know and enjoy – then nothing is permitted. This God stubbornly remains a *sinthome*. Even well-analysed subjects promise nevertheless still to perseverate in respecting the stale, stereotyped images of religious and pseudo-secular theisms whose styles and contents are properly perverse/*père-vers*. These subjects' libidinal economies, on the other side of their completed analyses, continue to require leaning upon fantasies of transcendent all-enjoyers and unbarred big Others, prohibited Elsewheres of speciously possible absolutes. How else to avoid being crushed by the trauma of the second of Oscar Wilde's 'two tragedies' ('There are only two tragedies in life: one is not getting what one wants, and the other is getting it')?

In the twenty-fourth seminar (*L'insu que sait de l'une-bévue, s 'aile à mourre* [1976–7]), the very late Lacan speaks somewhat enigmatically of striving 'towards a new signifier'.[233] In terms of Lacan's interlinked theories of signifiers and mathemes, perversion involves, for him, the perverse subject attempting to turn S($\bcancel{A}$), the signifier of the barred Other, back into S(A), the signifier of the unbarred Other. This leads to the idea of an analysis that possibly could assist in inventing an alternative to *père-version* in which new signifiers tied to S($\bcancel{A}$), rather than to S(A), become the nodal anchors of transformed libidinal economies, the *points de capiton* of renewed *désir*.

Lacan's atheism hence points to an anti-Heideggerian 'only we can save God'. More exactly, only we can save ourselves through inventing a new *sinthome* for our desiring lives instead of staying stuck in theistic *père-versions*. Once earthly as well as heavenly fathers have been demystified, can another figure different in kind from them take their places? Can we move in a direction other than one 'from Dad to worse' (*du père au pire*), as the later Lacan describes it?[234] Is our only choice really between, to paraphrase Friedrich Engels, paternalism and barbarism? Are we condemned to the perverse game of continuing to buttress the paternal *imago* during its long decline?

One of the final Lacan's hopes is that a desirable, rather than desire-extinguishing, atheistic alternative to *le Nom-du-Père* and its ilk, a fundamentally new S_1, just might arrive at some point. This strain of Lacanianism would involve, like Marxism, a messianic atheism: We at last will be redeemed from our redeemer – without, for all that, falling into (self-)condemnation. One fine day, God finally no longer will arrive. We will have transubstantiated Him into something else – *a*-men.

6. Lacan's Pascal, Pascal's Lacan: From Jansenism to Freudianism

In addition to the evidence I have examined thus far, the true stringency of Lacan's thoroughgoing atheism is fully on display, perhaps surprisingly, in his engagements with Pascal. This might come as a surprise due to Lacan exhibiting fascination with a historical figure aggressively championing Christianity against all comers at the dawn of modernity. *Contra* unbelieving debauched libertines, morally lax Jesuit casuists[235] and rationalist thinkers such as Descartes rendering the divine just another object before the tribunal of secular philosophical judgment, Pascal upholds 'the God of Abraham, Isaac, and Jacob' as an inaccessible, unknowable transcendence to be followed on faith rather than proven (or disproven) by reason.[236]

If Lacan really is an uncompromising and especially virulent atheist, as I contend, then what does he see in Pascal? Do not Lacan's lingerings over Pascal's writings suggest, contrary to my assertions of the former's unwavering atheism, an enduring affinity on the part of Lacan for the religion of his childhood? Relatedly, what about the deep faith of his adored younger brother, the Benedictine monk Marc-François Lacan?

Lacan evinces interest in many of Pascal's contributions to the history of ideas, including the latter's mathematical labors as anticipating such subsequent developments as cybernetics and game theory, developments dear to Lacan.[237] Yet, as for so many readers, Lacan understandably is most attracted to the later Pascal's literary, philosophical and theological masterpiece, namely, the unfinished set of fragments known as the *Pensées*. Lacan does not wade into the thick of scholarly controversies about whether or not Pascal's conversion experiences, especially that of the night of 23 November 1654,[238] mark a discontinuity between a younger scientific Pascal and an older religious Pascal.

However, Lacan's lengthy set of reflections on the wager in the *Pensées* indicate that he assumes the post-conversion Christian Pascal not to be utterly discontinuous with his previous scientifically focused self. In fact, one of the many appealing aspects of the *Pensées* for Lacan likely is what he takes to be its undermining of the ostensible zero-sum conflict between science and religion. This undermining is effectuated through Pascal's integration of mathematically informed reasoning into a planned apology for Christianity – with *le pari de Pascal* treating God's existence according to the procedures of the mathematized probability theory Pascal himself helps to found. As with Pascal's blending of mathematics (as science) and Christianity (as religion),[239] Lacan similarly brings various formalisms to bear on the existentially charged field of psychoanalysis.

A number of other features of the Pascal of the *Pensées* in particular are registered by Lacan as resonating with Freudian psychoanalysis. To begin with, Pascal's talk of 'the heart' (*le coeur*) as unknown to and uncontrollable by 'reason' (*la raison*) easily can be interpreted as one of the many historical precursors of the idea of the unconscious as disclosed by Freud (with the Pascalian heart as the primary processes of the Freudian unconscious and Pascalian reason as the secondary processes of Freudian preconsciousness as well as consciousness).[240] The best-known *pensée* in this vein is the one declaring that 'The heart has its reasons of which reason knowns nothing' (*Le cœur a ses raisons, que la raison ne connaît point*).[241] And, just as, for Pascal, the sub- and/or super-rational heart is not without its own rationality ('the heart has its reasons'), so too for Freud and Lacan: Although different from and largely invisible to consciousness with its logic, the unconscious is not without its own logic.

Secondly, Pascal tirelessly emphasizes the divided nature of the human being[242] (as thereby '*un monstre incompréhensible*'[243]). A multitude of entries in the *Pensées* stress the inherently split status of humans.[244] This Pascal observes that 'Man's dualism is so obvious that some people have thought we had two souls' (*Cette duplicité de l'homme est si visible, qu'il y en a qui ont pensé que nous avions deux âmes*).[245] In the *Pensées*, we are said to be riven by an array of overlapping, cross-resonating oppositions, including those between instinct and reason,[246] the animal and the angel,[247] the innate and the acquired,[248] innocence and corruption,[249] greatness and wretchedness,[250] fallenness and redemption,[251] the rational and the passionate[252] and good and evil.[253] Lacan, with his theory of the subject as structurally split along multiple axes and fault lines, cannot fail to appreciate this prominent and fundamental aspect of the later Pascal's account of the human condition as inherently and internally conflicted. The key difference is that whereas Christianity is put forward by Pascal as promising an overcoming of the oppositions cleaving humans into irreconcilable halves,[254] Lacan makes division and discord into ineliminable, insurmountable dimensions of subjectivity.[255]

Of course, part of what splits the Lacanian subject, as the 'barred' S ($) *qua parlêtre*, is nothing other than what Lacan baptizes 'desire' (*désir*). I will say a lot more below about Lacan's distinctive metapsychological conception of desire in relation to his readings of Pascal. For the time being, I merely want to highlight those moments in the *Pensées* when Pascal foreshadows Lacan's concept of *désir* in ways Lacan clearly appreciates.

In two fragments, Pascal very succinctly summarizes the human situation: '*Man's condition*. Inconstancy, boredom, anxiety' (*Condition de l'homme: inconstance, ennui, inquiétude*)[256] and '*Description of man*. dependence, desire for independence, needs' (*Description de l'homme: dépendance, désir d'indépendance, besoin*).[257] As will be seen shortly, this second fragment's talk of both desire (*désir*) and need (*besoin*) in relation to human dependence can be heard as echoed by Lacan's stress on uniquely human prolonged prematurational helplessness (i.e. Freud's *Hilflosigkeit* as entailing a lengthy period of childhood dependence on adult significant others) and the genesis, out of this helplessness, of the Lacanian need-demand-desire (*besoin-demande-désir*) triad.[258] That noted, a plethora of other fragments in the *Pensées* repeatedly emphasize, in line with Pascal's just-quoted two hyper-compact characterizations of the misery of the human condition, how desiring repeatedly disturbs the peace of the person. It causes him/her the pain and suffering of craving, dissatisfaction, yearning and the like. Pascalian desire is a ceaseless restlessness that never arrives at fulfillment and contentment, that always finds itself lacking and constantly looking elsewhere to other people, places and times for its perpetually missing gratification.[259]

Even if and when desire gets what it supposedly wants, it finds itself suddenly disappointed and deflated. With this in view, the author of the *Pensées* remarks that 'It is not good to have all one needs'[260] (recalling that, for Lacan, desire is what remains unsatisfied after the demand to satisfy a need has been met[261]). Pascal also maintains, apropos the '*inconstance*' involved in human nature, that 'What causes inconstancy is the realization that present pleasures are false, together with the failure to realize that absent pleasures are vain' (*Le sentiment de la fausseté des plaisirs présents, et l'ignorance de la vanité des plaisirs absents causent l'inconstance*).[262] No sooner does desire attain what it has been pursuing than it generates a disenchanting anti-climax (i.e. 'the realization that present pleasures are false'). But no sooner does the desiring creature experience such anti-climactic disenchantment than he/she again sets up yet another new lost-in-the-past and/or expected-in-the-future satisfaction (i.e. 'absent pleasures'), never learning the lesson of the intrinsic vanity of desire's ends. For anyone even minimally familiar with Lacan's own account of *désir*, Pascal's characterizations of desire in the *Pensées* cannot but appear as foreshadowing this account.

To have recourse to contemporary parlance, the Pascalian desiring person becomes an addict chasing the dragon of a state of completion impossible to attain (at least, for Pascal, in this world). As another *pensée* puts it apropos humans as addicted to desire, 'They do not know that all they want is the hunt and not the capture'.[263] The agitated anticipation of the journey, while pleasure remains absent, is preferable to the quiet repose at the destination, which brings with it the pain of boredom, of Pascalian *ennui* (incidentally, recent affective-neuroscientific research into the so-called 'SEEKING system' of the brain likewise suggests that humans and various other animals, even at the neurobiological level, have an inclination to prefer goads, however unsettling, to goals, however satisfying). As Exhibit A of all this, Pascal has in mind the wealthy hedonists and libertines around him, whose miserable jadedness reveals the spiritual dangers of satiety and the futility of the life of desire.

Such jaded aristocrats and their ilk, frittering their money, lives and even souls away at opulent gambling tables, are afflicted by an insatiable desire for 'diversion'. Such *divertissement*, according to the *Pensées*, is basically an attempt by those seeking it to divert their attention away from the wretchedness of their own all-too-human lives (as lives of desire). For Pascal, games and other amusements, embodying the desire for (other) distracting desires, are essentially defensive.[264] Yet, such diversions, as themselves fueled by desire, perpetuate the very misery they are meant to combat in a self-defeating vicious circle. From a Lacanian standpoint, one could say that Pascal's discussions of *divertissement* outline in advance certain contours of Lacan's analytic theory of the repression of *désir* as constitutive of the psychoanalytic unconscious (with Lacanian repression being also always the return of the repressed,[265] being always incomplete, flawed and partial).

Finally, there is Pascal's Jansenist scorn for the vanity of both the self and the world. As regards selfhood, Pascal laments and lambasts what he identifies as human beings' inherent narcissistic tendencies.[266] The self forming the object of these tendencies is rendered by Pascal in terms strikingly similar to how Lacan depicts the ego (*Ich, moi*). Both the Pascalian self and the Lacanian ego are self-objectifications composed out of internalized socio-symbolic roles and beguiling for the subject's conscious and unconscious libidinal dynamics.

For Pascal, the world reflected in and by the self – this would be, for Lacan, the socio-symbolic order reflected in and by the ego – is just as vain as the self itself (with the vanity-*qua*-narcissism of the self mirroring the vanity-*qua*-futility of the world). This world, withdrawn from by Pascal's fellow Jansenist travellers sheltering in the abbey of Port-Royal-des-Champs, is depicted in the *Pensées* as nothing but lies, as a tissue of falsehoods, illusions, mirages and the like.[267] Lacanian 'reality', a hybrid Imaginary-Symbolic construct distinct from the Real, closely resembles the Pascalian world as a web of deceit composed of fictions, fantasies, etc.[268]

Also, there is a particular one-liner from Pascal's *Pensées* from which Lacan draws much inspiration – 'Men are so inevitably mad that not to be mad would be to give a mad twist to madness' *(Les hommes sont si nécessairement fous, que ce serait fou, par un autre tour de folie, de n'être pas fou)*.[269] Lacan quotes this line directly on several occasions.[270]

Already in the 1946 *écrit* 'Presentation on Psychical Causality', Lacan observes, likely inspired by this same Pascalian aphorism, that 'if a man who thinks he is a king is mad, a king who thinks he is a king is no less so' (*si un homme qui se croit un roi est fou, un roi qui se croit un roi ne l'est pas moins*).[271] In Lacan's synopsis of his third seminar (i.e. the *écrit* 'On a Question Prior to Any Possible Treatment of Psychosis' summarizing the academic year on *The Psychoses* [1955–6]), he likewise credits Pascal with having established the concept of 'social psychosis'.[272] Pathologically delusional self-identification (e.g. 'a man who thinks he is a king') is just a more obvious and exaggerated version of the inherently delusional quality of all 'normal' ego-level self-identifications (such as 'a king who thinks he is a king' or even a philosopher who thinks 'I = I'). This normality is the majority of persons' investments in the Imaginary and Symbolic fictions and fantasies making up the everyday madness (i.e. the 'social psychosis') of who and what self-deceiving humans (mis)take themselves to be as individuals and even as whole societies.

The later Lacan's '*les non-dupes errent*' (the non-dupes err), the title of *Seminar XXI* (1973–4) and homophonous with the original title of Lacan's aborted version of *Seminar XI (Les Noms-du-Père)*, gestures at Pascal's pithy sentence about madness. For Pascal, not to be mad is itself an even madder form of madness than the ordinary madness of a thoroughly mad world – with Lacan, in the 1949 *écrit* on the mirror stage, speaking of 'the most general formulation of madness (*la plus générale de la folie*) – the kind found within the asylum walls as well as the kind that deafens the world with its sound and fury (*de son bruit et de sa fureur*)'.[273] Likewise, from Lacan's perspective, not to be taken in (i.e. duped) by the omnipresent illusions woven of images and words pervading the human condition leaves one incapable of understanding (with this incapacity as erring in relation to) others' and one's circumstances in connection with them.[274]

Nonetheless, as I already indicated, the famous 'wager' (*pari*) from the *Pensées* and bearing Pascal's name is what attracts the bulk of Lacan's attention. Lacan references Pascal's wager on numerous occasions. Moreover, he devotes a sequence of sessions of *Seminar XVI* to commenting on this famous *pari*. He even writes of Pascal's wager that 'what it conceals . . . is inestimable to psychoanalysts'.[275] Lacan's glosses on *le pari de Pascal* have been taken up by a number of interpreters, including Jean-Pierre Clero,[276] Cormac Gallagher,[277] Dominiek Hoens[278] and a handful of others. On this occasion, I will not pretend to offer an exhaustive unpacking of Lacan's often cryptic remarks about Pascal. I merely wish to show that and how the properly Lacanian handling of Pascal's wager brings out the profoundly atheistic nature of the psychoanalytic experience and the theory entangled with it. This is so despite the fact that Pascal presents his wager as part of a spirited, multi-pronged defence of Christianity in the face of the rise of modern rationality and science (with Lacan crediting Descartes, one of Pascal's intellectual nemeses, with helping make the subsequent advent of Freudian psychoanalysis possible, thanks to Descartes's central historical role in laying the philosophical foundations of scientific modernity).

7. Of games and sacrifices: Giving the other its want

Obviously, the primary puzzle I must solve is how Lacan extrapolates atheistic consequences from Pascal's wager, intended by its author to compel even jaded unbelieving hedonists to change their ways, return to the fold, and at least act as though they faithfully uphold the Christian God's existence. Relatedly, Lacan's occasional sympathetic and even admiring remarks about Pascal might lead some to go so far as to take these as signalling Lacan being receptive to the sort of Christianity defended in Pascal's works.[279] Lacan's references to other Christian figures and contents certainly appear to encourage some more religiously-minded readers to attribute a Christian/Catholic outlook to Lacanian psychoanalysis. But, as I am about to show in the case of Lacan's appropriations of Pascal, such religious, Christian and/or Catholic attributions to Lacan and his teachings are fundamentally unsound and erroneous.

To begin with, one must bear in mind that Lacan's various positive statements about Pascal are offset by multiple more critical and cautious notes he sounds in response to this seventeenth-century thinker. For instance, in *Seminar IX* (*Identification* [1961–2]), he utilizes the field of mathematics, as contributed to by both Descartes and Pascal, so as to render even more dubitable the very existence of either the Cartesian philosophical God or the Pascalian religious God. Despite Descartes's and Pascal's differences apropos their discourses on the divine, they both depict God as unconstrained by the strictures of finite human rationality, so much so that He even can bend and break such elementary rational rules as those governing arithmetic.

For example, God, in His free-willed omnipotence, is capable of making two-plus-two not equal four, despite adequately numerate human beings finding it impossible to deny the seemingly self-evident truth of $2 + 2 = 4$. Yet, as Lacan observes in the ninth seminar, the absence of observed instances in which core mathematical propositions taken to be timelessly true are somehow discovered at points in time to be false and no longer to hold – an example of this would be a discovery suddenly calling into question the *apriori* veracity of $2 + 2 = 4$ – suggests the absence of a divine agent or authority willing and able to meddle in matters of mathematical reasoning.[280] Despite mathematics's appeals to and affinities with metaphysical realist sensibilities, themselves often part of or reinforcing mystical, religious and/or spiritualistic worldviews, this same field is turned by Lacan against both the Cartesian and Pascalian renditions of the divine.

Then, in *Seminar X*, Lacan pointedly self-identifies as being among the 'complete unbelievers' (*absoluement incroyants*) when describing Pascal's neurotic and proto-existentialist *horror vacui*,[281] with Lacan already having highlighted this Pascalian terror in *Seminar II* (*The Ego in Freud's Theory and in the Technique of Psychoanalysis* [1954–5]) in particular.[282] As I will underscore shortly, this Pascalian horror of the void contains aspects crucial to Lacan's psychoanalytic appropriation of Pascal's wager. That said, Lacan, on several subsequent occasions, reiterates his assessment of Pascal as an especially anxious neurotic.[283] He blames Pascal's excessive anxiety for what are alleged to be a number of metaphysical blunders on his part.[284] And, in *Seminar XIII*, Lacan characterizes Pascal's wager as 'absurd' (*ce pari absurde*).[285] Similarly, the sixteenth seminar, during its discussion of the Pascalian *pari*, dismisses religiosity in general as '*connerie*' (i.e. stupidity and/or bullshit).[286]

Apart from the wager itself, another illustration of Pascal's alleged anxiety-induced metaphysical missteps brought up several times by Lacan also is to be found in the *Pensées*. At one point therein, Pascal, after emphasizing the cosmos's unimaginable vastness, declares:

> Nature is an infinite sphere whose centre is everywhere and circumference nowhere. In short it is the greatest perceptible mark of God's omnipotence that our imagination should lose itself in that thought.[287]

Nature's vastness reflects that of its creator, namely, God Himself. In a very traditional vein, Pascal associates divinity with both the spherical and the infinite. But, according to Lacan, Pascal's recourse to the image of the infinite sphere proves to be self-defeating given his purposes.

To be more precise, Lacan's contention is that the infinitization of the spherical results in the center being nowhere rather than, as Pascal asserts, 'everywhere' (or, a center that is everywhere is, in effect, nowhere and, thus, is not even a proper center). Treating both nature and God as infinite spheres hence leaves Pascal having inadvertently stranded himself in the same center-less cosmic expanse as the modern scientific universe he seeks to problematize in the name of a Christian *Weltanschauung*. He hoists himself by his own mathematical and metaphysical petard here.[288]

The preceding evidence ought to be enough to establish that Lacan's approach to Pascal and his wager is not that of a Christian believer or even that of someone vaguely tempted by religious faith of any sort. Lacan not only sees fit to remind his audiences of his atheism while reflecting on things Pascalian – he goes out of his way to stress that, in his view, Pascal's larger metaphysical framework is fatally flawed and that his attempts to defend the old God of Abraham, Isaac and Jacob against the onslaughts of modernity are unsuccessful. But, to echo the title of Gallagher's essay on Lacan *avec* Pascal, what is it Lacan nevertheless considers theoretically valuable and psychoanalytically relevant about Pascal's wager in particular?

The 20 November 1963 opening session of the abruptly cancelled original version of the eleventh seminar (*Les Noms-du-Père*) contains an important observation about Pascal's God. Therein, Lacan remarks:

> *God of Abraham, Isaac, and Jacob, not of the philosophers and the scientists* (savants), writes Pascal at the head of the manuscript of his *Pensées*. Concerning which may be said what I have gradually accustomed you to understand: that a God (*un Dieu*) is something one encounters in the real (*ça se rencontre dans le réel*), inaccessible (*inaccessible*). It is indicated by what doesn't deceive – anxiety (*ça se signale par ce qui ne trompe pas, l'angoisse*).[289]

After linking the Pascalian divinity to the register of the Real *qua* 'inaccessible' – elsewhere, Lacan likewise qualifies God as unknowable[290] – Lacan's lecture introducing the theme of 'The Names-of-the-Father' goes on to reflect on Abraham's sacrifice of Isaac and its famous artistic depiction by Caravaggio.[291] This same Lacan also invokes a central thesis from his immediately preceding tenth seminar of 1962–3: According to psychoanalysis, anxiety is the one affect that does not deceive[292] (with all other affects compromised in their veracity by repression and other intra-psychical defense mechanisms).

Indeed, the Old Testament God of the binding of Isaac fairly can be described by Lacan in his own terms as a transcendent, alien Real who, in His enigmatic opacity and unpredictable inscrutability, arouses anxiety in His faithful subjects. Pascal himself already emphasizes, against Cartesian rationalism and similar epistemologically confident and ambitious forms of modern philosophy and science, God's unsettling unknowability for finite human minds.

Starting in *Seminar X*, Lacan develops an account of sacrifice, epitomized by the one Pascal's God demands of Abraham (Lacan additionally brings up Jewish ritual circumcision in this same vein[293]), with transformative implications for various conceptions of the divine. For Lacan, Pascal's anxious emphasis on God's inaccessibility and unknowability brings to light the character not only of the deity of Abraham, Isaac and Jacob but also of gods in general. All gods, given the difference-in-kind between the human and the divine, are strange, foreign and at least partly impenetrable. What is more, this divine inscrutability, in the context of humans' perceived frailty and dependence *vis-à-vis* their god or gods, arouses anxiety. This anxiety can be expressed in the form of certain existentially-pressing questions such as: What does this divine alterity want? Who or what are we for our god or gods? Are we pleasing to our deities? What do we have to be or do in order to placate them?

Of course, religious sacrifices are attempts to curry favour with the divine. The crucial twist Lacan adds to this is his contention that the strategy of engaging in sacrificial practices (as epitomized by religious rituals in which offerings are made to the gods) is not one where the sacrificing subjects are guided by a prior self-assured certainty resulting from the gods having handed down precise dictates and instructions making clear their interests and appetites. The desires of the gods are mysterious and disconcerting, since, for believers, everything seems to depend upon whether or not these unknown whims are satisfied. Sacrifice, Lacan claims, aims at 'capturing' this enigmatic, elusive Otherness, snaring it by forcing a determination of what it wants via sacrificial gifts. Through the framework of the ritual, the gods are made to desire what is offered to them. Their terribly silent mouths are preemptively stuffed with supposedly appeasing objects.[294]

On Lacan's reading, Pascal's wager is a means of coping with anxiety in the face of a deified-but-cryptic Other, a means calling for sacrifice.[295] This wager's sacrificial dimension consists of its participation in a Christian ethic of renunciation,[296] specifically 'the renunciation of *jouissance*'[297] (with this *jouissance*, for Pascal, amounting to, for example, the depraved excesses of sinful libertines). Those who wager on the Christian God's existence and at least outwardly behave as if this God exists bring their manifest behaviour into line with Christianity's renunciative ethos in which immoderate extremes involving pleasures and pains are forsaken.

Lacan links the wager with Pascal's contributions to game theory. Pascal is known for, among many other things, mathematically taming chance as it features in the gambling pastimes of his aristocratic contemporaries (enabling the determination with numerical precision of exactly how a pot of money is to be divided among players of a game that must be brought to a premature halt). Such gambling contemporaries are among the addressees of the *pari* famously featuring in the *Pensées*. Lacan depicts Pascal's wager as a combinatory game resembling the games of chance entertaining his dissipated peers.[298]

Lacan, in *Seminar XII* (*Problèmes cruciaux pour la psychanalyse* [1964–5]), makes some pointed remarks about Pascal's wager as a combinatory game of chance. He states, 'The stake is, in a way, what masks the risk. Nothing, when all is said and done, is more contrary to risk than a game. The game caps the risk' (*L'enjeu est en quelque sort ce qui masque le risque. Rien, en fin de compte, n'est plus contraire au risque que le jeu. Le jeu encapuchonne le risque*).[299] Games and game theory are at least as much about minimizing the risk of loss as maximizing the chance of gain.[300]

From a psychoanalytic standpoint, games, including Pascal's wager, are inherently defensive. They are ways of containing, controlling and minimizing risks that otherwise might overwhelm potential and actual players with anxiety or that already did overwhelm them in the repressed past (such as with the *Fort-Da* game of Freud's grandson, in which this game with spool and string is a response striving to domesticate previous painful experiences of the unpredictable intermittent departures of the child's mother[301]). Pascal himself, in his contributions to game theory, mobilizes his considerable mathematical and intellectual talents to circumscribe and rein in what otherwise are unruly contingencies.[302] Thanks to the field of mathematized probability theory, a 'science of uncertain things' (as G.-T. Guilbaud puts it in an overview of cybernetics likely known to Lacan[303]) whose foundations are laid in Pascal's correspondence with Pierre Fermat, the distance between the present and the future goes from being totally opaque to becoming partly translucent.[304] Risks ahead thereby can be foreseen and, hence, managed.[305]

Also in the same session (19 May 1965) of the twelfth seminar, Lacan soon adds, 'This is the relationship of the game to fantasy. The game is a fantasy rendered inoffensive and conserved in its structure' (*C'est là le rapport du jeu au fantasme. Le jeu est un fantasme rendu inoffensif et conservé dans sa structure*).[306] Lacan's comments in *Seminar XII* about Pascal and games indicate that Pascal's wager both is an exercise in defensive risk and anxiety management as well as 'a fantasy rendered inoffensive and conserved in its structure'. But this indication raises a number of questions: What risk(s) does the wager seek to 'mask' (*masquer*) or 'cap' (*encapuchonner*).? What risk(s) might the wager itself run in turn? And what is the fantasy sublated/sublimated, simultaneously defanged and preserved, by the particular combinatory game of chance that is Pascal's wager?

As for what risk(s) the wager seeks to mask and cap, Lacan provides a hint about this through comparing Pascal's wager to Hegel's celebrated dialectic of lordship and bondage from the 1807 *Phenomenology of Spirit*.[307] Lacan depicts this particular dialectic as also involving a wager – specifically, a gamble on the part of he/she who becomes master by unflinchingly playing chicken with the 'absolute master', namely, death. In Lacan's eyes, the Hegelian master–slave scenario is, as he puts it on one occasion, 'more honest' than Pascal's wager.[308] This is because Hegel's master-to-be really risks complete annihilation without any intimations or prospects of a death-defying existence in Heaven or Hell. In Hegel, there is a real risk of losing everything with no compensation whatsoever, neither a better life in this world nor an afterlife in another world.[309] Lacan sees Pascal as employing his wager in order, at least in part, to contain and close off this risk of total loss.[310]

This is not to say that death is entirely occluded within the parameters of Pascal's wager. If it turns out that (the Christian) God does not exist, then, for Pascal, there is no life after death. Yet, according to the combinatory schema of his wager, the absence of an afterlife still can be paired with either way of wagering, whether for or against the being of the divine.

If one wagers that God exists but it turns out He does not, Pascal, in his religiosity, contends that one still gains the benefit of living a better life acting as though God exists (as I will show subsequently, this contention, based on Pascal's faith in Christian ethical teaching about the good life, is directly challenged by Lacan's Freudian 'ethics of psychoanalysis'). A person allegedly will be happier and more fulfilled in this world by behaving in a God-fearing manner, regardless of whether he/she eventually gets rewarded for such behaviour in a heavenly afterlife.[311] As Pascal reassures his addressees apropos his wager, 'if you win you win everything, if you lose you lose nothing',[312] with him soon referring to the latter outcome as 'a loss amounting to nothing' (*la perte du néant*).[313] This reassurance is likely what prompts Lacan to depict Pascal as minimizing or eliminating risk and to contrast his wager with Hegel's master–slave dialectic.

For Pascal, even if God does not exist, conducting oneself as though there is no divinity, afterlife and the like results in a miserable life of ennui, unrest, longing and degeneracy. This is so despite the lack of any punishments inflicting eternal suffering in the infernal abyss. In Pascal's view, the life of the wanton, unrepentant libertine is already on its own a harsh punishment needlessly inflicted by such a hedonist on him/herself, regardless of whether or not there is an omniscient and omnipotent Other to mete out judgement after death. By simply wagering that God exists and living accordingly, one easily avoids both the possibility of an afterlife in Hell as well as the actuality of a hellish life here on earth. One has nothing to lose, as Pascal himself emphasizes. But, as Lacan implies, a wager in which one has nothing to lose is not much of a wager.[314]

8. Risk management of the family firm: The Pascalian *horror vacui*

But what are the precise contours of the life-and-death risk, akin to that run by the Hegelian master, tamed and domesticated within the confines of the Pascalian wager's combinatory of outcomes? What version(s) of life-threatening danger(s) does Lacan see Pascal as defending against? Lacan drops a key clue to answering these questions in his tenth seminar devoted to the topic of anxiety.

At the end of the 12 December 1962 session of *Seminar X*, Lacan explicitly invokes Pascal. In particular, he focuses on Pascal's experimental-scientific efforts to refute Aristotelian plenism as per '*Natura abhorret vacuum*' (a phrase attributed to Aristotle but coined by François Rabelais in the 1530s). After noting Pascal's *horror vacui* and his foreshadowing of existentialist sensibilities, Lacan comments:

> Pascal . . . touches us still, even those of us who are complete unbelievers. Being the good Jansenist he was, Pascal was interested in desire (*désir*), and that's why, I'm telling you in confidence, he carried out the Puy de Dôme experiments on the vacuum (*le vide*).[315]

He continues:

> The vacuum doesn't interest us at all from the theoretical point of view. It's almost meaningless for us now. We know that in a vacuum there can be hollows, plenums, masses of waves and anything else you like. But for Pascal, whether or not nature abhors a vacuum (*que la nature ait ou non horreur du vide*) was essential, because this signified the abhorrence that all the learned men of his day had for desire. Until then, if not nature, at least all thought had abhorred the possibility that somewhere there might be a void.[316]

Lacan takes advantage of the fact that Pascal himself rejects holding strictly apart, on the one side, the ontological, theoretical and descriptive dimensions of the natural sciences and philosophies of nature and, on the other side, the ethico-moral, practical and prescriptive dimensions of theology and theologically informed philosophical anthropology. Hence, for Pascal, there are fundamental implications for the human condition on a practical-philosophical level flowing from the controversies over Aristotle's plenism.

Lacan capitalizes on this, drawing parallels between Pascal's fascination with the topic of the vacuum (*le vide*) in physics and Pascal's own (arguably neurotic) recoiling in terror from the silent and largely empty vastness of the physical universe of Cartesian and Galilean scientific modernity. Indeed, Pascal evinces a certain proto-existentialist horror at his own experimental confirmations – his 1647 and 1648 work related to the Puy de Dôme experiments verifies Evangelista Torricelli's 1643 experimental results – of the existence of vacuums within a modern image of nature that itself disturbingly appears to Pascal as mostly just one giant cosmic void. Even if the being of nature does not abhor a void, the thinking of Pascal certainly does ('if not nature, at least all thought had abhorred the possibility that somewhere there might be a void').

Moreover, Lacan draws a further parallel in the passages just quoted from the tenth seminar. This would be a parallel between voids in non-human nature (whether as the vacuum at issue in debates over Aristotelian plenism or modernity's infinite physical universe as a largely empty vast expanse of black space) and the void at the very heart of human nature, namely, the negativity of Lacanian desire in its precise metapsychological sense. As Lacan notes, Aristotle's *horror vacui* as well as the pre-modern pictures of nature of which it is a part long ago ceased to be of concern to the modern mindset, given this mindset's reliance on post-Aristotelian natural science ('The vacuum doesn't interest us at all from the theoretical point of view. It's almost meaningless for us now'). Ancient and medieval plenism, along with the larger pre-modern notion of nature (whose foundations are provided by Aristotelian physics) to which it was wedded, was thoroughly undermined by the progress of the empirical, experimental sciences of nature over the course of the seventeenth and eighteenth centuries.

But, as Lacan underlines, Pascal and the Christian traditions on which he relies, at the level of their theosophical anthropologies, recoil in terror and disgust from a uniquely human void. In *Discours sur les passions de l'amour* – admittedly, there are some doubts about the authorship of this text containing multiple anticipations of psychoanalytic ideas[317] – Pascal observes that 'When one loves, one persuades oneself that one would discover the passion of another: thus one is afraid' (*Quand l'on aime, on se persuade que l'on découvrirait la passion d'un autre: ainsi l'on a peur*).[318] Relatedly, one of the fragments in the *Pensées* even refers to some persons fearing the void denied by Aristotelian plenism as though this natural vacuum were somehow a sentient and sapient other.[319] This would be the inner emptiness driving humans towards enslavement to the excesses of gnawing, ceaseless cravings (i.e. Lacanian desires), to the squandering of lives lived perpetually chasing after elusive private pleasures and satisfactions. This inner emptiness is, in Lacan's terms, the 'vacuole' of 'the Thing' (*das Ding, la Chose*)[320] fantasmatically filled in by the spectral presence of the object-cause of desire, namely, *objet petit a*. Pascalian Christianity abhors the black-hole-like void at the gravitational centre of the human libidinal economy as per psychoanalysis ('for Pascal, whether or not nature abhors a vacuum [*que la nature ait ou non horreur du vide*] was essential, because this signified the abhorrence that all the learned men of his day had for desire').

My reading of these concluding remarks from the 12 December 1962 session of the tenth seminar is reinforced by what Lacan has to say at the end of the immediately subsequent session (19 December 1962) of this same seminar. A week later, he brings up the Old Testament God, the deity partly at stake for Pascal himself in his reflections on the divine. Lacan associates this God with the '*Che vuoi?*' of the Lacanian Other, namely, the question of what the subject wants in the face of, when confronted by, this impenetrable alterity's mysterious, opaque desire, a desire that perturbs and animates the subject's own desire[321] (in line with the Hegelian–Kojèvian mantra, embraced by Lacan, having it that 'man's desire is the desire of the Other'). Furthermore, he grounds this subject-Other desiring relationship in the Freudian Oedipus complex.[322] Finally, Lacan concludes this seminar session by linking the Old Testament God and/as the Other asking '*Che vuoi?*' with the Greek goddess Diana and/as Lacan's *Chose freudienne* of the 1955 *écrit* of this title ('The Freudian Thing, or the Meaning of the Return to Freud in Psychoanalysis').[323] As will become apparent soon enough, this link is crucial for understanding Lacan's critical assessment of Pascal's wager.

On two other roughly contemporaneous occasions, Lacan reiterates this connection between the paternal Old Testament God and the maternal Thing. First, in the final session (24 June 1964) of *Seminar XI* (*The Four Fundamental Concepts of Psychoanalysis* [1964]), Lacan invokes the mysterious spectre of what he dubs '*the dark God*' (*le Dieu obscur*).[324] This would be the divine Other as 'dark' *qua* obscure, as a being whose desire (including this being's underlying affections, attentions, inclinations, intentions and the like) is inscrutable and unpredictable (along the lines of Freud's *Nebenmensch-als-Ding*, which becomes Lacan's *Chose maternelle*). Lacan then proceeds to talk about God and divine dictates as they feature in both Spinoza's and Kant's philosophies.[325] On the heels of this, and at the very close of the eleventh seminar, he brings up his concept of 'the paternal metaphor'[326] (about which I will say more soon).

The second occasion when Lacan echoes the linkage he makes in *Seminar X* between the God of someone like Pascal and the Thing of Freudian psychoanalysis occurs in the *écrit* 'Science and Truth', itself the transcription of the opening session (1 December 1965) of the thirteenth seminar. Therein,

Lacan touches upon multiple thinkers' conceptions of God, including a number of figures important or related to Pascal and his ideas about the divine. These figures include Saint Augustine, Descartes, Angelus Silesius and Spinoza. Lacan immediately follows this rapid-fire tour of the God of certain philosophers with another self-reference to 'The Freudian Thing' and the enigmatic alterity of its *Chose qui parle*.[327] Lacan likewise mentions '*La chose freudienne*' in proximity to referencing Pascal in *Seminar XVI*.[328]

Grasping what is entailed by Lacan's association of the Pascalian God with the Freudian Thing requires appreciating his recasting of Freud's Oedipus complex (with Lacan being acutely aware that select details in Pascal's life history suggest Pascal struggled mightily with some severe Oedipal issues[329]). This recasting starts with emphasizing a fact noted by Freud: Human beings are born stranded in a prolonged state of prematurational helplessness.[330] In *The Future of an Illusion*, Freud, with the topic of religion squarely in view, associates human helplessness with a 'longing' (*die Sehnsucht*) for the father and the 'protection' (*der Schutz*) he provides.[331] Lacan crucially adds that the protection the helpless child longs for is from nothing other than the mother herself as the menacing Real of *das Ding*, as the ominous opacity of maternal desire. Freud's association of childhood *Hilflosigkeit* with a yearning for fatherly safeguarding harbors profound implications for Lacan's understanding both of the paternal figure in the Oedipus complex and, relatedly, of the deity of Judeo-Christian monotheisms (Pascal's included).

Compared with other animals, human infants spend a relatively lengthy period of time in a state in which they are utterly and completely dependent upon others for the satisfaction of their basic bodily needs.[332] This physiological reality of 'prematuration', of a primordial *Hilflosigkeit*, is responsible for humans being (as Elizabeth Grosz nicely phrases it) 'naturally social',[333] namely, biologically inclined towards a matrix of more-than-biological structures organizing what comes to be their reality. According to both Freud and Lacan, human nature is naturally predisposed to the predominance of nurture over nature.[334]

For Lacan, the neonate, as 'still trapped in his motor impotence and nursling dependence',[335] is propelled into a series of social relations by the initial catalyst of its simple helplessness. These social relations ultimately are underpinned by a 'symbolic order' as a network of codes, meanings, norms, representations and rules shaping inter-subjective interactions, namely, an enveloping, overarching system into which the neonate is inserted and inscribed even before the actual moment of biological birth. The family is the earliest sphere in which the child collides with a realization shattering the sense of omnipotence connected with his/her infantile narcissism. This realization is nothing other than the child's dawning awareness that he/she is 'not all', that there are other people with their own needs and desires, that everyone is subjected to orders and authorities transcending their immediate inclinations.

At a certain point during the child's initial condition of total dependency, he/she encounters the mother ("*l'Autre primitive*") as an 'all-powerful Other'[336] who could, at any moment, withdraw her vitally indispensable love.[337] Once the mother is constituted as another with her own desires, figuring out what this Other wants becomes, for the not-yet-independent child, almost a matter of life and death. Hence, as Lacan claims, the question '*Che vuoi?*' ('What does the Other want?) lies at the heart of the Oedipus complex as one of the key mysteries confronting the nascent subject, the answer to which is determinative of his/her very existence as a desiring being.[338] Along related lines, Žižek insists that 'the subject "is" only through its confrontation with the enigma of *Che vuoi*? ("What do you want?") insofar as the Other's desire remains impenetrable, insofar as the subject doesn't know what object it is for the Other'.[339] The implication here is that the refusal or abolition of this question correlatively entails the absence of full-fledged subjectivity proper.[340]

Another detail from Freud's corpus relevant to Lacan's revision of the Oedipus complex resides in the 1895 *Project for a Scientific Psychology*. Therein, Freud briefly touches upon what is involved in the psychical-cognitive establishment of a relation to another person, to what Freud dubs the '*Nebenmensch*' (neighbor). He affirms that, given 'the initial helplessness of human beings', extraneous individuals are essential in the procurement of 'satisfaction' (*Befriedigung*), with this being the initial impetus behind both communication and morality.[341] As Alphonse De Waelhens notes, 'This immaturity entails the fact that our original and inescapable lot is dependence.'[342]

In the 1895 *Project*, Freud goes on to remark that the other person, as a mental object, can be decomposed into two core constituents. On the one hand, there is the other as a 'thing' (*Ding*), as something with a 'constant structure' (*konstantes Gefüge*). On the other hand, there is the other as 'understood' (*verstanden*) on the basis of memory and the acquired knowledge it contains.[343] This suggests that the Other-as-thing is an enduring mystery, something that fails to fall easily into the grasp of an understanding grounded upon experientially registered data (such as the observable overt behaviour of the other as a sensible physical object within the perceptual field).

Lacan, in his rightly celebrated seventh seminar – a large portion of this academic year is devoted to dealing with Kant's practical philosophy – highlights Freud's comparison of the other person with 'the Thing'.[344] Is it any accident that the German word used by Freud is the same one employed by Kant to designate that which forever remains radically unknowable for the thinking subject (i.e. the noumenal *Ding an sich*, the constitutively inaccessible thing-in-itself)? An irreducible margin of alterity, of permanent foreignness, remains a constant (if not always acknowledged) feature of all inter-human relationships.

This unknowable alterity is, at the everyday level, typically covered over by ubiquitous transferential fantasies and related psychical productions filling in the many gaps and cracks in the fabric of experience resulting from this inherent ignorance. Such psychical productions serve as compensations for a constitutional lack of telepathy *qua* an impossible mind-to-mind symbiosis (as should go without saying, a lot would be different if human beings were mentally transparent to one another). Reality itself would not be what it is as something seemingly stable and negotiable without these 'fictional' elements that mitigate the thing-like opacity of the Other.

In fact, Freud's discussion of the other person as a mental object in the 1895 *Project* provides one way of construing Lacan's distinction between the lower-case 'o' other (i.e. the 'little other') and the upper-case 'O' Other, the latter having two separate senses. The little other is to be situated in the Lacanian register of the Imaginary. It is the other insofar as he/she is assumed to be 'like me', to be an alter-ego whose motives and impulses are capable of being transparently understood.

By contrast, the upper-case 'O' Other designates, in Lacan's vocabulary (and depending on the context), either of two aspects of alterity. On the one hand, there is the Real Other (i.e. the Other *qua* Thing) as something radically alien and eternally enigmatic. On the other hand, there is the Symbolic Other, often referred to in Lacanian parlance as the 'big Other' (*le grand Autre*) of the symbolic order. This third dimension of otherness interposes itself between the Imaginary other and the Real Other.[345]

The big Other of the symbolic order, as, in part, a normative social and conceptual framework, transcends individual ego-level relationships, with this framework operating as something regulative in a law-like way. This order is a mediating third standing over-and-above the confrontation between ego and alter ego. Additionally, this same Symbolic Other simultaneously helps tame and domesticate the Real Other in sustaining an organized network of shared patterns and meanings, that is, in supporting a sort of consensus reality in which others are not too other, too strange and incomprehensible. Žižek observes that 'In order to render our coexistence with the Thing minimally bearable, the symbolic order *qua* Third, the pacifying mediator, has to intervene: the "gentrification" of the Other-Thing into a "normal fellow human" cannot occur through our direct interaction, but presupposes the third agency to which we both submit – there is no intersubjectivity (no symmetrical, shared relationship between humans) without the impersonal symbolic Order.'[346] Or, as he words it elsewhere, 'For Freud and Lacan, "neighbor" is definitely one of the names of *das Ungeheure*, of the Monstrous: what is at stake in the process of "Oedipalization", the establishment of the rule of the paternal Law, is precisely the process of "gentrifying" this monstrous otherness, transforming it into a partner within the horizon of discursive communication.'[347]

For Lacan, the paternal function, itself an indispensable component of the Oedipus complex, serves to initiate the child, as a young subject-to-be, into the human universe of languages, laws, norms, meanings and codes. This function marks one's initiation into the domain of the symbolic order as a trans-subjective matrix governing both intra-subjective and inter-subjective dynamics. Furthermore, from a Lacanian perspective, one essential aspect of the symbolic order is that it exists as a solution to the 'other minds' problem, as a way of making co-habitation with one's opaque and mysterious neighbor-Things tolerable (apart from the more obvious role it plays in appearing to guarantee stable social cohesion by regulating the actual conduct of individuals in relation to one another).

Lacan explicitly identifies the mother (in terms of her being the archaic significant other for the child, the original caregiver as Freud's 'primary love-object'[348]) as the figure via which the child first encounters *das Ding*.[349] The maternal figure is that through which the perturbing and unsettling Real Other as Thing is introduced into the field of the child's psychical and libidinal life – 'the whole development at the level of the mother/child interpsychology . . . is nothing more than an immense development of the essential character of the maternal thing, of the mother, insofar as she occupies the place of that thing, of *das Ding*'.[350] The maternal caregiver is no longer, as she supposedly was during the reign of infantile primary narcissism, simply part and parcel of an other-less whole or continuum, a mere extension of the neonate's corporeal-libidinal existence. She comes to be recognized as beyond the whims and fancies of 'his majesty the baby'. What is more, there is much about her speech and behaviour that starts to show itself as strange and somewhat unclear in meaning. And, as yet another crucial aspect of the gradual implosion of the infant's narcissistic universe, the child also begins to realize that there are, to put it succinctly, other others, that he/she is not the sole object of affectionate interest for the mother.

How does the child respond to this difficult discovery of alterity? How does he/she deal with the loss of the earlier illusory monopoly over the mother's love and attention? Not only must this loss be coped with – Lacan argues that, in addition, an anxiety-provoking situation ensues in which the desires of the maternal Thing must be deciphered, in which what she wants becomes crucial for the child's own interests. On a Lacanian account, some of the earliest childhood identifications are precipitated as answers to questions concerning what captures the love of this maternal figure.

Indeed, Lacan's revision of his theory of the mirror stage in the eighth seminar on *Transference* (1960–1) emphasizes that the identification with the reflected image of the *moi-Gestalt* is activated by adult cues and encouragement.[351] In the twelfth seminar, the example Lacan uses to illustrate this contention is the mother holding the child up in front of a mirror and saying, 'That's you there!'[352] Furthermore, this aspect of the inner workings of the mother–child dyad is precisely what propels the child towards the paternal figure, rather than this figure forcefully intruding from the outside into the confines of a closed binary system.[353]

Although Lacan retains the Freudian theme of paternal authority as a prohibitory force, he nonetheless repeatedly emphasizes that, even in the earliest moments of the Oedipus complex, the father is more than just a threatening rival whose interference in the relationship with the mother is simply resented. Lacan sometimes speaks of what he calls 'the Name-of-the-Father' (*le Nom-du-Père*) as 'the paternal metaphor'. He states that this metaphor stands in for the 'desire of the mother'.[354] What does this mean?

In the typical, relatively healthy version of the Oedipus complex, the child initially concludes that what mother wants is nothing other than father. The paternal figure is identified as possessing those qualities and attributes capable of capturing the mobile, mysterious desires of the maternal figure – 'the mother's desire is for the father (or whatever may be standing in for him in the family), and . . . it is thus his name which serves this protective paternal function by naming the mother's desire'.[355] The father's features represent, as a 'metaphor', the desire of the mother. This metaphor signifies what she wants and what one must be to win her love, thus reducing anxieties arising from utter uncertainty in this regard.[356] Lacan similarly defines the phallus as whatever 'x' the child presumes the paternal figure to have by virtue of which he occupies a privileged position with respect to the maternal figure.[357] Lacan maintains that the paternal metaphor's significance resides in the phallus, as a guiding coordinate for the mother's desires,[358] and even that the father's main function consists in being the bearer of this phallus.[359]

During the seventeenth seminar, Lacan provocatively summarizes his recasting of the Freudian Oedipus complex. He declares:

> The mother's role is the mother's desire. That's fundamental. The mother's desire is not something that is bearable just like that, that you are indifferent to. It will always wreak havoc. A huge crocodile in whose jaws you are – that's the mother. One never knows what might suddenly come over her and make her shut her trap. That's what the mother's desire is.[360]

Lacan continues:

> Thus, I have tried to explain that there was something that was reassuring. I am telling you simple things, I am improvising, I have to say. There is a roller, made out of stone of course, which is there, potentially, at the level of her trap, and it acts as a restraint, as a wedge (*ça retient, ça coince*). It's what is

called the phallus. It's the roller that shelters you (*vous met à l'abri*), if, all of a sudden, she closes it.[361]

He promptly adds, 'I spoke . . . about this level of the paternal metaphor. I have only ever spoken of the Oedipus complex in that form.'[362] How is Lacan's summary of his take on matters Oedipal to be unpacked and deciphered?

From a Lacanian standpoint, the paternal metaphor stabilizes the early Oedipal situation by providing the child, via 'the signification of the phallus', with a means of psychically avoiding the perceived danger of maternal desire – and this thanks to the paternal metaphor offering a provisional answer to the question ('*Che vuoi?*') of maternal desire.[363] The jaws of the crocodile mother cannot now suddenly snap shut, since the child, through reference to the paternal position, believes him/herself to have discovered the triggers for the opening and shutting of these jaws, the magic 'open sesame' commanding this movement. The child's first social sphere (i.e. the Oedipal family unit), as the ontogenetic foundation for the subject's subsequent establishment of places in larger social realities, thereby becomes a little bit more predictable, a little bit more manageable. As Charles Shepherdson explains:

> The 'father' is a metaphor, in the sense of being that which the child substitutes as an answer to the enigma of maternal desire. Faced with the lack in the Other (the gap opened by the question 'What does the Other want?'), the child produces an answer in the form of the 'father,' whose essential function is to provide a symbolic point of reference, a localization, a grounding point that will give the lack in the Other a limit and a place.[364]

Richard Boothby likewise remarks that 'The function of the paternal metaphor is to submit the desire of the Mother (which is of the order of the Thing) to the law of the Father (which comprises the totality of the signifying system, the structure of the symbolic order).'[365]

This image of the crocodile as an illustration of the relation between maternal desire and the paternal metaphor also hints at another aspect of the father's function in Lacanian theory. In addition to metaphorically signifying maternal desire – Lacan states that the Name-of-the-Father 'names' the desire of the mother, fixing and pinpointing it through the effects of nomination and symbolization[366] – *le Nom-du-Père* is the original incarnation of what Lacan refers to as 'the Law' (with a capital 'L').[367] That is to say, the Name-of-the-Father represents whatever is responsible for instituting a series of rules and orders as barriers structuring the relationship between mother and child.[368]

By describing the confrontation with the desire of the mother as akin to the situation of being caught in the fanged mouth of a giant carnivorous reptile, Lacan alludes to Freud's comments about the childhood fear of being devoured by the mother. And, Lacan's Lévi-Straussian descriptions of paternal authority's function of prohibiting incest – throughout his teaching, he insists that this is the first and foremost function of the father[369] – point to something identical. Paternal authority forbids the mother from 'reabsorbing' her progeny, from ravenously reuniting herself with what should become separate ('You must not reintegrate your product!').[370]

The Lacanian Oedipus complex is as much about setting boundaries for the parents, boundaries of which the child is eventually cognizant, as it is about introducing the young nascent subject to the world of laws and restrictions. Bruce Fink succinctly delineates the twofold natures of the paternal metaphor and the desire of the mother as follows:

> the father keeps the child at a certain distance from its mother, thwarting the child's attempt to become one or remain forever one with the mother, or forbidding the mother from achieving certain satisfactions with her child, or both. Stated differently, the father protects the child from *le désir de la mère* (which means both the child's desire for the mother and the mother's desire) – that is, from a potential danger.[371]

The paternal figure operates so as to cover over the disturbing enigma of Real Otherness, as first embodied in the guise of the maternal figure, by demystifying the desire of the mother (namely, by providing an answer to the question 'What does mother want?'). The father also appears to ensure that the hidden intentions and impulses lurking within the dark abyss of the (m)Other can only go so far, that these urges too are subjected to norms and constraints preventing them from running amok.[372] Paul Verhaeghe claims that 'the prohibition on incest of the Oedipal period is first of all directed at the mother'.[373] Similarly, Moustapha Safouan describes Lacan's paternal metaphor as a kind of guarantee against the Other 'irreducible to any transparency',[374] against the anxiety-inducing proximity of the (m)Other.[375]

The maternal Other unregulated by the Law of *le Nom-du-Père* is a figure of *jouissance* (albeit, perhaps, exclusively a fantasmatic figure). As is well known, Lacan distinguishes between *désir* and *jouissance*. Lacanian desire refers to libidinal pursuits as submitted to the parameters of governing influences (such as social regulations, the reality principle and so on), whereas *jouissance* refers to an enjoyment exceeding the boundaries and limits under which human desire normally operates. Simply put, desire is mediated by the Law, whereas *jouissance* bypasses (or, at least, attempts to bypass) this mediation.

Lacan treats desire and the Law as inextricably intertwined.[376] Furthermore, the literal translation of *jouissance* as 'enjoyment' is problematic because, according to Lacan, this so-called enjoyment is far from enjoyable. In the Lacanian view, libidinal life is tolerable only insofar as its intensity is tamped down and modulated by various factors. Too much pleasure becomes unpleasurable. The violent, overwhelming upsurge of *jouissance*, short-circuiting, for instance, the regulated equilibrium between the pleasure and reality principles, threatens to engulf and annihilate the subject, to submerge and consume its very being.[377]

Desire, which comes into existence through the individual's ontogenetically original cathexes being disrupted, through the loss of the primordial drive-object(s), is a sort of defense against this *jouissance*. More specifically, the maternal Thing is retroactively rendered desirable after the fact of the pacifying paternal prohibition having partially eclipsed her unsettling presence. During a lecture on the topic of psychosis, Lacan maintains that the realm of the fully and properly human is founded upon a 'holding in check' (*refréner*) of *jouissance*[378] (with it being safe to presume that this means both one's own *jouissance*, as the unrestricted machinations of the drives, and others' *jouissance* in relation to oneself). He reiterates this point verbatim on another occasion too – 'Every human formation has as its essence, and not as an accident, the holding in check of *jouissance*' (*Toute formation humaine a pour essence, et non pour accident, de réfréner la jouissance*).[379]

Žižek highlights one of the consequences of Lacan's reconsideration of the Oedipus complex in terms of how Freud's example of the *Fort-Da* game from *Beyond the Pleasure Principle* is to be interpreted. The standard reading of this example is that the child's game with the spool is an attempt to secure a degree of pleasurable active mastery over the painfully passive experience of being left behind by the mother. The child consoles him/herself by being able to control the comings and goings, the appearance and disappearance, of the little object (in lieu of being able to control the mother herself).[380] In light of the Lacanian depiction of the maternal figure, Žižek suggests turning this interpretation of the game on its head:

> we should *invert* the standard constellation: the true problem is the mother who *enjoys* me (her child), and the true stake of the game is to escape this closure. The true anxiety is this being-caught in the Other's *jouissance*. So it is not that, anxious about losing my mother, I try to master her departure/arrival; it is that, anxious about her overwhelming *presence*, I try desperately to carve out a space where I can gain a distance toward her, and so become able to sustain my desire. Thus we obtain a completely different picture: instead of the child mastering the game, and thus coping with the trauma of his mother's absence, we get the child trying to escape the suffocating embrace of his mother, and construct an open space for desire.[381]

Symbolization, whether sustained by the paternal function or, in this example, a game – one should recall Pascal's preoccupation with games (specifically, games of chance) – provides the child with a way out of a stifling enclosure. The displacement of the cathexes invested in *das Ding* (as the original mother-

Thing) onto a series of substitutes (i.e. 'metaphors' as subliminatory stand-ins) opens up some psychical breathing space for the young subject-to-be. This displacement involves loosening the ties that tightly bind the libidinal economy to the maternal primary love-object. Short apron strings strangle the desiring capacities of whoever is too tightly tied to them.

A genuinely human life, characterized by a flexibility and mobility of desires, requires the distance from *jouissance* (one's own as well as that of the Real Other) made possible by Symbolic identifications, practices and transformations. Put differently, one cannot become a human subject per se without undergoing 'castration' *qua* the (painful) separation from the archaic Thing of the drives. The split characteristic of Lacanian subjectivity (as the 'barred S' [$]) is, at one level, a splitting off from *das Ding*.

Lacan contends that the true import of the myth of Oedipus, as relevant for psychoanalysis, is actually revealed by Freud's tale of the primal horde from *Totem and Taboo*.[382] What consequences does this contention entail? In *Totem and Taboo*, the band of brothers, instead of rejoicing once they succeed in doing away with the autocratic 'primal father' (*Urvater*), are so upset by their accomplishment that they immediately agree upon the institution of a set of laws forever prohibiting anyone from acting as they did. In other words, rather than enjoying libidinal liberation (à la the free circulation of women) in the wake of having liquidated the external obstacle to gratification (incarnated by the primal father), the fraternal horde re-imposes upon itself a set of restrictions forbidding unlimited enjoyment. As Lacan has it, the *Urvater* returns, in a spectral fashion, as the body of laws enacted following his physical demise. This is what Freud means when he says that 'The dead father became stronger than the living one had been. . . . What had up to then been prevented by his actual existence was thenceforward prohibited by the sons themselves.'[383]

Re-reading Sophocles's *Oedipus Rex* through the lens of *Totem and Taboo*, it can be seen that something similar happens in the case of Oedipus himself. Upon discovering that he has lived out what Freud alleges to be one of the most basic repressed fantasies structuring everyone's unconscious (i.e. the *jouissance*-laden fantasy of killing the father and sleeping with the mother), Oedipus, instead of savoring the attainment of this forbidden fruit, tears out his own eyes and voluntarily exiles himself from Thebes.[384] For Lacan, the common lesson of both Sophocles and Freud is that Oedipal victories are always Pyrrhic, that circumventing desire in directly seizing *jouissance* leads to the unbearable implosion of the libidinal economy itself.[385] As regards the Oedipus complex, the mother is tolerably desirable (as opposed to intolerably proximate, to the mother as smothering) only so long as she remains inaccessible behind the screen of paternal law – 'The father, the Name-of-the-father, sustains the structure of desire with the structure of the law.'[386]

The subject perceives a risk of *jouissance*-induced obliteration (akin to Ernest Jones's 'aphanisis'[387]) in approaching the prohibited maternal Thing too closely. Moreover, the child requires protection from the *jouissance* of this Real Other (in the sixteenth seminar, Lacan defines the *Nebenmensch* as 'the intolerable immanence of enjoyment'[388]). The establishment of a stable governing framework in the Oedipal situation (i.e. the Name-of-the-Father's founding of an enveloping trans-individual authoritative order to which all familial actors, the father included, are answerable[389]) partially shields the fragile young subject from the arbitrary and incomprehensible caprices of its first significant others. Becoming the sole object of its mother's desire is, for the child, a Pyrrhic Oedipal victory, landing him/her in a situation fraught with many psychical dangers. In this sense, Lacan's thinking implies that there is something relieving for the child in finding out that the mother is interested in others such as the father, that he/she is not the sole focal point of the mother's interest left to carry the burden of her desire alone.

Why and how is appreciating Lacan's just-glossed recasting of the Freudian Oedipus complex important for making sense of his musings about Pascal's wager? Why did I take this apparent detour in the midst of discussing Pascal *avec* Lacan? The crucial upshot of this seeming digression is that Lacan subtly utilizes his version of Oedipal structures and dynamics to depict *le pari de Pascal* (and, along with it, Judeo-Christian monotheisms generally) as a sort of compromise formation. This would be a repression that also, as Lacan has it, is simultaneously a return of the repressed. Pascal's wager, on this Lacanian rendition, is an instance of the paternal metaphor (in the guise of the Symbolic Other of Christianity's God-the-Father, with His grace and judgement) defensively substituting for and partially eclipsing the desire of the mother (as the original, primordial Real Other, with her spectral libidinal webs of opaque *jouissance*, drives, fantasies, etc. into which one is hurled at birth and within which one is left helplessly entangled). I now will set about elaborating and defending this line of argumentation.

9. 'You bet your ass!': Choosing between neurotic pathos and ordinary suffering

So, what evidence is there that Pascal's wager is a compromise formation, simultaneously a repression as well as a return of the repressed, along the lines insinuated by Lacan? To begin with, Pascal, responding to anyone who might be inclined to reject choosing according to the parameters of his *pari*, insists on the unavoidability of this choice between betting for or against the Christian God's existence. He responds, 'but you must wager. There is no choice, you are already committed' (*mais il faut parier. Cela n'est pas volontaire: vous êtes embarqué*).[390]

Foreshadowing the Sartrean existentialist 'condemnation to freedom',[391] Pascal maintains that one cannot choose not choosing. For the author of the *Pensées*, with his Jansenist 'all or nothing' approach to various religious issues[392] – the text of the wager is headed by the ultimate all-or-nothing of the alternative between '*Infinity–nothing*'[393] – one either chooses to believe in the Christian God or one does not. The second option of this wager, choosing not to believe in the Christian God, contains not only the choice of atheism. It also contains: one, choosing to believe in a non-Christian God or gods (recalling Spinoza's dictum according to which all determination is negation' [*omnis determinatio est negatio*],[394] with belief in a non-Christian God or gods as a determination negating belief in the Christian God); as well as, two, agnosticism as not choosing to believe by (vainly) attempting to avoid the very choice itself.

Yet, there is no avoiding the choice ('you must wager. There is no choice' [*il faut parier. Cela n'est pas volontaire*]). The attempt at avoidance is already itself a choice not to wager in favour of the Christian God's existence. Moreover, according to Pascal, even if one never bothers explicitly to consider God and the question of His existence or non-existence, one implicitly gambles for or against this divine being each and every day of one's life, through one's thoughts and actions ('you are already committed' [*vous êtes embarqué*]). One's habitual quotidian cognition and comportment already tacitly testify to whether or not one is wagering that God exists. For as long as one is alive on this earth, one always already has embarked on a journey in which, Pascal insists, the fateful decision of *le pari* is omnipresent and inescapable.

Lacan sees fit to underscore Pascal's 'you are already committed' (*vous êtes embarqué*) on several occasions.[395] What, from a psychoanalytic point of view, is attention-worthy in this specific aspect of the Pascalian wager? More precisely, how might this textual detail from the best-known fragment in Pascal's *Pensées* be interpreted in light of Lacan's rendition of the Oedipus complex?

Well before Martin Heidegger and his concept of 'thrownness' (*Geworfenheit*), Marx already emphasizes (most famously, at the start of 1852's *The Eighteenth Brumaire of Louis Bonaparte*) that birth tosses human beings into vast, intricate constellations of collective structures and dynamics, into a sprawling social history already well underway.[396] Like both Marx and Heidegger on this particular score, Lacan too foregrounds in various ways the fact that, in his terms, each and every subject-to-be, through being born, falls into the enveloping nets of symbolic orders as trans-subjective big Others. Starting with the family as itself a social unit inseparably bound up with its surrounding *grand Autre*, strands of socio-symbolic mediation are brought to bear on *le-sujet-à-être* (or *à venir*) even before the actual event of physical birth. Such mediation suffuses, creates and sustains the very existence of the 'speaking being' (*parlêtre*). In Lacan's eyes, there simply is no subjectivity whatsoever without this mediation (although, at the same time, this is not to say that Lacan reduces the subject entirely to the register of the Symbolic and its signifiers). Ontogenetically, beginning with this 'throw' (*als Wurf*) of birth, with everyone embarking (*à la* Pascal's '*vous êtes embarqué*') on life thusly, the human psychical organism finds itself confronted with the thereafter lifelong challenge of orienting and situating itself with respect to the two types of capital-O Otherness identified by Lacan. As I explained earlier, these two types are Real Otherness (Oedipally associated with the maternal figure as the initial embodiment of the Thing [*das Ding, la Chose*]) and Symbolic Otherness (Oedipally associated with the paternal figure as the initial embodiment of the authority of socio-linguistic Law). For Lacan, the Oedipal familial drama fundamentally is about the child's struggle to find a safe place in relation to these two registers of alterity.

Of course, the throw of birth is also a hurling into the biologically preordained state of prolonged prematurational helplessness. Such helplessness would count as an aspect of what Pascal repeatedly characterizes, almost *ad nauseam*, as humanity's congenital 'wretchedness' (*misère*). Indeed, and along these very lines, the author of the *Pensées* at one point states, '*Description of man*. Dependence, desire for independence, needs' (*Description de l'homme: dépendance, désir d'indépendance, besoin*)[397] Furthermore, the authoritative English translator of Pascal, Alban Krailsheimer, goes so far as to maintain, apropos the *Pensées*, that 'The categorical statement that man is wretched constitutes the basis of Pascal's entire argument.'[398]

The particular wretchedness of Freudian–Lacanian *Hilflosigkeit* entails the child's ontogenetically fateful complete dependence for his/her very survival and well-being on its adult significant others (i.e. the parental figures as Real and Symbolic Others). For the child, thrown into such helplessness and dependence, properly situating him/herself in relation to his/her Real and Symbolic Others (as per the Lacanian version of the Oedipus complex) is, in a way, a matter of life and death. Without their love, approval, care and concern, the child faces one or more existential threats: literally perishing, becoming a terribly malformed subject burdened with one or more crippling pathologies, or even failing to become a proper subject in the first place.

This last dangerous possibility could be described, paraphrasing the Lacan who speaks of a 'second death' over and above the literal physical perishing of the individual organism, as being deprived of a 'second birth' (as a secular Lacanian twist on the Protestant theme of being 'born again'). After being biologically born as a human being *qua* organism belonging to a specific primate species, one also can and should be socio-symbolically born as a speaking being *qua* subject recognized both inter-subjectively (in Lacan's terms, by tamed and domesticated alter-egos as little-o others who are comprehensibly 'like me') and trans-subjectively (in Lacan's terms, by big Others as anonymous mediating

Thirds, as shared collective frameworks of customs, ideals, institutions, mores, norms, representations, rules, traditions, values and so on). Related to this notion of a second birth, one might recall the anecdote about the German idealist philosopher J. G. Fichte throwing a party to celebrate the first time his son employed the first-person pronoun '*Ich*' (I). In Fichte's view, the initial uttering of 'I', and not the date of the biological occurrence of physical birth, is the true birthday of the person *qua* genuine subject. Without this second birth, the human being is left to languish in a living death of one or more sorts of grave psychopathology.

Taking into account the immediately preceding, it becomes clear that, from Lacan's perspective, Pascal's stress on the inescapability of his perilous, high-stakes wager ('but you must wager. There is no choice, you are already committed') cross-resonates with developmentally primary thrownness-into-helplessness as highlighted specifically by psychoanalysis. For humans, being hurled into existence is tantamount to embarking (*embarquer*) on a course in which they have no choice but to choose (or wager) how to position themselves as regards their this-worldly bigger significant Others. Likewise, Pascal's wagerer must decide, whether he/she wants to or not, how to situate him/herself vis-à-vis the otherworldly divine big Other and the combination of potential outcomes allowed for within the parameters of *le pari*.

If things go awry in this Oedipal ontogenetic process, the uncertain child might find him/herself condemned to the psychotic Hell of never acceding to the status of being a full-fledged subject *qua parlêtre*. A severely neglected child might even die as a result of not being in the attentive graces of a merciful parental caretaker. When Lacan, many times, contends that a psychoanalytic interpretation of Pascal's wager reveals that this gamble is more about the being of the 'I' (*Je, Ich*) than the existence of God,[399] this arguably is what he has in mind.

In Pascal's wager, the fate of one's soul in the afterlife is potentially at stake. In what Lacan alleges is the ontogenetically original version of this Pascalian existential scene of choosing, the fate of one's soul in this life is actually at stake. Related but in addition to the threat of both literal death and socio-symbolic death (i.e. non-recognition by *le grand Autre*), there is, Lacan maintains in *Seminar XIII* apropos Pascal, a 'vague anxiety of the beyond that is not necessarily a beyond of death'.[400] What is this other 'beyond' (*au-delà*) distinct from that which, whatever it is, lies on the hither side of the end of life?

I would contend that this other beyond and the anxiety it arouses refer back, in Lacan's eyes, to the Oedipal familial drama as he recasts it. This has everything to do with the desire of the Other.[401] More precisely, it has to do with the withdrawn and inaccessible Real Otherness of the maternal Thing, namely, the 'beyond' of the (pre-)Oedipal inferno of the infant rather than that of a potentially blissful afterlife on the other side of biological perishing. As Lacan knows well, Pascal's Augustine-inspired and anti-Pelagian Jansenism stresses the subject's total and complete reliance on the Other in the guise of the fallen human being's abject dependence for renouncing sin and achieving salvation on the unpredictability of God's infallibly efficacious grace. Indeed, the concept of grace is central to Pascal's thinking and at the center of controversies among his contemporaries in which he intervenes.

In *Seminar XVI*, Lacan, in the context of discussing Pascal's wager at length, goes so far as to claim that the degree of theoretical interest Christianity has for psychoanalysis is tied specifically to its idea(s) of grace.[402] For Lacan, grace as per Christianity is a sublimated form of what originally is the desire of the (m) Other *à la* his version of the Oedipus complex. From Pascal's own Christian perspective, the human condition is one of fallenness into the errors and miseries of sinfulness, a condition from which humans can be saved only by the grace of an unknowable and inscrutable God. From Lacan's psychoanalytic perspective, this echos the ontogenetically archaic and primary state of the young human child being thrown into the world helplessly reliant for his/her very survival and health on the desires (as attention, concern, love, etc.) of seemingly all-powerful bigger Others (i.e. parental caretakers). Accordingly, Lacan repeatedly draws parallels between the desire of the maternal Real Other of psychoanalysis and the grace of the paternal Symbolic Other of Pascal.[403]

During the one and only session (20 November 1963) opening Lacan's aborted 1963–4 seminar on 'The Names-of-the-Father', he mentions 'a book I have promised for six months from now'.[404] As a footnote to the 1990 English translation of this seminar session states, 'This book was never published.'[405] However, in 2021, the manuscript of this unfinished book, interrupted by and abandoned in favour of work on what became 1966's *Écrits*, was posthumously published under the title '*Mis en question du psychanalyste*'. It contains a line of thought especially relevant to my present reflections on psychoanalysis and religion.

In the manuscript of '*Mis en question du psychanalyste*', Lacan again associates Christianity with his motif of *le désir de l'Autre*. In so doing, he floats a particularly interesting hypothesis on this occasion. According to this Lacan *circa* 1963, the figure of Jesus Christ and the accompanying doctrine of the incarnation have more to do with making an all-too-human life in this world at least tolerable, rather than having to do primarily with otherworldly transcendence and possible afterlives.

Viewed from a Lacanian angle, the distinctively Christian account of God becoming human is, in part, about rendering the Other's desire less enigmatic. This is accomplished by having the incarnation concretely incarnate *qua* express God's desire. And what desire does the incarnation express? In '*Mis en question du psychanalyste*', Lacan answers that it incarnates the divine Other's desire to be like us, even to be one of us. That is to say, Christ embodies the Father's affirmation of the very desirability of the human condition.[406]

Earlier, I reminded readers of Lacan's commitment to the Hegelian–Kojèvian dictum having it that 'Man's desire is the desire of the Other.' Recalling this dictum in conjunction with Lacan's just-explained claim about the Christian doctrine of the incarnation, the figure of Jesus Christ *vis-à-vis* God-the-Father can be taken as representing an effort by this faith's believers to convince themselves that, as it were, man's desire is the desire to be man (a far from self-evident assertion). This is a matter of rendering their own otherwise miserable and wretched lives desirable, of making this vile world livable through turning flesh-and-blood human existence into a desideratum of the divine Himself. If God wants it, how can we not want it as well?

With Christian grace *à la* Pascal bringing up for Lacan his account of *désir*, it should come as no surprise that Lacan's reflections on Pascalian thought also mobilize the Lacanian concept of *objet petit a*, the object-cause of desire. Lacan repeatedly maintains that object *a* is the real central stake of Pascal's wager.[407] How so?

Whole books can be and have been devoted to clarifying the exact nature of Lacan's *objet petit a*, with Lacan crediting himself with having invented this particular concept as his main contribution to psychoanalysis.[408] In what is about to follow, I will not pretend to furnish an exhaustive elucidation of the crucial Lacanian metapsychological category of object *a*. Considering the focus of my elaborations here, I will devote myself below to clarifying the role of object *a* in what Lacan has to say regarding Pascal's wager specifically.

Lacan indicates that the gambler who assents to *le pari de Pascal* is making a bet in which his/her own life must be placed on the figurative gaming table in order for him/her to take up this particular wager.[409] Lacan also alleges that one's own life, at least when wagered on Pascal's terms, is rendered equivalent to being an instance of *objet petit a*.[410] Furthermore, Lacan contends that Pascal wrongly equates the *a* of one's wagered life with nothing, with absolute nullity.[411] What does all this mean?

By Lacan's lights, Pascal's wagerer offers up his/her life as an object presumably 'causing' (*qua* steering and governing) the desire of the divine Other, as the *objet petit a* of the God who may or may not really exist. He/she who wagers on God's existence and indeed acts accordingly offers up the sacrifice of his/her self-objectified life to a presumed transcendent alterity/authority. This sacrifice entails renouncing earthly life as the libidinal creaturely existence of pursuing one's insatiable passions broadly construed, namely, the life of desire (i.e. life-*qua*-*a*).

Hence, in Lacanian terms, Pascal's wagerer objectifies his/her own life of desire (as, in its entirety, an object *a*) and sacrificially proffers it to a (dark, obscure, hidden) God who is assumed to desire such a sacrifice. This sacrificed life thereby functions as the *objet petit a* fixing and directing (i.e. 'causing') this divine Other's *désir*. Without such fixing and directing, God's desire would remain ominously cryptic and impenetrable, like the anxiety-inducing desire of the maternal Thing as menacing Real Otherness presumably animated by an enjoyment (*jouissance*) operating lawlessly and unpredictably. This contrasts sharply with the lawful, predictable, rule-governed reign of the pacified (or, at least, pacifiable) Symbolic Other as Christianity's God-the-Father, Himself the epitome of Lacan's paternal metaphor (involving both the Name-of-the-Father and the phallus) as per the Lacanian Oedipus complex.

The combinatory game of the four possible outcomes entertained by Pascal in his *pari* is, in Lacan's view, a means of coping with and fending off an anxiety ontogenetically originating for all subjects, Pascal included, in the helpless infant's confrontations with the threatening opacity and indecipherability of the desire of the (m)Other *qua Ding/Chose* on which the child is wholly dependent for his/her very life. As seen, Lacan treats this game of wagering (and most games in general) as defensively managing risk by capturing chance in the nets of mathematical-style calculation of probabilities and payoffs. Yet, for all Pascal's straining to present his wager as not really a wager – as I underscored earlier, Pascal stresses that one has nothing to lose and everything to gain by wagering that God exists and behaving accordingly – Lacan argues that this same Pascal actually fails to minimize and avoid the sort of risk concerning him.

This is where Lacan's 'ethics of psychoanalysis' collides with Pascal's Christian-Jansenist ethics. A Lacan I cited a short while ago condemns Pascal's equation of the life of desire (i.e. life as *a*) with mere, sheer nothing(ness) as false. This Lacan is taking issue with the claim in the *Pensées* that the life of desire, to be renounced by the wagerer who acts in line with wagering on God's existence, is so irredeemably worthless (or 'wretched' [*misérable*]) that its sacrifice to God and His laws does not even count as a loss whatsoever. For this Pascal, one has nothing to lose but loss and nothingness themselves. By contesting Pascal's religious outlook on this score,[412] Lacan makes the Pascalian game of the wager truly risky, no longer just a game,[413] precisely at the point where Pascal discounts any true risk.

In the sixteenth seminar's extended musings on Pascal's wager, Lacan, as is his characteristic wont, repeatedly has recourse to various and sundry formalizations. This recourse is especially appropriate in relation to Pascal, given the latter's contributions to mathematics and the natural sciences. Apropos *objet petit a* and the Pascalian objectification of life-as-*a*, the Lacan of *Seminar XVI* puts forward an equation proposing that '$1 + a = 1/a$',[414] an equation he applies to the subject of Pascal's wager.[415] In having what is added to 1, through this very addition, become the denominator of a fraction with 1 as its numerator, the larger the number assigned to *a* (i.e. the more instances of *a*), the smaller the sum resulting. In Lacan's equation involving *a*, addition strangely and counterintuitively results in a sum smaller than the values added to produce it. It seems that Lacanian desire has its own law of diminishing returns: The more living desire repeatedly pursues iterations and incarnations of its object-cause (*a*), the less one ends up possessing. With *objet petit a*, it indeed looks as though more is less.

As regards these mathematical-style assertions concerning *désir*, the Lacan of the sixteenth seminar contends that Pascal simply reduces *a* to 0, the life of desire to 'infinitely nothing'.[416] Yet, if '1 + *a* = 1/*a*', as Lacan also maintains, then Pascal's equating of living desire with absolute nothingness is incorrect. However much one gives oneself over to desire, however large the value of *a* gets, it will never be the case that 1/*a* = 0. The lower limit of 1/*a* might be almost nothing in its smallness, but it never becomes completely nothing.[417]

Freud famously depicts the therapeutic progress of a successful analysis as a process in which neurotic pathos is turned into ordinary suffering.[418] The Lacan who challenges Pascal's reduction of life-as-*a* to nothing(ness) is essentially saying to Pascal that the best humans can hope for is not renouncing their passions, but transforming their desire from being mired in Freud's 'neurotic pathos' into becoming instead a source of much milder 'ordinary suffering' (a suffering not unaccompanied by an entourage of compensatory little pleasures). Correlatively, Lacan also is saying that attempting to sacrifice this one-life-to-live-as-*a*, rather than resulting in the gratification of living a satisfying life in this world as promised by Pascal, only worsens and intensifies neurotic pathos. One thereby condemns oneself to a Hell on earth, namely, the misery of a life lived under the lashes of excessive super-ego-inflicted guilt (about which I will explain more momentarily).

If God does not exist but one lives as though He does, then, contrary to what Pascal himself says, one has gambled away the virtual nothing of desiring life for utterly nothing whatsoever. Even worse: One has wasted and ruined even the few small gratifications obtainable in the virtual nothing of this one life in this one world. Instead of successfully avoiding danger through game-theoretic risk management, Pascal's wager contains the real danger, obfuscated and denied by Pascal, of a version of making the perfect (as Pascal's 'eternity of life and happiness' [*éternité de vie et de bonheur*], 'an infinity of infinitely happy life' [*une infinité de vie infiniment heureuse*][419]) the enemy of, if not the good, then at least the not totally awful and worthless (i.e. life-as-*a*, living desire). And, Lacan insists that his insight into the inherently 'barred' ($\cancel{A}$), inconsistent and fragmentary, status of any and every big Other indicates that there is no deity worth wagering on along Pascalian lines[420] – a sentiment echoing the virulent atheism of Freud himself.

10. Whose desire should, and whose should not, be ceded?: From Pascalian to Lacanian ethics

In the seventh seminar, entitled *The Ethics of Psychoanalysis*, Lacan makes a now-renowned observation, according to which, 'from an analytical point of view, the only thing of which one can be guilty is of having given ground relative to one's desire' (*la seule chose dont on puisse être coupable, au moins dans la perspective analytique, c'est d'avoir cédé sur son désir*):[421] Elsewhere, I have argued against construing this as an imperative, as a sort of Lacanian eleventh commandment.[422] Without me rehashing those arguments here, suffice it to say for now that I understand this celebrated statement from *Seminar VII* as more descriptive than prescriptive, as more explanatory than justificatory.

Lacan's oft-invoked line about guilt and 'ceding' (*céder*) one's desire ought to be read as of a piece with his larger 'return to Freud'. More precisely, I take this statement to be a distillation of one of Freud's insights regarding the super-ego. The later Freud alights upon a type of paradox exhibited particularly by those who can be characterized as 'moral masochists', whether zealous adherents to a demanding religious way of life or garden-variety secular perfectionists of whatever stripe. Counterintuitively, the closer such individuals get to embodying their normative ideals through self-imposed discipline (enforced by the super-ego), the more guilty they feel. Such seemingly excessive and unwarranted guilt fixates upon the remaining small flaws and imperfections sustaining a stubbornly persistent narrow gap between the person's ego and ego-ideal.[423]

For this Freud, moral masochists' extreme and unjustified guilt, expressed in their needlessly harsh self-reproaches and the like, is to be explained through recourse to two of his theses regarding the super-ego. First, the super-ego is intra-psychically omniscient, registering everything transpiring within the psyche consciously, preconsciously and unconsciously. Second, the super-ego refuses to register any difference between, on the one side, fantasies, ideas, inclinations, urges, etc. and, on the other side, behaviours, conduct, deeds, etc.; for this psychical agency, a mere desire or wish within the mind alone, even if thoroughly repressed and never actually acted upon, is the same as the enactment in the external world of this desire or wish. The super-ego refuses to distinguish between intention and act, treating the former as equivalent to the latter.

So, how do these two Freudian theses apropos the super-ego permit explaining the perplexing intensification of moral masochists' guilt the closer they get to incarnating their ideals? Such masochists' rigid self-discipline in pursuit of perfection requires a significant amount of renunciation and repression of any impulses that might interfere with this pursuit. But even when rendered fully unconscious, such tendencies and urges neither go away nor become invisible to the super-ego.

Instead, under the pressure of repression, these impulses, pent-up and unsatisfied, become only more intense and insistent. Although the conscious portions of the ego remain unaware of all this, the intra-psychically omniscient super-ego is quite cognizant of these repressed impulses and their growing vividness and urgency. And since the super-ego treats intentions as equivalent to actions, it punishes the rest of the psyche of the moral masochist by making him/her feel just as guilty as though he/she had really acted out all of his/her most strongly repressed desires and fantasies. Therefore, considering the over-the-top strength of the repressions moral masochists impose on themselves in their futile quests to completely close the gap between their egos and ego-ideals, it now looks to be no wonder that they become more guilty and self-punishing the closer they get to such closure.

In Lacan's terms, Freud's moral masochists 'give ground' (*céder*) on their *désir*. In so doing, they render themselves all the more guilty before the tribunals of their own super-egos. Whether they are guilty at the level of being, in terms of inter- and trans-subjectively determined ethical, legal or moral culpability, is irrelevant. If anything, analysis's moral masochists usually appear to others as the opposite, namely, as irreproachable exemplars of certain high-minded principles and values. But, to themselves, they appear to be criminals, failures, incompetents, reprobates, sinners, wretches and so on. They feel guilty, even if they are not guilty. For Freud and Lacan alike, not only does no good deed go unpunished – no repressed bad intention goes unpunished either. The greater the goodness achieved by the moral masochist through 'ceding' his/her desires, the greater the negative affective punishment of super-egoistic guilt endured by him/her.[424]

Apropos the likes of Pascal and the Jansenist residents of Port-Royal, their Christian asceticism would qualify as an instance of what Freud identifies as moral masochism. In Lacan's parlance, these Christians practice a way of life insisting upon 'giving ground' relative to their desires. Such ceding intensifies, rather than ameliorates, their sense of *apriori* guilt, of fallenness into misery and sinfulness, before God-the-Father-Almighty. As regards Pascal's wager specifically, the *Pensées* make abundantly explicit that an individual wagering on God's existence dictates him/her *céder son désir*, as Lacan would put it.

As seen, the Christian ethics informing and relied upon by *le pari de Pascal* promises that even if God does not exist, living as though He does (i.e. conducting oneself along the lines of a Christian ascetic) results in a happier life. Pascal's Jansenism involves a belief that living a life of self-renunciation (i.e. of Lacan's 'giving ground relative to one's desire'), regardless of questions of God and an afterlife, results in eudaimonic well-being and contentment, namely, a Christian 'good life' *qua* happy existence. This belief is precisely what Freud's economic paradox of moral masochism and Lacan's famous rephrasing of it in *Seminar VII* attack.

If indeed 'the only thing of which one can be guilty is of having given ground relative to one's desire', then behaving according to a wager on God's existence, as Pascal recommends, produces only more misery for the wagerer. He/she thereby ends up leading a life burdened by ever-growing guilt and related negative affects. Even if God exists, this is a life of neurotic pathos, of gratuitous self-flagellation, in this world. Lacan thus elevates the stakes of Pascal's wager, turning it from a probability-theoretic game in which players having nothing to lose into an existential drama with real risks. The wagerer now truly has something to lose, if only the almost-nothing of a one-and-only desiring life as ordinary suffering.

The Freudian–Lacanian re-description of guilt, on the basis of the psychoanalytic theory of the super-ego, here begins to shade from description into prescription. More specifically, Lacan's redeployment of Freud's reflections on moral masochism enables him to pit a distinctive 'ethics of psychoanalysis' against the ethics of Christianity dear to Pascal and integral to his wager. In the sixteenth seminar, Lacan even mentions Pascal's *Pensées* in connection with ethics generally and the ethics of psychoanalysis (as per the seventh seminar) specifically.[425]

Especially with the benefit of hindsight provided by Lacan's *Seminar VII*, one can see both Pascal and Kant as thinkers interested in ethical dimensions 'beyond the pleasure principle' (as per the title of Freud's 1920 book introducing the theory of the death drive [*Todestrieb*]). However, both of these modern thinkers fail to achieve the formulation of an ethics uninfluenced by the pleasure principle, namely, by tendencies to pursue gratification, satisfaction, etc. and correspondingly to avoid pain, suffering, etc. Kant gets much closer to such an achievement by comparison with Pascal. But even he ends up succumbing to one of the features of Pascal's ethical perspective inevitably reintroducing the influence of the pleasure principle upon ethics.

Two aspects of the position of the Pascal of the *Pensées*, including the author of the fragment on the wager, ensure that his Christian ethics remain under the sway of the pleasure principle. First, and as I noted a moment ago, there is a eudaimonic side to the Pascalian ethical perspective – and this apart from the promise of infinite happiness in the afterlife. To be precise, Pascal maintains that one of the reasons for wagering on God's existence and behaving accordingly is that such behaviour, even if God and Heaven are non-existent, is conducive to a more pleasant and fulfilled life in this world.

As I just explained, Lacan's psychoanalytic ethics directly challenges this Pascalian eudaimonism in which goodness and happiness remain conjoined. Moreover, and as Lacan himself stresses, Kant's deontological ethics of pure practical reason revolutionarily rejects eudaimonism and, in so doing, separates goodness from happiness, from any and all considerations of (positive) emotions, feelings, sentiments and the like. This ethical bracketing of (eudaimonic) happiness broadly construed is Kant's step *Jenseits des Lustprinzips*.[426]

Yet Kant shares in common with Pascal a retention of the figure of God as indispensable for an ethical disposition. In Kantian ethics, the deity of Christian monotheism functions as a 'postulate of pure practical reason'.[427] By this, Kant means that the ethical subject, acting on the basis of a good will, necessarily must, in so willing and acting, hypothesize or suppose (or, one could say, wager upon, with Kant himself alluding to *le pari de Pascal*[428]) something very much along the lines of Christianity's divinity. Although, according to Kantian critique (as well as according to Pascal[429]), God cannot be proven to exist at the level of theoretical philosophy (i.e. epistemology, ontology and metaphysics),[430] He must be assumed to exist at the level of practical philosophy (i.e. ethics, morality and politics) so as to provide agents with the hope, one central to Pascal's wager too, that behaving ethically will lead to future happiness in Heaven at the side of the divine Creator.[431] Without such hope, what is the point of living ethically? Why bother?

Kant's insistence on God as a necessary hypothesis of ethical agency, as an essential postulate of pure practical reason, compromises what Lacan identifies as constituting the real radicality of the Kantian deontological revolution in ethics. This radicality resides in elevating the good 'beyond the pleasure principle'. Kant's ethical revolution arises precisely from his rupture with both eudaimonism and utilitarianism insofar as these other two ethical orientations (apart from Kantian deontological ethics) tightly tie goodness to happiness – with happiness being what Kant treats as human-all-too-human 'pathological' inclinations and feelings involving contentment, gratification, satisfaction and so on.

By holding onto God as a regulative 'as if' (*als ob*) accompanying ethical *praxis*, Kant allows happiness (in the guise of hope for it in the afterlife) to continue exerting a gravitational pull inflecting the practical subject's willing and acting. Even if this subject expects no happiness-inducing rewards for ethico-moral goodness in this life and this world, it looks as though Kant permits this same subject at least to expect such rewards in another life and another world. Despite the deontological repudiation of the good-*qua*-happy life of eudaimonism and utilitarianism, happiness continues to haunt Kantian ethics in the guise of what Lacan would call Kant's 'God hypothesis'[432] (i.e. the divine as a postulate of pure practical reason). Furthermore, especially considering Kant's proto-psychoanalytic suspicions according to which even the seemingly purest good willing might be undetectably compromised by impure unconscious motivations,[433] it is surprising he does not appear to worry about the postulation of God inevitably tainting the will with the influences of a pathological transactionalism threatening to turn the unconditional categorical imperative into just another conditional hypothetical imperative.

Through the wager of the *Pensées*, Pascal blatantly appeals to the transactional sensibilities of the cynically non-believing aristocratic libertine who enjoys betting on games of chance. Pascal intends to employ the rewards and punishments of the wager's possible outcomes as initial incentives to begin acting in conformity with a Christian ethical way of life. But, as merely initial concessions and inducements to the likes of the jaded hedonistic free thinker, Pascal anticipates the eventual blossoming in the wager-persuaded convert of an inner belief from which will flow purer motives than those of a strictly transactional nature concerned only with carrots and sticks.[434]

However, whether with Pascal, Kant or whoever else, retention of God as an authoritative judging big Other, as a transcendent power distributing salvation (as pleasure, happiness, etc.) and damnation (as pain, suffering, etc.), cannot but leave ethics tainted by a whiff of the transactional. This whiff is ineradicable so long as probabilities of divine rewards and punishments are assessed to be non-nil values. Whether as the divinity of Pascalian belief or the holiness of Kantian faith, the spectre of God as redeemer or condemner cannot but influence the subjective agent at the level of his/her affects, desires, drives, emotions, fantasies, feelings, inclinations, motivations and the like as all arrayed along the spectrum between the pleasurable and the painful. Such a deity inevitably sustains the primacy of the pleasure principle within the field of the ethical.

Lacan's psychoanalytic ethics aims to remain faithful to the true radicality of Kant's step beyond the pleasure principle – with Kant himself, as just seen, blunting this radicality through his retention of God as a postulate of pure practical reason. For Lacan, and with reference again to Pascal, wagering against God's existence, consequences be damned, is a necessary condition (albeit not, by itself, a sufficient condition) for ethical willing and acting. Why?

As Kant himself stresses throughout his practical philosophy, the will can be unconditionally good only if and when it categorically disregards the willer's pleasure, pain, happiness and well-being (as bound up with the external worldly consequences of actions). Yet, insofar as the God hypothesis of the likes of Pascal and Kant inevitably and unavoidably brings with it considerations of pleasure, pain, happiness and well-being, it cannot but dilute the goodness of the will at the heart of Kantian ethical agency. From a Lacanian standpoint, one extending the authentically revolutionary side of Kant's ethics as *Jenseits des Lustprinzips*, exclusively if and when the subject acts with no hope whatsoever of any payoff beneficial to his/her person, including divine approval and recompense, does he/she have the chance to be, if just for a moment, genuinely ethical as also thoroughly non-transactional. From this standpoint, the crucified Christ's loss of faith in a transcendent God-the-Father, with his dying cry of 'Father, why hast Thou forsaken me?,' is precisely what endows his promptly ensuing death with its sublime aura of being an act of supreme goodness.

Disbelief in anything like an authoritative praising-and-blaming God would be a prerequisite for maximally good willing and acting according to the standards of an ethics that is wholly and completely beyond the pleasure principle. In *Seminar XX*, Lacan counterintuitively proposes that only clerics and theologians can be true atheists[435] (this is because 'clerics' and 'theologians' designate, in this context, those who have thought especially hard about God and related matters). Similarly, I would claim now, still in a Lacanian vein, that only atheists can be truly ethical.

Obviously, this claim directly contests the age-old apology for religion according to which without belief in God, faith in the afterlife and the like, people would not behave ethically. Even non-believers often will accept, with however much resignation and cynicism, that widespread religious belief is necessary for sustaining intact the moral fabric of societies. Both Pascal and Kant evince adherence to the notion that ethical comportment requires divine orientation.

Lacan's radicality resides in suggesting not only that these two (i.e. ethical comportment and divine orientation) do not automatically go hand-in-hand but also that the divine is antithetical to the ethical. Pascal's wager does not even entertain the possibility that one might bet on God's non-existence but conduct one's life in what could be deemed a good manner even by Pascal himself. However, Lacan insists on keeping this possibility in view when analytically evaluating *le pari de Pascal*.

Lacan's anti-Pascalian wager is that solely by betting on God's non-existence is one potentially able to accede to proper goodness as untainted by the sordid, self-serving transactional calculations of the pleasure principle. Again, for any ethics *Jenseits des Lustprinzips*, only atheists have any chance of being able to will and act in a purely ethical fashion. Only they can be 'good for goodness's sake', rather than for the sake of a heavenly afterlife or other divine favors.

As I noted a while ago, Lacan recasts Pascal's wager as a scenario in which Pascal encourages the wagerer to offer up his/her desiring life as an *objet petit a* in relation to the presumed desire of a supernatural Other (in this instance, the Christian God). Combining Lacan's glosses on *le pari de Pascal* with his ethics of psychoanalysis as per *Seminar VII* especially, one could say that Pascal's wagerer is urged by the author of the *Pensées* to 'give ground' (*céder*) on his/her desire by making it into an object to be sacrificed to the supposed desire of an enigmatic, unknowable Real Other. For Lacan, God-the-Father is a disguised permutation of Mother-the-Thing, of *la Chose maternelle* as Lacan's rendition of Freud's *Nebenmensch-als-Ding*.

Viewed from a Lacanian angle, the sacrifice of one's objectified desiring life (as *a*) called for by the Pascalian wager on God's existence is, in truth, a desperate defensive maneuver by such a wagerer. It is an attempt to 'cause' *qua* control (with *a* as Lacan's 'object-cause of desire') what would otherwise manifest as the threatening and anxiety-inducing opacity, the night-like abyssal void, of the Real of the Other's desire. And Pascal promises whoever decides to gamble on God's existence at least a eudaimonistic life of happiness and well-being in this world, if not also maximal infinite ecstasy and enjoyment in the other world of the afterlife.

Incidentally, during a 1972 public lecture at the Université catholique de Louvain, Lacan refers to an anonymous analysand's 'Pascalian dream' of an infinity of (after)lives, with Lacan reading the maximum gain of Pascal's wager as an infinity of infinitely happy lives in the plural (a reading on display throughout Lacan's various meditations on Pascal under consideration by me here). Yet, this dream is said by Lacan to have been experienced by his analysand as so nightmarish that she awoke from it 'almost mad' (*presque folle*).[436] Lacan's insinuation with respect to Pascal himself is that, so to speak, he should be careful what he wishes for – that the '*jouissance* expected' of living infinitely after this life would not be the same as the '*jouissance* obtained' were one to end up in the existential insomnia of eternal life.[437] At Louvain, Lacan even claims that the prospect of death as final, as bringing finite life to a permanent close, is the sole thing that makes this life bearable – 'Death is of the domain of faith. You are quite right to believe that you surely will die; it supports you. If you didn't believe it, could you handle the life you have?' (*La mort est du domaine de la foi. Vous avez bien raison de croire que vous allez mourir bien sûr; ça vous soutient. Si vous n'y croyez pas, est-ce que vous pourriez supporter la vie que vous avez?*).[438] Perhaps hitting the jackpot of Pascal's wager would be the greatest Pyrrhic victory ever.

Indeed, Lacan's '1/*a*' matheme from *Seminar XVI* and its discussion of *le pari de Pascal* can be interpreted as indicating precisely that winning this wager would be a Pyrrhic victory. As I already noted, Lacan insists on reading the purported maximum gain in Pascal's wager as an infinity of infinitely happy lives (rather than an infinitely happy [after]life in the singular, as it appears in the text of the *Pensées*[439]). If wagerable-because-objectified desiring life equals *a*, then making $a = \infty$, as Lacan does in how he portrays the outcome of betting on God existing and God really existing, results in $1/\infty$. But $1/\infty$ amounts to an asymptotic approach towards 0. In short, what Pascal-the-Christian depicts as the biggest win (infinity) Lacan-the-psychoanalyst depicts as total loss (zero).

Apart from Lacan's theoretical and metapsychological reasons for not believing in Pascal's Christian God and Heaven, Lacan also warns, as a psychoanalyst, that the reward in this world for the sacrifice of one's desire will be anything but the promised contentment and joy of the good life. Instead, and as per 'from an analytical point of view, the only thing of which one can be guilty is of having given ground relative to one's desire', Pascal's self-sacrificing wagerer on the existence of the Christian God can expect nothing but the Hell-on-earth of steadily intensifying neurotic guilt, of ever more gratuitously self-inflicted negative affective pain and anguish. No good deed goes unpunished by the psychoanalytic super-ego.

In what could be called Lacan's wager, Lacan suggests to his audiences that refusing to 'give ground relative to *one's* desire' by atheistically rejecting the self-sacrificial giving ground relative to the divine Other's desire (as in Pascal's wager) is one's only hope of avoiding condemnation to a this-worldly life of misery and masochism. With respect to Pascal, Lacan likely would endorse Gilles Deleuze's now-familiar warning – 'Beware of the other's dream, because if you are caught in the other's dream you are screwed' (*Méfiez-vous du rêve de l'autre, parce que si vous êtes pris dans le rêve de l'autre, vous êtes foutus*):[440] As Lacan would put this *vis-à-vis* Pascal's wager, beware of the divine Other's desire, because if you are caught in this Other's desire, you are fucked. Moreover, for a psychoanalyst, one has much more reason to fear this-worldly damnation at the hands of one's own super-ego than to fear other-worldly damnation at the hands of a judging deity. Taking into account the analytic clinic of neurotic guilt, the very probability theory Pascal helps invent and utilizes in the calculations of his famous wager would recommend to any chancers to opt for Lacan's wager rather than Pascal's.

Lacan's is the better bet. This wager on atheism both makes real ethicality possible and facilitates ordinary suffering in place of neurotic pathos. One should not fall prey to making the improbably perfect the enemy of the not-entirely-bad – with the latter as, to paraphrase Žižek, slightly more than nothing (i.e. the Lacanian 1/*a* of *Seminar XVI* and its discussion of *le pari de Pascal*).

Despite Lacan's many divergences from and disagreements with Pascal, there is an implicit aspect of Pascal's wager of which Lacan approves. This aspect is associated by Lacan with his interpretation of Hegel's dialectic of lordship and bondage – an interpretation, as seen, he sometimes refers to in connection with his commentaries on Pascal. Lacan, in his 1972 Louvain lecture, proposes that Pascal's wager and Hegel's master–slave dialectic both teach that life is worth living only if one's own desire is invested in causes, ideals or values for which one would be willing to risk life itself.[441] Pascal's wagerer puts his/her objectified existence at stake. Hegel's master wins his authority through refusing to flinch in the face of the danger of literal death (with death as the Hegelian 'absolute master').

Whereas Pascal focuses his utterances and desire on the possible outcomes of his wager, Lacan shifts attention to wagering itself. At the risk of oversimplification, one could say that Pascal-the-Christian is obsessed with the result-as-destination, while Lacan-the-psychoanalyst is concerned with the process-as-journey. Lacan recasts Pascal's 'man infinitely transcends man' (*l'homme passe infiniment l'homme*)[442] as the this-worldly immanent transcendence of brute animal life by a desire that repeatedly, restlessly strives towards *teloi* other than the simple preservation and reproduction of mere creaturely existence. What Pascal describes as the wretchedness of desire's 'perpetual motion' (*mouvement perpétuel*),[443] of its agitated wanderings, is all we have, until we no longer have even it. If we cannot bring ourselves to make it into something livable, we truly will have lost everything.

11. The unlikely actuary: Pascal and Christian capitalism

Several times during the sixteenth seminar, Lacan identifies Pascal as a contributor to the foundations of modern capitalism.[444] He goes so far as to label

Pascal 'a pioneer of capitalism'.[445] What justifies these assertions by Lacan? And what are their implications?

Pascal's multiple contributions to making capitalism as we know it possible are of two basic sorts: first, his more obvious contributions along these lines flowing from his mathematical and scientific labors, and second, his less obvious contributions along these same lines arising from his religious reflections. As for the first sort, Pascal's key role in laying the foundations of mathematically precise probability theory arguably is his single most significant and influential contribution to facilitating the capitalist mode of production. In rendering the *à venir* calculable and predictable with numerical exactitude, Pascal helps make possible such capitalism-essential functions and institutions as insurance policies, market forecasts, futures speculations and on and on. He also invents a working calculator and an early form of public transportation, with such machines and services destined to feature ubiquitously in modern industrial societies.

As a pioneering figure in modern mathematics and science, Pascal participates in a broader seventeenth-century paradigm shift fundamental to the character of modernity as a whole. Along with the likes of Galileo Galilei and Descartes, he is involved in a historical process of mathematizing not only natural, but also human, realities (as Lacan points out in the sixteenth seminar, Pascal's wager attempts to render life itself an objectified, calculable value[446]). This mathematization, starting in the seventeenth century, of so much under the sun, manifest through a combination of scientific *savoir* and technological *savoir-faire*, goes hand-in-hand with the contemporaneous historical development of early capitalism. Without delving into the details at present, suffice it to note that the limitless extension of quantification to anything and everything whatsoever is essential to capitalism both infrastructurally and superstructurally.[447]

In 1848's *Communist Manifesto*, Marx and Engels famously describe capitalism as dissolving whatever it comes across into the 'icy water of egotistical calculation' (*eiskalten Wasser egotisticher Berechnung*):[448] Thanks to this dissolution into quantification, 'All that is solid (*Ständische und Stehende*) melts into air, all that is holy (*Heilige*) is profaned.'[449] It would not be inaccurate to claim that, for Marx and Engels, modernity's techno-scientific mathematization of reality is integral to capitalism's spontaneous desacralizing and desecrating thrusts.

In the light of this Marxian motif from the *Communist Manifesto*, Pascal can be seen to be an unwittingly ironic figure. The irony of Pascal's historical role in relation to the development of capitalism has to do with his modern mathematizing tendencies in relation to his intense Catholic piety as a militant Jansenist. As Lacan is not alone in appreciating, Pascal's wager in particular, contained in the *Pensées* of the later highly religious Pascal, amounts to a synthesis of Pascal's mathematical and religious passions. In *le pari de Pascal*, formalistic probability theory is deployed so as to lure sceptics and non-believers onto a path leading to full-blown (re)conversion to the Christian faith.

Yet, interpreted from a Lacanian vantage point, Pascal inadvertently ends up being complicit in something for which he reproaches Descartes. As I highlighted some time ago, Pascal takes issue with Descartes allegedly reducing God to being a mere object subservient to the judgements of the tribunal of human rationality. Cartesian rationalism purportedly brings the highest and holiest down to the level of what can be assessed, evaluated, grasped and manipulated by the same sort of this-worldly reasoning operative in secular philosophy (especially metaphysics) and mathematics (especially geometry).

Pascal disapprovingly regards this aspect of Descartes's thinking as emblematic of the profaning narcissistic pride of finite human reasoning. In an implicit foreshadowing of Marx and Engels's 'All that is solid melts into air, all that is holy is profaned', Pascal basically warns that the application by Descartes of a mathematical-geometric style of reasoning to sacred subjects inevitably leads to a desacralization of the objects to which it is applied. In Pascal's view, God cannot but be debased and insulted by this alleged Cartesian rationalistic arrogance.

Nonetheless, even if only as an initial tactic for seducing the unfaithful, Pascal's wager also applies mathematical-style reasoning to the very question of God's existence. Admittedly, there are non-negligible differences between the Cartesian and Pascalian applications of formalistic reasoning procedures to the metaphysical and theological issue of whether or not God exists. Descartes, partly relying on Anselm of Canterbury's 'ontological argument' in the *Proslogion*, purports to prove the necessity of God's existence as a perfect (as well as infinite, omniscient and omnipotent) being beyond any shadow of doubt whatsoever. By contrast, Pascal denies that human reasoners can attain such Cartesian absolute certainty about God. But, he still contends that, in place of God's existence as a rationally known necessity, God's existence and this existence's possible consequences for human beings nevertheless can be treated as reasonably calculable probabilities for a mathematics of foreseeable future contingencies.

Whereas Descartes maps the methodological and inferential framework of geometry onto God and His existence, Pascal brings to bear the machinery of probability theory upon the same. But, in both cases, the mathematical (of whatever exact type) is handled as applicable to the religious. Lacan, with an acute awareness of all this, hints that Pascal inadvertently participates through his wager in launching a capitalist-style mathematization of all things, God included. This mathematization leads into the 'icy water of egotistical calculation' in which holiness, piety, sacredness, etc. get diluted and dissolved – an outcome of history's ironic dialectics diametrically opposed to Pascal's own original intentions. And Lacan, through introducing psychoanalytic considerations into an examination of *le pari de Pascal*, exploits and recalibrates the wager's probabilistic reasoning so as to suggest that the best bet is not what Pascal says it is (with me having explained this Lacanian line of argumentation above).

Furthermore, a specific textual fact further justifies me bringing Marxist elements into play with respect to Lacan's psychoanalytic employments of Pascal. On two occasions, in the thirteenth and sixteenth seminars, Lacan approvingly mentions French Marxist Lucien Goldmann's 1956 book *Le Dieu caché*, a study devoted to Pascal and Jean-Baptiste Racine. In *Seminar XIII*, Goldmann is depicted accurately as treating Pascal's wager as a prelude to Marxism's wager on the advent, sooner or later, of revolutionary proletarian class consciousness.[450]

In *Seminar XVI*, delivered in the immediate aftermath of the leftist student-and-worker upheaval of May 1968 in France, *The Hidden God* is praised as a 'very beautiful work'.[451] But Lacan promptly goes on to remark, 'That doesn't make the author more popular with me' (*Ça ne me rend pas l'auteur plus fréquentable*).[452] Whatever ambivalences Lacan feels with respect to Goldmann, Lacan's extended elaborations on Pascal's wager in the sixteenth seminar occur simultaneously with a largely sympathetic revisitation of Marxism by the older Lacan of the late 1960s and 1970s.[453]

Lacan's Oedipal reinterpretation of Pascal's wager in particular defensibly can be portrayed as in line with some of what is operative between Feuerbach and Marx as regards the critique of religions and religious ideologies. The fourth of Marx's 1845 'Theses on Feuerbach' concludes with Marx declaring that, 'once the earthly family is discovered to be the secret of the holy family, the former must then itself be destroyed in theory and in practice' (*die irdische Familie als das Geheimnis der heiligen Familie entdeckt ist, muß nun erstere selbst theoretisch und praktisch vernichtet werden*).[454] Marx here foregrounds both the core of Feuerbach's critical thesis regarding religion generally and Christianity especially as well as the historical materialist step beyond Feuerbach.

As is well known, Feuerbach, particularly in his 1841 *magnum opus The Essence of Christianity*, contends that the secret of all theology is anthropology.[455] Hence, as Marx's Thesis Four indicates, the Feuerbachian gesture apropos Christianity's other-worldly 'holy family' (as theological) is to reveal it to be derived from the this-worldly 'earthly family' (as anthropological). But for Marx, leaving the critique of religion at this is far from fully satisfactory, particularly for a materialism at least as concerned with practice as with theory (a concern most famously conveyed in the eleventh and final of Marx's 'Theses on Feuerbach'[456]). Marx calls for not only Feuerbach's theoretical dissolution of the religious holy family (e.g. the Christian Trinity and accompanying figure of the Virgin Mary) but also the practical in addition to theoretical dissolution of the social earthly family (e.g. the bourgeois and proletarian familial structures bound up with the capitalist mode of production and its accompanying religious ideologies).

Like Marx, Lacan adopts and extends further a Feuerbach-style critical stance *vis-à-vis* religious matters (e.g. in a 1975 lecture, Lacan grounds the Christian Holy Trinity in the psychoanalytic triad of his metapsychological, register-theoretic Borromean knot as the Real of this monotheistic Trinity, and pointedly not *vice versa*[457]). Of course, Freud himself, in texts such as *Totem and Taboo* and *The Future of an Illusion*, already situates psychoanalysis in a Feuerbachian vein by indeed, as Marx would put it, uncovering the immanent-earthly behind or beneath the transcendent-heavenly family. Building on Freud's work, Lacan makes explicit two uniquely psychoanalytic twists on such Feuerbachianism.

First, Feuerbach himself emphasizes that the theological emanations from the anthropological amount to humanity, in a self-alienating self-objectification, misattributing its best features to its God or gods. From Feuerbach's perspective, religious divinities are, in essence, projections of human beings' natural virtues into a beyond such that these virtues appear in the (dis)guise of transcendent supernatural entities. By contrast, for both Freud and Lacan, religions' deities are at least as much projections of humanity's vices as of our virtues.

This contrast reflects the fundamental difference between, on the one hand, Feuerbach's more rosy and romantic positive view of human nature and, on the other hand, psychoanalysis's darker and more pessimistic assessment of who and what we really are in truth. Moreover, Freud's and Lacan's insistences that theologies also reflect humans' nastier, uglier features have as a side benefit psychoanalysis's greater explanatory power apropos religious phenomena. For instance, the Old Testament fire-and-brimstone God (a figure discernible in Pascal's writings) is something that seems to be able to be done much greater explanatory justice to by psychoanalysis than by a more idealistic and romanticizing Feuerbachianism.

The second psychoanalytic twist to Feuerbach's critique of religion is forged by Lacan largely on the basis of his recasting of the Freudian Oedipus complex. Freud tends to portray the heavenly Father as a spectral reflection, a sort of Feuerbachian projection, of the earthly (primal) father. But with Lacan, one could say, again with reference to Feuerbach, that the secret of paternal theology is maternal anthropology.

According to the Lacanian account of Oedipal dynamics, the paternal metaphor as a lawlike Symbolic structure stands in for, and defends against, the mysterious, threatening and unpredictable desire of the mother as Real Other. And as I went on to show in my unpacking of Lacan's interpretations of Pascal and his wager, Pascal's Christian God-the-Father can be analytically decrypted as a paternal metaphor simultaneously concealing and revealing (as a repression that also at the same time is a return of the repressed) the desire of the (m)Other as the *Nebenmensch-als-Ding* (i.e. *la Chose*). From this Lacanian angle, Pascal's Christianity generally and the enigmatic divine Other of his wager particularly amount to transformations of the maternal into the paternal. These transformations serve defensively to eclipse the presupposed lawlessness of the anxiety-provoking Real Thing behind the shield of the lawfulness signified by the Name-of-the-Father.

In the mid-1960's manuscript '*Mise en question du psychanalyste*', posthumously published in 2021, Lacan at one point therein discusses religion and class side-by-side. This cross-resonates with Lacan's references to Goldmann in particular, given that Goldmann's *The Hidden God* brings together Christianity and Marxism through its historical materialist reassessment of Pascal. Apart from '*Mise en question du psychanalyste*', I know of no other place in which Lacan contrasts religious and class identities as he does in this newly-available manuscript.

Therein, Lacan, echoing statements he makes elsewhere, suggests that analysis can, and indeed sometimes does, bring about losses of religious faith in analysands, converting them from pre-analytic believers into post-analytic non-believers.[458] Apparently, analysts sometimes can accompany their patients to the point of taking a Lacanian rather than Pascalian wager (in which one bets on this life of desire in the *hic et nunc* as 1/a rather than, à la Pascal, betting on the renunciation of this life as mere, sheer 0, as utter nothingness, vanity, etc.). But Lacan claims that, by sharp contrast, analysis seems to have no effect whatsoever on investments in socio-economic systems – 'we have never seen psychoanalysis tear anyone away from their bourgeois ties, from their class determinations' (*on n'a jamais vu la psychanalyse arracher quiconque de par son cours à ses attaches de bourgeois, à ses déterminations de classe*).[459]

According to this Lacan, identifications with capitalist class positions are among the most stubborn and persistent ego-level cathexes. With capitalism having been born roughly 300 years prior to psychoanalysis – and, of course, analysis is born at the start of the twentieth century within a European capitalist socio-historical context – it remains to be seen whether or not this obduracy of class identifications is peculiar to capitalism. Tellingly, Lacan writes of '*attaches de bourgeois*' here, thus hinting that the phenomenon in question might be specific to subjects within capitalist societies.

Regardless, between Pascal writing at the dawn of capitalist modernity and Lacan doing so in the thick of it, things likely have shifted significantly in terms of the degrees of relative inflexibility between religious and class identifications. Yet, as I have argued on other occasions,[460] the capitalist social history of the modern era, particularly in its consumerist phase of the past half-century or so, looks to have made people secular where they believe themselves to be religious and religious where they believe themselves to be secular. Consistent with this line of argumentation, perhaps the inflexibility and refractoriness of capitalist class identifications is another symptomatic indicator that the invisible hand of the market really has replaced the invisible hand of God for most, if not all, of us.

For Lacanian psychoanalysis, our simultaneously both libidinal- and political-economic investments in economic identities and the social systems in which they are inscribed may well be the *sinthomes* of subjects suffering under capitalism (i.e. the symptoms essential to the very being of capitalist subjectivity). If there is to be a cure, albeit one admittedly that will entail a great deal of pain and hardship, it perhaps starts at a point indicated by Goldmann's Marxist reading of Pascal. This starting point could be called 'Marx's wager'.

As with Pascal's jaded aristocratic libertines, capitalism's dulled cynical subjects perhaps initially are unable to bring themselves to experience first-person conscious disbelief in and disidentification with capitalism and its class identities. But, they might begin by at least acting as though capitalism is not eternal, that, like all preceding modes of production and socio-economic systems, it too is historical-*qua*-transitory. Through evidence and arguments concerning capitalism's self-destructive tendencies and/or socialism's and communism's feasibility and preferability, capitalist subjects perhaps preliminarily can be persuaded to take their first steps away from a system governed by the logic of capital alone. Even if these first steps are motivated by cold probabilistic calculations still concerned with egoistic self-interest, of saving oneself from the sinking ship of a rotten social formation, they still would amount to the promise of a new beginning.

Apropos Pascal, there is no certainty that the free-thinking degenerate gamblers he addresses truly will develop heartfelt religious belief if enticed to bet along the lines encouraged by the set-up of Pascal's wager. Apropos Lacan, there is no certainty that capitalism's subjects can be led to disinvest from their class identities. Yet, if there remains a place for faith, it would be here.

12. 'Get thee to a monastery!': Jacques, Marc-François and the Roman Catholic Church

I already have mentioned in passing a couple of times Lacan's beloved brother.[461] Pascal's younger sister Jacqueline withdrew to the solitude of the abbey of Port-Royal-des-Champs so as to be a Cistercian nun. Likewise, Lacan's younger sibling Marc-François withdrew to the solitude of the Abbaye de Hautecombe so as to be a Benedictine monk. It seems not unreasonable to suppose, especially from a psychoanalytic perspective, that this striking biographical parallel, involving French Catholic culture, played some role, however minimal, in attracting Lacan to Pascal's work.

Lacan's best-known biographer, France's preeminent historian of psychoanalysis Élisabeth Roudinesco, stresses that Jacques's deep affection for and closeness to Marc-François by no means indicate the former's sympathy for the latter's religious convictions. Yet, other commentators on Lacan occasionally refer to Marc-François so as to insinuate or even assert (often in a disingenuous *'je sais bien, mais quand même'* mode) that Marc-François's life and beliefs can be interpreted as testifying to a lingering (Benedictine) Catholicism on Jacques's part too.[462] In a moment, I will substantiate, *contra* such insinuations and assertions, Roudinesco's insistence on Lacan's atheism as unwavering even in the face of his adored younger brother and this brother's deep Catholic faith. I will do so utilizing the newly available evidence of a just-published tranche of correspondence between the two Lacan brothers.

Roudinesco recounts Jacques being dismayed, saddened and even angered by Marc-François's 1929 departure for Hautecombe and its cloistered environment[463] (just as Pascal, despite his Catholic piety, had his own misgivings about his younger sister's decision to sequester herself at Port-Royal). By the time of this departure, Jacques already had 'violently rejected . . . the Christian values he had been brought up in'.[464] When Marc-François eventually was ordained in 1935, 'Jacques was present at his brother's ordination. After that he never went to Hautecombe again.'[465] Jacques's post-1935 lifelong avoidance of Hautecombe suggests a lasting aversion to his brother's vocation and its institutional setting.

In 1933, Lacan got married for the first time to Marie-Louise Blondin (a.k.a. Malou). Regarding this event, Roudinesco comments:

> At the end of 1933 Lacan let himself in for a regular marriage with all the trimmings, blessed by the Roman Catholic Church. Had he forgotten that only a few months earlier he had been writing to his mistress from Spain about his strong anti-Christian convictions?[466]

She soon adds of this wedding:

> the religious ceremony was designed to meet the requirements of the Lacan family. Lacan himself was fascinated by the rituals of the church and wished to keep up Catholic appearances. And he didn't want to disappoint his mother, who would never have accepted the idea of her son being married without the blessing of the church. So Lacan asked Dom Laure, the abbot of Hautecombe, where his brother Marc-François was a monk, to perform the ceremony at the church of Saint-François-de-Sales.[467]

In these two passages, Roudinesco firmly distinguishes, in the case of Lacan, between 'strong anti-Christian convictions' and 'Catholic appearances'. As she knows well, the French Freud enjoyed toying with the imagery and symbolism of Catholicism, thereby bringing psychoanalysis into connection with a French

Catholic culture he shares with many of his interlocutors and much of his immediate audience.[468] But, as I believe Roudinesco rightly maintains, such playings with appearances by no means testify to a profound and/or hidden religiosity on Lacan's part.

For Lacan, God indeed does not exist. Nevertheless, God's lingering imagistic and symbolic traces, entangled with this-worldly customs, habits, institutions, practices, rituals and the like, can be manipulated and appreciated even by those fully aware of these undead forms' lack of any actual other-worldly backing. Reverence is not necessary. One can enjoy irreverently playing with these traces.

As will be evident shortly, the failure of Lacan's first marriage features centrally in the recently published correspondence between him and his younger brother. Without rehearsing all of the biographical details of this, Marc-François was troubled by and disapproving of how his older brother treated Malou as well as women in general (including his eventual second wife, Sylvia Bataille).[469] Roudinesco states that 'Marc-François . . . loved his brother very much but thought that he hadn't been sufficiently Christian in his dealings with women.'[470] After quoting from a conversation with the Benedictine monk, she observes:

> It had been a very long time since Lacan had shared the Christian spirituality to which Marc-François had consecrated his life. But had he really been a Christian up to the age of sixteen? It's doubtful. In any case, by the end of the Second World War his atheism was so evident he no longer needed to identify himself with the Antichrist, as he had in the past. Even so, he still valued some of the conventions of the respectable bourgeoisie.[471]

With the interrogative second sentence here, Roudinesco suggests that Jacques lost his religion even earlier than dated by Marc-François (with her associating this loss with the young Jacques's early-adolescent enthusiasm for Spinoza's philosophy[472]). Moreover, she again emphasizes the sharp split straddled by Lacan between virulent atheism and adherence to 'some of the conventions of the respectable bourgeoisie'[473] (including especially aspects of French Catholic culture[474]).

In addition to the failed first marriage to Marie-Louise Blondin, another focus of Jacques's correspondence with Marc-François is the former's desire to obtain an audience with Pope Pius XII. In 1953, the year Jacques delivers the oral version (i.e. the so-called Rome Discourse) of his middle-period (i.e. the period of the Saussurian 'return to Freud') manifesto 'The Function and Field of Speech and Language in Psychoanalysis', he asks his brother to look into arranging with the Vatican authorities for such a meeting.[475] Although Marc-François was unable to arrange for an audience with Pius XII in 1953, with the Pope's office declining Jacques's request, Jacques nonetheless still visited the Papal Palace of Castel Gandolfo while in Italy[476] (and also at one point tried to get a copy of the

Écrits delivered to the Pope via a cardinal in Rome of Lacan's acquaintance[477]). Interestingly, in one of Marc-François's 1953 letters to his older brother, he appeals to Pascal as a source of inspiration shared between him and Jacques as both ostensibly concerned with the 'freedom' (*liberté*) and 'liberation' (*libération*) of humanity via Christianity (Marc-François) or psychoanalysis (Jacques).[478]

It appears Marc-François allowed himself to believe that his older brother's interest in a Papal audience signaled a reconversion to the Catholic faith. Of the younger brother, Roudinesco declares:

> he sincerely believed his brother had been reconverted to Christian doctrine. In his eyes, though Jacques was still leading a life of sin, he was saved now by his teaching, which showed at last a wonderful return to the values of Catholic spirituality.[479]

Roudinesco clearly considers Marc-François mistaken in this assessment of the import of his brother's desire to meet with the Pope. The younger Lacan looks to have fallen prey to his own wishful thinking. As late as a 1992 interview with the historian of psychoanalysis Paul Roazen, Marc-François, just two years prior to his death, continues to plead for the compatibility between his own Catholic faith and his brother's version of Freudian psychoanalysis.[480] To this end, the devout Benedictine monk appeals to certain of Lacan's overtly Catholic followers, mentioning the Jesuits Louis Beirnaert and Denis Vasse by name.[481]

As Roudinesco underscores, one must bear in mind that Jacques, at the same time as he is enlisting his brother to help arrange a *tête-à-tête* with the Pope, is also engaged in a parallel process of courting the leading lights of the French Communist Party (Parti communiste français [PCF]).[482] During this period, Lacan is simultaneously wooing Catholic believers and communist non-believers alike. This fact does not exactly bear witness to the most sincere and committed Catholicism on Lacan's part.

While Marc-François was at least momentarily inclined to interpret Jacques's request for an audience with Pius XII as indicative of a return to the fold of the faithful, Roudinesco portrays it as of a piece with quite secular concerns about garnering cultural and political support for psychoanalysis. After asserting apropos Jacques that 'His desire to meet the Pope was based on a coherent political position'[483] – note that this 'position' is 'political' and not religious – she explains:

> In his concern to privilege a subject constituted by the desire of the other, in his references to the mystical tradition, in his manifold winks at the technique of directing consciences, and finally in his quest of a Trinitarian order opening,

through the symbolic, onto the prevalence of a divine word, Lacan translated Freudian discourse into a language familiar to Catholic tradition. In following his own discourse, men accustomed to theological debates were apt to rediscover the Rome of the Vatican or the spiritual exercises of Ignatius of Loyola. All that was easier to digest for them than Freud's apparent positivism, his excessively radical critique of religious illusions, the remains of his biologism, and finally his violent affirmation of the primacy of sexuality. In brief, Lacan charmed the priests, but did not fool them as to the atheistic character of what he was up to. He was interested in the Pope without seeking God, and in religion without rekindling faith. His dream was that a two-thousand-year-old institution could serve as a source of support for the recognition of his doctrine and his person. That is why he encouraged his disciples who were priests not to leave their orders, just as he had advised others to study medicine, and still others not to break with the restrictive superego of existent institutions. There developed in his orbit, starting with the *Rome Discourse*, a veritable 'current' of Catholic inspiration.[484]

Roudinesco is even blunter about the true motives behind Lacan's coquetting with the Vatican, side-by-side with approaching the communists, on a more recent occasion – 'He saw both the Church and the PCF as potential reservoirs for recruits for his own movement.'[485] If indeed this is the case, then Lacan is not interested in what he can do for the Roman Catholic Church, but what the Church can do for him ('His dream was that a two-thousand-year-old institution could serve as a source of support for the recognition of his doctrine and his person'). Those Lacanian 'currents of Catholic inspiration' tend to ignore all this, including Lacan's fidelity to a Freudianism that, audience-aware French Catholic repackaging of it aside, is indeed fundamentally at odds with religion generally as well as Catholicism specifically.

Jacques's myriad dalliances with the Church and its traditions are not about him converting back to Catholicism (*pace* Marc-François), but about converting Catholics to him and his version of Freudian analysis. With his analytic acuity, he knows what his Catholic listeners want to hear, seductively pandering to them through 'references', 'winks' and other sorts of intellectual flirtations. As I will show soon, Jacques's letters to his younger brother certainly reveal that he knew what Marc-François wanted to hear, that the latter desperately wanted to believe that his older brother believed again (or was close to believing again and could be brought to it).

In the above block quotation, Roudinesco sounds overly confident and categorical about Lacan failing actually to take in his Catholic addressees ('In brief, Lacan charmed the priests, but did not fool them as to the atheistic character of what he was up to'). She evinces too much faith in the faithful here. In the cases of Marc-François as well as various others past and present, there are those among the religiously inclined or convinced who stubbornly hope for or attempt to bring about a rapprochement between Lacanian psychoanalysis and Christianity. As regards the cases of Catholic Lacanians, one might be tempted to paraphrase Abraham Lincoln: Lacan at least manages to fool some of the Catholics some of the time.

Flashing forward to 1981, Marc-François presides over mass two days after Jacques's death on 9 September of that year. Roudinesco recounts:

> On Friday the eleventh, the fiftieth anniversary of his taking orders, Marc-François celebrated mass in the church Saint-François-de-Sales. . . . Lacan was an atheist, even if, out of bravado, he had once dreamed of a great Catholic funeral. Marc-François asked the congregation to pray for his brother, recalling that all his work was steeped in Catholic culture, although 'the church and the gospel' were not essential to it.[486]

Marc-François, over the course of his life, seems to waver between lamenting his older brother's atheism, lauding his Catholicization of the Freudian field, and a number of stances between these two extremes.[487] In ceremonially marking Jacques's passing (and doing so in the same church in which the abbot of Hautecombe presided in 1933 over Jacques's first wedding), Marc-François appears to occupy one of these in-between positions, portraying Lacanianism as culturally but not doctrinally Catholic.

So, what about the newly released samples of correspondence between the Lacan brothers? What, if anything, do these letters reveal about the rapport between Lacanianism and Catholicism? Long before their posthumous publication, Marcelle Marini comments in passing that, 'A correspondence between the two brothers . . . might illuminate some aspects of Lacanian thought.'[488] We now shall see whether it does.

As regards the letters published in 2021 in the *Lacan Redivivus* special issue of the Lacanian journal *Ornicar?*, Jacques's missives to Marc-François involve him asking his younger brother to help not only in winning an audience with the Pope but also in securing a Papal annulment of his first marriage to Blondin. My readings of select moments of this correspondence are informed by an acute awareness of the older Lacan brother's larger agenda both: one, to garner cultural-political support for psychoanalysis via the Holy See, as well as, two, to maintain Catholic appearances (as Roudinesco would put it) through having the Church officially declare his failed marriage never really to have been a true marital bond. Jacques's positive pronouncements about Catholicism in the context of these letters to Marc-François must be examined in light of these underlying motivations.

In a letter dated Easter (5 April) 1953, Jacques spends much of his time imploring Marc-François to assist with getting the Church officially to annul his first marriage.[489] The choice of Easter as the date for this letter already likely is meant to appeal to Marc-François's Christianity and accompanying sensibilities. Amidst the pleas for an annulment, Jacques intersperses a number of statements about himself intended to help sway his younger brother to aid and abet his efforts to symbolically obliterate the failed marriage to Malou as never having existed in the eyes of such big Others as the Roman Catholic Church and the French bourgeoisie culturally loyal to it. Jacques evidently is anxious to save particular appearances with respect to these Others. As Jacques's former mistress Catherine Millot recounts about him, 'He liked to claim that he was faithful.'[490]

In this same 1953 letter to Marc-François, Jacques proposes that his psychoanalytic vocation and his brother's religious calling are allied in their shared struggle to defend un-objectifiable subjectivity against modern socio-economic and techno-scientific objectifications. Both Freudianism and Catholicism are said by this Jacques to belong to the same 'great tradition' (*la grande tradition*), one for which 'man can never be reduced to an object' (*l'homme ne saurait jamais être réduit à un objet*).[491] This manner of identifying an overlap between psychoanalysis and religion is far from implausible within certain limits. Lacan's version of analysis indeed can be seen to involve a theory of the subject resistant to various and sundry standard fashions of problematically collapsing the subjective into the objective.

Much less plausibly, Jacques soon proceeds to profess to Marc-François his sincere personal belief in the sacredness (*sacrée*) of the idea and institution of marriage.[492] The older brother obviously feels the need to reassure his junior sibling that his request for assistance in winning an annulment from the Church is not made lightly or on the basis of suspicious non-religious motives. This felt need already is telling in and of itself.

Moreover, much in Jacques's conduct of his private life, both during and long after his first marriage (indeed, up to the very end of his life), bears witness to the contrary, namely, his blithe disregard for any sort of sanctification of middle-class Catholic monogamy manifest in his personal behaviour. Nobody with knowledge of Jacques's biography and lifestyle can read his profession to Marc-François about 'the sacred conception that I have of the commitment of marriage' (*la conception sacrée que j'ai de l'engagement du marriage*)[493] without at least some degree of sceptical reaction. Maybe Jacques, accustomed to leading double lives at this point thanks to having lived with Sylvia while still married to Marie-Louise, is banking on his younger brother's non-knowledge of his intimate affairs, thanks to the latter remaining at a comfortable distance from Paris, sequestered away in the monastic solitude of the Abbaye de Hautecombe.

Towards the end of his Easter 1953 letter to Marc-François, Jacques, after repeating how important the annulment of his first marriage would be to him, returns to the topic of the intersection between psychoanalysis and religion. He points out to his younger brother that there are many Catholics among his students and followers[494] (with him mentioning, in a subsequent letter to Marc-François, dated 5 September 1953, the Jesuit priest Beirnaert in particular[495]). He also anticipates in this letter his planned outreach to the Pope as well as his upcoming (September 1953) address in Rome (i.e. the shortened oral version of 'The Function and Field of Speech and Language in Psychoanalysis', the so-called Rome Discourse).[496] Jacques then equates the 'language' of central concern to his upcoming Rome Discourse with the (Christian) concept of 'logos'.[497] Jacques's rapid-fire insistences on the proximity between Freudian psychoanalysis and Catholicism cannot but appear in this context as all attempts at wooing Marc-François to the cause of a Papal annulment – and, subsequently, to the cause of a Papal audience too.

Jacques's 5 September 1953 letter to Marc-François contains the direct request for assistance in being granted a one-on-one audience with Pius XII. Jacques states that he is making this request partly thanks to the urgings of the Catholics among his adherents (whom he somewhat suspiciously crowns here '*Mes élèves les plus sage et les plus autorisés*').[498] This letter speaks of 'the future of psychoanalysis in the Church' (*l'avenir de la psychanalyse dans l'Église*) and of his and Marc-François's 'common Father'[499] (apropos this '*Père commun*', Jacques might really have in mind the tyrannical Catholic patriarch of the Lacan clan, namely Émile Lacan, his and Marc-François's grandfather, whose name, as *le Nom-du-Père*, they both bear – with Jacques expressing pronounced loathing for this paternal figure whom he credits with teaching him 'the essential act of cursing God' as well as 'being the sort of father who gave fatherhood a bad name'[500]). Again, as with the earlier petition for assistance with an annulment, Jacques appears to lay it on thick apropos his supposed Catholicism when seeking something he desires (in this instance, a Papal audience) from his younger brother. And as Roudinesco would remind readers at this juncture, Jacques is flirting with the atheistic communists of the Moscow-loyal PCF at the same time as he is trying to seduce his sibling into seeking personal and political favours on his behalf from the Vatican.

The final detail from the Lacan brothers' correspondence I wish to highlight is to be found in a 3 January 1962 letter from Jacques to Marc-François. Therein, Jacques mentions his (partly Spinoza-inspired) account of desire (*désir*) as 'the essence of man'[501] (incidentally, in a 1982 letter to Jacques Sédat, Marc-François utilizes Spinoza's orientation towards an 'ethics', as per his 1677 *magnum opus*, and investment in biblical exegesis as a means to draw Jacques, with his debts to Spinoza, back towards theology and religion[502]). Jacques then claims as regards this desire that 'I try to found the topology of its transcendence' (*Je m'essai à fonder la topologie de sa transcendance*).[503] The invocation of 'transcendence' in particular is almost certainly intended to be agreeable to Marc-François's religiosity, given the transcendent status of Catholicism's God-the-Father and much bound up with Him.

Yet, two features of Jacques's talk here of 'the topology of transcendence' render this pitch to Marc-François quite dubious. As regards transcendence, if Lacanian desire specifically is qualified as 'transcendent', it would be so in an immanent, this-worldly manner, and not as something other-worldly, connected with or stretching into any sort of supernatural realm standing above and beyond earthly existence. Given Lacan's irreligiosity, desire's transcendence indeed would have to be an immanent transcendence, one very much of this world. Moreover, Lacan himself demonstrates, as a theorist, that there is no incompatibility between an atheistic metapsychology and recourse to a suitably qualified transcendence. Transcendence alone, despite the insinuations Jacques directs towards his younger sibling, does not automatically suggest pious belief on the part of anyone who invokes it.

What is more, and as Jacques himself knows well, the very phrase 'the topology of transcendence' is, in a sense, a contradiction-in-terms. This is because the mathematical discipline of topology could be said to be inherently immanentist. Topology is concerned with the continuous transformations of single surfaces, lone planes of immanence, such as to produce a variety of spatial configurations (including such favourites of Lacan's as the cross-cap, the Klein bottle, the Möbius strip and the torus). Any apparent transcendences, in terms of inner-outer, recto-verso or upper-lower divisions, are, specifically in terms of the topological objects frequently gestured at by Lacan, merely apparent. In truth, they are effects of folding and twisting a unique and undivided surface – with all of this subtly harbouring atheistic implications for any standard monotheistic notions of transcendence (as is the case too for the Spinoza dear to Lacan, the radical immanentist of *The Ethics*). Jacques seems to be counting in this 1962 letter on Marc-François being unaware of the true nature of his metapsychological recourses to topology.

My above analyses of specific moments in the correspondence between the Lacan brothers admittedly casts Jacques in a somewhat unflattering light. It certainly looks as though the older brother manipulates the younger brother, the former coquetting with Catholicism precisely when wanting something from the latter (such as an annulment by or audience with the Pope). Yet although the portions of Jacques's letters to Marc-François I have highlighted reveal a certain amount of dishonesty and deception on the part of Jacques, there is something fundamentally truthful in Jacques's conduct.

To be more exact, Jacques's artful appropriations of Catholic images and symbols is a consistent feature of his conduct in both his private and public lives. In his teaching as well as his familial existence, Jacques continually tries to have it both ways, being a virulent atheist in practice as well as in theory while also relishing his participation in the spectacles of traditional Catholicism's pageantry and ceremonies. In this way, he tacitly rejects Pascal's all-or-nothing approach to religious issues.

Talk of dishonesty and deception typically entails the idea that such thus-labelled instances of behaviour deviate from the default *modus operandi* of the person responsible. Yet, Jacques's default *modus operandi* itself involves straddling the fence between committed atheism and the maintenance of Catholic appearances. In light of these considerations, it would be defensible to claim that Jacques is basically honest with Marc-François insofar as he (Jacques) conducts himself with his younger brother in a manner entirely consistent with his general fashion of living and acting.

There is nothing especially inauthentic or misleading about Jacques's putting on of Catholic airs specifically with Marc-François, since Jacques regularly put on such airs with just about everyone else too, perhaps himself included. Jacques liked to play the Catholic, although he definitely did not want to be Catholic. Maybe such playing was Jacques's way of making light of and taking distance from a religious background which, as an analyst, he knew all too well could not simply be erased from his ontogenetically formed being as a speaking subject (*parlêtre*) by mere, sheer intellectual fiat.

Instead of the ponderous cerebral atheism of certain philosophers and ideologues aiming to render God essentially dead, Jacques's psychoanalytic atheism lightens the religious loads of one's life history by irreverently aestheticizing the High and the Holy. Traditional atheistic ponderousness amounts to a persisting participation in the affective atmosphere of the religions supposedly opposed by atheism. By contrast, specifically Lacanian atheism works in part by turning the sacred relics of one's past, once one accepts that these possessions cannot be voluntarily discarded and left by the historical wayside, into toys providing at least a measure of amusement, if nothing more. With the analyst's awareness that one cannot simply kill off for good the God of what one could call one's 'mother religion' (soaked up from birth onwards along with one's 'mother tongue' [*la langue maternelle*], not to mention mother's milk too), Jacques seeks to turn this indestructible ontogenetic revenant into a source of aesthetic and intellectual enjoyment (rather than masochistically letting it remain a source of guilt and other forms of joyless suffering). He does so by transforming God from being a living substance to be obeyed to becoming an undead semblance to be exploited.

Although one cannot negate God once and for all, Lacan shows that one can quite effectively and impiously sublimate or sublate (*als Aufhebung*) Him. From Lacan's perspective, this is the only viable mode of atheism. The gloominess of religious piety is best fought with the lightness of parody and humour, rather than with equally gloomy secular or atheistic doctrines. Reverence is undone by irreverence, not more reverence.

If Marc-François wanted to know nothing of the religion-related contradictions at the heart of his older brother's split subjective character – it certainly looks as though the Benedictine monk continually hoped in vain that his psychoanalyst sibling eventually would wager on Catholicism like Pascal's jaded libertine – that was his problem. Jacques left Marc-François the gift of the analytic tools to diagnose and treat such a religious passion for ignorance. This gift is partly wrapped in the colours of their shared French Catholic culture, a culture for which, of course, the Pascal of the *Pensées* is a central figure.

Psychoanalysis and agnostic atheism

Lorenzo Chiesa

La question de dieu se pose à chacun, comme chacun sait, même aux athées.

ANONYMOUS INTERVENTION IN LACAN'S SEMINAR
'LA TOPOLOGIE ET LE TEMPS'

Il est très, très difficile de parler a-substantivement, surtout que nous nous imaginons chacun être une substance. Il est évidemment très difficile de vous sortir ça de la tête, quoique tout démontre que vous n'êtes au plus chacun qu'un petit trou.

LACAN, 'DES RELIGIONS ET DU RÉEL'

Paul then stood up in the meeting of the Aeropagus and said: 'People of Athens! I see that in every way you are very religious. For as I walked around and looked carefully at your objects of worship, I even found an altar with this inscription: TO AN UNKNOWN GOD. So you are ignorant of the very thing you worship'.

ACTS OF APOSTLES, 17:22

1. 'I do not know, and you cannot know either': Freud's agnosticism?

1.1. Illusion and delusion

Famously, in his 1927 *The Future of an Illusion*, Freud claims that religion is an *illusion*. Far less famously, in the same context, he also specifies that illusions should be distinguished from *delusions*. Delusions are manifestly in conflict with reality and belong to the field of psychiatry. Illusions are indeed equally sustained by deep-seated subjective wishes but are not inevitably in conflict with reality. In this sense, 'an illusion is not the same as an error, it is indeed not necessarily an error'.[1] Following a cautious logic of double negation, unlike a delusion, an illusion need not be 'unrealizable'.[2] Freud provides a series of examples to substantiate the difference and overlapping between illusion and delusion, which we could systematize as follows:

a. Illusions that proved delusional, such as Aristotle's belief that vermin evolved out of dung and the belief that children are without sexuality.

b. Illusions that proved delusional, yet were somehow matched by reality, such as Columbus's circumstantial discovery of America while trusting to be on a new sea route to India.

c. Illusions that increasingly appear non-delusional, as is the case with alchemy to the extent that modern 'chemistry no longer considers a transmutation of metals into gold as impossible'.[3]

d. Illusions that have come true.

Regarding this last instance – illusions that have come true – Freud bizarrely refers to 'a poor girl [who] may have an illusion that a prince will come and fetch her home'.[4] He then adds in all seriousness: 'It is possible. Some such cases have occurred'.[5] It is striking how Freud here immediately shifts his focus to religion. The prince at stake metonymically conjures up the Messiah. On the one hand, the coming of the Messiah and his founding of a golden age should be regarded as 'much less probable'[6] than the poor girl's becoming a princess. On the other hand, we are invited to rationally contemplate the hypothesis that religious ideas may *not* necessarily turn out to be *delusional* illusions. Epistemologically, the future of the illusion that religion is does not automatically entail its refutation as an error.

Throughout Chapter 6 of *The Future of an Illusion*, Freud prolongs and intensifies the seesaw inherent to his overall argument. Some religious doctrines as illusions are so farfetched with respect to what we scientifically know about the world that we should treat them as de facto delusions – Freud does not say which, but elsewhere he shows a strong aversion to the Christian Trinitarian dogma.[7] Yet with respect to others – even 'most' – it is simply too early to make a call. We cannot judge their 'reality value': 'Just as they cannot be proved, neither can they be refuted. We still know too little to approach them critically'.[8]

In line with the same oscillation between an enthusiastic anticipation of the logical triumph of atheism and a persistent justification of agnosticism as more rational, Freud has almost unlimited faith in the progress of science, but his own arguments also indirectly expose its limits. Scientific work is our only way to the refutation of religion. Scientific work will go as far as debunking the partisans of the 'why not?', namely, those who ask: 'If even the crabbed sceptics admit that the statements of religion cannot be confuted by reason, why should not I believe in them?'[9] That is to say, science will conclusively demonstrate that 'ignorance is ignorance'[10] and thus retrospectively persuade those we could call 'hypocritical theists' that they are now only deluding themselves into believing – namely, they are deluding themselves into a delusion – when actually, on an unconscious level, they are already unbelievers – or, we may say, 'closet atheists'.

However, at the same time, science itself can do nothing, both currently and in the future, against the supporters of the 'I believe because it is absurd to believe'. In a different passage of *The Future of an Illusion*, Freud discusses the *Credo quia absurdum* of the early Christian Fathers and presents it as a sort of desperate, albeit high-handed, effort of religion.[11] Here, religious illusions, especially in terms of de facto delusions, are themselves cheerfully embraced as avowed rational absurdities and taken as an irrational motivation to believe. As Freud puts it, the basic claim is that 'religious doctrines are outside reason's jurisdiction' and stand above reason.[12] For him, this position does not hold precisely because it amounts to a profession of *belief*, or faith, not reason. But he therefore does not seem to fully appreciate how it is precisely such a deliberate diminishing of reason that makes religious truths most irrefutable for rationalists: in a sense, religion's last card, the absurdist one, is also its strongest. Or also, in this instance, Freud in turn evades the problem of what he rightly considers as the religious-absurdist 'evasion of the problem'.[13]

And yet we witness to a further fluctuation in the general reasoning of *The Future of an Illusion*. Freud's most conclusive words on the stance psychoanalysis should adopt with regard to religious truths *do* seem to face the problem at stake, at least by opting to openly suspend it in an agnostic way: 'It does not lie within the scope of this enquiry to estimate the value of religious doctrines as *truth*'.[14] Instead, the *social* value of religion as an illusion must be investigated psychologically and superseded *practically*. On this socio-practical ground, religion ought not to have a future.

1.2. As if

These brief insights should already suffice to alert us about the complexity of Freud's positioning vis-à-vis religion and God. Sympathetic readers such as Oskar Pfister and Christopher Hitchens are, for opposite motives, both wrong in their clear-cut assessments. Against Pfister's attempted subsumption of psychoanalysis under Christianity,[15] for Freud, religion phenomenologically remains for all concrete purposes an infantile disorder of civilization, despite its ultimate theoretical irrefutability. But contra Hitchens's enlisting of the father of psychoanalysis as a fifth horsemen of 'antitheism', Freud was not an unequivocally optimistic champion of a new Enlightenment, although he would have gladly subscribed to Hitchens's slogan 'God is not great'.[16]

We have always to bear in mind that the however programmatic and assertive statements of *The Future of an Illusion* are far from intended as a conclusive manifesto. The book is in fact structured, in a convoluted manner, as a quasi-Platonic dialogue in which Freud anticipates and tackles – not always successfully – the objections of his potential opponents. As we saw, he thinks he has rationally done with the hypocritical theist. He underestimates but also circuitously acknowledges the irrational unassailability of the absurdist credo. Above all, once he has shifted his discussion to the pragmatic value of religion, the kind of critic he deals with most in depth, in different chapters and various guises, is what we could name the 'conservative atheist'. In short, according to the latter, religion as the opium of the people created by the people is indispensable for social control and averting chaos. Religious doctrines are untrue, but 'we are led to behave "*as if*" we believed in these fictions' because of their supposedly 'unequalled importance for the maintenance of human society'.[17]

We soon sense that the more Freud finds it difficult to exhaustively rebut this stance, that is, the more he is obliged to refine his dialectical arsenal, the less he manages to disguise his ethical and political contempt for the 'subtle and modern'[18] – or cynical – arguments he is countering. Here, it would seem that, in the end, and not without some vertiginous detours, it is precisely as a reversal of the conservative atheist's hypothesis that Freud's overarching motto emerges between the lines. We could phrase it as: 'It is highly unlikely that God exists, but we cannot prove it. For the *sake* of humankind, let's *try to behave as if there were no God!*'.

Now, Freud shares with the conservative atheist the methodological separation of the epistemological and practical levels of religion. Moreover, they both deem the second to be definitely more important. As the conservative atheist himself bluntly puts it, 'it is a practical problem, not a question of reality value'.[19] But the conservative atheist takes theoretically for granted the absurdity of religion only to strengthen it socially as a, on close inspection, self-interested fiction – and thus demands a compliance with the everyday conduct of the absurdist by, paradoxically, *not* having faith in a final and transcendent meaning of absurdity. Freud instead uses the *undecidability* concerning the theoretical truths of religion as a lever to promote an irreligious social experiment based on education. Insofar as we can historically ascertain that 'immorality, no less than morality, has at all times found *support* in religion',[20] theoretical agnosticism must give way to atheism as praxis. Such is our predicament. Here, Freud seems to suggest that we have nothing to lose in accepting this challenge.

1.3. Two arguments against conservative atheism

Freud puts forward two interrelated arguments against those who claim that, for social reasons, we should behave as if religious doctrines were true, although we know they are not. The first is rather implausible. The second is somehow stronger. In spite of sharing the flawed general presupposition of the first, it is then developed in a tactically promising way but, interestingly, ends with Freud *doubting* the most convincing and pragmatic part of his own atheistic conclusion.

In the first argument, the conservative atheist appears to be initially inclined to openly tell the masses that there is no God but that, to prevent unrest, they should act as if there were one. Freud, who tacitly shares his elitist division between 'philosophers' and 'the man whose thinking is not influenced by the wiles of philosophy',[21] objects that such a move would not work in the least. The masses will never accept the 'as if' and would 'turn away in disdain'.[22] He compares them with one of his sons who, when told that a fairy tale that fascinated him was not a true story, completely stopped paying attention to it.

Here, Freud's assumption is naïvely pre-psychoanalytic. It clashes with some of the most basic tenets of his theory of the unconscious and specifically with his notion of negation. In short, moving from a position of overt repression for which God is not dead (God is) to the recognition that he is dead (God is *not*) is far from sufficient to dispel the belief in God. Not only, on a first level, the conscious statement 'God is not dead' always already goes together with the unconscious premise 'God is dead', but also and especially, on a second level, the conscious acknowledgement that God is dead still inevitably evokes an unconscious clinging to God.[23] To put it in more Lacanian terms, the unconscious truth that God is dead – the truth of incompleteness and of the absence of a meta-language – cannot but structurally sustain itself by *in turn* sustaining the – however repressed – imaginary belief that God is alive. In this sense, for Lacan, 'God is unconscious'.[24] Or paraphrasing Octave Mannoni's famous description of perversion as *je sais bien, mais quand même*, I very well know that the universe is godless, but nonetheless . . .[25] Thus, the masses will continue to uphold religious ideas in spite of their claims to the opposite and ostensibly profane behaviours. Mutatis mutandis, the same arguably also applies to the alleged intellectual superiority of the philosophers of the 'as if' and their practical fictions as well as to Freud's rejection of them. In other words, what Freud misses here is the dimension for which the very existence of the unconscious as he himself understands it implies God as a *transcendental* – species-specific – illusion in a Kantian way.[26]

Leaving aside this issue, which by itself condenses Freud's severe underestimation of the power of religion, *The Future of an Illusion* advances a second argument on why the strategy of the conservative atheist would prove ineffective. Freud seems to anticipate the prospect that the latter might be tempted *not* to inform the masses about the groundlessness of the 'theoretical truths' of religion. Philosophers know they are untrue, yet in behaving as if they believed in them humankind will by default remain religious and civilization will not descend into chaos. For Freud, this is not a viable solution either. On the one hand, he seems to be alarmed by the manipulative and exploitative involutions such a paternalistic and undemocratic kind of leadership may give rise to – whereby the opium of the people created by the people would actively and cynically be administered by a restricted number of people. On the other hand, and most importantly for the overall economy of his reasoning, this scenario fails to take into consideration that humankind is in any case fast abandoning religious fairy tales, independently of the desperate and contrasting efforts of the philosophy of the 'as if', and there really is no way back.

According to Freud, the best thing we can do in the present situation is therefore preparing the masses for the inevitable. This means instructing them about the necessary function religion has exercised in history and how best to overcome it, since we have finally reached adulthood as a species. While it is undisputable that religion 'has contributed much toward restraining the asocial instincts',[27] this has clearly not been enough, and we have come to a point where 'the question arises whether we are right in considering it necessary for mankind'.[28] In a different passage, Freud goes even further and states that he is 'prepared to defend the statement that culture incurs a greater danger by maintaining its present attitude to religion than by relinquishing it'.[29] Religion now counters civilization.

However, at the same time, Freud promptly concedes that his pedagogical mission is incredibly arduous: he 'hardly know[s] where to begin', and 'certainly' he might be asked why he puts forward these points if he is unconvinced by their effectiveness.[30] In yet another passage, when pressed by the conservative atheist to fully assume the potential consequences that a removal of religious inhibitions could entail for humans as beings ruled by passions and the claims of instincts, Freud both insists on the fact that our sole hope for the future rests on the experiment of a non-religious education and, in short succession, bitterly admits 'the possibility that I too am chasing after an *illusion*'.[31] All in all, he says, 'I do not know, and you cannot know either'.[32] The irreligious future of an illusion might well turn into the illusion of a religion-free future.

1.4. Helplessness or instinctual vigour?

Freud provides us with two contrasting atheistic accounts of the socio-psychological origins of religion and the idea of God. According to the former, which he already delineates in his 1907 article 'Obsessive Action and Religious Practices', religion emerges out of a partial renunciation of our *anti-social instincts*. As for the latter, elaborated in *The Future of an Illusion*, religion derives from an attempt to cope with the *helplessness* of humankind before nature.

According to the first account, religion should be regarded as an ambivalent 'compromise' formation.[33] It is based on a suppression of socially harmful instincts, without which civilization could not have been established, that, however, always proves inadequate. Religious life thus amounts to an interminable process whereby suppression is inevitably followed by 'backsliding into sin', which in turn gives rise to penance.[34] In this sense, religion stands as a 'universal obsessional neurosis',[35] since obsession itself revolves around a similar unending conflict: the obsessional's repression[36] of instincts is only partly successful and his conscientiousness remains continuously threatened by temptations and an accompanying anxiety, or expectation of misfortune, connected with the idea of punishment. This state of affairs coalesces in obsessional and religious ceremonials alike, which should be understood as both a defence against the renewed temptation and the ill expected and, simultaneously, as a representation of something that 'is not yet absolutely forbidden',[37] that is, a displaced reproduction of the instincts these same ceremonials are designed to prevent.

We should take notice that, for Freud, such a compromise manifests itself more widely in religious practices in a twofold way. First, the iniquities humankind renounces are projected onto the deities, who are allowed to indulge in them. In their most elemental configuration, gods are evil. Second, humankind is itself not prevented from carrying out iniquities if it does so in the name of the deities. The ambivalence of the religious compromise can therefore be summarized in one concise sentence: 'All acts which religion forbids are committed in the name of religion'.[38] In the end, religion thus overall contributes to the development of human civilization *and* threatens it.

Freud's second and more sophisticated account of the socio-psychological origins of religion has, at first sight, much in common with the first. The arguments proposed in 'Obsessive Action and Religious Practices' are incorporated into those advanced in *The Future of an Illusion*, but they ultimately clash in my view, and their tension, if not contradiction, is tentatively solved only through a dubious subterfuge – the axiomatic postulate of the Father of the horde.

Again, for Freud, individuals are inherently enemies of civilization; civilization must be defended against individuals; because of that, civilization can only be built on an instinctual renunciation; and, in this respect, religious ideas are both 'the most important part' of civilization and a source of perpetual danger we should finally have done with.[39] Yet, in this second account, Freud also repeatedly claims that religion originates as a protection from a more fundamental coldness, cruelness and callousness of nature. What is primarily at stake is our being helpless as a species. The 'principle task' of civilization as a whole is 'to defend us against nature', and religion in particular 'is born of the *need* to make tolerable the helplessness of man', ultimately by invariably furthering the illusion that wretched 'life in this world serves a higher purpose'.[40] From this perspective, it is only in a derivative manner that religion also protects us from – and exposes us to – anti-social instincts. As Freud seems to be implicitly sensing at one point, without fully acknowledging it, these instincts cannot but be 'the evils of *society*'.[41]

More to the point, it seems to me difficult to reconcile the precondition of a species-specific *helplessness* as a ground zero of our natural predicament with the assumption that there is '*too great instinctual vigour*' in humankind.[42] The latter would still affect the masses Freud scornfully refers to as 'lazy and unintelligent'.[43] What he fails to grasp, or at least elucidate, is the properly Lacanian move whereby the anti-social 'instincts' to be curbed duly *coincide* with our helplessness. Or better, Freud misses the fact that religion (and civilization in general) as a human-made protection that soon turns into a Pandora box should be investigated starting from our *instinctual* helplessness, our being derailed on the very level of the instincts. In other words, and this is his untenable stratagem, Freud still somehow *believes* in a human 'state of nature', in which, oxymoronically, due to our hardwired anti-social-as-pre-social instincts, nature would 'destroy us [. . .] through what has caused our satisfaction' – incest, cannibalism and murder – yet that would still be to the eventual libidinal benefit of 'only one single person', the Father of the horde, who could enjoy without restrictions.[44] We are all speciated as helpless, here especially because too great instinctual vigour as naturally self-destructive satisfaction actually amounts to helplessness, *but nonetheless*, once upon a time, there existed a Man who positively satisfied his instinctual vigour.

Rephrasing this through Lacan's parlance, we could say that Freud thus ends up mitigating his intuition of onto-anthropological helplessness as irremediable not-Oneness by positing an exceptional One of enjoyment as a really existing historical figure. Helplessness and the killing and subsequent divinisation of the Father of the horde would be part of the same primaeval scenario and equally responsible for the emergence of religion: 'The longing-for-the-father explanation [of religion] is identical with the other, the need for protection against the consequences of human weakness'.[45] Moreover, in *The Future of an Illusion*, the Father of the horde from *Totem and Taboo* strikes back and is resurrected in the guise of the 'tyrant or dictator'[46] – about whom Freud does not say much. We should infer that his atheistic assessment of the social origins and value of religion is itself thereby permeated by a significant, unrecognized and recurrent religious relapse.

1.5. The past of an illusion

Having outlined this general impasse in Freud's reasoning, which I think he does not manage to solve, what should nonetheless interest us is his specific step-by-step *genealogy* of religion and the idea of God as dependent on our structural and never fully eliminable natural helplessness. Chapter 3 of *The Future of an Illusion* presents us with a temporal sequence that proceeds dialectically. The arguments are only sketched but overall compelling.

The first and most basic form of defence against the brutality of nature is achieved through a humanization of the elements of nature. More precisely, our desperate predicament would supposedly follow from the 'violent act of an *evil* Will', which we can attempt to exorcise, appease and bribe.[47] This enables us to overcome a fundamental anxiety. In short, 'we are perhaps still defenceless, but no longer helplessly paralysed'.[48] Unlike what claimed in 'Obsessive Action and Religious Practices', anxiety here appears to predate the temptation to indulge again in the instincts we renounced. But, as in this earlier text, embryonic religion is closely related to the projection of human iniquities onto transcendence.

The second step involves turning such a purely evil Will into an *ambivalent* Father figure. This alleviation of transcendent violence, which further reduces our impotence, would result from a social transposition of the fact that, ontogenetically, as children, we all both fear the father and rely on his protection.

In the third stage, nature is detached from human evil insofar as we start to observe some regularity and order in its phenomena. Yet, our helpless state persists, especially through the experience of death. The preservation of our species thus still requires confidence in father-like gods. The latter are both instated as 'the lords of nature'[49] and deemed *inscrutable* to the extent that we essentially remain without remedy.

At this point, thanks to the increasing separation of nature from gods – and its subjection to them – morality becomes the primary domain of religion. Having sedated the dangers of nature, gods must now make amends for the evils of society. The laws of civilization are credited to have divine origins and must be obeyed unconditionally. As divine, they also apply to nature in its entirety. In the end, this amounts to positing that the apparent meaninglessness of earthly life and its lingering human horrors should be subsumed under the conclusive meaning of an immortal and blissful life after death, which our soul could participate in. So, notwithstanding its 'devious ways',[50] there exists a superior Intelligence, who is severe but *benevolent*. Or, we could add, divine paternalism follows from and sublates divine evil, divine ambivalence and divine inscrutability.

This state of affairs leads to the emergence of monotheism. If the moral laws that are divine also govern the whole universe, then there must eventually exist *one* divine being. Freud concludes that the monotheistic God is at the same time, dialectically, a return to the historical beginnings of religion as derived from our species-specific helplessness. That is to say, the monotheistic God reveals the father-nucleus of all religions. Most importantly, monotheism therefore epitomizes the way in which religious doctrines genealogically contain historical truths that, however, are as distorted and systematically disguised as 'when we tell the child that new-born babies are brought by the stork'.[51]

1.6. The present of an illusion

For Freud, at present, religion can and must be overcome. It *can* be overcome because, in spite of our enduring structural helplessness,[52] we are somewhat *less* helpless thanks to scientific progress. It *must* be overcome because, precisely in light of our increased control over nature, religion by now proves to be on the whole detrimental to the species. Religion in fact stabilized our primordial helplessness, by giving it a meaning, only at the cost of what we could call a volatile libidinal economy of aggressiveness, which eventually in turn amounts to an *enhancement* of helplessness. In short, the convoluted sublation of the evil Will allegedly responsible for our predicament into a benevolent God and the prospect of an otherworldly life of bliss inevitably paves the way for the further division between the brotherly neighbour who worships the same God and the infidel enemy who does not. In Freud's own words, while 'the narcissistic satisfaction provided by the cultural ideal is also one of the forces that effectively counteract the hostility to culture within the cultural group', cultural ideals become nonetheless 'a source of discord and enmity between different cultural groups'.[53] In Lacanian terms, the other as counterpart turns into the ultimate cause of our lack of enjoyment, since he mythically stole it once upon a time. In the name of the benevolent God, every otherwise prohibited behaviour is licit in order to convert or exterminate the inimical other.

Freud straightforwardly claims on at least two occasions that the overcoming of religion is now possible simply by *acknowledging our helplessness* – and thus also the material-biological basis on which the historical foundation of religion rests. Humankind 'will have to confess [its] utter helplessness and insignificant part in the working of the universe'.[54] More conclusively, 'he who humbly acquiesces in the insignificant part man plays in the universe is [. . .] irreligious in the truest sense of the word'.[55] Yet several more or less explicit and undeveloped tensions emerge in Freud's discussion.

First, as Freud must concede to the conservative atheist, there is no guarantee that a scientifically mediated irreligious education will work. To begin with, we should aim at 'reducing to a minority the majority' of religiously asocial masses.[56] At worst, we will have to conclude that this is unfeasible, and Freud's own future of an illusion proves illusory. At best, a future without religious illusions will be achieved only by means of a long-term, and asymptotic, transition. It is indeed hopeless to try and eradicate religion 'by force and at one blow'.[57] In this regard, even the intriguingly 'great cultural experiment' carried out in the USSR seems to lead us nowhere.[58]

Second, and quite surprisingly, in one isolated passage Freud seems to be fully aware of the fact that science may well be transformed into a new religion, in the precise sense that it would dialectically both sublate (religious-aggressive) helplessness and present it again in an enhanced form on another, more dangerous, level. 'Human creations are easy to destroy, and science and technical skill, which have built them up, can also be turned to their destruction'.[59]

Third, the self-identification of technologically and militarily advanced Christian America with 'God's own country' already anticipates this contradictory passage.[60]

1.7. 'Optimism without foundation': 'Optimistic enough'

On close inspection, Freud's doubts about the effectiveness of non-religious education are even more deep-seated than they appear to be at first sight. In the final chapters of *The Future of an Illusion*, his teetering between hopeful optimism and anxious pessimism becomes extremely pronounced and almost uncontrollable. I think it closes with a somewhat forced declaration of blind faith in science's capacity to eradicate religious practice.

Let us summarize Freud's overall stance. Religion is initially indispensable for communal existence. It gives a meaning to meaningless helplessness. In providing information that 'should solve for us the riddles of the universe',[61] it offers some form of wish-fulfilment. Religion also channels asocial instincts while remaining, conflictingly, an *affective* instinctual renunciation.[62] Still, it has not made the greater part of humankind happy or moral; it has not turned it into 'supporters of civilization'.[63] In addition to that, science is increasingly detecting religion's errors and there is no stopping to this process.[64] More knowledge equals less religion. If people do cling to religion, it is because of their obscurantist religious upbringing. An uninfluenced child would not bother about God and the afterlife.

But perhaps this child would anyway repeat the mistakes of his ancestors. *But* maybe he would not, and the 'intellectual degeneration' of religion is only a 'secondary nature'.[65] *But* it could well be the case that this very assumption stands itself for an illusion: 'I do not know, and you cannot know either'.[66] *But* we should admit that there is hope for the future and the experiment of a non-religious education is worthwhile. *But*, again, 'perhaps even the hopes I have confessed are of an illusory nature'.[67] *But* Freud's illusions would, in his view, still definitely not be delusions: 'My illusions [. . .] are not, like the religious ones, incapable of correction, they have no delusional character".[68] *But* probably non-religious education will not alter much our psychological-religious nature in any case and 'our god *logos* is not perhaps a very powerful one'.[69] *But*, ultimately, supported by science, we can increase our rational power, since science has supposedly demonstrated in a conclusive manner that 'it is no illusion'.[70]

The socio-political considerations that accompany this disorienting seesaw are not only equally undecided but also quite problematic in terms of what they surreptitiously end up proposing in practice. Already in the opening chapters of

The Future of an Illusion, Freud's overall 'defence of culture' seems to support two apparently incompatible libidinal economies. On the one hand, he thinks civilization should aim at diminishing instinctual sacrifices, identify those that remain necessary while reconciling us with them and compensate us for this renunciation.[71] On the other hand, he appears not to be opposed to a *less* permissive civilization in which the super-ego is strengthened and 'yet other wish-gratifications, which are today entirely permissible, will appear just as disagreeable as those of cannibalism do now'.[72]

The more specific question concerning the future of religion is itself suspiciously treated through a similar dichotomy. Freud's hesitations enable us to glimpse three different scenarios. According to the first, non-religious education proves successful thanks to science. Useless religious prohibitions are revoked. The consolation of religion and the aggressive satisfaction that goes with it are *rationally* renounced; that is, humankind realizes that laws serve their interests. This renunciation is compensated by the fact that laws become less rigid, which in turn prompts people to have a 'more friendly attitude to them' and aim at improving them.[73] Abandoning religion thus amounts to a process of gradual social growth orchestrated by 'sensible teachers' who know how to temper the force of the onset of a new development.[74]

As for the second scenario, evoked only in passing, the experiment proves unsatisfactory, and we return to religion. However, this is a possibility that Freud himself elsewhere categorically rules out as impracticable. In fact, as seen, the masses will soon 'infallibly' discover that there is no God even if they are not told about it. Freud's call for non-religious education originates precisely from the assumption that the masses 'are ready to accept the results of scientific thought' without being ready for it.[75] As the social victims of a 'surplus of privation', the masses are resentful 'enemies of culture' and will not think twice before manifesting their hostility to it once they discover there is no God and stop fearing punishment.[76]

This leads us to a third and very bleak scenario as, for Freud, the only actual alternative to the liberal wager of a non-religious education. If we do not confide in the latter's possible triumph – and Freud's own reservations are far from minor – we should carry out 'the most rigorous suppression of these dangerous masses and the most careful exclusion of all opportunities for mental awakening'.[77]

There is eventually a very thin line separating Freud's aristocratic, misguided (if God does not exist everything is permitted?) and frankly indefensible socio-political position from that of the conservative atheist, his alter ego.

1.8. *Unglaubensgenossen*: Atheism or agnosticism?

Freud's final eulogy of science and its *logos* does not go without a subtle and crucial retraction that, beyond his avowed intentions, opens again the question of religious *truth* – and the existence of God – as epistemologically and ontologically *undecidable*.

For Freud, science is certainly no illusion. Although scientific ideas can be developed and ameliorated – 'a rough approximation to the truth is replaced by one more carefully adjusted, which in its turn awaits a further approach to perfection' – they already provide us with 'an assured and almost immutable core of knowledge' that, arguably, cannot be revolutionized.[78] Thanks also to the psychological insights of psychoanalysis, science thereby leads our non-religious education as fundamentally based on an acknowledgement of helplessness and aimed at the establishment of a non-oppressive, or at least more tolerable, civilization of 'comrades in unbelief' (*Unglaubensgenossen*).[79] Yet – and this is very important – Freud specifies that science's task has to be procedurally confined to 'showing how the world must appear *to us*', since the question of the world irrespective of our perspective is just an 'empty abstraction without practical interest'.[80] Comrades in unbelief must focus all their emancipated efforts on a pragmatic improvement of earthly life and should refrain from wasting energy in metaphysical speculation.[81]

Freud's general stance on atheism and agnosticism becomes here even more convoluted and ambiguous. As seen, he methodologically starts off with an *agnostic* delimitation of religious truth, which would lie beyond the scope of psychoanalytic investigation. However, he subsequently appears to be claiming that psychoanalysis can deliver the historical truth that religion is a human-made production, revolving around human helplessness, which is already reflected in disguise within religion itself and can be confirmed beyond reasonable doubt by science. Recognizing all this would suffice to make us irreligious. But does this mean that such a historical truth about religion also provides us with the ultimate truth about religious truth and that thus Freud's position is at bottom not agnostic but *atheistic*? I do not know, and Freud does not seem to know it either![82]

There are two further complications. First, by Freud's own admission, the above holds exclusively with respect to the world-*for-us*. Helplessness, or not-Oneness, is scientifically *our* ultimate horizon. But might this very not-Oneness be (contained by) the One in the world as *in itself*? To the extent that, in the very last page of *The Future of an Illusion*, Freud ends up implying this metaphysical question, only to leave it aside for its supposed lack of practical value, his general orientation turns out to be again more agnostic than atheistic, despite and thanks to his full commitment to a scientific outlook.

Second, even if we were to privilege the atheistic Freud, for whom a science that includes psychoanalysis would be enough to have done with religion once and for all, his atheism remains, for lack of a better word, *weak*. He does not realize how the conclusion 'the not-One is', when directly applied to the world as in itself, inevitably conjures up a far more insidious One and definitive religious meaning, namely, the *God* of atheists, the *logos* for which 'there is no meta-language' is necessarily instated as a meta-linguistic statement. Ultimately, as observed, Freud's entire rational-scientific atheistic account of the origins and overcoming of religion itself depends on the positing of a really existing Father (of the horde) that does not stop returning in a symbolic form after he was slaughtered at the dawn of history.

2. Lacan and the new triumph of religion

2.1. Freud's alibi

Lacan's return to Freud *initially* involves an appreciative assessment and appropriation of Freud's stance on religion. The latter is treated most thoroughly in the context of the delineation of an ethics of psychoanalysis.

As spelled out in 'Discourse to Catholics' (delivered in 1960), in spite of his anti-religious penchant, Freud rightly situates religion at the 'forefront of moral experience'.[83] More to the point, following the Freudian theme of helplessness and specifying it further, for psychoanalysis, religious morality stands as an initial attempt at coping with a structural and species-specific frustration regarding enjoyment, or better, with the fact that there is 'something irremediably awry in human sexuality'.[84] Freud would also fittingly see that the outcome of such a process remains far from successful. According to Lacan, this very frustration is sublimated through religion only by associating it with a greedy prohibiting Law that concurrently creates the mirage of a primordially lost libidinal Thing and an ensuing aggressiveness.

In other words, and still in line with Freud, religion makes civilization possible to begin with, but it also ends up 'aggravating' our predicament.[85] It produces a discontent whose generalized suffering does not match the effort. Here, Lacan unhesitatingly subscribes to Freud's proposed solution to the religious impasse, which would amount to the kernel of Freud's own ethics: religion can and must be superseded by fully assuming our unsurpassable helplessness. In Lacan's more openly anthropo-ontological terms, this means the following: through reason we need to reconcile with a 'nature [that] mysteriously opposes itself',[86] namely, a nature that appears to be, at least through our human lack-of-being, fundamentally denatured.

'Discourse to Catholics' never criticizes Freud, not to mention his pronouncements on religion. Lacan even seems to endorse what he defines as Freud's anti-humanistic humanitarianism.[87] In short, a future without religious illusions is built upon tolerance and temperance (humanitarianism), yet this does not entail being progressive or confiding in freedom or the masses (antihumanism). Lacan argues here that it is precisely insofar as Freud grasps that there is no highest good as a goal and that a utilitarian approach to morality is unviable – since the well-being of the group necessarily goes together with an evil for those who lie outside it – that he thinks we should not abandon the field of ethics to religion and instead recover it 'at man's level'.[88]

However, the same text equally abounds in my view with arguments that, against Lacan's intentions, already challenge Freud's problematic position, both socially and epistemologically. First, from a social perspective, Freud's conservative disdain for the masses is strictly related to his assumption that the proclamation of the death of God and the disclosure of religion as an illusion would unleash their destructive libidinal tendencies, which can be averted only through a careful and gradual irreligious education. On the contrary, as Lacan never tires of repeating, if 'God is dead nothing is permitted anymore'.[89] This is precisely what *Totem and Taboo* itself would show by stressing the correspondence between the killing of the Father of the horde and the emergence of a prohibiting Law. In other words, for Lacan, Freud's greatness rests on having formulated the founding *myth* of *modernity* – 'insofar as modern man is the one for whom God is dead' – and grasped modernity's subjection to the tyranny of the superego as a 'durable' repressive agency that internally 'heaps reproaches'.[90] *But*, and Lacan overlooks it here, for Freud, this myth is at bottom not at all a myth. It is a *really existing* event that founds history and civilization tout-court, which then modernity runs the risk of compromising by revealing how the law and the death of the Father retrospectively transformed into God have always been coextensive. According to the Freud of *The Future of an Illusion*, the second killing of the Father – the Nietzschean death of God, if you wish – is inevitable and supposedly final, yet it could have potentially disastrous consequences, since the basic fabric of civilization might be destroyed by a resurgence of instinctual vigour. To sum up, for Freud, if the Father of the horde is dead, then nothing is permitted anymore, as he is turned into God; however, if God is dead, then everything is potentially permitted, at least in the direction of the species' collective self-annihilation.

The second main issue tackled by Lacan in 'Discourse to Catholics' that implicitly contradicts Freud, epistemologically in this case, concerns the distinction between knowledge and belief. We discussed how, in *The Future of an Illusion*, religious belief, especially in the guise of the 'I believe because it is absurd to believe', is both precipitously liquidated as irrational (ignorance is ignorance) and more prudently identified as rationally unassailable. However, this second approach inevitably institutes religious belief as a separate domain. Freud's *agnosticism* – not just his atheism – is in turn in this sense weak. It follows what Stephen Jay Gould has named the doctrine of the non-overlapping magisteria (NOMA),[91] whereby science and religion each have its own legitimate authority and area of inquiry. Without mentioning Freud, Lacan firmly contests this stance as a 'strange division', which in the name of tolerance gives rise to a 'curious neutrality'.[92] Those who, like Lacan, do not profess any religious affiliation should rather closely examine religious belief through knowledge, that is, *rationally* interrogate the very impregnability of irrational belief for reason. To begin with, this is needed to the extent that, for believers, belief is itself a kind of knowledge.[93] Conversely and more importantly, irreligious minds must also address the belief component of knowledge, or *knowledge*'s own belief.[94] Lacan is thus led to denounce the 'flippancy' in the way science disposes of religion,[95] which, unsurprisingly, is sooner or later accompanied by a tacit transformation of science into a novel kind of faith.

As seen, Freud senses the latter issue although he does not unfold it. Lacan reminds us that throughout his work Freud is also profoundly aware of the tight link between the vicissitudes of human sexuality as fundamentally flawed and a *cupido sciendi*, or desire to know.[96] Yet Freud never really questions the alleged objectivity of science's pursuit of knowledge as itself motivated by an essential quest of the subject for an ultimate meaning that would heal our 'existential gap' or 'fault line'.[97] Like religion, science in turn depends on this structural anthropo-ontological horizon. In Freud's jargon, for Lacan, science is itself a form of 'wish-fulfilment'.

Only three years after 'Discourse to Catholics', in 'Introduction to the Names-of-the-Father' (1963), Lacan can thus less supportively conclude that condemning religion as an illusion stands for nothing more than an 'alibi'.[98] Illusion – or semblance, to use a more Lacanian term – turns out to be far more extensive, pervasive and resilient than the traditional field of religion. Freud is fighting a straw man while underestimating the emergence of new idols. His 'crude' materialism,[99] as still sympathetically presented in 'Discourse to Catholics', now increasingly becomes *grossier* in the sense of coarse, inaccurate and clumsy. The later Lacan will distance himself from it in no uncertain way.

2.2. Freud is religious

In Seminar II, during a lively question-and-answer session, Lacan vehemently disputes Hyppolite's conclusion that, in spite of the fact that through psychoanalysis Freud was of course not openly 'engaging in a new religion', he nonetheless would in the end put forward a 'religion against religion'.[100] On the contrary, in Seminar XVII, Lacan scorns Freud, to the point of ridiculing him, for after all 'retaining in fact, if not in intention, [. . .] what he designates as being the most essential in religion'.[101] That is to say, as implacably reiterated and specified in two distinct lessons from Seminar XIX, 'Freud promotes the One' and thus falls back into the very 'sermonizing' he abhorred.[102]

I think that Lacan's understanding of Freud's position on religion and God always remains the same. What instead changes radically is the value he attributes to it for the sake of a truly irreligious psychoanalysis. Starting from the 1960s, Lacan can no longer support Freud's stance, even when it appears to adopt a straightforwardly atheistic approach, for which, again, due to helplessness, the One is not and the not-One is. This is primarily due to Lacan's own investigations of that period into the paradoxical implications of the incompleteness of the symbolic order – and, in short, civilization – as stemming from our most basic species-specific trait, namely, language's inability to fully represent sex. The logic of the paradox at stake already emerges embryonically, if only on an ethical-existential level and unaware to Lacan, in the passage from 'Discourse to Catholics' we commented on earlier. Nature opposes itself through the helplessness of the animal that happens to speak and be at odds with sex; superseding religion involves rationally acknowledging this state of affairs; but, for Freud, it is still a question of finding an '*agreement*' with and '*repose*' in such an unredeemable predicament.[103] In other words, put simply, a direct promulgation and endorsement of the not-One as *conclusive* gives rise to the One (not-One), the Being of the lack of being, the ultimate Meaning of 'there is no ultimate meaning'.

Hyppolite is totally correct on this point. Freud's anti-religious crusade triggers a *religion* against religion. As he goes on to argue in Seminar II, Freud's works are afflicted by a serious conflict. On the one hand, he is a 'pure speculator', who discovers the death instinct – as inextricable from helplessness, we should add – and stumbles upon it as something 'enigmatic' that, at the same time, concerns 'a knowledge of an entirely different depth'.[104] Here lies the grandeur of Freud's materialism. On the other hand, against this orientation and far less originally, there is a naively *rationalist-humanist* Freud 'who thinks it is possible to rationalise humanity' in a comprehensive fashion.[105] For Hyppolite, *The Future of an Illusion* epitomizes the latter Freud insofar as in this text he aims at lifting all illusions in the name of a 'reinforced ego' and 'freed humanity', however much they depend on the recognition of finitude.[106]

In Seminar II, Lacan underestimates Hyppolite's subtle reasoning. At this stage, there is for Lacan only one Freud, the irreligious one. Even *The Future of an Illusion*'s optimism and utopianism would be subservient to a reason that never abdicates and in this way (anticipating Lacan's own notion of the 'real') shows that 'no matter how far one extends [. . .] rationalisation, it will necessarily blow up somewhere'[107] – which is precisely what Hyppolite advances with respect to the deeper knowledge associated with the death instinct. Misunderstanding this last point, Lacan then attacks Hyppolite for positing that Freud would stop before 'the opaque and the ineffable'[108] – which Hyppolite never contends and, as seen, is instead precisely what Freud himself does in *The Future of an Illusion* in his weakly agnostic moments.

But by the time of his Seminars of the late 1960s, Lacan digests Hyppolite's critique and radicalizes it. Freud's stance on religion becomes indefensible in at least three overlapping manners, which also tend to contradict each other if one juxtaposes his texts. Schematically, Freud promotes the One in that he:

   a. preserves an absolute One that is also instantiated in language;
   b. understands the language-based oscillation between and co-dependence of not-One and One (symbolic differentiality) but makes it dependent on the disappearance of a pre-linguistic absolute One;
   c. fosters a metalinguistic One (not-One).

First, at his most unsophisticated, Freud clings to a fundamental 'principle of union', which he names Eros and considers as the 'founding force of life'.[109] This is the case especially in his metapsychology and *Beyond the Pleasure Principle* in particular. The same principle acquires anthropomorphic traits, both phylogenetically and ontogenetically, through the figure of the all-loving father: 'The father is love, the first thing to be loved in this world is the father'.[110] Freud thus retains 'the very substance' of religion.[111] More specifically, he turns out to be much closer to Christianity than he is prepared to concede.[112]

Second, as detailed in *Totem and Taboo*, the all-loving father (the One) necessarily refers to a dead father (the not-One). Religion, civilization and 'order' as such are established on the 'love of the dead father'.[113] Yet, and this is crucial, for Freud, the father is dead only because his sons murdered him and obliterated his boundless enjoyment (the absolute One) at the dawn of history. Treating this coarse myth, 'the nonsensical story of *Totem and . . . Beginning*',[114] as a really existing event Freud fails to realize that 'the father is, from the origins, castrated', not just from the presumed historical beginning.[115]

Third and most importantly for Lacan's own reflection, in his allegedly most atheistic moments – such as in some passages of *The Future of an Illusion* – Freud appears to forget the linguistic co-dependence of not-One and One he elsewhere intuits and ends up paying a high price for it. On the one hand, Freud fathoms that the dead father is not incompatible with religion but always goes together with it.[116] On the other, he very bizarrely trusts that he has done with religion simply by revealing that 'the support of religion is nothing other than the [living but mortal human] father' and God is thereby dead.[117] Religion would instantaneously evaporate as soon as we appreciate that God as an illusion is nothing more than an emanation of the all-loving father who protects the child from his structural helplessness.

In this context, Lacan goes far beyond Hyppolite's denunciation of the humanist Freud. Not only does Freud's attack on religion pave the way for a religion against religion, but gross materialists like him are 'the only authentic believers'.[118] We move from a religion *against religion* to a *religion* against religion that is actually a *religion* (against religion). In other words, in claiming that, as nothing other than a creation of human helplessness and the father-complex, God is most definitely dead and we only need to accept it in order to be irreligious, Freud supports the *God* that guarantees there is no God or, which is the same, an unconditional belief in the meaning of unsurpassable meaninglessness. Although he himself advances the theme of the all-love of the dead father, Freud does not come to terms with the logic according to which 'there is no metalanguage' invariably turns into a metalinguistic statement when it is not problematized as such.

Regarding this issue, we should note that, as early as 1927, Pfister already formulated a similar, and even more intriguing, objection in an intense letter to Freud. Independently of Pfister's untenable hijacking of psychoanalysis in favour of a Protestant 'autonomy' and 'complete moralisation', the pastor lucidly infers that the scientific world of the 'end of illusion' as 'our highest knowledge' and, importantly, a 'whole' does not eventually sit on the immanence of blind chance, as envisioned by Freud, but on a transcendent Satan.[119] We should also observe that, curiously, this One (not-One) – which Pfister very aptly calls 'the Devil's island'[120] – as the kernel of Freud's purported atheism somehow returns to and rehabilitates the evil Will he himself identified as the most elementary form of religion in both *The Future of an Illusion* and 'Obsessive Action and Religious Practices'.

The agreement with and repose in helplessness finally correspond to a diabolical yet *reassuring* reconciliation.

2.3. Religion's invincibility

In what is arguably one of his most mature, extensive and explicit dissections of religion vis-à-vis science and psychoanalysis, the 1974 interview 'The Triumph of Religion', Lacan goes as far as systematically turning the clichéd rationalist-humanist predictions of *The Future of an Illusion* on their head. I think this has not yet been sufficiently emphasized by commentators. The scenario he sketches is very bleak and totally anti-Freudian: psychoanalysis does not hold any key to the future; religion will almost certainly triumph again over psychoanalysis; perhaps psychoanalysis itself will become a religion; psychoanalysis can at best survive.[121] As for science, the only way in which it would really manage to triumph, demonstrate human superiority and not be reabsorbed within religion is by annihilating us once and for all (for instance, by creating 'bacteria that would be resistant to everything' and clear the globe of human 'shitty things').[122] Leaving aside this apocalyptic ending, which is likely to remain just a megalomaniac fantasy, religion looks 'invincible'.[123]

And yet, according to Lacan, the fact remains that psychoanalysis has historically been a privileged moment as an 'intrusion of the real'.[124] Psychoanalysis will fail and be reduced to a mere flash of truth in between two religious worlds only *if and when* religion will indeed triumph again in the future.[125] Avoiding, or at least delaying, this however likely outcome involves, in short, 'getting used to the real'.[126]

Here, Lacan bluntly but effectively defines the real as 'what isn't going well' and, at its utmost, 'what doesn't work' at all.[127] Psychoanalysis revolves around both levels of the real. On a first level, it detects, circumscribes, treats and provides a formulation of 'what isn't going well' in the guise of the symptom. On a second level, it then refers the symptom to a structural point of impossibility, the not-working of the sexual relationship as the most fundamental characteristic of the animal that happens to speak. Lacan implies that, in this second and more thorough sense, not only does the human world as what appears to work symbolically (One) always evoke the real as what does not work (not-One) – and vice versa – but also this very oscillation as a '*difference*' (One/not-One, or not-two, or better, no-two-as-One), which is finally what *is* real, shows that 'there is *no* such thing as a world' for us (not-One).[128] That is to say, the not-One is *phenomeno-logically* conclusive.

Moving from these premises, religion can generally be understood as a versatile and thereby incredibly powerful disavowal of a thus-conceived real. It is therefore diametrically opposed to psychoanalysis in a twofold way: religion is both 'designed [. . .] so that [we] do not perceive what isn't going well' in the semblance of the world, and, when this semblance becomes untenable, it still succeeds in giving meaning to what does not work at all.'[129] Religion gives meaning to 'absolutely anything whatsoever', including 'all the distressing things science is going to introduce' – and their leading to the increasing scientific evidence that there is no such thing as a world – because it always finds a 'correspondence between everything and everything else'.[130]

At this stage, we also need to appreciate Lacan's complex positioning on the role of modern science vis-à-vis religion, which clearly emerges in 'The Triumph of Religion'. The least we can say about this difficult topic is that, for him, modern science has an ambivalent relation with the real. It is an illusion but not simply a religion. On the one hand, modern science is definitely driven by a desire to know oriented towards an ultimate meaning or absolute knowledge whereby everything would work. On the other, this very movement – passed off as an accumulative progress – is contradictorily propelled by nothing other than a repeated and exponential encounter with the real as meaningless. While religion recovers a correspondence between everything and everything else, modern science on the contrary unmasks that there is no agreement 'between our intuitions and the world' – as Lacan already puts it in 'Discourse to Catholics'.[131] In other words, ever since the refutation of the geocentric model of the universe, science has more and more demonstrated that physical reality is 'totally inhuman'.[132] For us, moderns, the crucial question is thus no longer that of the 'conaturalness' of appearances and the transcendence they would depend on and open onto, but that of what we make technologically appear in the real 'disjunctions' secreted and augmented by our science.[133] In this way, it would seem that earth and heaven are scientifically 'devoid of God'.[134]

Yet 'The Triumph of Religion' adds a further turn of the screw to this argument. However little awareness science has of its contradictory trajectory and however much it instead continues to be motivated by the pursuit of absolute knowledge, the real will nonetheless undoubtedly 'expand' and 'religion will *thereby* have still more reasons to soothe people's hearts'.[135] Lacan concurs that, as Freud already claimed in *The Future of an Illusion*, religion consisted in its beginnings in giving anthropomorphic meaning to meaningless natural things. But the fact that science now produces less and less – so to speak – 'natural' things precisely at the place where, through the real, it de-natures nature, or better de-anthropomorphises it, does not in the least entail that religious meaning will diminish, not to mention vanish. Again, religion can very well prosper as the categorical meaning of a nature that opposes itself through us: 'Religion will find colourful meaning for [. . .] the oddest experiments', including those that could potentially destroy our species.[136] So, in the end, against Freud and against Lacan's own support of Freud's position in 'Discourse to Catholics', accepting the not-Oneness of nature as it seems to transpire by means of the sexual and epistemological vicissitudes of the linguistic animal does not suffice to dispose of religion and even ends up reinforcing it.

2.4. The future of psychoanalysis: Getting used to the real real

We now need to ask: What does Lacan specifically mean by 'getting used to the real' in this context? How does this way of countering religion differ from Freud's, only at first sight very similar, acknowledgement of helplessness and thus avoid falling back into the indirect promotion of the One, or better, the *One* (not-One)?

In short, in 'The Triumph of Religion', Lacan seems to think that Freud stops at the level of the symptomatic real, what is not going well yet can be delimited as such. Or more to the point, Freud senses the more structural level of the real as impossible, what does not work at all, but reduces it to the symptomatic level. He does so precisely by turning unsurpassable helplessness – as already linked to the linguistic animal's being at odds with sex – into yet another pacifying 'conception of man',[137] whose rationalist-humanist function fundamentally lies in protecting us from anxiety (at the cost of presupposing a diabolical worldview).

But, on closer inspection, according to Lacan, Freud's mistake is due to his blindness to the impossible real of modern science itself. The latter remains for Freud a veritable taboo.[138] So much so that he is also responsible for our own current difficulty to confront it.[139] On the one hand, *Freud* does not see that his proposed overcoming of religion by acquiescing in our insignificance preserves religion also and especially because he maintains the idea that science will be able to *confirm* this state of affairs – the absence of an ultimate meaning – as an ultimate and hence religious meaning. This is after all how science makes us less helpless. On the other hand, *Lacan* puts science's impossible real at the centre of the irreligious future of psychoanalysis as a verbal praxis distant from any 'confession' of finitude and as a knowledge of the 'totally inexplicable fact that man is a speaking animal' for which there is no sexual relationship.[140]

'The Triumph of Religion' concludes with a series of bold considerations and a renewed anti-religious warning. Psychoanalysis needs to go beyond the symptom as 'not yet truly real' but simply the fashion in which the real manifests itself through the discontent of the speaking being as a thus-*demarcated* 'sick animal'.[141] Getting used to the real means getting used to the 'real real', or 'true real', that is accessible by the scientific pathway of little equations and formulas, or better – Lacan here fails to specify it – of the scientific *impasses* that give rise to further equations and formulas as well as further impasses.[142] What we can therefore scientifically reach and have a tangible technological impact upon is nothing other than what we continuously 'miss',[143] what is given to us as the non-correspondence between our intuitions and the inhumanity of physical reality, the not-Oneness of the world.

Yet, importantly, Lacan insists that this real real from which we are in a sense always 'separated' is *not* 'transcendent' to the symptomatic real.[144] The not yet truly real and the truly real are two sides of the same coin, namely, the absence of the sexual relationship, language's impossibility of representing sex. While the symptomatic real witnesses to the fact that symbolic sexuation always falls short of the sexual relationship, science accesses the real real precisely insofar as it cannot provide the formula of the sexual relationship.[145] Or, from a slightly different perspective, we could say that the real real amounts to the not-Oneness of the world as the *in itself for us*. Positing it as the not-Oneness of the world as the *in itself for itself*, independently of us, always requires a transcendent 'act of faith'.[146] Similarly, Lacan repeatedly cautions us against claiming that the real real as the not-One is necessarily *all* there is,[147] since such a move inevitably institutes the transcendent *One* (not-One) – and, albeit more sophisticatedly, only redoubles the mistake of Freud's weak atheism. This is the initial kernel of Lacan's *strong* agnosticism.[148]

Getting used to the real as the real real first and foremost involves getting used to not submitting it to *any* totalizing worldview, kicking the habit of *Weltanschauungen* in order to become addicted to the productivity of the impossible.

2.5. Becoming an atheist and the true religion

Throughout Lacan's works, there are undoubtedly some passages that, if taken out of their polemical context, seem to embrace atheism as a straightforward fait accompli. For instance, in addition to asserting that he does not profess any denominational affiliation, he equally regards the Gospel as nonsensical, a fairy tale.[149] He states that his teaching has absolutely nothing to do with attempts at misappropriating it in view of a religious hermeneutics.[150] Most emphatically, 'I do not believe in Him'.[151] With regard to psychoanalysis in general, Lacan deems it to be devoted to a demystification of religion.[152] Conversely, religion provides answers to the question of truth that are totally incompatible with those of psychoanalysis.[153] An unedited version of 'The Triumph of Religion' makes it crystal clear that there can be no amicable relation between psychoanalysis and religion: 'In the end, it's either one or the other'.[154]

Yet, whenever Lacan openly tackles atheism, he presents it as a difficult and interminable *process*. At best, we are always only *becoming* atheists. In this sense, Seminar XVII identifies atheism with the 'pinnacle' of psychoanalysis.[155] The *pointe* at stake is never a consolidated point but an asymptotic peak, tip or extremity. In other words, as suggested in an address to Italian psychoanalysts, we should keep on trying to exit religion as an illusion that – in agreement with Freud – was useful in the past and – against Freud – will certainly continue to affect us in more or less disguised forms even beyond its expiration date.[156] Lacan dwells on these issues in Seminar X: actual atheism can only be conceived of as a practice of 'asceticism' facilitated by psychoanalysis; its fulfilment would require 'doing away with the fantasy of the Almighty', that is, *any* dimension of a presence that circumscribes the world.[157] To the extent that alleged atheists still believe in some kind of 'universal eye' that looks at them from the outside, there unconsciously persists a 'God in whom everybody believes without believing'.[158] As specified in a later discussion with Yale students through an oxymoronic formulation that resonates with what I called the God of atheists – or One (not-One) – not only 'everybody is religious, even the atheists', but also 'atheism is the disease of believing in God, believing that God does not intervene in the world'.[159] For this reason, peremptory statements such as 'I do not believe in Him' should immediately be followed by a far less solemn 'but who gives a fuck' about it.[160] That is, independently of our seeming disbelief, we count with a thus-defined God of atheists and have to come to terms with him. It is only by assuming his inevitability that 'perhaps psychoanalysis is capable of creating a viable atheist', which is to say, 'somebody who does not contradict oneself all of the time'.[161]

Now, while supposed atheists invariably believe in not believing, because they do not believe they believe, it is instead believers, who can never really believe,[162] and the contradictions of religious doctrines that can teach us something about atheism: 'The force of atheism, of the impasses in the notion of the divine, is not in atheistic arguments, which are often much more theist than the others. The lesson is all the same to look for them among the theologians themselves'.[163] Yet – and this is crucial – such productive impasses remain after all religious; they disavow the real in that they are subsumed under a however inconsistent ultimate meaning and must accordingly be challenged. Lacan is not ingenuously saying that if atheists are theists, then theists are atheists, although at times he may give the impression of adopting this sophistic line of reasoning.

In this light, we can also better assess Lacan's notoriously ambivalent stance on Christianity. I would suggest understanding it on three related levels of increasing importance. First, there is an overt acknowledgement of the profound influence of the Christian, and Catholic in particular, tradition on his upbringing (especially through his attending a Jesuit school) and psychoanalytic theory at large (suffice it to mention a key notion such as the Name-of-the-Father).[164] Second, Lacan often provocatively flirts with some of the most outrageous tenets of Christianity in order to counter the falsely irreligious assumptions of his opponents. This is most noticeably the case with the recurrent motif that the problem of anthropogenesis can better be approached materialistically from a re-evaluation of the Biblical notion of creation ex nihilo and St John's 'in the beginning was the Word' than from the lingering theo-teleology of mainstream evolutionary theory – by means of which 'man will continue to believe he is the flower of creation, and this is the fundamental belief of what institutes him as a religious being'.[165] Third and most significantly, drawing on Hegel and anticipating many arguments later popularised by Žižek, Lacan recovers a hidden atheistic kernel in Christianity,[166] which nonetheless must be superseded since it eventually ends up only reinforcing religion as an illusion.

As I discussed elsewhere, such a tension within Christianity is extensively investigated in Seminar XX and 'The Triumph of Religion'.[167] On the one hand, the 'essence of Christianity' lies in a 'filthy truth' (*vérité d'immondice*):[168] the truth that the world is not-One, that the universe as a *uni*-verse is a 'flower of rhetoric',[169] again, fundamentally because there is no sexual relationship, that is, because sex does not have a meaning for the speaking animal and enjoyment can only be given as a lack of enjoyment. Note that Lacan is as always very careful in choosing his words: the truth *d'immondice* is literally *im-monde*, from the Latin *immundus*, where the prefix 'im' negates the *mundus*, or world. The filthy truth of Christianity certainly 'inundated what we call the world', destroyed the 'miraculous, universal balance' phantasmatically established by the Greeks and Romans (including the latter's 'baths of jouissance sufficiently symbolized by those famous thermal baths').[170] But, on the other hand, Christian filthiness equally 'revives the religion of men'.[171] Lacan's main argument here is that Christianity paradoxically strengthens religion by means of a filthy truth (the truth of incompleteness) that is as such disavowed by any religion, including Christianity.

We can better appreciate this issue if we dwell on Lacan's contentious suggestion, repeated several times, that Christianity is the 'true religion' ('that it is the true religion, as it claims, is not an excessive claim'; 'the Gospels [. . .] you can't speak any better of the truth').[172] Christianity is a *true* religion because the birth and death of Christ, as God's Word or *logos* incarnated in the body of a miserable member of the *Homo sapiens* species ('the Word was made flesh and dwelt among us'[173]) who is then murdered, strikingly *redoubles* the predicament of the linguistic animal, 'a repugnant carnal being' that is 'ravaged by the Word'.[174] In this sense the statements 'in the beginning was the Word' and 'the speaking being is a sick animal' – first and foremost sexually, for language cannot represent sex, which hence remains a logical impossibility – point in the same atheistic direction.[175]

Yet Christianity fully remains a *religion* in that it also disavows the very real it evokes. Christ's coming into existence in this world is ultimately aimed at disavowing the logical impasse concerning the contingent emergence of language in humans and the concurrent absence of the sexual relationship – that is, the question of anthropogenesis, the real question about existence. It does so by dogmatically giving this truthful impasse an unprecedented *meaning*: Christ, the embodied Word, has become one of us to spread the word, the good news that the love of God can eventually save us.[176] Salvation is thus preserved by replacing the classical illusion of enjoyment with the abjection of *this* world (brought to the point of the killing of God at the hands of a repugnant carnal being) only to oppose the latter to *another* world of eternal life in which it will be resolved. More specifically, while Christianity as a 'true' religion is the least untruthful and hence most meaningless of all religions – it even makes God forsake himself on the cross – it nonetheless consolidates meaning (salvation and eternal life) precisely thanks to the disclosure of truth as meaninglessness (the abjection of this world). God saves us only if we first crucify him and thereby enable resurrection, namely, if we save the Saviour from truth *through* his own filthy truth.

2.6. Overcoming Christianity: Minorizing truth

For Lacan, Christianity as the least untruthful religion therefore becomes one of psychoanalysis's worst enemies, namely, 'the true *within* religion'.[177] Simply put, in it, incompleteness provides the ultimate reason to believe in completeness. The Christian revelation of our 'misfortune' eventually only sustains the Church's religious intention 'to carry the species [. . .] right up to the end of time' through a carefully supervised veiling of the absence of the sexual relationship.[178] Along the same lines, the obscenity of Christ's tortured body on the cross does not really disrupt the onto-theo-totology of Aristotelian animism – that is, its founding the being of the world on the perceived Oneness of the human body, understanding the soul as the identity of this body and setting up a (religious-sexual) theory of knowledge on their supposed correspondence.[179] The death of Christ in fact prepares nothing less than his return among us as a body: 'Christ, even when resurrected from the dead, is valued for his body, and his body is the means by which communion in his presence is incorporation', so much so that 'Christ's wife, the Church as it is called, contents itself very well' with that.[180]

However, the outcome of such a complicated preservation and successful relaunching of religion cannot but in turn lead to a 'precarious' God. [181] This is especially evident at the level of his supposed being at once one and trine. Either he becomes a count – 'one-two-three' – 'only retrospectively after Christ's revelation', and in this case 'it is his being' – his being also trine – 'that suffers a blow', or, alternatively, 'the three is prior to him, and it is his unity that takes a hit'.[182] In short, in spite of resurrection, Christianity either saves being at the expense of the One or saves the One at the expense of being. Lacan thinks that this theological impasse in the notion of the Christian divine, the latter's inability to smoothly be accommodated into onto-theo-totology, opens the field of psychoanalysis as an atheistic praxis directed at 'separating severely'[183] the One from being.

But the other side of the lesson to be learnt from the vicissitudes of Christian theology is equally if not more seminal to the process of becoming an atheist: Christianity's betrayal of its filthy truth markedly illustrates and skilfully profits from the fact that the truth of incompleteness can only be *half*-said. Incompleteness, the not-One, and the absence of a meta-language cannot really be maintained, or thought, without promulgating the semblance of completeness, the One, and a meta-language. Christianity transforms such a structural oscillation into a static dogma, that is, the neat separation between the abjection of our world and the perfection of the world to come that will have redeemed it. In Christianity, a profound awareness of the co-implication between the not-One and the One is *explicitly* stabilized as a historical fallen One (not-One) to be providentially recomposed as a messianic *One*.

For Lacan, psychoanalysis therefore needs to 'minorise'[184] the truth of incompleteness already brought about by Christianity and successively obscured by its religious status. It is first certainly a matter of 'displacing' or 'dislodging' any notion of completeness – as Christianity initially does with its filthy truth of abjection – but we should then also be cautious not to 'disturb' or 'undermine' it too much.[185] That is to say, independently of a Christian dogmatic transvaluation of incompleteness into completeness, directly promulgating incompleteness as truth still goes together with a return to completeness, saving God, in spite of one's alleged atheism. Moreover, unlike Christianity, weak atheism promotes the *One* (not-One) *without* even comprehending it. What psychoanalysis should instead do to begin with is 'putting truth in its place',[186] that is, acknowledging that, at least with respect to the dimension of language as the natural habitat of the human animal, incompleteness and the mirage of completeness are structurally inextricable.

3. The God hypothesis
3.1. *Le Dieur*

At this stage, we should pay particular and renewed attention to what Lacan calls 'the God hypothesis'. In Seminar XX, he famously claims that 'as long as someone says something, the God hypothesis will be there [*sera là*]'.[187] Two important clarifications are needed not to miss the centrality of this statement in Lacan's delineation of a strong agnosticism and ascetic atheism as well as his concomitant critique of both theism and weak atheism. First, taking the passage above at face value, as it should be taken, God amounts to a *hypothesis*. Saying immediately institutes God as a hypothesis, the hypothesis that language is One – or, which is the same, that there is a meta-language – and this hypothesis will be there as long as there is language. The God hypothesis, which could also be understood more bluntly as an unconscious '"faith" in the coherence of sense-making',[188] remains structurally necessary for speech to be even minimally operative. In this sense, whatever he says, *Homo sapiens* always speaks as a *dieur*, a 'God sayer'. The animal that happens to speak and be at odds with sex cannot but put forward the God hypothesis. Yet, by the same token, Lacan is not in the least identifying God with speech or language, which would result simply into a trivialized reiteration of the Christian *Logos*, as instead several commentators maintain in a more or less nuanced manner.[189] Lacan seems to anticipate such a flagrant equivocation in Seminar XXII and categorically dispels it: 'I have never said that God is *in* language'.[190] Quite the contrary, God, that is, the God hypothesis, 'consists of the set of *the effects of language*'.[191]

Second, on a *logical* level, the God hypothesis amounts to a necessary symbolic *existence* for each and every speaking animal. But the perennial 'being there' of the God hypothesis, which Lacan also expresses as 'there is something of the One' (*il y a de l'Un*) and 'there exists one' (*il existe un*), does not imply an underlying *ontological* divine *essence*, or unity of substance. That is to say, God as a structural hypothesis – and even as structure's most structural hypothesis – coincides with the impossibility of proving it, or better, of proving the existence of an essence that would confirm the hypothesis.[192] Because of such a coincidence, the God hypothesis is also *real* in the specifically Lacanian meaning of the term. As epitomized by the contradictions of theologians, the symbolic hypothesis of the One inevitably leads to the real not-One. Yet conversely, and most importantly, any attempt at disproving the symbolic hypothesis of the One in the name of an ultimate real not-One ends up not only reinforcing the existence of the former but also attributing it an essence. Again, weak atheists are the only authentic believers. Weak atheism's direct positing of the absence of a meta-language, the truth of the incompleteness of structure, goes together with the implicit affirmation that the absence of a meta-language is a *meta*-language, the truth about truth, and consequently that God – meta-linguistically as *extra*-linguistically – *is* in such a fashion a unity of substance.

So, on close inspection, what Lacan is thinking through the God hypothesis is the continuous oscillation between the One and the not-One as the two poles of the set of the effects of language. Insofar as the not-One pole is irreducible to another One – it is Other-than-One – the set (One, not-One) turns out to be an open set, which can more accurately be understood as a *not-two* or no-two-as-One. The not-One thereby re-emerges in the not-two and seems to be preponderant over the One. To the best of our knowledge, this not-Oneness is final with regard to the effects of language. But as soon as we reach this conclusion, the effects of language are turned into a conclusive set, externally circumscribed as a bracketed not-One by the One/God that guarantees there is no God. This is, at bottom, a consciously deceiving God, whose metalinguistic status equates with the fact that, for us, there is irrevocably no meta-language. Using Lacan's jargon, the not-Oneness of the field of the effects of language, as well as of the world at large as effected by language, can therefore only be half-said.

Lacan's passionate opposition to weak atheism in both its humanist and allegedly anti-humanist guises is a constant in his work. Already in Seminar II, where his arguments on the topic are introduced as not yet forming a clear-cut hypothesis, he launches at the 'sentimental atheism' that is typical of modernity, scientism and their 'deluded anthropomorphism'.[193] Lacan senses the audience's unease with his references to God. He specifies that his conceiving of a *Deus ex machina*, a God extracted from the machine – that is, a God hypothesis as a structural symbolic effect of language – is the only possible alternative to surreptitiously extracting the machine from God.[194] In other words, we must avoid reifying the machinic *automaton* of symbolic intersubjectivity, and the phenomena of consciousness it gives rise to, as the product of some kind of 'cosmic' subjectivity or soul.[195] The 'idiocy of scientific atheism' does instead carry out precisely such a reification.[196] Its rejection of anything that could be considered as a recourse to God fully resorts to God. That is, it swiftly moves from the assumption that everything can be humanly explained to a notion of deified consciousness that, hijacking evolutionary theory, 'mak[es] consciousness the high-point of all phenomena'.[197] Mutatis mutandis, this also applies to the supposedly anti-humanist as anti-scientistic scenario that ends up presupposing the God who would consciously deceive us – and, we should add, a direct promulgation of the truth of incompleteness still remains a vertiginous claim to a universal explanation. Such is the twofold 'illusion' we have fallen prey to nowadays.[198] As Lacan concludes, a king continues to be a king, independently of all efforts to turn his absolute power into an apparently more constitutional one.[199]

In Seminar IX, Lacan discusses some contiguous issues by now openly framing them within an embryonic version of the God hypothesis. He turns his critical attention to the pseudo-atheistic formula 'God is dead. Everything is permitted'. Based on his previous point in Seminar II, we should read it not only morally but also epistemologically, as 'God is dead. Everything can be explained'. Lacan notices how the original version of the formula as articulated by Dostoyevsky followed an assertive logic – '*since* God is dead everything is permitted/can be explained' – while it is today strangely rendered in a hypothetical mode – '*if* God is dead, then everything is permitted/can be explained'.[200] This simple grammatical shift by itself indicates that self-professed 'free thinking' unconsciously abides by the God hypothesis.[201] Insofar as it is clear that everything is not permitted/cannot be explained, '*in the hypothetical formula* it is imposed as necessary that God exists'.[202] But, for Lacan, this is not a mere illusion to be cast aside. Although free thinkers do not assume it, they de facto demonstrate that the God hypothesis stands as a precondition at the heart of all 'valid thinking', that is, of securing at least the means of seizing the 'shadow of a certainty'.[203] Because of that, psychoanalysis is not best defined as an atheistic project.[204] Endorsing Dostoyevsky's assertive formula is not an option either, for it would eventually only translate into 'since God is dead nothing is permitted/can be explained' – which is paradigmatically witnessed by the deceiving God as the definitive outcome of the atheistic argument. With the historical death of the traditional God as a guarantor of absolute Oneness and the emergence of the truth of incompleteness, psychoanalytic thought must instead proceed in three stages of increasing importance. First, it is a matter of acknowledging that the dead God sustains the *opposition* not-God/God, or not-One/One. Second, we need to better grasp such an opposition as a ceaseless *alternation*, from not-One to One, to not-One, to One etcetera, whereby the terms of the opposition 'determine one another very closely'.[205] Third, we should not overlook the fact that although this mutual determination makes the terms '*rejoin* one another', as a not-two, the very rejoining also amounts to 'an *open* field', or no-two-as-One.[206]

Seminar XIV elaborates a similar anti-atheistic tirade from a slightly different and more complex angle. Here, Lacan returns to St Anselm and, through a close reading of Chapter II of *Proslogion*, shows that the latter's focus is not, as suggested by philosophy handbooks, on how the most perfect essence would necessarily imply existence but, quite the contrary, on highlighting the necessary symbolic existence of the 'function of the Other' – or God hypothesis – *independently* from demonstrating the existence of a perfect Being that would underlie this function.[207] According to Lacan, what is crucial in St Anselm's argument is therefore the refutation of the position of the atheist who, in saying 'there is no God', does not know what he is saying, is a 'fool', and actually evidences a structural 'impotence of thought'.[208] St Anselm very well knows that it is *not* sufficient for the *idea* of the most perfect Being to exist as an idea, for this Being to exist. Yet, as long as the foolish atheist considers that he himself has the right to have the idea of the most perfect Being, that the latter exists as the idea of a Being that, for him, does not exist, and as long as he cannot prove that this most perfect Being does not exist, should the latter per chance exist, the atheist would only demonstrate that his own idea of the most perfect Being is an *inadequate* one – since it would be separated from the existence of the most perfect Being, which is more perfect than the existence of the idea that does not imply this Being's existence.

More generally, in Seminar XIV, Lacan reiterates that, whatever we say, it is not only possible but also necessary to establish oneself in the function of the Other, or God hypothesis. This is what psychoanalysis should urgently re-examine in an age when, nominally, everyone is an atheist, nobody believes in the Other and anything that is based on *any* form of existence of this Other is seen as philosophically indefensible. Obviously, in so doing, psychoanalysis does not at all aim at 'remitting ourselves to the Other', religiously going back *into* it as a perfect Being.[209] On the contrary, it aims at 'perceiving the caducity of everything that is founded simply on this recourse to the Other'.[210] Furthermore, such an assumption of how the inexorable evocation of the Other as One only paves the way for the Other as not-One in turn shows that the caducity of *all* things we have thus derived cannot be maintained without again making recourse to the Other as One.

As made clear in the following lesson of Seminar XIV, the Other as not-One, which Lacan now writes as A barred, $\bar{A}$, should *not* be the endpoint of psychoanalysis, even after appreciating its dialectical relation with the Other as One. This would inevitably reinstate the latter by default. Instead, psychoanalysis should stress that the not-One *is* such, the 'open field' of Seminar IX, only inasmuch as the One is negated in and by language – that is, only to the extent that, to the best of our knowledge, 'we *posit* that there is no locus where the truth constituted by speech can be assured'.[211] In other words, and this is crucial, what matters is not $\bar{A}$, which especially in the world of dogmatic weak atheism does not do more than 'blowing on a shadow',[212] or kicking at an open door – whereby we eventually only re-enter Being as the unity of substance through the back door, one way or another (Christianity itself already goes full circle here). What matters instead is the bar, that is, the mark: 'What is meant by capital A marked by a bar? Well, then, I have just said it, I do not need to go looking for it any further. *It is marked* [. . .] we cannot conceptualise our experience unless we start from the fact that the Other is marked'.[213] And this barred A as marked cannot but be marked by a signifier, $S(\bar{A})$. As plainly expressed in Seminar XX, 'I marked [the locus of the Other] by redoubling it with the S that means signifier here, signifier of A insofar as the latter is barred: $S(\bar{A})$. I thereby added a dimension to A's locus, showing that qua locus it does not hold up, that there is a fault, hole, or loss therein'.[214]

However, for Lacan, this signifier itself conveys nothing more than a *hypothesis*. It does say, 'there is no such thing as the Other as One'. Yet this signified is not necessarily definitive; it does not unavoidably concern the 'foundation of things',[215] unless we are paradoxically content with placing ourselves here and now in the – after all comforting as totalizing – hands of the deceiving God. Only the latter would indeed irrefutably prove the hypothesis as 'there is no such thing as the Other as One because there is an ultimate (Other as) One that guarantees the Other as not-One'. Once more, the truth of incompleteness, which is not the *truth* about truth but the 'conditional of a truth' that is articulated and verified logically,[216] can only be half-said. Still, what we can fully assume, unlike weak atheists, is that, as soon as we say it, we conjure up the possibility of a diabolical meta-language.

3.2. God as real: The mystical God

We should now make a third and most significant clarification about the God hypothesis as the structural effect of language. The God hypothesis has two poles (One, not-One) also in the sense that, qua hypothesis, it displays two faces of *God*.[217] *Both* poles of the oscillation can be reified in the name of the divine. While the not-One emerges as the impossibility of proving the One and it indirectly promotes the One by means of its pseudo-atheistic absolutization, it may in fact even be taken straightforwardly as the locus of *the One*. This is the dimension Lacan refers to as God as *real*. We would negatively yet directly be granted access to God precisely through what does not work in the symbolic, its impasse. In Seminar XX and elsewhere, this is discussed in terms of mysticism. For mysticism, the phenomeno-logical not-One amounts to the ultimate ontological *One* tout-court. The mystic would thus be experiencing a *transcendence*-in-immanence.

According to Lacan, the God as real of mysticism thereby differs from the metaphysical God of (non-negative) theology and philosophy, although they share the *same* objective, that is, the Oneness of Being.[218] As he plainly puts it in Seminar XIV and in a contemporary 1967 conference, in spite of being 'less stupid than the philosophers' due to their focus on immanence, the mystics still assume 'a certain universal Being [. . .] *beyond* reality [that] manifests itself *in* reality'.[219] This, he adds, is equally incompatible with psychoanalysis. Mysticism's direct access to God through the phenomeno-logical not-One amounts to a quintessential fantasy – of the subject's absorption by the object – that ends up bordering on psychosis.[220] Reaching the metaphysical God as the perfect Being that would underlie the symbolic existence of the phenomeno-logical One requires instead a complex phantasmatic detour: first, isolating the One pole of the God hypothesis from its not-One pole; second, relegating the not-One pole to worldly abjection or at least to a lesser degree of being; and, third, solving their fabricated contradiction onto a transcendent otherworldly level that only retroactively accounts for and includes immanence through some sort of salvific history or ascent.

In Seminar XX, Lacan also famously discusses the metaphysical God in relation to man's subjectivity and enjoyment and the mystical God in relation to woman's subjectivity and enjoyment. While I have examined these intricate issues in detail elsewhere and cannot rehearse them here in a few sentences,[221] it is nonetheless crucial to introduce a disambiguation. Notwithstanding some misleading pronouncements ('it is insofar as her jouissance is radically Other that woman has more of a relationship to God'[222]), which could be interpreted in various ways, Lacan does *not* intend to equate feminine enjoyment with mysticism.[223] To put it bluntly, feminine enjoyment is *not* a transcendence-in-immanence, the not-One *as One*. It is instead the most radical phenomenological experience of the *not*-One the speaking animal can have – independently of its biological sex but subsequently to its symbolic sexuation as woman.

More to the point, feminine enjoyment amounts to an experience of *incompleteness as undecidability*, that is, the undecidability between the One and the not-One as mutually effected by language. This is to say that the not-One pole of the oscillation does not alone, so to speak, suffice for incompleteness – since it springs back to the One pole, or is itself reified as One – and that the not-One of incompleteness actually *results from* the very undecidability between the One and the not-One. In a sense, the *not*-One of incompleteness is the incompleteness *of* 'there is (only) something of the One', where, again, the One is not a mere semblance but a necessary symbolic existence that nonetheless necessarily entails the no-two-as-One.

Lacan's understanding of feminine enjoyment in terms of infinity should also be read in this context. What is immanently infinite as *not*-One is the undecidable *space between* the One and the not-One poles, or the 'impossibility of numbering',[224] which only woman inhabits as such, regardless of the oscillation but with reference to it as delimited by the two poles. On the contrary, the mystic is fascinated and captured by the not-One pole in the guise of the *'imagination of the hole'*, by the hole-as-One.[225]

In order to properly appreciate these arguments, we should not lose sight of the fact that feminine enjoyment at the same time both has to do with the infinite not-One of incompleteness (non-phallically) *and* is oriented towards the *One* (phallically yet differently from man).[226] The two elements of woman's enjoyment remain inextricable. She cannot preserve her non-phallic enjoyment without her own phallic enjoyment. Instead, it is the mystic who severs the not-One pole of the oscillation from the One pole only to *short-circuit* the former with the latter for the benefit of the latter. As Lacan has it incontrovertibly in Seminar XVI, 'the mystics seek in their own way the relation between enjoyment and the One'.[227] The kernel of mysticism thus lies in an *attempted isolation of feminine non-*

phallic enjoyment that, by levelling it down to the not-One pole of the oscillation, actually turns the not-One pole into a variation of man's phallic enjoyment.[228] At the risk of oversimplifying, mysticism is closer to man's enjoyment than woman's enjoyment, including when we are dealing with 'woman' mystics. Namely, mystics still echo man's desperate clinging to the One pole, whereby incompleteness is experienced merely as a *lack* to be compensated with a desire for the One Being supposedly underlying the symbolic existence of the One, that is, for the God of metaphysics.

More generally, against widespread interpretations coming from both religious and pseudo-atheistic quarters,[229] Lacan vehemently and repeatedly separates psychoanalysis from mysticism: 'Freud follows a thread, which is what we could call the most opposed to mystical confusion. Mystical confusion is what always threatens us'; 'The world we call mystic [. . .] might just as well be called mythic or indeed illusory'.[230]

3.3. God as real: Abraham and Moses

The issue of the two faces of God (the masculine metaphysical One and the mystical not-One *as One*) qua reifications of the two poles of the God hypothesis – of its continuous oscillation between the One and the not-One – is raised prior to Seminar XX. Lacan discusses it already in the first session of his interrupted Seminar on 'The Names of the Father' (1963) in a way I find more transparent, consistent and nuanced.

Here, what is first and foremost clear is that the mystical experience of the phenomeno-logical not-One, the abysmal real as what does not work in the symbolic order, fundamentally amounts to a 'headlong plunge into the enjoyment of *God*' as a supposed ontological One.[231] Appropriately, Lacan does not refer to woman's enjoyment in this context. We can find a similarly drastic distancing from mysticism in one of his last Seminars, Seminar XXV, where he compares it to nothing less than a 'flagellum', or 'scourge'.[232] Asking in a rhetorical fashion whether every man falls under the 'burden' of religion – which by extension suggests woman does not necessarily – Lacan also specifies that some people, women *and* men, 'fall into' the trap of mysticism.[233]

Secondly, at the other end of the religious spectrum with respect to the mystical God, 'The Names of the Father' locates the God of metaphysics. This is God as *Being*, or better, as One transcendent Being, the God that 'asserts his identity with Being'.[234] It is important to stress that such a God is, for Lacan, equally the 'God of philosophers' – of the canon of modern Western philosophy, if not already of Aristotle – *and* the God of mainstream Christian theologians. In this occurrence, Lacan speaks of Augustine's God ('I am the one who I am'),[235] but in other Seminars, he associates it with Descartes's, Newton's, Leibniz's, Voltaire's and even Einstein's God.

Thirdly and more crucially, in 'The Names of the Father', Lacan introduces two further *profiles* of the two faces of God, showing their dialectical reversibility and thus avoiding some of the ambiguities of Seminar XX. These are the God of *Abraham* (and, mutatis mutandis, of Pascal in a Christian context), at the not-One pole, and the God of *Moses*, at the One pole, which need to be distinguished but, by the same token, only evidence a continuity. The former is for Lacan a *real* God, the God of the meaningless request to sacrifice Isaac after the same God, in a most inconsistent way, granted Abraham an unexpected child and made a pact with him and his descendants. Lacan presents Abraham's God as 'encountered in the real' and, more to the point, phenomeno-logically experienced as anxiety.[236] Yet, unlike the experience of God as real of mysticism, which leads to an illusionary dissolution or *realization* of the symbolic in God's alleged enjoyment – the mystic 'feels it but knows nothing about it'[237] – Abraham's real God signals the *real*-of-the-symbolic, of the incessant oscillation between the not-One and the One, as the traumatic point of origin of the symbolic. What is at stake in Abraham's God is the emergence of the productive enigmaticity of *desire* (the desire of the Other, in both an objective and a subjective sense).[238] Encountering the meaningless real, Abraham does not plunge into God's alleged enjoyment, which would turn the not-One into the One. While remaining *religious* through faith in a transcendent One, he instead exposes himself to and sustains the full impact of a fundamentally unanswerable 'What does He want from me?', even if not especially after God sends an angel to rescue Isaac.[239]

According to Lacan, with Moses's God, the not-One as enigmatic desire is undoubtedly codified. Moses delimits divine desire by means of a set of specific commandments. His God is a God of the Law. But at the same time, this is a God of the 'singular equilibrium' between the Law and desire.[240] Such a 'co-conformity'[241] of the two means not only that God desires the Law but also that desire now ultimately amounts to the divine Law's own erratic desire – a point which Paul further unravels and complicates in Christianity. Most importantly, for Lacan, the thus-conceived God of Moses cannot be reduced to the God of philosophers. The latter is a One Being; the former is a *One of existence*. Unlike Augustine's God ('I am the one who I am'), the God of the Burning Bush says to Moses, '"I am the Existent," and not Being'.[242] This is a subtle yet crucial distinction, given what we have discussed so far.

In more Lacanian jargon, Moses's God is anchored to the One pole of the oscillation of the God hypothesis, that of 'there is something of the One', but its symbolic existence does not imply an underlying imaginary essence or unity of substance (hence, for instance, the centrality of the prohibition of idolatry). In other words, as Lacan insists in 'The Names of the Father', Moses's God as symbolic existence corresponds to nothing other than a *name*: 'The name of this God is but *The Name*'.[243] Or better, we could add, there is no other meaning to be granted to the God who introduces himself as '"I am the Existent," and not

Being' – that is, 'I am not "I am the one who I am"' – than that of being the Name 'I exist'.

Here, on the one hand, we should not lose sight of the fact that, of course, Moses's God himself remains a *religious* One. Bluntly put, he is indeed *anchored* to the One pole of the oscillation, that is, somehow detached from the not-One pole of Abraham's initial encounter with the meaningless real – out of which he was nonetheless developed and with which he forms a structural continuum. Although uncoupled from a substantial imaginary essence (the God Seminar XV refers to as 'the old man with a beard'[244]), symbolic existence may in turn be reified into a transcendence. In a sense, Moses's God conclusively *is* a non-hypothetical symbolic existence. But, on the other hand, Yahweh still does *not* know what he wants. To use a well-known expression from Seminar XVII, the only *attribute* of his being is a 'ferocious ignorance',[245] notwithstanding the establishment of a Law that in fact resolves itself into the Law's own erratic desire. At bottom, 'Yahweh's adjurations to his people [. . .] contradict one another from one line to the next'.[246]

In spite of its religious transcendent reification, the God of Moses is in this way seminal for Lacan because he hints at the dimension of the *One as real*, of the real-of-the-*symbolic*. The real cannot be confined to the not-One pole of the oscillation of the God hypothesis for it conditions the oscillation as such, or structure. On close inspection, the symbolic One exists only as real since it remains 'all alone'.[247] More precisely, the contingent happening of the necessity of the symbolic existence of the One ('there is something of the One') is given exclusively along with the *not*-One as a point of impossibility. Or also, the One happens 'all alone' in that it structurally lacks another One and thus never accesses the two, the two-as-One. While, fundamentally, 'there exists only the One', namely, the One of 'there is something of the One' as all alone, this at the same time means that the One 'becomes something that undoes itself'.[248] It happens in an instant only to vanish. And, in *this* way, 'there is something of the One' – the necessity of the symbolic existence of the One – indicates that which exists by *not* being One *Being*.[249]

3.4. Dio-logy

The One-as-real facet of the God hypothesis has not yet sufficiently been appreciated by commentators. In light of the above considerations, we should in passing revisit and complement some of the however incisive arguments François Balmès puts forward regarding Lacan's treatment of the divine.

Balmès's greatest general merit is having drawn attention to the fact that a simplistically atheistic stance for which 'there is no God' is, based on textual evidence, totally incompatible with Lacanian psychoanalysis.[250] More in particular, I completely agree with his claim that, for Lacan, the question of atheism 'remains methodical', namely, 'the place of God is necessary in it' and, at best, we can 'do without [this place] only on condition of using it'.[251] Better said, psychoanalysis singles out different 'points of *structure* that are necessarily given in everyone's experience, whether one believes one believes or one believes one does not believe, which correspond to what [religious] tradition has called God'.[252] As Lacan himself succinctly puts it in Seminar XX, 'the symbolic' – or even language tout-court as not limited to the symbolic – 'is the basis of what was made into God'.[253]

Precisely insofar as I share this differentiated structural approach, there are two closely related issues where I think Balmès's investigations partly fall short. To begin with, Balmès fails to distinguish the God of Moses – the real of the *symbolic*; the *One* as real – from the God of Abraham – the *real* of the symbolic; the *not-One* as real. He conflates the former with the latter as both indicating a 'God of faith' to be opposed to the 'God of reason' of (Christian) philosophers and theologians.[254] But, as seen, a distinction between the God of Abraham from the God of Moses – as the individuation of the two poles of a continuum – is precisely one of the main arguments Lacan puts forward in 'The Names of the Father'. He keeps on insisting for pages that Moses's Hashem cannot be reduced to Abraham's El Shaddai, and vice versa.[255] The first is a powerful yet ferociously ignorant *Master*, whose moronic name indeed means 'The Name'.[256] The second is not the Almighty with which he is often misleadingly translated, Lacan specifies,[257] since he instead signals the very place of an anxiety-inducing *break* in what appeared to be the promise of an alliance with his people.

Although Balmès is right in saying that the God of Moses corresponds to 'the symbolic inasmuch as it is determined by a flaw, a central hole',[258] the emphasis here should definitely be put on the fact that this is the *symbolic's* flaw and central hole, without which there would be no symbolic *order*. What is fundamentally at stake with the God of Moses as understood by Lacan is not so much an 'ineffable name' (leading to a mystical Kabbalah)[259] as, again, The Name that in naming only itself does not actually name anything, the existence of the One that is not One Being and the persistence of a desire continuously undetermined by its own determination. On the other hand, Abraham's God marks the initial irruption of such an enigmatic desire – which, with Moses, will have retrospectively been the 'desire *of a God*'[260] – that is, the cut that interrupts the cohesive myth of unspeakable divine enjoyment, the latter's sheer indetermination qua as such fully *determined*. Through the aborted request to sacrifice Isaac, 'we see the sharp divide', the literal 'knife-edge [*le tranchant du couteau*] between God's jouissance and what, in this tradition, is presented as His desire'.[261]

The distinctiveness of Moses's God features even more prominently in Lacan's 1967 article 'La méprise du sujet supposé savoir', which Jacques-Alain Miller convincingly reads as a sort of continuation of 'The Names of the Father'.[262] Here, Lacan restates the opposition, derived from Pascal, between the God of philosophers and the God of Abraham, Isaac, and Jacob. However, not only does he, like in all the other instances in which the phrase 'God of Abraham, Isaac, and Jacob' recurs in his work, refrain from adding Moses to this list, but he also surprisingly associate Moses with James Joyce. Moses would be the initiator of a 'dio-logy',[263] of a discourse on the One as real and as not aiming at Being, that in spite of its religious reification paves the way for what in his late Seminar on Joyce Lacan will call a 'sound logic'.[264] In a nutshell, the latter amounts to a demystification of the 'theo-logy' of philosophers, where the attempt at securing Being inevitably turns the One into an imaginary subject-supposed-to-know.[265] For Lacan, theo-logy underlies every allegedly non-theological *theorein* or, we may say, extracts ideo-logy from dio-logy. As Miller puts it, theoretical knowledge is thus always related to 'a subject who would already know it' and, in this sense, 'there is no theory that is atheistic'.[266]

It is fair to admit that Lacan never expands on 'dio-logy'.[267] It is also important to stress once more that, obviously, the God of Abraham, Isaac and Jacob, on the one hand, and that of Moses, on the other, are given as the two reversable extremities of one and the same structural oscillation – which is religiously reified, yet far more visible as an oscillation than in the God of philosophers and of mysticism. But, still, their distinction should be maintained if we wish, as Balmès does, to highlight the different 'points of structure' that Judeo-Christianity made into God. In line with my considerations, in Seminar XVII, returning to Freud's *Moses and Monotheism* and adopting a more historical perspective, Lacan himself goes as far as suspecting that monotheism only emerged with *Moses*, initially in the guise of the One as real, and was retrospectively applied to the not-One as real of the Abrahamic threshold between divine enjoyment and divine desire.[268]

Bearing in mind all this, the second and closely connected problem with Balmès's account is the way in which he seems to underestimate the dialectical ramifications of the division between the (Judaic) God of *faith* and the (Christian) God of *reason*. Most likely, this is also due to Lacan's own hesitations and at times incongruous statements on the matter. To put it simply, it should be apparent by now that the God of reason requires faith just as the God of faith exposes the kernel of reason. On the one hand, in order to move from the One that exists as all alone to the One-All-Being, the 'theo-logy' of philosophers depends on an 'act of faith' in the subject-supposed-to-know.[269] Moreover, with and after Descartes, this faith becomes more specifically a, however repressed, 'scientific' faith in the fact that the God of reason, the subject-supposed-to-know, does not deceive us. On the other hand, faith in reason cannot but go together with reason in faith. That is, the backbone of our phenomeno-logical structure, or, if you wish, of the species-specific transcendental of the speaking and thinking animal, basically consists of the One as all alone tackled by Moses's 'dio-logy' – albeit religiously. As discussed, Lacan posits that structure as real corresponds to the oscillation between the One and the not-One (or 'One missing'), which prevents us from isolating the former from the latter and can better be rendered as the 'bifidity of the One'.[270] The God of Moses, whose only attribute is his ferocious ignorance, is a bifid God.

Another way of summing this up would be to say that dio-logists religiously believe only in the *formal* (non-imaginary) aspect of the One, as a de-essentialized existence. This makes them lay the foundations for a logical-mathematical approach to the One. But, at the same time, this also establishes them as the most coherent, and thus inflexible, *mono*-theists. Or also, dio-logists religiously believe in the formal aspect of *belief* that weak atheists wrongly do not believe they believe in. Dio-logy reifies the very fact that our linguistically transcendental condition cannot but create the One.

4. Polytheism, monotheism and science

4.1. Polytheism and monotheism: From the real to the symbolic

Throughout his work, Lacan opposes any neat division of a God of reason from a God of faith. In fact, his main assumption in these matters is that there has been no historical progress of reason, and specifically no increasing rationalization of religion – whether one favours it, like Freud, or decries it, like Pascal. However, in some instances, Lacan himself seems to encourage the idea of such a progress. This tension is most evident with regard to the two conflicting genealogical narratives he puts forward to explain the passage from polytheism to Judeo-Christian monotheism. According to the first, which I claim should be rejected as ingenuously teleological and thus in conflict with Lacan's own premises, monotheism *symbolizes the real* of polytheism. As for the second narrative – far more dialectically complex and aligned with what I have argued so far – monotheism does instead disrupt the *imaginary* of polytheism by putting at centre stage the *real of the symbolic*. Yet, at the same time, through Christianity, monotheism both radically imaginarizes the real of the symbolic and nonetheless enhances the latter's anti-imaginary function.[271]

Let us consider this tension in more detail, which in my opinion cannot be solved solely via a reference to Lacan's teachings – although it must be said that he seems to be leaving the first account aside after the early 1960s. Especially in Seminars VII, VIII and IX, Lacan repeatedly states that the gods of paganism are *real*: they 'quite certainly belong to the real', 'are found in the real', 'are an element of the real', 'were real and real alone'.[272] He further understands them as a 'numen', namely, a 'real shining and appearance'[273] that not only encompasses the connotations traditionally ascribed to it by the likes of Lucretius – confusion, panic, disorder, anarchy[274] – but also displays the distinctive mark of the Lacanian real, namely, it is an *'unthinkable'*,[275] a point of logical impossibility. In addition to that, such evental dimension of the gods as real would be generalized in the ancient world: it 'rises up at every step, at the corner of every road'; it 'proliferates and intervenes everywhere in human experience'.[276]

In this context, Lacan diametrically opposes monotheism as symbolic to the real of polytheism, substantiating his claims with reference to both Freud's and Hegel's take on the history of religions. Discussing *Moses and Monotheism*, in Seminar VII, he approvingly points out that, for Freud, 'there is no doubt that [the monotheistic message] contains an incontestable weight of *superior* value over any other' and that this temporal hierarchy and the pursuit of the monotheistic 'goal' are compatible with Freud's atheism.[277] The God of Moses would introduce a *'rationalist* cause' that 'contrasts greatly' with the 'pandemonium of gods'.[278] More specifically, the God of Moses should be conceived of as *delimiting* the pervasive appearance of the real in polytheism by means of the Law. Here, the *Name* of the Father, his existence without essence, is not addressed by Lacan as a ferociously ignorant God but, quite the contrary, as the God of the ten commandments, which, whether or not we obey them, 'in their indestructible character [. . .] prove to be the very laws of speech', 'the condition of all social life' and, in short, 'the *effective* law'.[279] With Judaism, the real of the polytheistic gods would thus only residually persist through God's ignorance and jealousy in a 'hidden' and, so to speak, linguistically-legalistically sublated form.[280] The real would safely be kept 'at a certain distance'. This would be epitomized by the fact that the assembled Jews cannot come near to the burning bush (which Lacan refers to as 'Moses's Thing').[281]

Christianity would then successfully reinforce, if not conclude, such a process of rationalization of the divine real, whereby, as moderns, 'we no longer have anything more to do with [the gods]' or, at least, they become 'outdated, obsolete'.[282] Of course, what Lacan has in mind here is the direct and explicit identification of Christ with the *Word* or Logos, through which the real would be contained and sublated symbolically. More precisely, first, the pagan man encountered multiple revelations in the real of a disorder that punctuated his everyday life, where what was revealed was fundamentally an unthinkable. Second, Judaism only delimited these real revelations *at a distance* (also in the sense that it did not rule out the existence of gods other than Yahweh outside of Canaan[283]). Third, these real revelations are unified in Christianity by subsuming them *under* the Revelation of the Logos and its providential history, 'at the level of the signifying articulation'.[284] According to this very Freudian Lacan, even the most mysterious aspect of such a unification, the fact that the Christian God is one and yet trine, reflects nothing other than 'the most purely symbolic' relationship of kinship, that between father and son, with love as the third mediating term.[285]

Because of this destruction of the gods, Lacan concludes that Hegel is right in recovering a certain *atheistic* message in Christianity. Optimistically, he even adds that we should locate the Christian message 'at the midpoint [. . .] between theogony and atheism'.[286] We are thus left to infer that, in agreement with the understanding of the end of the psychoanalytic treatment proposed in the early Seminars, full-fledged atheism would in this context simply coincide with so-called full speech. Namely, it would amount to the subject's symbolic fulfilment, or dis-alienation, of his real desire once he recognizes his own positioning in the signifying articulation as externally guaranteed, and therefore completed, by the – psychoanalytic and supposedly irreligious – Name-of-the-Father.

4.2. Polytheism and monotheism: From the imaginary to the real-of-the-symbolic, and back

In striking contrast with this, the second account Lacan offers of the passage from polytheism to monotheism and its development delineates a far-from-linear trajectory. This trajectory does not teleologically culminate in a, frankly quite naïve, rational achievement of atheism.

To begin with, throughout his teachings, Lacan also often firmly associates the pagan gods with a neat prevalence of the order of the *imaginary*. As early as Seminar II, he speaks in their regard of a 'very different structuration of human experience' primarily characterized by a '*concord and harmony between humankind and the world*'.[287] As late as Seminar XX, he insists on the same motif using a more philosophical jargon: the 'fantasising of antiquity', its mythology, fabricated shovelfuls of gods as 'rather *consistent* representations of the Other'.[288] Polytheism would therefore persuasively manage to reduce the Other as structurally not-One to the Other as another One. In a mythical way, the One is not yet all alone. Predictably, according to Lacan, such a harmonic or consistent – but phantasmatic – representation relies at bottom on an effective cultural implementation of the *semblance* of a sexual relationship that blocks the real of its impossibility as the ineliminable invariant of the species that happens to speak. In short, this is the semblance of a 'state' where 'each and every guy correctly fucks his "one gal"'.[289] By means of a concerted practice of sexual rites and festivals, which unite the community with divine enjoyment, polytheism would thus more precisely amount to a *symbolic imaginarization of the real*, that is, the blatant *opposite* of the unthinkable 'real appearances' Lacan elsewhere deems to be its kernel.

We could attempt to reconcile these two contrasting understandings of polytheism (bluntly put, as *either* real *or* imaginary) by arguing that the frequent 'real appearances' of the divine – the diffuse '*presence* of the gods in human affairs' as opposed to a transcendent and thereby *hidden* divine Providence[290] – used to be immediately and, again, effectively imaginarized in an *immanent* manner. Lacan seems to be pointing in this direction when he suggests, in passing, that 'the numinous rises up at every step but, *conversely*, I would say that *every step* of the numinous *leaves a trace*'.[291] That is to say, 'it *did not take much* for a new temple to be erected, for a new religion to be established'.[292] So, eventually, instead of being a bearer of disorder, 'the numen *weaves* human experience *together*'.[293] Lacan's later claim that in polytheism there is 'a relationship that blends supernatural agencies in with nature itself' could be interpreted along the same lines.[294] But if the synthetic reading I am now proposing conveyed Lacan's final stance on the matter, then his pairing of polytheism with the real as *un*thinkable would remain, at least terminologically, unwarranted and misleading.

In any case, what is most evident in the second account of the emergence of monotheism provided by Lacan is that its originality lies in a break with and vocal denunciation of pagan 'prostitution'.[295] The real made palpable by Judaic religion coincides with the real of 'There is no sexual relationship'[296] as the structural point of impasse of the symbolic(-imaginary) order. Yahweh is a One-all-alone, and thus real, precisely in the sense that he in vain attempts to fill in the gap of a missing Goddess by means of an alliance with his people,[297] who keep on betraying him yet not without returning to him. With the same move, their participation in divine enjoyment gives way to God's inscrutable desire – the Law's own desire – whose jealous and ferocious ignorance indeed revolves around his loss of a mythical sexual knowledge.[298]

As already considered, Lacan thinks that Christianity perpetuates the Jewish highlighting of the real of the symbolic. This is certainly the case with regard to the fact that its 'filthy truth' of earthly abjection itself concerns the absence of the sexual relationship and targets the semblance of a satisfying enjoyment – the Ancients' jouissance which Paul colourfully scorned as *porneia*.[299] Yet, more importantly, Christianity goes further and radicalizes the visibility of the incompleteness of the symbolic and the ensuing 'negation of [imaginary] harmony'[300] by presenting us with the *crucified* Christ, who is not only foolishness to the Greeks but also a *skandalon* to the Jews. The Christian God is such only by making himself being killed. The One as real is such only by turning itself into the not-One as real. Or also, the real One is here all alone not just because it is solely qualified by its ferocious ignorance but because this ignorance duly corresponds to its own Passion. Christ's inconsolable loneliness reaches an extreme level whereby he even forsakes himself on the cross. Against those instances in which Lacan sees Christianity in terms of a facile symbolic rationalization and draining of the real, here the Word/Logos patently reveals itself as fundamentally il-logical in its very functionality.

But, concomitantly, Christianity also carries out an unheard-of imaginarization of the il-logicality of the Word. Insofar as the death of the Word as embodied in a man-god is followed by his resurrection, and the promise of an otherworldly eternal life for all those who believe in him, the Christian Logos advances a 'precise *solution* to the mystery of the relations between man and speech'[301] – that is, to the real of the symbolic. For Lacan, the Christian return to the imaginary should not only be understood in terms of its *personalization* of God, which against the Jewish prohibition lends itself to idolatry and becomes particularly evident in Catholic art and the cult of saints. Nor should it be limited to the fact that such a – corporeal, anthropomorphic – personalization goes together with the 'imaginary idea of the whole',[302] of a now transcendent One-All-Being, which as transcendent *universalizes*, and thus enhances, the pagan mirage of spherical harmony (of an immanently 'good form of satisfaction'[303]). According to Lacan, the Christian return to and amplification of the imaginary even directly denies the absence of the sexual relationship it otherwise *mono*-theistically promotes. That is to say, it disavows the ground zero of the truth of incompleteness for which 'the signifier is not made for the sexual relationship'.[304] Indeed, the resurrected Logos becomes essentially a body in incorporated communion with 'Christ's wife, the Church as it is called'.[305] The Church is thus 'so well *grounded* in the gap peculiar to the sexuality of speaking beings' that, by means of a strict regimentation of sexual life symbolically consonant to this scenario, it will 'carry the species [. . .] right up to the end of time' and conclusive Salvation.[306]

On close inspection, the Christian relapse into imaginary polytheism has therefore primarily to do with the re-emergence of what, in a brilliant presentation delivered during Seminar XX, Récanati refers to as the 'two gods' (male and female) and the conversion of this re-emergence into what Lacan prefers to call the 'two God'.[307] Such a contradiction in terms well conveys the imaginary synthesis attempted by Christianity notwithstanding its uncovering of the real of the symbolic – the absence of the sexual relationship. As should already be clear, Lacan does not regard poly-theism as fundamentally concerning *many* gods but as an immanent *pan-theistic bi-theism*. Polytheism is the religion of the semblance of the *two*-as-one or, better, of the One-and-the-Other-as-One as a harmonious one-*all*. Christianity itself ends up with a One-All, but it requires *transcendence* to posit it. In other words, the Other as not-One of the structural oscillation One/not-One can be sublated into One only by resorting to an ulterior and thereby omni-*comprehensive* level, that of the One-All-*Being*. Or also, unlike in pantheism, in Christianity, the not-One can at no point be taken as a *different/ second* God. More concretely, this means that the semblance of the sexual relationship orchestrated by the Church is symbolically *less* effective than that installed by polytheism. That is the case since it depends on the fulfilment of a providential History that will eventually redeem this abject world – and thus immanentize transcendence. In this sense, as evidenced by the Reformation (Lacan singles out Luther's saying that we are 'waste matter which falls into the world from the devil's anus'[308]), Christianity remains *hic et nunc* a religion of real earthly abjection, all the more it insists on a, in turn eventually pan-theistic, One-All-Being to come.

It is in terms of this *ambivalent* movement of 'deny[ing] the gods', instead of in those of an increasingly atheistic rationalization of religion, that we should read Lacan's claim that Christianity and Western philosophy follow a parallel path, if not that they should be merged into a single theology-philosophy ('there is not but one philosophy, which is always theological').[309] Put simply, with its juxtaposition of hyperbolic doubt and *cogito ergo sum* (Descartes), infinitesimal and *clavis universalis* (Leibniz), inaccessible noumena and categorical imperative (Kant), contradiction and absolute knowledge (Hegel), will to power and Life (Nietzsche), modern philosophical ontology itself remains Christian, whether professedly so or not. This is the case in the specific sense that, in spite of its variations, it persists in giving rise to a more or less *closed* dialectic of the *trou*/hole and the *Tout*/Whole,[310] of how the real of the symbolic is imaginarily subsumed under a *Being* supposed to know (the philosopher's own system) that nonetheless does *not* fully manage to *enclose* the hole.[311] In short, modern philosophical ontology invariably falls back into a *Weltanschauung*, literally, a vision of the world as supposedly seen from *outside* it. A passage from Seminar XX, whose richness would necessitate a book of its own to be meticulously unfolded, is very clear on this point:

> For quite some time it seemed natural for a world to be constituted whose correlate, *beyond* it, was *being itself*, being taken as eternal. This world conceived of as the *whole*, with what this word implies by way of limitation, regardless of the openness we grant it, remains a conception [. . .] a view, gaze or *imaginary* hold. And from that results the following, which remains strange, that some-one – a part of this world – is at the outset assumed to be able to take *cognizance* of it. [. . .] Therein has always lain the *impasse*, the vacillation resulting from the cosmology that consists in the belief in a world.[312]

4.3. Of no-things and Christian science

According to Lacan, modern and contemporary *science* would only intensify, albeit in a greatly effective and tangible manner, this theological-philosophical see-saw of the W-hole and bring it to its *pseudo*-atheistic completion.

With regard to the hole, syncretically drawing from Koyré's and Kojève's work on the scientific revolution,[313] Lacan deems the substitution of the infinite universe for the closed world of ancient *episteme* to be in continuity with the Christian characterization of this world as abject, as no uni-verse, as well as with the corporeal fragmentation of Christ on the cross. With Copernicus, Galileo and Newton, the epistemological break of monotheism theologically initiated by the Judaic One as real – the ignorant God – and consolidated by the Christian

(One as real *as*) not-One as real – the *dead* ignorant God – is directly applied to the investigation and manipulation of *physical* reality. As discussed, Lacan deems that, following the collapse of the geocentric hypothesis, modern science operates on the basic assumption of the non-agreement between human intuition and sense-perception, on the one hand, and nature, on the other. This is its far-reaching novelty. To the extent that pre-modern – late-classical and medieval – Judeo-Christian science is still dependent on the co-naturalness of nature and the unified body of the animal that happens to speak it is still fundamentally pagan.

Lacan repeatedly returns to and refines his understanding of such a real break of modern science, its uncovering of 'a world in decomposition, *thanks [to] God*',[314] and especially of what has been made of it. Science as we have it now, present in our world, far surpasses the assumption that the idea of knowledge has always implied, namely, the 'imagined ideal unification' of knowledge.[315] Indeed, science does *not* promote a more comprehensive knowledge of the world but introduces in it 'things that did not in any way exist at the level of our perception'.[316] Science thereby manifestly problematizes the allegedly empiricist principle according to which 'nothing is in the intellect that was not earlier in the senses'.[317] More specifically, we could say that modern science unbinds *sensus* from sense perception – from which follows the etymological polyvalence if not antitheticality of this primary word for us. *Sensus* is reduced by mathematized science to what can be counted ('taking what is our *sensus* at the level of the ear or eye, for example, leads to counting vibrations'[318]). The ensuing play of numbers, *sensus* in the sense of symbolic *meaning*, produces novel effects that have nothing to do with our sense perception ('the world that is assumed to have always been ours is now populated [. . .] without your having the slightest suspicion of it, by a considerable and interesting number of what are called waves'[319]).

Lacan's overall argument is here particularly bold. It is not only the case that the agelong monotheistic engagement with the real of the symbolic – as opposed to its pagan imaginarily successful containment – is radicalized through the scientific acknowledgement of the non-agreement between human sense perception and nature. It is also the case that science's effectiveness in symbolically/mathematically manipulating this physical real gives rise to a vertiginous challenge to the Christian *ontological compensation* for the *immundus* Christianity nonetheless solicited. That is to say, Being as an underlying and all-inclusive unity of substance is increasingly countered by a pullulating swarm of 'in-substances'.[320] Seminar XVII singles out Hertz waves, but this paradoxically intuitive point could today be rendered through even more perspicuous examples from quantum mechanics, astrophysics, not to mention the more mundane field of information technologies.[321] Lacan salutes the emergence of these 'no-things' (*achoses*).[322] He claims that it is on their basis that we can finally – atheistically – think materialism in a completely different sense, that is, relinquish the 'ideality of matter' vulgar materialism clings to.[323] He also insists on how this materialism focused on the, so to speak, immaterially material effects generated by science rests on an appreciation of the fact that this very effectiveness necessitates repeated encounters with the real. What *sustains* science is, in short, the creative displacement of the meaningless real emerging from the non-co-naturalness of human sense perception into symbolic *sensus* or meaning itself. In other words, the mathematical formalization through which science operates effectively deals with the real only insofar as it always returns to an impossibility, whereby 'in every formalized field of truth there are truths that one cannot demonstrate'.[324] Or also, scientific laws as *scientific* cannot but continuously be juxtaposed in a at bottom non-cumulative manner. Moreover, there are good reasons to assume that each of them changes over time.[325]

But, concomitantly and with the same movement, science also veils the epistemological *and* ontological truth of incompleteness. The more science's effectiveness depends on an unstoppable uncovering of in-substances, the more it recovers (in both senses of the verb) this space, the space of *para-ousia*,[326] through and with the semblance of new *ousia*. That is to say, while science constructs itself 'out of something of which there was nothing beforehand' – since this in-substantial something only becomes some-thing symbolically and takes form with reference to mathematical formalization – it also 'forgets this very effect'.[327] Simply put, we could suggest that the symbolic operations of real science are always accompanied by the imaginarization of what they operate on.[328] The truth of incompleteness is thus invariably reduced to what Lacan aptly calls the 'aletho-*sphere*'.[329] The no-things *qua* counted as some-things (no-things that could not be such without the count) are being put to the service of the One-Thing.

In the wake of my reading of Lacan's considerations on Christianity's theological relapse into the imaginary, I think this process can itself be better understood in three overlapping ways. First, and most visibly, science gives rise to an unprecedented level of idolatry. Thanks to its 'curious' – that is, far from predestined or at least unsurpassable – 'copulation' with capitalism, and commodity-fetishism in particular, scientific technology inundates the field of *aletheia* with myriads of so-called 'gadgets'.[330] For the time being, this has been the most sensational outcome of the enormous apparatus of science and its accessing the real by means of numbers and letters.[331] While it is doubtless the case that '[we] are now, infinitely more than [we] think, [these] instruments' subjects', for they are turning into 'the elements of [our] existence'[332] – Lacan's privileged examples, in the 1970s, remain the automobile, the television and rockets sent to the moon as watched on television, but the list could easily be expanded and updated – it remains to be established whether in the future these gadgets will even manage to 'truly animate us'[333] – namely, engulf us into a plan of artificial immanence similar to that of paganism.

More to the point, gadgets function like idols precisely insofar as they occupy the place 'of what we lack in the relationship of knowledge'.[334] They cork the very hole made apparent by science's acknowledgement of the non-agreement between human sense perception and the world, from which science contradictorily derives its effectiveness. In so doing, they provide us with ersatz counterparts. Not coincidentally, they also tend to culminate in products that, recuperating in a new way the basic animistic assumption for which the world thinks like we do, are increasingly in our idealized image and likeness – whether in a strictly anthropomorphic sense (humanoid robots) or not (generic artificial intelligence).[335]

Second, according to Lacan, science's own relaunching of the epistemic fantasy of imaginary completion, fuelled by the fabrication of counterfeit *ousia* as ersatz counterparts, cannot but more widely rest on the domain of sexuality. Fetishized gadgets voraciously gobble up our desire with the promise of surplus, if not absolute, enjoyment (nowadays, paradigmatically, in the guise of sex-bots, virtual sex, designer babies, not to mention the seeming availability of equally endless and disposable sexual identities[336]). But the fact that, for instance, we come to treat 'an automobile like a fake wife'[337] more generally indicates how the discourse of science, entwined with that of capitalism, restores and serially multiplies the semblance of the sexual relationship. In this way science loses the hallmark of what characterizes its break with previous kinds of knowledge, namely, its departure from the latter's dependence on the myth of the complementarity between the sexes (be it that of the Western matter and form couple or that of the Eastern Yin and Yang pair), which is itself ultimately responsible for any harmonic vision of the world as a Whole.[338] The technological transformation of in-substances into merchandise, pivoting on a 'propaganda [of] happiness' and an ensuing 'sexomania', only keeps on prolonging and boosting the ridiculous masterly attempt at in-forming the not-Oneness of woman.[339]

Last but not least, science remains an imaginary discourse even in that it *explicitly* attempts to put forward a harmonic vision of the world as a Whole. Or better, its serial production of – sexualized – gadgets clearly runs parallel to a burgeoning series of *Weltanschauungen*. Despite their apparent incompatibility and consequent ephemerality, each *Weltanschauung* involves an underlying claim to be final, or at least one step closer to finalization, preferably in the guise of a synthesis of pre-existing visions (for instance, string theory or quantum gravity should accommodate the competing findings of relativity theory and quantum mechanics). In short, as Jean-Claude Milner has convincingly argued, *modern* science still aims at instituting itself as an *ideal*, that is, *pre*-modern science.[340] The juxtaposition of scientific laws innovatively obtained through a mathematical formalization that accesses the real turns into their accumulation as subservient to a renewed religious totalization. In Seminar XVII, Lacan understands such a regressively fideistic movement of modern science in terms of its loss of 'hesitation', or doubt.[341] On the one hand, we would be wrong to regard science as a mere theo-philosophical concoction, because of its continuous and ever more frequent exposures to the real – it keeps on bumping into new (no-)things within the same totalizing process with which it betrays itself. But, on the other, given such self-betrayal, it is more than legitimate to ask whether physics as we know it today actually amounts to a supreme *meta*physics.[342]

Especially but not exclusively in his very last Seminars and related writings, Lacan adopts an even harsher stance. It is not simply the case that, as in 'The Triumph of Religion', modern science will be reabsorbed by religion. Modern science is and has always been as such religious, and specifically (Judeo-)Christian. We are dealing with a 'theology of science'.[343] Its dialectic between the real and the imaginary is and has always been unbalanced towards the imaginary, that is, devoted to the production of an all-encompassing meaning externally guaranteed by a subject-supposed-to-know, a 'subject supposed *by* knowledge', or God.[344] Lacan often conveys this denunciation by means of extremely disparaging comments: 'Galileo worked for the Pope'; Newton's law of gravitation finds its truth in his apocalyptic book on the prophet Daniel; Einstein's relativity theory is firmly anchored to the Biblical 'Let there be light!'.[345] Overall, science amounts to a *Dieu-lire*, a delirious reading-God and reading-of-God.[346]

4.4. The negative Weltanschauung

The crucial albeit only sketched and highly speculative point that powerfully emerges in this context is that science also currently endeavours to occlude its increasing encounters with the real through a, so to speak, *negative Weltanschauung*. In other words, we would be witnessing a tendency to search for a new kind of synthesis that *totalizes the real* as an acausal and chaotic universe – a notion with which we can nowadays associate many more scientific theories than in Lacan's times. At stake in science's religious relapse is neither simply what Žižek rightly describes as a vestigial Ptolemization, where new theses are somehow forcedly adjusted to a previous framework thanks to spurious complications, nor just an accelerated Copernicization, in which novel paradigms rapidly replace one another without renouncing their profession of – mutually exclusive – exhaustiveness, nor even solely, in the fashion of contemporary physicists such as Carlo Rovelli, a merging of clashing paradigms into an expanded 'unitary field'.[347] Beyond this, for Lacan, science is heading in the direction of what we could call the synthesis of 'there is no synthesis', or the absolutization of the real hole as *itself* a definitive Whole.

In a little-known, short, yet incredibly rich 1975 article, 'Des religions et du réel', he argues that even in this radical configuration, which grasps and tries to come to terms with the deadlock of any positive *Weltanschauung*, science further confirms its inability to do without an 'encompassing' or 'circular' horizon posited in relation to the body of the speaking animal that inhabits the real.[348] Science thus still 'introduces the One into the real'.[349] It turns it into a paradoxical uni-verse. What science should instead seriously consider is the hypothesis that the 'real is not everything'[350] or, better, that the *real not-all is itself not necessarily all there is – although it might well be*.[351] This move would presuppose not only relinquishing every specific constant or 'constancy', such as energy or matter, which is in fact invariably reintroduced in an inverted 'real' form (dark energy, anti-matter and so on), but also and especially focusing exclusively on local occurrences of 'consistency' and related inconsistency, like set theoretical mathematics already does.[352]

Developing on Lacan's concise and cryptic hints, we could suggest that a negative *Weltanschauung*, especially a truly negative one not limited to appending gloomy prefixes to previous positive visions, proves to be much more *solid* than a positive *Weltanschauung*. Simply put, it potentially even allows for a kind of totalization – unnoticed or at least underestimated by Lacan – that instead of operating by means of accumulation does postulate the Whole through the very juxtaposition of local, and mutually inconsistent, consistencies. In brief, we can already envision a scientific *Weltanschauung* of every possible incompossible present and future *Weltanschauungen* (the idea of a so-called multiverse made of parallel universes points that way and is indeed no longer confined to the realm of science-fiction). By absolutizing the field of inconsistencies, such a chaosmos would seemingly also provide us with a way out of what Lacan sees as the logical impasse of the Christian theo-philosophical compensation for the abjection of this world, namely, the idea of a Being that is contradictorily a part of this abjection only by taking providential/salvific cognisance of it as a whole from the outside. *But*, as should now be evident, in opposition to Christianity's initial goal (the final parousia of Being among beings), this solution comes only at the high price of tacitly relying on a *deceiving* God, or God of atheists, whose malefic cognisance remains by definition forever inaccessible to us. In such a scenario, the nowadays fashionable and apparently ready-at-hand 'great outdoors'[353] turns out to be on closer inspection nothing more than an indoor pool – or a devilish island – of an irredeemably *far-out* divinity. If, as Lacan assumes to be the case, modern science was theoretically founded upon Descartes's axiomatic exclusion of the hypothesis of the evil genius, and further embedded into Einstein's consideration that 'God does not play dice with the universe',[354] then science here religiously goes full circle. And if this seems a plausible outcome of the trajectory of modern science, then, as Lacan puts it in 'The Triumph of Religion' in order to resist it, 'I think we would do better to avoid saying that the real [as not-all] *in any way whatsoever* forms a whole.'[355]

More in general, Lacan is also well aware of the fact that, owing to the nature of language and the concomitant absence of the sexual relationship, science's *Weltanschauungen* – whether positive or negative – cannot truly be successful, for structural reasons. It is precisely the continuously failed but always more thorough and extensive attempt at containing the real that by, as it were, compressing it renders it exponentially uncontrollable and explosive. This process has also significant political repercussions. Since his early writings, Lacan has insisted on associating the repeated foundering of the semblance of imaginary completeness with the inversely proportional enhancement of the aggressiveness inherent to the project of global domination and world administration.[356] On the one hand, putting no-things – such as, of course, atomic energy – into the explicit or implicit service of the One-thing no doubt potentially increases the chances of the self-annihilation of the animal that happens to speak, or symbolic nothingness (the total indifferentiation of symbolic difference as otherwise *sustained* by no-things).[357] Yet, on the other, we should also be critical of hastily and complacently taking the apocalypse for granted – as our titillation with statistics of extinction, this uber-negative and yet perversely reassuring *Weltanschauung*, currently does, bordering on prophesising.[358] According to Lacan, the possibility that science actually manages to achieve military, ecological or viral/bacteriological Armageddon (negative totalization) remains no less unlikely than the possibility that it obtains the formula of the sexual relationship and thus transforms us into another posthuman species (positive totalization).[359] What instead seems to await us in the near future is a somehow scarier intensification of the movement from the imaginary to the real and back, with the establishment of prolonged periods of techno-religious – if not neo-pagan – obscurantism in which science is repressively used to put a leash on itself.

5. Towards agnostic atheism as strong atheism

5.1. Of God and the half-God

We examined how, for Lacan, the so-called God *hypothesis*, that is, the continuous oscillation between the One and the not-One, amounts to a structural effect of language as such and thus to an inescapable condition of the *Homo sapiens* species. On this level, Lacan most definitely already parts ways with Freud and unexpectedly comes close to the position of those contemporary cognitivists who regard our theo-*logical* propensity as favoured by certain hardwired aspects of brain function.[360] Importantly, according to Lacan, the oscillation between the One and the not-One of the God hypothesis is then religiously *reified* into an explicit-conscious or at least implicit-unconscious belief in a transcendent or immanent divine, and the question is to establish whether this second, and retroactive, *theo*-logical level is equally necessary. Very bluntly put, can we *structurally* not believe in some kind of *God*?

Lacan genealogically details the divine extracted from the God hypothesis through different figures of the ultimate One, which we could summarize as follows:

    a. The not-One *as immanent One* of polytheism. Through an effective imaginarization of the real, operated symbolically in the guise of fertility cults and the like, the not-One pole of the oscillation of the God hypothesis is turned into another One, the Goddess, which sustains and cements the semblance of the two-as-one. The real not-One frequently irrupts as a 'crisis of presence', but it is at each turn immediately and fully contained in this way. There is, strictly speaking, no real not-One as *un*thinkable.[361]

    b. The *existence* of the *transcendent One* of monotheistic Judaism or, more precisely, the *One* (One $\rightleftarrows$ not-One).[362] Judaism carries out a religious reification of the very *oscillation* of the God hypothesis or, if you wish, of our species-specific *transcendental* structure. The two immanent poles of the oscillation (One; not-One) are treated as distinct in their continuity and as *both* real: the *real* not-One of the symbolic epitomized by the Abrahamic encounter with an inscrutable desire issued as a command and the real One of the *symbolic* epitomized by the Mosaic Law of desire as ignorant and all alone. Yet the two poles are as such nonetheless divinized as One God. This transcendent One exists but is not the All-Being.

    c. The *transcendent One* as *One-All-Being* of monotheistic Christianity or, more precisely, the One (not-One) → *One*. Christianity carries out a religious reification that chiefly revolves around the immanent not-One pole of the oscillation of the God hypothesis, that is, the real abjection of this world. The immanent One pole of the oscillation only signals our being ravaged by language as the absence of the sexual relationship, and it is thus reduced to the not-One pole. Yet this very predicament, epitomized by the death of the Logos tout-court, functions just as a necessary prelude to the providential history of a transcendent One. God's love has always-already taken abjection into account and will finally solve it messianically through the universal and salvific revelation of himself as One-All-Being.

    d. The not-One *as the transcendent-in-immanence One* of (Christian pseudo-feminine) mysticism. Through a far-from-optimal imaginary realization of the symbolic, which materialises phenomenologically as an increasingly painful yet soon abandoned pleasure-in-pain, the immanent abysm of the real not-One pole of the oscillation of the God hypothesis is as such explicitly conflated with the transcendent One-All-Being of Christianity. Mysticism therefore somehow marks a failed return to polytheism or better to pagan divine enjoyment,[363] in the context of a monotheistic God of desire and love – still obviously worshipped by the mystic – that by definition opposes it.[364]

e. The *implicitly transcendent One* (not-One) of weak atheism, which science ends up partaking of or, more precisely, the not-One → One (not-One). The process of secularization of the Christian abjection of the world, now devoid of any providential order, leads to the proclamation of an ultimate not-Oneness, or chaosmos. This time God is allegedly dead for good, yet, by the same token, the immanent not-One pole of the oscillation of the God hypothesis – a structural oscillation which the weak atheist underestimates and fails to confront as such – is also contradictorily absolutized, for instance, as the absolute necessity of contingency. The direct assertion that the real not-One is all there is, immanently, tacitly entails the automatic instatement of a *forever* transcendent One that guarantees this very state of affairs – as its subset – from the outside, or God that guarantees there is no God. This God consequently amounts to a *deceiving* God, the God of the lie that the not-One is as *our* ultimate truth.

In a little-known lesson of Seminar XXII, Lacan seems to be attempting to overcome all these variants of the religious reification of the God hypothesis,[365] which in different ways and to different extents sense the prevalence of the not-One in the structural oscillation One/not-One only to disavow it directly or indirectly. He does so by putting forward the notion of the 'half-God'.[366] In previous years, he already insisted on how the truth of incompleteness, as, more specifically, the truth that the oscillation One/not-One issues into the *no*-two-as-*One* of structure as such, can only be half-said, if we are not to relapse into any metalinguistic whole truth as ultimate One, especially (and more consistently) that of the deceiving God. Here, it is instead primarily a matter of emphasizing the other – oblique and more intricate – side of the same coin: the awareness of only half-saying the not-One as truth should be accompanied by the appreciation that this very *half*-saying cannot but also half-say the One as God.[367] In other words, the other half of half-saying the truth is half-saying God. Unless we accept this matter of fact, we are not truly half-saying the truth but kept hostage by the *dieur*, whom we then, willingly or unwilling but inexorably, transform into an ultimate religious One. When isolated, half-saying the truth always says too much.[368]

Lacan goes as far as claiming that a thus-conceived half-God is 'right'.[369] Acknowledging and working through the half-God is no doubt 'rare', but it 'will renew' the subject by paving the way for an unexplored dimension of the speaking animal that appears to acquire both epistemological and ethical traits.[370] Linking this succinct passage with some of the most incisive and appropriately laconic mottos from Seminars XIX and XX, and the former's own title in particular, . . . *or Worse*, I would suggest that Lacan is here putting forward a threefold argument. First, we either say the truth of incompleteness or say worse[371] (that is, directly invoke some kind of ultimate One). But, second, we either *half*-say the truth of incompleteness or say *the worst*[372] (that is, indirectly invoke the ultimate One as a deceiving God). Yet, third, half-saying *God* along with half-saying the truth of incompleteness is the *best* – and in the end only – way of half-saying this truth (which left by itself would fall back into a direct or an indirect invocation of the ultimate One).

In short, in this instance, the late Lacan contends that the half-God manages *not* to reify religiously the God hypothesis as our transcendental. Such is in my view the theoretical and practical kernel of his *ascetic* atheism. The laborious and repeated, in fact never-ending, juxtaposition of half-saying the truth of incompleteness with the open invocation of the half-God – namely, on closer inspection, of the One pole of the oscillation of the God hypothesis – would enable us to exorcise our (tacit) reliance on God as the ultimate One.

The problem with this conclusion is that Lacan does not appear to realize that half-saying God cannot really be confined to the level of the One *pole* of the God *hypothesis*, since it already somewhat involves the level of the allegedly *ultimate* One. Or also, half-saying God already says *more* than the half-God. In order to successfully detach the God hypothesis from its religious reification and truly half-say the truth of incompleteness as this hypothesis's outcome – that is, again, the not-One as no-two-as-One, which is derived from the enduring co-implication of the One and not-One poles of the oscillation – we would actually need to continuously stick to the structural see-saw of what we earlier referred to as the One that 'undoes itself'[373] as soon as it emerges. The latter is indeed *less* than a half-God. Vice versa, and with the same move – bearing in mind that *both* poles can be reified religiously – we would also need to keep to the saw-see of the not-One that immediately 'makes' the One (which in turn undoes itself into the not-One, which makes the One, and so on). Dwelling on either of the two poles dissolves the potentially atheistic credentials of half-saying the truth and of the half-God. Yet, as conscious subjects, we cannot but – even alternately – dwell on one of the two poles, and thereby, at least in our hegemonically (post-)Christian tradition, either reify the One as all *alone* into an ultimate salvific One or reify the *not*-One into an ultimate deceiving God. Half-saying thus remains, at best, just a more sophisticated version of weak atheism and saying the worst.

In other words, here Lacan's ascetic atheism becomes in my opinion unfeasibly ascetic. At the risk of oversimplifying an admittedly complex and as-yet-unexplored matter, I am tempted to claim that ascetic atheism inevitably fails *de facto* because it would necessitate the adoption of an unbearable and untenable subjectivized *cognisance* for which 'there is no One, but as soon as I say it I turn it into One, but there is no One, but as soon as I say it I turn it into One', etcetera, *ad infinitum*.[374] Moreover, against Lacan's plans, what consequently looms in the background of ascetic half-saying is the reappearance of a – naïve (post-) Freudian – psychoanalysis idealistically devoted to a conscious drainage of the unconscious, which he always vociferously condemned as a mirage, and which in this context would result into a conscious mimicking of the unconscious.[375] In a nutshell, my allegation is that if, with Lacan and contra or beyond Freud, God is *unconscious*, to the point and in the precise sense that the oscillation of the God hypothesis amounts to our species-specific transcendental, then it is difficult to see how our being *conscious* of God as unconscious could dispose of him without disposing of ourselves.

This strategy clearly does not work for at least two additional and related reasons. First, and straightforwardly, given Lacan's own psychoanalytic tenets, we are at most only partly conscious of what is unconscious. Second, our very *self*-consciousness, our 'being-me-to-myself', the semblance of our 'making One',[376] rests as such precisely on an *unconscious* and *ur*-religious *sedimentation* of the oscillation of the God hypothesis, a ground-zero reification (or fundamental fantasy) of which self-consciousness constitutes the most obvious and everyday ossification. God is unconscious not only in the sense that our conscious profession of alleged atheism remains unconsciously theistic but also and especially in the sense that the unconscious is *itself*, in its own terms, already proto-religious through the fundamental fantasy. The fundamental fantasy functions as the most basic containment of the continuous movement from the One that undoes itself to the not-One that makes One (and back), in favour of the latter.[377]

Taking this into account, there are some cryptic remarks, in the works of the early 1970s, where Lacan seems to surmise this impasse, suspend his cogitations on the *half*-saying as inconclusive and abide by a minimalist handling of the truth of incompleteness *and* the tolerance of the paradoxes that *necessarily* come with it. We should simply say the truth of incompleteness or say worse.[378] More precisely, first, we should say the truth of incompleteness or say worse (the salvific God). But, second, saying the truth of incompleteness comes with the worst (the deceiving God). Yet, third, we should nonetheless say the truth of incompleteness and its inherent worst, or say even worse[379] (the worse than the worst of the recurrence of the salvific or deceiving God through half-saying). I think such a capitulation to the resilience of God as unconscious should be read as an admission of defeat of ascetic atheism. This is the case at least with respect to the guise in which ascetic atheism is formulated on the plane of saying and critique.

5.2. Half-saying better and more-than-half-saying

The other related, and more general and important, problem with the allegedly atheistic programme of ascetic half-saying is that it indeed limits a priori the question concerning a viable and non-weak atheism to a question of *saying*, of the constraints of language or, which is the same, of the God hypothesis as our transcendental. I think Lacan's confinement of things religious to this loosely Kantian – and Freudian – *critical* horizon is in the end also responsible for the capitulation we have just described.

The most emblematic condensation of such an approach can be found in the previously cited prescriptive recommendation from 'The Triumph of Religion' for which 'we would do *better* to avoid *saying* that the real in any way whatsoever forms a whole'.[380] At face value, this amounts to just another warning against unintentionally embracing weak atheism and its deceiving God, the worst as the God that guarantees there is no God. As soon as we say that the real not-One is all there is, we turn it into the *One* (not-One). To resist this outcome, we should ascetically practice half-saying the truth of incompleteness – and the half-God as its other half. However, on closer inspection, Lacan's own saying, his recommendation aimed at a cautious half-saying, happens to say much more than intended. It insinuates: 'The truth of incompleteness can only be half-said, *but* the not-One really *is* all there is, the problem is simply we cannot *say* it'. As should be evident by now, such a blind reliance on an ultimate ontological not-Oneness supposedly obfuscated by the finitude of our linguistic-logical condition only reinforces weak atheism through the very endeavour to defuse it. If, beyond the wall of language, and the illusory fabrications of the One it gives rise to, the not-One is *all* there is, then this *a fortiori* requires the deceiving God, one who is now being specified as not only deceiving us but also, *extra*-linguistically, the whole of Creation – as still seen from an *intra*-linguistic perspective (Lacan's). Here, the *fideism of the not-One* strikes back harder and, by means of Lacan's for once gullible words, highlights the vengefulness of the deceiving God towards those who try to eradicate him. Taking the path indicated by Lacan on this occasion to obviate a new triumph of religion can eventually only make it triumph again. Let us recall that, by his admission, religion gives meaning to 'absolutely anything whatsoever'.

Moving from this series of deadlocks, and trying to overcome them, it is however crucial to stress that this is not Lacan's last word on the matter. We should return to and seriously consider the already commented pronouncement from the late text 'Des religions et du réel' according to which, *perhaps*, 'the real [not-One] is not everything' there is, or, conversely, 'it is not certain' that the real not-One is everything there is.[381] This is patently a much stronger, ontological as *meta-critical*, claim than the unfruitful one for which 'we would do better to avoid *saying* that the real in any way whatsoever forms a whole'. It bypasses the strictures of our linguistic transcendental as fundamentally irrelevant – since, after all, for Lacan, the wall of language is such only as structurally *holed* – and directly posits the daring[382] and strongly agnostic possibility that there *might* eventually be some form of ultimate One. In my view, it nonetheless does so – in an embryonic manner that needs to be patiently developed, ameliorated and systematized beyond Lacan – precisely for the purpose of averting *per viam negationis* the stubborn and unconscious resurgence of the deceiving God and, more to the point, the unwanted but, at this stage, seemingly unavoidable passage from 'the not-One is everything there is, full stop' to 'the not-One is everything there is and, precisely because of the full stop, it is such *as a whole*'.[383]

What is still, first and foremost, at stake in this highly speculative context (that of a renewed first philosophy that takes its cue from the most advanced aspects of Lacan's psychoanalysis) is the very concrete search for an atheistic formulation of the truth of incompleteness that does not end up contradicting itself, that is, turn into a truth about truth and thus into some figure of God. In other words, it is a matter of recognizing the dead end of *ascetic* atheism as *critique*, which in being reabsorbed by *weak* atheism only perpetuates the *undeadness* of the dead God, and of replacing it with the *meta-critical* delineation of *agnostic atheism* as *strong* atheism.

This ambitious programme should avail itself of two straightforward questions, which have guided my investigation since its inception, informed the various exegeses I have carried out so far and must now be made crystal clear. First, can we *half*-say the truth of incompleteness in a *better* way than by surrendering to the half-*God*, whose 'rightness', or righteousness, we have just proved to be *wrong*? Second and more boldly, is it possible to *more*-than-half-say this truth without being spoken by the *deceiving* God? My personal wager, still Lacanian in inspiration, in what follows is that we can and must answer positively to these queries. To put it briefly and anticipating a more thorough scrutiny,[384] first, *a better way of half-saying the truth of incompleteness*, namely, 'creating a viable atheist', *can only go through an attempt at more-than-half-saying it meta-critically*. Second and without solution of continuity, this tortuous but indispensable tactical detour also enables us to think the *being* of the not-One – or, better, of the no-two-as-One as *Homo sapiens*' conclusive phenomeno-logical predicament[385] – *as such*, that is, *irrespective of* – yet also thanks to – the derivation of the not-One from our species-specific transcendental (the structural-linguistic oscillation between the One and not-One poles of the God hypothesis).

For the sake of clarity, let me restate and spell out some broad definitions with which I have already been operating and which from now on will become even more central to my arguments.

I call *weak agnosticism* the position that posits the possibility of an ultimate One but does not investigate it as it would be a priori impenetrable to reason.

I call *weak atheism* the position that posits the impossibility of an ultimate One but does not investigate it as it would already be demonstrated by reason, and thus implicitly posits the *One* (not-One).

I call *ascetic atheism* the position that problematizes weak atheism but, remaining confined to a critical, or transcendental, treatment of reason, implicitly or explicitly returns to either weak atheism or theism tout-court.

I call *strong agnosticism* the position that problematizes both weak *and* ascetic atheism and posits the possibility of an ultimate One by investigating the not-One *of* reason *meta*-critically or ontologically. More precisely, I call strong agnosticism, in its strongest version, the position that rationally first contemplates and then debunks the possibility of an ultimate *One* (not-One), or deceiving God, as still reliant on the belief in a diabolical reconciliation. Strong agnosticism replaces such a possibility with the more logical and less religious possibility of an ultimate One that is not-One and ultimate not-One that is One, without solution of continuity and alternation, or *self*-deceiving God.

I call *agnostic or strong atheism* the position that *decides* for a *practical* atheism of the not-One on the basis of the undecidability obtained through strong agnosticism's ontological meta-critique.

5.3. Behind and beyond the hole in the wall

Regardless of his deep-seated vetoes against first philosophy,[386] Lacan himself tries to more-than-half say the truth of incompleteness, sporadically yet insistently. The passage from 'Des religions et du réel' we have just examined is not an isolated instance in his oeuvre. In doing so, within a wider psychoanalytic framework and its search for a feasible atheism, Lacan also contravenes Freud's purportedly scientific-as-anti-religious injunction, in *The Future of an Illusion*, to always remain confined to 'showing how the world must appear *to us*' so as not to step into the domain of 'empty abstraction without practical interest'.[387]

One of the works in which this understated Lacan emerges most clearly is Seminar XIX. He sets the tone for strong agnosticism already in lessons II and IV. While 'it is clear that God exists', he nonetheless does not exist 'more than you' do.[388] Again, God as the God *hypothesis* – or, more selectively here, as the phenomeno-logical symbolic existence of the One as all alone, the One pole of the oscillation One/not-One – goes together with the species that happens to speak insofar as it coincides with its transcendental structure. The existence of God, which in this sense has a limited meaning, thus rests on the 'precarious', or contingent, status of the signifier.[389] *But* – Lacan adds, and this is methodologically crucial – 'this doesn't get us very far'.[390] We must go *further* than this conclusion and the associated strategy of half-saying. That is to say, we must acknowledge that it just *seems* to be the case that the dimension of *necessity* originates from and pertains only to the speaking animal's contingent production of the phenomeno-logically symbolic existence of the precarious One.[391] Such an incontrovertible contingency of necessity should not be taken as the only kind of necessity there necessarily is, unless we are content with transforming it into the necessity of contingency and the deceiving God it presupposes.

Hence, closely following Lacan's further arguments, on the one hand, the belief in a more than human-made God who made the world from nothingness 'on no account will [. . .] be sufficient for us'.[392] It is 'belief in itself', an *ur*-dogma to which every sort of belief eventually comes down.[393] As such it must rationally be invalidated, against the resigned quietism of weak agnosticism and the counterproductive arrogance of weak atheism. Here, *strong* agnosticism works on the assumption of the *unlikeliness* of an ultimate One, that is, as a meta-*critique*. However, on the other hand, despite such an opposition to our hardwired 'need for belief' and along with it, Lacan also plainly admits that 'nothing in this realm is certain'.[394] The possibility of an ultimate One, posited also by some great modern mathematicians,[395] must itself be rationally investigated so as not to leave it to the resourcefulness of religious theism and its systems of belief. Here, an equally fierce strong *agnosticism* works on the assumption that the phenomeno-logical conclusiveness of the truth of incompleteness, the not-One as no-two-as-One *and* its inherently paradoxical status, should *not* be taken *in itself* as conclusive and requires *meta*-critical elucidation.

These issues are then delved into in lessons V and VIII. In lesson V, Lacan's strongly agnostic more-than-half-saying intriguingly takes its cue from a problematization of the work of contemporary mathematician René Thom (a recipient of the Fields Medal and the founder of catastrophe theory) and his self-professed 'extreme metaphysics'.[396] According to Thom, as read by Lacan, logic as a formal discourse obtained within and applied to *Homo sapiens*' linguistic horizon, the 'wall of language' in Lacan's parlance, cannot account for number and the mathematics that follows from it. On the contrary, it is number that accounts for logic. Here, as elsewhere, Lacan sympathizes with this position.[397] Thom equally contends that number, algebra, functions and especially topology can linguistically account for what happens *behind* the wall of language. More radically, in his admittedly Platonic view,[398] number would also *extra*-linguistically function in nature as such through a, however differentiated, general topology uniting – phylogenetically and ontogenetically – pre-linguistic life, the origins and typology of natural languages and the advent of formal logic.[399]

In this regard, Lacan's stance becomes threefold. First, and in agreement with Thom, 'there can be no doubting' that modern science rests on number, function and topology, and that, more importantly, thanks to mathematics, science as a discourse 'has found the means to construct itself behind the wall'.[400] For Lacan, although we are unsurpassably placed *in front of* the wall of language, a wall that basically consists of the oscillation One/not-One, we can nonetheless mathematically access what is *behind* the wall, precisely because the wall is *holed*. The holed wall indeed coalesces in the *no*-two-as-One. Moreover, it is *only* by means of number that we can access what is behind the wall: 'It's quite certain that we cannot form any other idea' of the behind the wall.[401]

But, second, and on an already *strongly* agnostic level that challenges Thom's extreme metaphysics, it is not necessarily the case that the behind-the-holed-wall-of-language, which is the *real* as such for us, does *itself* work mathematically *beyond* language or, better, independently from it. 'Perhaps' it does, perhaps it does not, Lacan adds.[402] In other words, the hole in the wall of language – through which we mathematically access what lies behind it – still witnesses to 'the cleaving performed by the wall'[403] between language and what is not linguistic. Our scientific manipulations of what we could now call the *real-behind*, in an apt de-sublimation of Meillassoux's solemn 'great outdoors', both enlarge the hole in the wall and reinforce the latter as a holed *wall*. To put it very simply, entering the real does not entail exiting language. Or, more in detail, before considering 'the *meaning* of what *perhaps* is to be seen beyond the wall'[404] (a meaning that Thom takes for granted and deems to be numerical), we should not lose sight of the fact that the real that for us works mathematically, as the *behind*-the-holed-wall-of-language, fundamentally manifests itself as an *impossible*. Even in his more metaphysical digressions, the real first and foremost remains for Lacan a meaningless *dis*function, from which scientific effectiveness originates and to which it repeatedly returns, as we saw earlier. Following Lacan's understanding of the impossible in this specific context, we could suggest that the behind-the-holed-*wall* regarded as *beyond* the wall (which in a sense it is; it all depends on how we look at the holed wall, Lacan insists) shows that 'there is only, to the best of our knowledge' – note this further agnostic emphasis – 'this real that precisely signals itself as the impossible, the impossibility of reaching it beyond [as independently from] the wall'.[405] Yet, and this is even more crucial, 'it no less remains that this is the real'.[406]

Third, and most importantly, even if the real *were* to work mathematically in itself beyond the wall of language – as assumed by Thom's avowed plan to relaunch 'natural philosophy'[407] – to the extent that the real is already given to us through the hole in the wall of language as number's own inextricability from an impossible, or an 'impossibility of numbering',[408] an inherently mathematical nature could not but a fortiori be *meaningless* for us. Here, Lacan decidedly sides against Thom. On the one hand, according to Lacan, 'what I do believe I can formulate clearly, and in this respect I believe I am in agreement with everything that is most serious in scientific construction, is that it is strictly *impossible* to endue with the faintest shadow of *meaning* anything whatsoever that is articulated in algebraic or topological terms'.[409] On the other, according to Thom's 'generalised theory of meaning', as Miller forces him to acknowledge in an intense and often brusque 1978 conversation, mathematical 'signification is inherent to nature' as such and language tout-court is fully absorbed by it.[410] Hence, as Miller has it, on close inspection, catastrophe theory is hardly catastrophic.[411] Instead, it is ultimately a 'theory of resonance and reflection' and the 'transference of forms'.[412] As Milner then spells out, in postulating that insofar as catastrophe theory is true of nature, it is also true of the speaking animal, Thom eventually falls back into the pre-modern assumption of an a priori harmony between macro- and microcosm.[413]

For Lacan, obviously, there is meaning for those who stand *in front of* the holed wall, a meaning that in his own view is indeed, in front of the holed wall, mathematical prior to being logical not to mention pertaining to everyday speech. But – through yet another meta-critical hint – 'we *cannot* content ourselves with these con-fusion-meanings', since, as essentially devoted to veiling the absence of the sexual relationship ('this serves only to reverberate on the lyre of desire, on eroticism'), they both stem from the phenomeno-*mathemato*-logical existence of the One of the oscillation One/not-One and concomitantly avoid the question 'How does [this] One make an entrance?'[414] In other words, we need to tackle the impossible of the no-two-as-One, namely, the kernel of the behind-the-holed-wall-of-language, the *meaninglessness* of meaning, as first and foremost evidenced by mathematics itself.

Moving from this problematization of Thom's stance for whom, in the end, 'it is the numbers that know what they do',[415] and thus there is an ultimate meaningful *One*, we can also better appreciate how Lacan's stance nevertheless remains strongly *agnostic*. His problematization of Thom is in fact clearly neither intended nor presented as a refutation. Namely, we should unravel what remains implicit in Lacan's claim that 'perhaps' nature as such does not work mathematically beyond language, but *perhaps* it *does*.

Let us first summarize Lacan's main *critical* argument against Thom. What, for Lacan, does not hold in Thom's reasoning is his association of the allegedly *numerical* status of the real as such, qua the natural real, with some basic *meaning* that our phenomeno-mathemato-logical meaning would partake of. Thom not only accepts Miller's suggestion that, in an 'anti-Galilean' manner, 'for you, spirit is in direct contact with reality' but also goes as far as advancing that 'whatever system' in the universe 'has some kind of psychism'.[416] Instead, according to Lacan, what is certain – to the best of our knowledge and precisely thanks to psychoanalytic and *mathematical* knowledge – is that our access to the real, as also natural, is indeed numerical but only to the extent that the meaning of our mathematizations concretely rests on an impossibility, the no-two-as-One of the truth of incompleteness, which is to say on the meaninglessness of meaning. This is witnessed by the very functioning of modern science and the effectiveness of its impasses. This is the real in itself *for us*. Now, if the extra-linguistic real in itself *for itself* were numerical, which is

Thom's claim, then, as things stand, it would itself result *for us* in a meaningless impossibility.

We are thus left with three *meta*-critical options:

a. The real in-itself-for-itself is, against Thom, *not* numerical, or better said – in my own jargon – it amounts to an *uncountable as indifferent not-oneness* that contingently gives rise to the oscillation One/not-One and number more in general. Namely, it gives rise to a *difference* from the perspective of which the uncountable coincides with an impossible (the no-two-as-One). We are in *this* sense still 'in direct contact with reality', albeit one that is *meaningless* and *thereby* retroactively mathematized. Such a contingent emergence of difference and number should not necessarily be confined to humankind, although other potential forms of difference and number would necessarily be screened as impossible by the wall of language.[417]

b. The real in-itself-for-itself is, following Thom, numerical, yet, beyond Thom's declared intentions, this is the case in the specific mathematical-*religious* guise of the *One* of Intelligent Design.[418] The natural 'instability', or 'points of catastrophe', associated with the inherently mathematical 'logoi' of each and every 'being',[419] in turn differentiated or 'exfoliated' according to a 'biological teleologisation of language' (acknowledged by Thom or at least by Thomians),[420] are eventually resolved into a divine self-identity, or Number as the subject-supposed-to-know. Like the entirety of Creation, we are always-already in direct contact with reality in a crypto-providential way. In spite of its apparent impasse, the linguistic microcosm reflects or is isomorphic to a meaningful macrocosm.[421] But this overarching design requires a, rationally unacceptable yet irrefutable, *belief* in some sort of salvific plan. In other words, what the believer in mathematical meaning cannot account for is the emergence of a (seeming) mathematical impossibility characteristic of language, the very same language which he still needs to account for the mathematical design that would conclusively explain it.[422]

c. The real in-itself-for-itself is, following Thom, numerical, but, following Lacan, it forever remains for us an impossibility; that is, we are being duped by the *One* (not-One), or deceiving God. There is an ultimate *meaning* of meaninglessness which for us coincides with the fact that we – and possibly albeit far from necessarily other differentiated areas of Creation – are deliberately excluded from it. In this now fittingly catastrophic sense, we will never be in direct contact with reality, by definition.

We should stress that on such a meta-critical level the deceiving God is no longer limited to an unwanted implication of weak atheism, whose naïve critique we need to criticize, and is instead directly posited as an option we must seriously take into consideration. If mathematical impossibility is also more concretely experienced as the impossibility of saying the whole truth of incompleteness, and if, bearing this in mind, we intend to prevent the relapse of the very conception of a non-numerical and meaningless real in-itself-for-itself[423] into weak atheism, then it becomes imperative 'to always call into question'[424] the ostensible likelihood of that conception as the speculative climax of psychoanalytic knowledge. In other words, as Lacan courageously concludes, we need to accept not only that mathematical science is basically meaningless but also that, in predicating this, psychoanalytic knowledge *might itself* be (navigating) 'an ocean of false science'.[425] Again, these would be the waters of the Devil's island.

5.4. The deceiving God, for real

Later in Seminar XIX, in lesson VIII, in a different context that however builds on his confrontation with Thom, Lacan himself comes very close to openly posit the ontological possibility of the deceiving God by means of a radical meta-critical either/or: 'Either [. . .] the unthinkable thinks, or it is the fact of saying it [the unthinkable] that can act upon the Thing, enough for it to turn out otherwise.'[426] In other words, either the real as a, for us, unthinkable not-One does actually in itself think as One Being, and insofar as we will never get to think what Being thinks as One, we are being deceived, or our numerical-scientific manipulations of the real as unthinkable do have an effect on the not-oneness of being in itself. Only if the latter is the case, can there be 'real thinking' that thinks itself, especially by means of scientific formalization.[427] Or also, leaving aside the issue of a non-deceiving God – which is at this stage redundant since his unthinkability is always-already not such through belief/faith in him, especially in the sense that we will in the end fully partake of his thinking – either the real as for us unthinkable is unreal, a lie that nonetheless amounts to our ultimate truth,[428] whereby we can at best think the unthinkable's thinking as in turn something unthinkable, or the unthinkable qua in itself unthinkable is the only background for the contingently impactful emergence of any kind of *res cogitans*.

Lacan's interest in the deceiving God and, specifically, the key role of such a meta-critical hypothesis in the search for a viable form of atheism have strangely been much underestimated, if not altogether overlooked. My general stance is that the issue of the *One* (not-One) can neither interpretatively be confined to the speculative excursuses of Seminar XIX, although, as we have just seen, it is perhaps in this Seminar that it most clearly resounds as an ontological ultimatum while not being called by its name, nor methodologically relegated to the innocuous status of a recurrent sophistic provocation. It remains a constant and serious preoccupation throughout Lacan's works because it profoundly influences the very field and future of psychoanalysis itself. If the unthinkable were to think, then 'there is no psychoanalysis'.[429] He explicitly, and at times repeatedly, discusses the deceiving God, in different ways and from various angles, in twelve out of twenty-seven Seminars and in at least half a dozen writings.

As early as Seminar II, we are told that 'the idea that God is no deceiver', which is still as necessary for Einstein as it was for Descartes, 'is precisely what we don't know'.[430] Seminar III adds that with and after Descartes's *cogito ergo sum* and the related birth of modern science as based on the hyperbolic doubt, independently of however much both repress it, 'the discussion of the deceiving God is' – should be – 'a step that is impossible to avoid'.[431] Seminar IX reiterates the same point and complements it by claiming that what is instead rationally indefensible is the idea of a *non*-deceiving God supporting the *cogito*: 'The word exists, but not Descartes's [good] God'.[432] From a slightly different and less epistemological perspective, Seminar VII poses the question of the blatant incompatibility between an allegedly 'reasonable' God and the miserable state of our world, independently of our actions, as 'the central problem of ethics'.[433]

As late as Seminars XXII, XXIII and even XXVII, the same basic leitmotif is still present, albeit in a more convoluted manner, in spite of the changes Lacan's psychoanalytic theory and practice underwent in the meantime: 'God's knowledge [. . .] for sure, we don't know if it exists [. . .] It -sists, *perhaps*, but we don't know where, all we can say is that what [phenomeno-logically] consists does *not* bear witness to it.'[434] So, on the one hand, 'God's knowledge, it's the one that was deemed to be that of our good, which is untenable'[435] given our structural predicament, and if there were a God, it would be a deceiving God. But, on the other hand, 'it is more than unlikely that this One', the One of the phenomeno-logical oscillation One/not-One, 'constitutes the Universe',[436] even if we were to understand our deceived One that undoes itself as dependent on the tricks of an ultimate One Deceiver. 'We have never observed anything that would show us that there is a deceiving demon somewhere at the heart of nature.'[437] In other words, the deceiving God himself remains an unprovable hypothesis. Our taking him for granted in turn results in a last desperate, resentful and yet paradoxically optimistic kind of religious belief, of closure, that psychoanalysis should fight against, including in a clinical way.[438]

5.5. Descartes: From the deceiving God to the good old God

By and large, Lacan's scrutiny of the deceiving God revolves around a critical dissection of Descartes's *cogito*. But, moving from there, by means of an innovative reading of apparently outlandish aspects of Cartesian theology, it also culminates in a series of bold meta-critical pronouncements on being qua being and the extra-linguistic status of the truth of incompleteness, which he elsewhere methodologically avoids and condemns.

Initially, Lacan focuses on the impasses of the *cogito* ergo *sum* and, specifically, of the *cogito ergo* ego *sum*, and the way in which these very impasses give rise to the split subject of both science and psychoanalysis as inextricable from the manifestation of the phenomeno-logical truth of incompleteness.[439] In short, Lacan's main claim here is that, in his search for *certitude*,[440] Descartes fails to *derive* being from thinking (*cogito* ergo *sum*) and a fortiori to *individuate* being as an ego, a being-me/One-to-myself (*cogito ergo* ego *sum*). What Cartesian philosophy does instead accomplish by default, and here lies its greatness, is characterizing the animal that happens to speak-think, the *parlêtre* whose being and thinking cannot be separated, as a being who *doubts*,[441] and who more precisely doubts as to whether being really gives itself as an *I am*.

Underneath Descartes's 'I think, therefore I am', Lacan recovers a 'I think "therefore I am"', where '*therefore* I am' is just a thought that is being thought and the thinking subject is that which thinks 'therefore I am'.[442] Or better, the '*I am*' does thus not secure any Oneness of being since it solely proceeds from an 'act of beingthinking'[443] or, we could add, from the indistinct factuality of the *parlêtre*. This is the case unless we posit from the outset that the *cogito* of '*cogito ergo sum*' already presupposes an *ego sum* (if I am the One who thinks, then, of course, I think therefore I am), which obviously results in a circular argument.[444] More to the point, according to Lacan, Descartes rightly infers that the subject *is* out of the sheer *fact* of thinking. But he does not see that the subject, as an *it* and not an I, also thinks 'where it is impossible for [the subject] to articulate this "therefore I am", since there it is structurally ruled out that [the subject] accesses [. . .] self-consciousness'.[445] Hence, from this wider stance that takes into account the unconscious, the generic *parlêtre* and its (f)act of beingthinking – the *res cogitans* as devoid of a first-person singular pronoun – turn into a split subject, for which being and thinking are convolutedly both divided and overlapping: 'I am not, where I am the plaything of my thought', namely, where I confuse the 'therefore I am' with a being-me/One-to-myself, and 'I think', unconsciously, 'about what I am where', consciously, 'I do not think that I think'.[446] After all, it is indeed insofar as Descartes's *cogito ergo sum* already embryonically contains the split subject of the psychoanalytic *cogito* '*ergo sum*' that Cartesian reasoning itself ends up posing drastic questions such as 'am *I* or am I *not*?', '*perhaps* I?' and '*where* do I think *from*?'[447] These are at bottom existential variations on the phenomeno-logical One/not-One oscillation we have been describing. Such questions are then consonantly followed by the hyperbolic doubt 'am I being *deceived* into thinking that I am or, equally, that I am not?'

Lacan does acknowledge and praise the ontological extremeness and rational cogency of the hyperbolic doubt. He distinguishes two stages in Descartes's deceiving God. The deceiving God is not simply a joyful prankster – or a miracle maker – who nonetheless remains fundamentally benevolent towards and comprehensible for us, but an absolutely evil genius, 'the radical liar, the one that leads me astray in order to lead me astray'. [448] Against traditional philosophical interpretations, there is nothing moderate, 'systematic' and 'methodical' in the hyperbolic doubt. It is neither a 'cold doubt',[449] a controlled exercise in metaphysical Scholastic *disputatio*, nor even a more challenging form of modern scepticism (Lacan refers here to the beginning of Hegel's *Phenomenology* and its knowledge as a knowledge that is nothing but a 'not knowing yet', which by the same token nevertheless presupposes a 'knowing already').[450] Instead, the hyperbolic doubt is a passage to the act.[451] In fact, we should add, unlike sceptical doubt, the hyperbolic doubt does not only involve a phenomeno-logical 'vacillation' of the I as ego – an 'am I or am I not One to myself?' which contents itself with concluding that our 'being only seizes itself as thought in a succession of alternating times', and for which the invocation of the deceiving God is moreover unnecessary.[452] Especially if read through a meta-critical lens informed by psychoanalysis, it also goes as far as problematizing the ultimate status of such a vacillation and of the split subject that sustains it, namely, the very being of our beingthinking. In other words, the latter's not-Oneness could itself be a lie we will never unmask. It is precisely in this sense – that of the possibility of the *One* (not-One) – that Lacan surprisingly tells us that, surpassing Hegel, the hyperbolic doubt is unfolded *beyond* the level of the *real* (the real as such for us) and that, by delving into 'the subject as an inaugural act', what it eventually puts into question is the nature of the real *in itself*.[453] And it is also in this sense that while, on the one hand, Descartes's deceiving God cannot but remain for us, by definition, 'nonsensical' and 'logically unjustifiable', on the other, this theme is nonetheless far from 'irrational', for it inherently and consistently arises from the empirical deadlock of the *cogito* itself.[454]

Obviously, Lacan is well aware that Descartes's itinerary does not stop at the deceiving God. For the latter, God cannot be a deceiver. God, the Being the idea of whom is within me, that is, the possessor of all the perfections, is instead supremely good and the source of truth. As Descartes puts it, 'it is manifest by the natural light that all fraud and deception depend on some defect', and hence not on God.[455] For Lacan, this unwarranted move – God is not a deceiver because God is God – is a paradigmatic case of (Christian) religious repression and reliance on a belief that can give meaning to absolutely anything whatsoever, and as such it inaugurates (scientific) modernity as having an ambivalent relation with the real. On the one hand, precisely thanks to the hyperbolic doubt's eventual reaffirmation of the good old God, 'the philosophical *cogito* is at the center of the mirage that renders modern man so *sure* of being himself in his uncertainties about himself'.[456] But, on the other hand, this certitude as a compromise formation does not actually hold in at least two interconnected ways and instead witnesses to a gigantic return of the repressed.[457]

First, on a historical level, as moderns, we are still not exonerated from the hyperbolic doubt, quite the opposite: 'The notion that the real [. . .] is unable to play tricks on us [. . .] is, though no one really dwells on this, quite essential to the constitution of the world of science'.[458] Our science continues to require an 'act of faith [. . .] in supposing that there is something absolutely nondeceptive'.[459] When Einstein claims that God is cunning but not dishonest, he is not simply teasing us but expressing something that is 'essential to his position, his organisation of the world';[460] namely, he is repeating Descartes's repression. And, we should add expanding on Lacan, on close inspection, the contemporary emergence of *negative* scientific *Weltanschauungen* that – by turning early modern physics on its feet – summon the deceiving God without acknowledging it make the by-now-unconscious re-enactment of this repression ever more urgent, frequent and frantic. In short, the scientific-religious logic at play here is the following: on a conscious level, the world is not-One and there is no God (which implicitly installs the deceiving God that guarantees there is no God). On an unconscious level (conscious in Einstein as read by Lacan), the world is not-One and there is no God *but* God is clearly not a deceiver.

Second, on a more speculative level, Descartes's own good old God, without which the *cogito ergo sum* is unsustainable,[461] turns out to be a much trickier notion than anticipated and enables us, today, to put forward a series of meta-critical hypotheses about the status of the real in itself and for itself undetected by Cartesian philosophy. We could also take them as a doubt about the hyperbolic doubt.

5.6. Descartes: From the good old God to the deceiving God, again

Although Descartes avails himself of both cosmological and ontological arguments to prove the existence of God, for Lacan, his non-deceiving God profoundly departs from a traditional Scholastic understanding of the divine. First and foremost, God is a *verissimum*, a super-Truth, needed to overcome the hyperbolic doubt, and not simply an *entissimum*, a super-Being.[462] More to the point, what fundamentally matters in such an updated version of the good old God is his *will* to truth, in the superlative sense that *whatever* he may wish is the truth. So, on the one hand, God is 'the truth about truth', namely, the guarantor that what is, for us, phenomeno-logically articulated as true and threatened by the deceiving God is indeed true because he wants it.[463] But, on the other hand, God all the more guarantees our truth and dispels the hyperbolic doubt precisely in that truth could be different if he wanted it, whereby our current truth would be an error.[464] According to Descartes, it is after all well possible that, in the realm of 'eternal' truths, 1 + 1 + 1 + 1 does not make 4 and instead makes 2 or 3 (or 2 *and* 3, or 4 *and* 2 *and* 3), depending on God's will. Truth is thus ultimately 'God's own business', not ours.[465]

For Lacan, this bold Cartesian move has historically one major consequence, namely, the separation of truth from knowledge and the ensuing emergence of modern science. While truth is generously entrusted to or cunningly dumped on divine arbitrariness, scientific knowledge has supposedly nothing to do with God.[466] In other words, after Descartes, truth no longer founds knowledge – except through the tacit assumption that God does not deceive us. Or better, we no longer search in vain for the way in which truth makes knowledge possible, which was impossible to find, and scientific knowledge directly follows from the acknowledgement of this impossibility.[467] The unproductive hunt for God's signature in the world (for instance, for how he created the world with the letters of the Hebrew alphabet, each corresponding to a number[468]) succumbs to the void of *res extensa* and its effective manipulation by means of the little letters and numbers of algebra, leading to an ever increasing accumulation of knowledge.[469]

So, to sum up, Descartes's trajectory starts off with his famous suspension of all acquired knowledge and an endeavour to secure a certitude qua truth on which to solidly anchor knowledge. Yet this process proves far more difficult than expected and, to rescue the ego from the deceiving God, he ends up founding a scientific knowledge that is severed from divine truth although the latter would still externally guarantee it – since, by definition, God is not a deceiver. The outcome of this fruitful impasse is that, for scientific knowledge, truth is given as an impossibility of knowledge, that is, of knowing how divine truth externally guarantees truthful knowledge. Bar a reference to God's will – truthful knowledge is such and such because he wanted it – the algebra initiated by Descartes does in fact, at least for us, acquire a meaning only retroactively through the order of the commutations of its combinatorial elements.[470] In other words, expanding on something Lacan seems to be suggesting in a quite extraordinary passage from Seminar XII,[471] if everything is possible for the Cartesian God (as the domain of eternal truths), all that is possible for us (as knowledge) must pass through the impossibility of knowing his infinite possibilities (as our truth). More precisely, if eternal truths are consigned to divine contingency, then, apart from his will to truth, nothing is necessary for God, not even $2 + 2 = 4$, and everything is in itself possible for him. But if everything is possible for him, then, strictly speaking, nothing is really possible for our knowledge, since, if God wants it, even $2 + 2 = 4$ is not only unnecessary for him but also impossible for us. Hence, all that we appear to know as possible if not necessary hinges on a real that, for us, fundamentally corresponds to the impossible, save for the fact that God, who is not a deceiver, lets us extract out of it a possible truthful knowledge guaranteed in one of his contingent truths.[472]

What Descartes therefore accomplishes with his good old God is a separation of divine truth from both human (scientific) knowledge *and* – insofar as there is no 'natural trace'[473] of the one in the other, only an axiomatic celestial infallibility at the lie detector – from our phenomeno-logical real as thus based on impossibility – that is, not simply on a downgraded level of nonetheless homogeneous being. On the one hand, Being is such precisely *as* truth, that is, truth 'is in no way [. . .] placed in the parenthesis of a dimension which distinguishes it from reality'.[474] There is no solution of continuity between God's being and his will to truth.[475] On the other hand, and for the same reason, what the 'I think' reaches as it '*topples* into the "I am" is a real', but one for which 'the true remains so *outside*', or, literally, so far out, that 'Descartes then needs to make sure of a non-deceiving Other' in whom the truth of this very real is secured.[476] Again, the hyperbolic doubt forces Descartes to go beyond the level of the real as such for us (the impossible, also in terms of the impossibility of being-me-to-myself) and resort to the real in itself (the ultimate truthful 'Thing'[477]) as irredeemably distinct. The alleged antidote of the good God ends up preserving and reinstating the same ontological division that the deceiving God promoted.

Leaving aside any thorough debate about the level of plausibility of Lacan's interpretation of Descartes – which, ingeniously reading the *Meditations* and *Discourse on Method* along with *The Passions of the Soul*, *The Rules for the Direction of the Mind* and *The Search for Truth* I deem both inventive and quite accurate, if at times somewhat forced – the crucial question we should ask with respect to the 'strange'[478] Cartesian revamping of the good God, and specifically the separation of divine truth from the phenomeno-logical real as impossible, is whether he can finally manage to rescue us from the deceiving God. I think the answer, not made explicit by Lacan, is negative.[479] In short, the good old God exorcises the deceiving God only at the cost of turning *himself* into a somehow deceiving God.

Lacan touches on the fact that a God for whom everything is possible, in the sense that whatever he wants is the truth, cannot but be characterized by an element of capriciousness.[480] He also briefly points out that Descartes's radically voluntaristic approach to the divine, God's 'having wanted everything' qua truth – as opposed to a rationalistic approach whereby God 'knows everything' and is thus impotently submitted to his knowledge – makes it difficult to separate his goodness from evil tout-court, to the extent that his will has precedence over any criterion through which one defines good and evil.[481]

Here, we should take a step further, that is, specifically consider whether, given Descartes's own premises, his good God can be absolutely non-deceiving. On close inspection, this scenario would entail reducing his eternal truths to those which guarantee our truthful knowledge. In other words, God *might have wanted* that $2 + 2 = 5$, yet such a different possible truth was, is and will always be a mere non-actualized potentiality, not really possible, and $2 + 2 = 4$ becomes de facto a necessary truth. But, if we are not to limit in this way the infinite possibilities of God's will to truth, a limitation which would enter into conflict with his not being bound to any kind of necessity apart from the necessary coincidence between his will and *any* kind of truth, why should he not have wanted, be wanting or want in the future that 2 + 2 = 5? For example, why should 2 + 2 = 5 not be, right now as we speak, true in a parallel universe with respect to which, for us and not for God, 2 + 2 = 4 is a lie? And – taking our cue from a provocative albeit fleeting remark Lacan himself makes in Seminar XI – why should historically, within our universe, 1 + 1 + 1 + 1 = 4 and the set-theoretical +(1+(1+(1))) . . ., which does not simply equal 4, not be *both* true, as equally guaranteed by God, while, relative to a given point in time (Descartes's or Cantor's), they are reciprocally false?[482]

The other and more insidious problem with understanding Descartes's good God as absolutely non-deceiving and thus restricting eternal truths to their guaranteeing our current truthful knowledge is that it completely begs the key question initially raised by the hyperbolic doubt. Namely, is there a deceiving God? The good God contains if not annuls the prospect of the deceiving God, for whom 2 + 2 = 5 is a truth and 2 + 2 = 4 a lie with which he deliberately deceives us, only insofar as for the good God 2 + 2 = 4 is a possible truth, which he wanted, *and* 2 + 2 = 5 is another possible truth, which he himself not only might have wanted but also perhaps actually wanted, wants or will want. This actuality may not just apply to some hypothetical rational beings inhabiting the Andromeda galaxy. 2 + 2 = 5 could still *actually* guarantee *our* own truthful knowledge, and, after all, *here* really lies the *goodness* of the good God – in the fact that 2 + 2 = 5 would be as true as 2 + 2 = 4 is in present circumstances – and what keeps the deceiving God at bay. On the contrary, paradoxically enough yet consistently, and this is crucial, if the good God never actualizes 2 + 2 = 5 (or another different truth, say, 2 + 2 = 22) somewhere and/or sometime, if he never lies to us *relative to* somewhere and/or sometime, then we are back to square one, that is, to Descartes's 'stove-heated room' on 10 November 1619, his decision to 'reject as if absolutely false everything in which I could imagine the least doubt', uphold only 'what presented itself to my mind so clearly and so distinctly that I had no occasion to doubt it' *and* the consequent consideration of a 'malicious demon of the utmost power and cunning'.[483] In short, 2 + 2 = 4 is true and 2 + 2 = 5 is false, but is the deceiving God lying to me? Could it not be that 2 + 2 = 4 is absolutely false and 2 + 2 = 5 is absolutely true? Bar the argument I unfolded, we can alternatively counter this predicament only with a fideistic tautology; namely, there is no deceiving God because God does not lie (which is basically Descartes's reply if taken in isolation). So, at this stage, the most convincing outcome of the hyperbolic doubt in a Cartesian context appears to be a rather menacing either/or: either the good non-deceiving God must actually deceive us in a however relative manner, or the deceiving God might be deceiving us in an absolute way.

5.7. Descartes and beyond: From the good deceiving God to the self-deceiving God

What Lacan also touches on at various points in his oeuvre without elaborating further is whether, given the somehow deceitful traits of the good Cartesian God, his final status should not, for us, today – from an aspiringly atheistic stance for which, differing from Descartes's, the endless accumulation of knowledge goes together with the phenomeno-logical truth of incompleteness – better meta-critically be thought of as that of a *self*-deceiving God. As clearly expressed in Seminar XII, 'it is not so much a question of knowing whether he is not a deceiver but, what Descartes does not bring up, whether he is not deceived'.[484] I take this to be Lacan's most advanced and strongly agnostic development of the hyperbolic doubt, his doubt about the Cartesian doubt. In Seminar XIII, the same argument is twice presented as *important pour nous* in the space of a few lines.[485] As late as Seminar XXI we are told that, if there were a God, what would matter above all is not that, because of his lies, blasphemously, he is a 'swine', but rather his being a 'schlepper'.[486] More accurately, in such a scenario, 'God is the potter [*potier*], that's true, but the potter is *also* a schlepper [*empoté*].'[487]

Anticipating an argument that will henceforth prove central to delineating agnostic *atheism*, and using my own jargon, we could suggest that the most extreme and difficult-to-dispose-of figure of the divine is that for which the One = not-One = One = not-One, and so on. This figure in fact no longer irrationally relies on an act of faith, not even on a negative faith in a supremely powerful and cunning evil spirit, since it does not accomplish any kind of transcendent closure and instead makes the One as such *fully coincide* with the not-One, and vice versa. Our phenomeno-logical not-Oneness, namely, the truth of incompleteness, is in turn *not* really ontologically divided from this state of affairs. If there is a God, and we have no faith in our otherworldly salvation, then he is One that deceives our not-One. Yet, if we also relinquish our lingering (conscious or unconscious) faith in being deceived, namely, in our worldly and irreparable damnation, he then deceives us only insofar as he, poor devil, cannot but first and foremost deceive himself.

Genealogically speaking, and in brief:

a. Descartes both evokes and represses the deceiving God.

b. The deceiving God returns in disguise in Descartes's non-deceiving God.

c. Modern science continuously reiterates the repression of the deceiving God, loses faith in the non-deceiving God who thus stops guaranteeing our knowledge, and yet, it both abides by a pre-Cartesian version of the non-deceiving God (as idealistic, positivistic, cognitivist, etcetera absolute knowledge) and, in its weak-atheistic form, through its negative *Weltanschauungen*, unintentionally resurrects the deceiving God in the shape of the God that guarantees that there is no God.

d. In its search for a viable form of atheism that overcomes the impasse of science's weak atheism, a contemporary first philosophy informed by Lacanian psychoanalysis and indebted to the most outrageous moments of Cartesian metaphysics must resume the question of the deceiving God, unveil its most rational-irreligious implications and thus carefully confront the self-deceiving God.

Returning to Lacan's hinting at Descartes's God as, in the end or at least retrospectively, self-deceiving, there are three major interrelated points we should single out. First, precisely insofar as the domain of the Cartesian God qua will to truth is separated from that of knowledge, his being traditionally the ultimate Subject-Supposed-to-Know is already inherently challenged – in spite of the fact that, out of sheer goodness, he still guarantees our truthful knowledge.[488] Second, following from this, the Cartesian God remains thinkable (as One) yet solely as a 'will in its most radical *unthinkability*', and this limitation does not only concern us – because of the relative lies that he is forced to tell us in order to save us from the deceiving God – but also his own 'understanding'; that is, we are primarily dealing with a 'divine impasse' that *is* God.[489] Third, and more conclusively, the Cartesian God, therefore, 'may well be the Master of eternal truths', yet, given their voluntaristic arbitrariness, 'it is not even guaranteed [. . .] that he himself knows it',[490] and in this sense, in not having any knowledge of truth, he is, or comes very close to, the self-deceiving God (the One = not-One = One = not-One, and so on).

Expanding on Lacan, here God is One as truth – as the infinite possibilities of the eternal truths he may want and are as such necessarily true (and eternal as possible) – and, at the same time and for the same reason, not-One (not a God) as knowledge – due precisely to his infinite possibilities. Or also, returning to our previous example and moving quickly, in this context *both* $1 + 1 = 2$-*as-1* (alleged completeness) and $+(1)$ . . . (alleged incompleteness) are absolutely true, not only because everything God wants is by definition true but also, more importantly, and bypassing any transcendent reassurance, because whatever he wants is One as true (including alleged incompleteness, the not-One) *and* at the same time not-One as not-known (including alleged completeness, the One). God is, of course, complete. But he is also, concomitantly, *off* course, as such incomplete, and, again, not-God. $1 + 1 = 2$-as-1 and $+(1)$ . . . are both, as his truths without knowledge, in turn equally complete and incomplete. In other words, at this point it is not even enough to claim that God is *the One* who, as truth, does not know *what* he wants – as his attribute – since not-knowing what he wants is, as not-One, as not-God, precisely what he, the One, is all about as truth. Having said this, for Descartes, he nominally remains the *Master* of truth, and thus the God who is not-God and the not-God who is God is still, in a very precarious manner, *God*.

I think it is this set of issues that leads Lacan, in his late and very late work, to repeatedly ask the question: If there were a God, whom we can think of independently of having faith in him, would such a God not be a God who does *not* believe in himself?[491] In other words, and more generally, moving from the phenomeno-logical and critical assumption for which the universe is apparently not constituted as One (that is, from the truth of incompleteness and, psychoanalytically, from the absence of the sexual relationship), is the *self-deceiving God*, the One = not-One = One = not-One etcetera, not meta-critically the most *rational* and parsimonious alternative to considering not-oneness as conclusive? Either the real not-One is, full stop, yet paradoxically we cannot ever truly posit it without installing a transcendent and deceiving One that contains it. Or the potter is a schlepper.[492]

Also note that on this meta-critical level, the potter qua schlepper and schlepper qua potter, the self-deceiving God, as *the truth without knowledge of itself* provides a further, and possibly final, meaning to the formula 'God is unconscious'. As Miller argues, the formula should certainly not be read as 'God is the unconscious' or 'the unconscious is God', namely, as a – quasi-Jungian – essentialization of the unconscious.[493] Lacan himself reproaches Jean Laplanche and Serge Leclaire precisely for 'bringing into play the signifier as *joined to itself*, as representing [an] *essence* [. . .], and operating as such at the level of the unconscious'.[494] But, going beyond Miller, neither is the formula simply to be limited to the critical level according to which, in short, (a) atheists structurally remain closet believers because (b) the unconscious is already a proto-religious structure through the fundamental fantasy. In other words, once again, we need to distinguish the unconscious as a One that undoes itself and as such makes One from the self-deceiving God as a One = not-One = One, etcetera (the further meaning of the formula 'God is unconscious'). While the former is given as a continuous oscillation One/not-One that also ossifies into the semblance of the One – retrospectively and through the subject's consciousness – the latter remains a sheer identity of One and not-One.

In this second regard, Lacan's elliptical remarks point in two directions. In Seminar XXI, he asserts that 'to say that "God does not believe in himself" is exactly the same as to say that "there is something of the unconscious"'[495] – which I think runs the risk of reintroducing an essentialization of the unconscious on the meta-critical level of the self-deceiving God. However, in Seminar XXVII, he more consistently seems to suggest that, while these claims need to be related, they cannot be equated. In other words, on the one hand, meta-critically, the possibility of the self-deceiving God stands as a refutation of any alleged divine knowledge, that is, 'the unconscious [is not] God's knowledge'.[496] On the other hand, critically, but without solution of continuity, there most certainly is an unconscious knowledge that stems from the very oscillation One/not-One, an acephalous and human-all-too-human knowledge for which there is *no truth of knowledge*. Thinking more thoroughly the continuity between a knowledge of truth without truth of knowledge, the human unconscious as critique, and the possibility of a truth of knowledge without knowledge of truth, the self-deceiving God as meta-critique, stands here as the next challenge on the agenda of a psychoanalytically informed first philosophy.

Lacan stops short of investigating this. But in the mid-1970s, his own meta-critical incursions into the self-deceiving God, as based on an updating of the Cartesian God and, in my view, aimed at the delineation of agnostic atheism, become insistent albeit always fleeting. In Seminar XXI, he claims that we should interpret Descartes's deceiving God as '*totally* deceiving', that is, as amounting to *God* tout-court, in the sense that God both 'made the real' (the not-One) and precisely in that he made it he is 'all the more *submitted*' to it.[497] Or also, while the Lacanian real is by definition that which does not work (not-One), at the same time, 'it works like that' (One),[498] and the more the self-deceiving God deceives himself, the more things will nonetheless work (not-One = One = not-One = One, etcetera).

In another lesson from Seminar XXI, the idea of the self-deceiving God, of a 'God [who] does not believe in God', is equated with that of nature's being 'not so natural', namely, naturally 'deranged' in itself.[499] And, we should add, this is not to say that nature is simply barred. It is barred and it is not barred. Or better, as barred it is not barred, and as not barred it is barred.

In Seminars XXII, XXIII and other texts of the same period, Lacan notes that God is the (Name-of-the-)Father but as such *inherently père-vers*.[500] Thus, the question concerning the supposed 'deceit value' of our phenomeno-logical horizon vis-à-vis noumena, the not-Oneness with which the deceiving God would allegedly deceive *us*, should be rethought accordingly: it is only us who may regard not-Oneness as deceitful, since for the *self*-deceiving God who does not know-believe in himself 'deceiving and being the truth is exactly the same'.[501] For him, the not-One is One (and hence he is deceiving us given our not-Oneness), yet the One is not-One (and hence he is telling us the truth), yet the not-One is One, and so on and so forth. In other words, unpacking and systematizing Lacan's point, God as truth is in a way *more* submitted to his lying than we are due to the truth of incompleteness, in that his lying is for him indistinguishable from the truth, whereas, on a phenomeno-logical level, we also contingently rely on the *oscillation* between the One and the not-One as distinct, not on their identity.

As late as Seminar XXVII, his last, Lacan claims that the question 'Does God believe in God?' is after all rhetorical, an 'answer-question', namely, God does *not* believe in himself.[502] Again, if there were a God, then he would be a self-deceiving God. *But* – and this is crucial – if this is the case, however much this question remains theoretically 'venomous',[503] then, as Lacan quips in 'La troisième', too bad if there is a God, 'too bad if God deceives me'[504] in first and foremost deceiving himself. That is to say, reversing Pascal's wager through a post-Lacanian and supremely rational updating of Descartes, as anticipated in Seminar XV, we should '*do as if* [God] were not there'[505] at all and found our *practical* – ethical and political – action on the not-One while not reifying it. Weak-atheistic reification can be avoided precisely by upholding at the same time the *theoretical* option of the self-deceiving God. In this sense, 'we can do without [God] provided that we use [him]'.[506]

We may read along the same agnostically atheistic lines even Lacan's programmatic claim, in Seminar X, that 'the atheist, as combatant, as revolutionary, is not one who denies God in his function of omnipotence, but one who affirms oneself as not *serving* any God', and that this is what makes the question of atheism passionate.[507] Tertullian's absurdist credo could thus in turn be reversed. For the militant agnostic atheist, non *credo*, I do *not* believe, practically, *quia* non *absurdum est*, because it is *not* absurd, theoretically. Or also, fighting perversion as a circumlocutory 'crusade' for 'the defence of faith in the Other'[508] on its own ground, *je ne sais pas bien, mais quand même*. I do *not* very well know that there is no self-deceiving God, but nonetheless I do *not* believe.

To sum up, insofar as, critically, truth (the not-One) can only be half-said, because it structurally brings with it the deceiving God, but we can also discuss it meta-critically, in the domain of 'first truths',[509] as long as we concomitantly tackle it in this domain as the alternative truth of the self-deceiving God (not-One = One = not-One = One etcetera) such a speculative undecidability turns truth into a concrete question of 'choice'.[510] Strong *agnosticism* promotes agnostic *atheism* as *strong* atheism.

6. A short manifesto for agnostic atheism

1. The God hypothesis, the oscillation between the One and the not-One, or not-two, is the phenomeno-logic of the animal that contingently happens to speak and be at odds with sex.

    1.1 Difference designates the continuous reversibility of the One and not-One poles of the oscillation, that is, the One that undoes itself into the not-One and the not-One that makes the One.

    1.2 The not-One pole of the oscillation corresponds to the zero, or void.

2. The phenomeno-logical truth of the God hypothesis, the death of God as the truth of incompleteness, is the no-two-as-One.

   2.1 Every necessarily inconclusive, albeit structurally unavoidable, attempt at sublating the not-One pole of the oscillation into One and thereby into the two-as-One results into a semblance that still rests on the truth of incompleteness.

   2.1.1 Religiously, this semblance amounts to God. Epistemologically, to absolute knowledge. Sexually, to the con-fusion with the other/partner counted as One. Existentially, to the ego elevated to being-me-to-myself.

3. From a *critical* stance that addresses the threshold of our phenomeno-logic, the not-two as no-two-as-One is the real not-One.

   3.1 The real not-One marks logically the impossible, numerically the impossibility of numbering or uncountable infinity (that is, the space between the One and the not-One, or zero, poles of the oscillation) and ontologically the point of in-difference as *pure* difference.

4. Positing the real not-One as necessarily final, phenomeno-logically treating the truth of incompleteness as the truth about truth that irrefutably holds irrespective of our phenomeno-logic, inevitably turns the not-One into *One* (not-One). The real not-One would be *all* there is.

   4.1 This is weak atheism, which is weak because it implicitly posits the God of atheists, the God that guarantees there is no God, the deceiving God.

5. From a *meta-critical* stance that tries to think the real not-One not only as the phenomeno-logical threshold of the in-itself-for-us but also as the in-itself-for-itself without assuming a priori the reduction of the latter to the former, conclusively, *either* the not-One is in-itself-for-us and for-itself (in which case it would be more correct to state that not-*oneness* is) *or* the not-One is *One* in-itself-for-itself.

   5.1 This is strong agnosticism, which is strong because it both rationally ventures into the metaphysical territory that weak agnosticism avoids and questions the theistic relapse of weak atheism.

6. If the real not-One *is* in-itself-for-itself, then, due to our phenomeno-logic, we still cannot think it as such without transforming it into One (not-One). But the either/or prevents us from surreptitiously yet directly positing the One (not-One).

7. If the real not-One is eventually *One*, then, starting from the phenomeno-logical truth of incompleteness, we can think of it as at least three broad variants of God, which are increasingly less irrational: the salvific God, the deceiving God, the self-deceiving God.

   7.1 The salvific God transcendently contains and finally sublates the real not-One: it is One (not-One) → *One*. The deceiving God transcendently contains but never sublates the real not-One: it is *One* (not-One). The self-deceiving God neither contains nor sublates the real not-One: it is not-One = One = not-One = One, etcetera. Here, the One and not-One poles of the phenomeno-logical oscillation are no longer distinct precisely in and through the real not-One of the truth of incompleteness.

   7.2 Positing the salvific and the deceiving God requires an act of – conscious or unconscious – irrational faith in the One, which is not phenomeno-logically granted.

       7.2.1 Belief in any kind of salvific God remains at bottom *quia absurdum est*.

       7.2.2 The deceiving God remains a, however negative, salvific God in that it provides some form of closure precisely by means of irreversible damnation.

   7.3 Positing the self-deceiving God does not require any act of irrational faith in the One. Still, the possibility of the self-deceiving God does not hold any rational precedence over the possibility that the real not-One conclusively is.

8. *Either the real not-One as conclusive not-oneness is or the self-deceiving God* (the not-One = One = not-One = One, etcetera) *is*. The alternative between the real not-One and the self-deceiving God remains rationally undecidable.

   8.1 From a more ontological perspective, either indifference is or the *identity* of indifference and the One, which is nothing other than the *indifference* between the One and indifference, is.

   8.2 If indifference is, it remains indifferent to difference. In other words, difference is *and* is not difference, for at its purest it *is* in-difference, namely, indifference that contingently becomes difference yet also remains indifferent to difference.

   8.3 If the self-deceiving God is, it itself remains indifferent to difference, for as not-One = One = not-One = One etcetera, it is *not* different from the real not-One of contingent in-difference.

9. While the either/or remains rationally undecidable on a theoretical plane, we should *practically*, and ir-rationally, act as if there were no God, for if there were One, he would only be an inconsistent God, who deceives us by first and foremost deceiving himself. With this passage, strong *agnosticism* becomes agnostic *atheism* as *strong* atheism.

   9.1 If we chose the self-deceiving God, and the latter were, we would lose pure difference and difference (and the semblance of identity), namely, what makes us human, without acquiring any conciliatory identity (as Logos, blessed Life or even Hell), since the identity of the self-deceiving God is reduced to indifference.

   9.2 If we chose the self-deceiving God, and the latter were not, the result would be for us the same, namely, sheer entropic indifference.

   9.3 Agnostic atheism remains, on a new level, an ascetic practice. Practically choosing the real not-One necessitates the theoretical maintenance of the either/or for the real not-One not to relapse de facto into the One (not-One).

      9.3.1 *Philosophy* is the theoretical discourse that meta-critically constructs and maintains the either/or and thus sustains such an ascetic practice.

10. *Ethically*, this means that evil amounts to losing difference. Evil is what indifferentiates difference – and, more precisely, what indifferentiates in-difference – ultimately in the sense of the self-extinction of the *Homo sapiens* species. The good is conversely bound to critically re-dis-covering the point of in-difference as pure difference against the temptations of the One as the indifferent One.

    10.1 Practically acting, in the name of in-difference, as if there were no self-deceiving God amounts to agnostic atheism's neo-Cartesian, and permanent, *morale par provision*.

11. *Politically*, this means establishing a critical discourse of the real not-One – of the pure difference of in-difference – that opposes any discourse of indifferentiating totalization and totalizing indifferentiation (leading to maximal entropy).

    11.1 Capitalism is a discourse that chose and tends towards the One = not-One = One etcetera. Capitalism is more and more a self-deceiving discourse of the indifferent One – hence our current fascination with 'fake news' that are actually true lies. The exponential proliferation of 'differences' (identity politics) under capitalism increasingly renders them indifferent. They serve only the One of Capital whose identity is in fact nothing other than the indifference between its global Oneness (money) and these very indifferences.

11.1.1 Science as a discourse of the One (not-One) is today practically subsumed under capitalism as a discourse of the One = not-One = One etcetera. Implicitly – or explicitly – championing the One (not-One) itself leads us to indifference, as evidenced by the potential for self-extinction made possible by military technology and the uncontrolled exploitation of natural resources.

11.1.2 Even when it seldom does not directly embrace capitalism through its defence of identity politics, 'liberal' politics is today practically subsumed under capitalism. Like science, which it unproblematically equals with our common good, and paradoxically in the name of anti-totalitarianism, it abides by a discourse of the One (not-One), of the ideology of the end of ideologies. The progressive fool who attempts to tell the truth about the truth of incompleteness, ending up instead with the Truth of incompleteness, paves the way for indifference, and thus becomes more and more indistinguishable from the capitalist knave.

Conclusion

The modest absolute: Or, why I am not an agnostic (or even an agnostic atheist)

Adrian Johnston

1. After faitheism: Undead divinities and the prospects for complete disbelief

I first became aware of the work of Lorenzo Chiesa thanks to the 2007 publication of his book *Subjectivity and Otherness: A Philosophical Reading of Lacan* in the Short Circuits series at the MIT Press. I read this monograph immediately when it became available and was impressed and intrigued by its author. However, it was not until 2011, at an event in Berlin on 'The Human Animal in Politics, Science, and Psychoanalysis' hosted by the KW Institute for Contemporary Art and partly organized by Lorenzo, that he and I finally had an opportunity to meet in person for the first time. Fortunately, we promptly hit it off personally in addition to intellectually.

Lorenzo and I have remained in continual contact ever since that first meeting in Germany over a decade ago – and this in addition to each assiduously following the other's textual outputs as these have materialized in print over the years. Lorenzo has visited Albuquerque a couple of times to give talks in the Department of Philosophy at the University of New Mexico as well as in order for us to have the sorts of intensive discussions and debates possible only in face-to-face conversation. Moreover, for many years now, we routinely have conferred about various matters of mutual theoretical interest via e-mail and Skype.

The idea for the present co-authored book, *God Is Undead: Psychoanalysis for Unbelievers*, grew out of exchanges between Lorenzo and me triggered by his 2016 book *The Not-Two: Logic and God in Lacan* (also published in the

Short Circuits series at the MIT Press). What became clear to us through these exchanges is that our similar-yet-distinct interpretations of Lacan's stances *vis-à-vis* religions and theisms, interpretations we lay out in the main body of the present book, crystallize more profound philosophical differences between the two of us. These differences involve foundational metaphysical matters having to do with naturalism, scientificity, negativity and anthropogenesis, among other topics. Although *God Is Undead* focuses on Freud's and, especially, Lacan's irreligiosity, its ultimate stakes concern bigger-picture metaphysical controversies.

Before addressing some of the disagreements Lorenzo and I have with each other, I ought both to explain our chosen book title, *God Is Undead*, and to foreground a foundational consensus between us despite our disagreements. Perhaps under the influence of the still-ongoing Covid-19 global pandemic, I am tempted to turn to viruses in order to help illuminate the recourse to the notion of undead-ness in the title. In biological terms, viruses are entities situated on the border between life and non-life, the organic and the inorganic. Although viruses' organization and self-replication make them resemble the living organisms on which they parasitize, their status as being nothing more than nucleic acid molecules encased in protein coats seems to qualify them as non-living matter. As non-living matter acting like a living organism, a virus resembles the entities called 'the undead' in horror fiction.

Another feature of the undead of horror fiction is their interminable, obstinate persistence. One of the tropes of such fiction is the standard scene of the undead antagonist tirelessly rising up again and again from its repeated apparent demises at the hands of the living protagonist to continue its fiendish pursuit of this protagonist. No matter how many times the zombies are killed, they keep getting back up to resume relentlessly shambling on. Sadly, the same looks to be the case with the seemingly unending coronavirus pandemic. In this real-life horror show, each time we believe ourselves to have vanquished Covid-19 and allow ourselves to exhale a collective sigh of relief, we come to discover that the virus has not been defeated, that it resurfaces to persist in its blind, destructive process of making yet more copies (and mutations) of itself. These repeated demoralizing shocks in response to the persistence of Covid-19 resemble not a little the horror induced in audiences by harrowing tales of the undead.

The undead-like persistence of the coronavirus is so strong that all epidemiologists worth their salt concur about how the current pandemic, rather than finally ending for good Hollywood-movie-style, instead will morph into being endemic. Covid-19 will fade into the background, joining there such other entities as the viruses responsible for seasonal influenzas, but it will not disappear altogether. The coronavirus will defiantly linger on, becoming a regular refrain within the annual rhythms and routines of our ordinary lives.

As I highlight both in the main body above and elsewhere,[1] Lacan dismisses Nietzschean declarations of God's death as inadequate expressions for a true atheism. The more one consciously writes off the divine as deceased, the less one is prone to keep peeled a vigilant eye for the tenaciously persistent yet sometimes subtle traces of lingering religiosity, traces sometimes cloaked in pseudo-secular, subliminatory coverings. Lacan's 'God is unconscious', his alternative to 'God is dead', is intended to capture, among other things, the fact that pre/non-analytic conscious atheisms (as insufficiently atheistic) tend to be oblivious to the disguised undead-ness, the stubborn underground continuation, of theisms through subtle and not-so-subtle means. 'God is dead' directly implies that the divine can simply die. Following Lacan, Lorenzo and I jointly consider this implication to be complacently optimistic about the prospects for a sufficiently atheistic atheism. If such prospects are to have any chance at all, they must preliminarily recognize that, as per our book's title, God instead is undead. Like Covid-19, theisms cannot be defeated so easily. Both ontogenetically and phylogenetically, they are surprisingly obdurate.

I can best describe my own assessment regarding the prospects for a truly atheistic atheism through reference to Marx. Specifically, Marx's eulogy for the Paris Commune, 1871's *The Civil War in France*, involves him holding up the Commune as proof of the real socio-historical possibility of purportedly 'impossible' communism (as per the anti-communist refrain, as old as communism itself, according to which materially egalitarian and fully classless societies are nothing but the futility of unrealizable utopian daydreams). Marx underscores that, in the midst of utterly inauspicious conditions for embarking on a socialist/communist-style remaking of society – Paris was left beleaguered, and then surrounded and besieged by hostile enemy forces, after France's defeat in the Franco-Prussian War – the Communards nevertheless put in place a working new post-capitalist social order, however short-lived.[2]

Marx's post-mortem on the 1871 Paris Commune indicates that, under more auspicious circumstances, socialist and communist experiments in remaking societies have better than non-negligible chances to last longer than the Commune and achieve enduring infrastructural and institutional advances. Yet, even if, unlike Marx himself, one were to be sceptical about the likelihood of future socialist/communist victories – admittedly, the 'barbarism' alternative of the 'socialism or barbarism' disjunction already is globally triumphing now at the geo-political level and seems likely to continue its awful world-historical march forward as the twenty-first century continues to grind on – the very fact that the Commune managed to arise in the first place and persist, even if only briefly, in the teeth of the greatest adversity proves that socialism and communism are anything but impossible. Improbability is not impossibility. The utterly unlikely occasionally comes to pass. In religious language, the seemingly miraculous happens once in a while.

What the just-summarized Marx of 1871 says about the possibilities for socialism and communism I would say about the possibilities for genuine post-analytic-type atheism. As I reveal earlier in the book's main body, Lacan proposes that the analytic experience, especially in the terminal phases of clinical processes, brings about an authentic atheism through inducing the (if only momentary) liquidation of the very figure/place of the subject supposed to know (*le sujet supposé savoir*). This is Lacan's version of Freud's dissolution of the transference as one of the criteria for ending analysis. The later Freud of 1937's 'Analysis Terminable and Interminable' warns that an adequately thorough analysis provides no immunization or prophylaxis against potential future outbreaks of psychopathology even in the best-analyzed analysand.[3] Similarly, Lacan insinuates that no analytically terminal experience of thoroughgoing atheism, in which not only gods but all other religious and/or secular embodiments of a big Other authoritatively 'in the know' disintegrate and vanish, is guaranteed to last.

If anything, various of Lacan's remarks about theisms and atheisms convey a profound pessimism on his part. He appears resignedly to anticipate that individual analysands are likely to revert post-analytically to investments in subjects supposed to know (even if and when these are new ones different from pre-analytic ones). He also cautions that the gods of old show no signs of imminent demise at the present stage of social history – and this contrary to the Enlightenment-inspired hopes and predictions of the likes of Marx and Freud.

But, to refer back to Marx *circa* 1871 once more, the analyst's ability to induce in his/her analysands even a transitory, fleeting passage through an especially virulent atheism bears witness to the possibility of human beings (and maybe even humanity as a whole) fully facing up to the absence not only of God, but of any and every representative of the structural role of *le sujet supposé savoir* and/or *le grand Autre*. To Marx's cry regarding the Paris Commune 'But this is communism, "impossible" communism!',[4] Lacan might add regarding the evaporation of transferential cathexes onto subjects supposed to know, 'But this is atheism, "impossible" atheism!' Perhaps like the Paris Commune itself, psychoanalysis in its entirety, as both a theory and a practice, might prove to be a short-lived experiment, one snuffed out by an unholy alliance of its enemies, nonetheless showing real future possibilities, however unlikely these may be.

As for the foundational consensus underpinning the present book, Lorenzo and I are united in our opposition not only to religious and religion-friendly readings of Freudian and Lacanian psychoanalysis but also to garden-variety atheisms exposed by analytic tools to be insufficiently atheistic. In the spirit of Lacan's own prolific neologizing – by one (under)count, he is responsible for coining 789 neologisms, many formed as portmanteau words – I can say that Lorenzo and I both reject what might be labelled 'faitheism'. This particular portmanteau-word neologism combines, on the one hand, 'atheism' with, on the other hand, not only 'faith', but a string of other f-words too: failed, fake, false, fantasmatic, fictional, flawed, fucked, etc.

Put more exactly in Lacanian parlance, instances of faitheism would be any atheisms that, despite denouncing gods and the like as non-existent (or 'dead'), fail to jettison the structural categories occupied by various and sundry divinities, namely, Lacan's metapsychological categories of the unbarred big Other and the subject-supposed-to-know. An obvious and familiar example of faitheism in this precise sense would be a typical naturalistic-scientific atheism that, despite insisting on the natural without the supernatural, turns nature itself into a self-consistent and all-powerful *grand Autre* and natural scientists into the priest-like human authorities through whom this Other articulates its edicts, laws and truths. Nature-with-a-capital-N is simply put in the same place from which God was removed by scientific faitheism – with this structural place being that of the self-consistent big Other and/or *sujet supposé savoir*. Especially in Lacan's wake, arriving at genuine atheism, rather than at its faitheistic semblance, requires leaving this place itself empty and drawing the myriad appropriate consequences from the absence of unbarred big Others and subjects-supposed-to-know (and/or supposed to [know how to] enjoy).

2. Not all is onto-theology: Ontologies avoidable and unavoidable

The preceding aside, I must limit this relatively brief concluding reassessment of the persisting disputes between Lorenzo and me to how our divergences feature in relation to psychoanalytic critiques of traditional religions and theologies. Such self-restraint obviously is in line with the overarching preoccupations of *God Is Undead*. Moreover, attempting to stage an exhaustive reckoning here between Lorenzo's and my philosophical positions would do anything but help conclude the current book.

From my perspective, the main fault line of tension between Lorenzo and me in *God Is Undead* has to do with the notion of agnosticism. In other words, the question of whether or not an agnostic dimension is to be attributed to Lacan's non-belief in any established theisms condenses much of what divides our positions. Although somewhat of a simplification, it would not be entirely inaccurate to say that Lorenzo advocates in favour of an atheism tempered by the purportedly ineliminable caveats, qualifications and reservations of a lingering agnosticism, while I argue for an atheism decisively dispensing with the sorts of doubts carefully retained in Lorenzo's 'para-ontological' synthesis of philosophy and psychoanalysis.

Indeed, I view what Lorenzo calls his 'para-ontology' as directly inspired by what one might describe as Lacan's apparent agnosticism with respect to ontology as a philosophical theory of being making strong claims about the nature of what exists in and of itself. On several occasions, and particularly in the celebrated eleventh seminar of 1964 (*The Four Fundamental Concepts of Psychoanalysis*), Lacan seems hesitant, wavering and sceptical as regards the prospects for a psychoanalytic ontology and even for ontology *tout court*.[5] In no small part on the basis of what looks to be Lacan's ontological agnosticism, Lorenzo argues that Lacan must be religiously agnostic too in however refined and sophisticated a fashion. More precisely, Lacan's disbelief must involve at least a slight margin of uncertainty, given his scoffing at the boldness of most canonical philosophers' proposals about being *an sich* (including the being traditionally named 'God' in a wide range of metaphysical systems scattered across the history of Western philosophy). For Chiesian para-ontology, any ontology untempered by doubts about its confident truth-proposals apropos being-in-itself is essentially onto-theological, namely, a dogmatic faith in a really existing Oneness grounding and encompassing everything that is.

Already as regards Lacan's various remarks about ontology and its (lack of) prospects, Lorenzo and I disagree. I interpret this Lacan differently.[6] And, these differences in how we read Lacan's pronouncements on theories of being are not merely exegetical. Through unpacking them, as I am about to do, I can begin bringing to light what are, as I see things, the major philosophical and theoretical bones of contention between Lorenzo and me.

Lacan, in the same seminar (eleven) in which he sounds evasive about the possibility of a psychoanalytically informed ontology, also admits that, 'of course, I have my ontology – why not? – like everyone else, however naïve or elaborate it may be'.[7] This admission importantly concedes that nobody is able to avoid 'having his/her ontology'. Obviously, handfuls of certain sorts of professional academic philosophers deliberately set out to elaborate comprehensive theories of being. Such thinkers indeed have their ontologies, and consciously so in the forms of carefully assembled conceptual and argumentative constructions.

But, as Lacan's just-quoted 1964 remark suggests, those who are not professional academic philosophers, whether they are highly cultured psychoanalysts like himself or anyone else (including the proverbial ordinary person on the street in his/her anti-intellectualism), also have their spontaneous ideas about the ultimate nature of reality, if only as implicit or unattended-to assumptions, beliefs, images, presuppositions, etc. (e.g. the so-called 'natural attitude' as characterized by Husserlian phenomenology). Hence, one implication of Lacan's observation about the unavoidability of ontological speculations is that one cannot opt out of thinking ontologically. In other words, one is compelled or condemned to choose between two ways of arriving at and adhering to an ontology: consciously or unconsciously, wittingly or unwittingly. I will come back to the question of whether this alleged inevitability of subscribing to an ontology dooms everyone, Lacan included, to (onto-)theological thinking too.

Relatedly, in *Seminar XIX* (*. . . or Worse* [1971–2]), Lacan predicts 'one day someone will come along to make an ontology out of' his disruption and dividing of any and every One-All. This would be a theory of being centred on what is designated by the Lacanian mathemes $\cancel{A}$ and S($\cancel{A}$) (i.e. the barred Other and the signifier of the barred Other, respectively).[8] My guess is that Lorenzo hears this forecast on Lacan's part as uttered with a discouraged, disapproving sigh. Heard thusly, this Lacan would be expressing a dismayed fatalism or weary resignation in the face of the prospect of future philosophically-minded others coming along and working up various of his statements (on the One and the Many, the infinite and the finite, the [in]consistent and the [in]complete, and so on) into an ontological framework or metaphysical system. On what I imagine would be the Chiesian para-ontological parsing of this 1972 prediction, Lacan's not-One thereby, through being integrated into an ontology or metaphysics, would be recaptured and domesticated by the One it is intended to disrupt.

By contrast, I do not construe this later Lacan of 1972 as entirely displeased by the prospect of a future ontological/metaphysical systematization of his metapsychological musings. Why not? To begin with, and as I already pointed out a moment ago, Lacan accepts that ontological thinking, if only unconsciously, is unavoidable and inescapable. Not only will others *à venir* ontologize Lacanian psychoanalysis – Lacan himself, by his own admission, cannot help but engage in spontaneous ontologizing. And, presumably, thinking ontologically is better done with than without the aid of psychoanalytic insights (as well as better done intentionally rather than unintentionally).

Although Lacan's 'return to Freud' often is associated by his readers specifically with the so-called 'middle period' of his teaching during the 1950s, his profound fidelity to the founder of psychoanalysis also remains unwavering from the 1960s until his death in 1981. Indeed, Lacan declares to his followers during one of his final public appearances, in Caracas, Venezuela, in August 1980, that 'It is up to you to be Lacanians, if you want. Me, I am Freudian' (*C'est à vous d'être lacaniens, si vous voulez. Moi, je suis freudien*).[9] And, there are two Freudian lines of thought relevant to the present consideration of Lacan's attitudes to ontology I consider Lacan to adhere to in ways that might problematize what I take to be Lorenzo's para-ontological renditions of Lacanianism.

The first of these two Freudian lines of thought is to be found in Freud's 1901 *The Psychopathology of Everyday Life* (with this early text, along with 1900's *The Interpretation of Dreams* and 1905's *Jokes and Their Relation to the Unconscious*, being especially crucial to Lacan's rendition of the analytic unconscious). Therein, Freud describes how one might 'transform *metaphysics* into *metapsychology*'.[10] This in itself already suggests a kinship between metaphysical and metapsychological speculations such as to allow for translations between them. But, whereas Freud appears only intermittently to pursue this project of the psychoanalytic transformation of philosophy, Lacan, as is common knowledge, constantly refers to myriad figures and orientations in the history of Western philosophy from the ancient Greeks to his twentieth-century contemporaries. These references are so frequent and prominent as to result effectively in a blurring of lines between the metaphysical and the metapsychological in Lacan's teachings. Likewise, Lacan, unlike Freud, liberally and unabashedly uses philosophical terms and concepts in articulating his own version of psychoanalysis. As I have argued in detail elsewhere,[11] Lacan is not nearly so 'anti-philosophical' as many have tried to make him out to be.

The second Freudian line of thought to which Lacan is faithful, one dovetailing with Lacan's above-discussed admission of the inevitability of ontological thinking, has to do with free association. Of course, analysands attempting to free associate, struggling to say whatever comes to mind as it comes to mind while lying on the analyst's couch with as little self-censorship as possible, is at the very heart of the clinical analytic process as an exploration of the unconscious. This is as much the case for Lacan, and for just about every practicing analytic clinician, as it is for Freud.

Yet, one of the things psychoanalytic experience reveals to each and every analysand is that free associations are not actually free. The analysand's monologue initially or superficially seems to (in)consist of disparate fragments of speech surfacing within a meandering, directionless monologue repeatedly punctuated by a series of random *non sequiturs*. But, these fragments, when carefully examined under the influence of the analyst's interpretations, turn out to be pieces of a puzzle which, when assembled, furnish a bigger picture of the (partly) organized formations of the unconscious. These formations dictate the hidden logic rendering apparently free associations really determined expressions of structural dynamics previously unbeknownst to ego-level (self-)consciousness. In the same final chapter ('Chapter XII: Determinism, Belief in Chance and Superstition – Some Points of View') of *The Psychopathology of Everyday Life* in which the transformation of metaphysics into metapsychology is mentioned, Freud indicates that the explicit non-systematicity of persons' associations belie an implicit systematicity in their (if only unconscious) thinking.[12]

These Freudian theses about (un)free association can be nicely encapsulated through a paraphrase of a famous observation the later Freud makes about the super-ego. In 1923's *The Ego and the Id*, Freud remarks, 'the normal man is not only far more immoral than he believes but also far more moral than he knows'.[13] The lustful, murderous id and the concealed portions of the super-ego are the 'immoral' and 'moral' faces, respectively, of the analytic unconscious. However, popularizations of psychoanalysis and vulgarizations of Freud tend to overemphasize repressed immorality and correspondingly neglect repressed morality.

As regards one of the lessons of free association in psychoanalysis, one could say (paraphrasing this just-quoted 1923 Freud) that, in our thinking and speaking, we are not only far more inconsistent and conflicted than we believe but also far more consistent and systematic than we know. Psychoanalysis and its unconscious are not just about discord, fragmentation, splitting and so on. In the Freudian field, previously unappreciated syntheses and unities inevitably are brought to light too. As Lorenzo might put it, the psychoanalytic unconscious involves both the One (i.e. coherence and integration) and the not-One (i.e. incoherence and disintegration).

Even for psychoanalysis, a certain degree of consistency and systematicity is inevitable and inescapable. I would contend that this is so not only for analysands' (un)free associations on the couch of the clinical setting but also for analysts' and analytically-inspired thinkers' theoretical reflections at the level of metapsychology (and/as metaphysics). I believe that Lacan, however happily or not, ultimately accepted all of this.

Furthermore, and regardless of Lacan's own attitudes apropos the preceding, I feel that Lorenzo concedes too much to religions, theologies, etc. in a couple of related manners. First, he looks to me as though he treats all confident invocations of truth, whether as a matter of correspondence or coherence, as symptoms of (lingering, unconscious) religiosity. Appeals to the certain, the indubitable and the like seem to be diagnosed by Chiesian para-ontology as vestiges of fervent belief and zealous faith, even if such convictions are not invested in any traditional versions of gods or the supernatural.

One might say that conviction itself is convicted by Lorenzo's position of being inherently religious. Hence, a self-assured atheism would be, for him, not really atheistic given its belief in itself as true. It would have faith in its own truth, thus rendering it still religious. The 'agnostic atheism' of Chiesian para-ontology can be viewed as an attempt to accede to an atheism purged of any theistic remainders in the guise of convictions suspected of being tainted as essentially theistic/theological by the intensity with which they are embraced by those who hold them.

Second, Lorenzo relatedly appears to equate every actual and possible systematic metaphysics with monotheism of one sort or another. For him, any consistent interfacing of ontology and epistemology (with a metaphysics amounting to a combination of an ontology with an epistemology) put forward as encompassing the most basic and overarching conception of what exists and can be known amounts to erecting in philosophical thought a "One" lording it over reality in a God-like manner. From Lorenzo's perspective, even an ontology/metaphysics fulfilling Lacan's 1972 expectations of being forged firmly and strictly on the basis of his concepts of the not-One, the barred Other and the like would be, in its argumentative systematicity in addition to its belief in the truth of its own claims, theistic. For para-ontology, all ontology not qualified by an agnostic 'para-' would be onto-theology as fidelity to a God or a God-like Being-with-a-capital-B.

But, strong senses of truth and strivings to account systematically for the grounds of all existence are too precious and worthwhile to abandon *in toto* to the religious, the superstitious, the theistic and so on. As a cliché saying has it, even a broken clock is right at least twice a day. For me, not all truths are religious, not all systems are theistic and not all ontologies are onto-theological. Just because such intellectual and philosophical elements have a long history of association or entanglement with religions – given the hegemony of religions across the vast arc of human history, one would be hard-pressed to find any ideational-cultural elements of whatever kind not historically colored by established and extant religious renditions of them – does not mean that these elements are intrinsically and irredeemably religious. To paraphrase Marx, there are rational kernels to be salvaged and extracted from even the most mystical and thick of shells.

In fact, and to go a step further, how could one critique and challenge religions, theisms, etc. without assuming or asserting, at a minimum, the truth of one's anti-religious (whether agnostic or atheistic) stance, a truth whose strength is adequate to contest the purported strong truth of believers' claims? In arguing against supernaturalistic and theistic worldviews, putting themselves forward as true ontological/metaphysical frameworks, how could one not end up, so to speak, fighting fire with fire (regardless of one's initial intentions)? Does not even the most principled agnosticism *vis-à-vis* religions implicitly, if not explicitly, advance itself as metaphysically truer, at least in terms of what human beings allegedly can and cannot know about being(s), than the religions it casts into doubt?

Chiesian para-ontological agnostic atheism substitutes indecisive vacillations between One and not-One, A and $\cancel{A}$ (i.e. the unbarred and barred Other, respectively) or what Lorenzo baptizes the 'self-deceiving God' and 'indifferent not-Oneness' for any confident decision one way or another about a monotheistic deity or other form of Oneness. Yet, how does this substitution evade being tainted by religion, theism and/or onto-theology? Does not para-ontology itself seek to speak the ultimate truth about certain human existential predicaments in a coherent (i.e. systematic, broadly speaking) fashion. In fact, one even could encapsulate formalistically Chiesian para-ontological agnostic atheism as insisting on $\forall x (x \wedge \sim x)$ or, put more precisely through recourse to Lacan's mathemes, $(\forall A [A \wedge \cancel{A}] \wedge \forall \cancel{A} [\cancel{A} \wedge A])$. Both $\forall x (x \wedge \sim x)$ and $(\forall A [A \wedge \cancel{A}] \wedge \forall \cancel{A} [\cancel{A} \wedge A])$ logically unify Lorenzo's infinite oscillation between the poles of his self-deceiving God and indifferent not-Oneness. By contrast, a (post-)Lacanian non-agnostic atheism, when all is said and done, finally would insist on $\cancel{A}$, full stop.

But, would not such logical unification signal that Lorenzo's position itself, his para-ontological agnostic atheism, cannot escape being yet another One – in this instance, the oneness of the formulae $\forall x (x \wedge \sim x)$ or $(\forall A [A \wedge \cancel{A}] \wedge \forall \cancel{A} [\cancel{A} \wedge A])$? If so, if even para-ontology cannot avoid resting on an ultimate all-encompassing Truth (if only as the formally encapsulated alternation between One and not-

One, A and A̸, etc.), then why worry about trying to achieve such an impossible 'agnostic' avoidance? Why not just drop the vain agnosticism and, given the inevitability of having to presuppose or posit what one takes to be a true theory of being, opt for a new ontology atheistically (un)grounded on A̸ and able to confront the theological residues clinging to so many previous, older ontologies?

3. Modesty is not a virtue: Against agnosticism

One of the ways Lorenzo characterizes his position is as 'meta-critical'. Of course, this adjective qualifying his stance cannot but call to mind Kantian critique and its legacy up through the present. Moreover, this association is further reinforced by Lorenzo's stress on the importance of agnosticism. The critical Kant too is interpretable as epistemologically arguing for a principled metaphysical agnosticism as regards any and all strong ontological claims about beings in and of themselves (in the guises of Kant's *Dinge an sich*).

To bring up the topic of Kant's (in)famous thing-in-itself and the metaphysical/ontological agnosticism going along with it is also to bring up the history of the controversies surrounding these core features of Kantian transcendental idealism. As is well known, Kant's contemporaries and immediate successors, including the three other giants of German idealism (i.e. Fichte, Schelling and Hegel), all take issue with the idea of inherently unknowable things-in-themselves lying on the inaccessible other side of the purported 'limits of possible experience' exclusively within which knowledge is attainable by minded human subjects. It would be inappropriate, distracting and impractical for me to rehearse in the current context the myriad details and nuances of the critical reception of Kantian transcendental idealism during the late-eighteenth and early-nineteenth centuries (not to mention onwards up through the twenty-first century). However, in what immediately follows, I will be selectively mobilizing a few post-Kantian (specifically Hegelian) problematizations of Kantian critique as a means for articulating additional pushback on my part against the critical-agnostic dimensions of Lorenzo's project.

Hegel's various reservations and objections *vis-à-vis* Kant, including with respect to Kant's thing-in-itself, are numerous and multifaceted. However, a particular Hegelian line of argumentation targeting *das Ding an sich* is especially relevant as regards some of the differences between Lorenzo and me. According to this Hegelian line, nothing is more knowable than the allegedly unknowable thing-in-itself. Why?

This is because, according to Hegel, one is perfectly capable of knowing how the Kantian noumenal 'x' is produced. To arrive at this 'x', one need only subtract and negate all perceptible and conceivable positive attributes, features, properties, etc. from any given phenomenal object of experience. Once one has done so, one has knowingly generated an instance of *das Ding an sich* as what looks to be an ineffable nothingness. What is more, as a thinking subject, one knows exactly how one has generated the pseudo-beyond of this abstract emptiness through a process of subjective theoretical acts of subtracting and negating all determinations constitutive of knowable objectivities. Consequently, with the unknowable thing-in-itself recast as the end result of a deliberate conscious movement of mental operations of subtraction and negation, this thing's inscrutability, opacity, transcendence and withdrawnness (as per the ontological agnosticism of Kantian transcendental idealism and certain of its offshoots) all vanish, leaving nothing more or less to be known but the concrete genesis of this intentionally fabricated nothingness itself.[14]

This same Hegel also paves the way for the non-agnostic irreligiosity of Feuerbach, Marx, et al. (with me advancing and defending this contention both in the main body of this book and on another occasion[15]). He does so by subtly applying to every god (*qua* objectified supernatural transcendence) the just-summarized claims he blatantly brings to bear on Kant's thing-in-itself. As seen, Hegel demystifies *das Ding an sich* by showing how this presumably given noumenal objectivity is actually and actively produced on the side of subjectivity through the subject shifting how it maps and relates to the field of its experience. Likewise, Hegel demystifies the divine by showing how this purportedly otherworldly Being of beings really arises through this-worldly groups of human beings projecting aspects of themselves into a supernatural Elsewhere (a projection process subsequently rendered as Feuerbachian 'alienation' [*Entfremdung*] *qua* humanity's self-objectifying self-estrangement in and through various supernaturalistic mythologies and religions). As with the Kantian *Ding an sich*, so too, for a Hegelian, with any god: Once one knows how, and even perhaps also why, such reified abstractions are constructed by human beings in this world, one knows all there is to know about them (in the same way that, in modern natural science, once one knows how to experimentally [re]produce a given natural phenomenon, one knows the phenomenon itself in question). There remains nothing left for either theisms or agnosticisms to latch onto so as to put off a decisive atheistic reckoning.

In a piece featuring in a collection edited by Lorenzo[16] – this piece also serves as a chapter of my 2013 book *Prolegomena to Any Future Materialism, Volume One: The Outcome of Contemporary French Philosophy*[17] – I observe that Lacan temporarily inclines towards a Kantian critical-epistemological agnosticism. He does so during his mid-1950's quasi-structuralist 'return to Freud' specifically in relation to questions about the origin of language. In a Kantian manner, Lacan maintains that, for us speaking beings (*parlêtres*) always-already initiated into one or more languages, what comes before such individual-ontogenetic and/or collective-phylogenetic acquisition of (and/or acquisition by) language lies on the inaccessible other side of the limits of linguistically-mediated possible experience.

Yet, Lacan's Kantian critical-epistemological agnosticism about the transition from unrecorded to recorded history goes hand-in-hand with a stunning momentary lapse by him into obscurantist comparisons of language (precisely as the symbolic order *qua* socio-linguistic big Other) with Christianity's Holy Spirit. It seems as though, in this passing instance, Lacan allows himself to indulge in theological confabulations, to fill the void of an ostensibly unknowable 'x' (in this case, the origin of language) with faith's fictions. Even the best of us lose faithlessness from time to time.

Without going into all the details, it can be said that Lacan's moves away from certain aspects of his middle-period, Freud-*avec*-Saussure handling of the register of the Symbolic (and with it, the unconscious-structured-like-a-language), moves first becoming visible at the very end of the 1950s, involve him implicitly pivoting from a more Kantian to a more Hegelian handling of everything that is irreducible to the structures and dynamics of signifiers and the socio-linguistic.[18] As is common knowledge, much of this everything is subsumed under the heading of the register of the Real. At the same time and in parallel (perhaps not coincidentally), beginning in such contexts as the tenth seminar of 1962–3, Lacan also is more consistently and full-throatedly atheistic in his pronouncements.

The contrast between Kantian and Hegelian perspectives also enables me to bring out significant differences in how Lorenzo and I make sense out of the later Lacan's admittedly rather obscure comments about a non-traditional portrayal of the divine. On Lorenzo's reading, these comments suggest the possibility of what Lorenzo labels 'the self-deceiving God'. For him, because there is this possibility in addition to the bare lone being of 'indifferent not-Oneness' – for me, the latter would be in line with what I have in mind with the concept of 'weak nature' – one must agnostically refrain from asserting the existence of one and only one possibility (as yet another One[ness]) in place of a traditional theistic deity. Additionally, the atheism part of Lorenzo's 'agnostic atheism' is the fact that neither of the alternatives he entertains, the self-deceiving God or indifferent not-Oneness, is a divinity of any recognizable creed.

Unlike Lorenzo, I construe the Lacanian self-deceiving God – in my contribution to this book's main body, I focus on God's self-doubt as per Lacan's 'God does not believe in God' – not as one of two (or more) real possibilities for what might exist in lieu of any traditional theism's deity. Instead, I understand Lacan here to be engaged in a Hegelian-style immanent critique of religiosity. More precisely, the later Lacan, like Hegel, Feuerbach, Chesterton and Bloch before him as well as Žižek after him (i.e. the leading representatives of the atheism-in-Christianity orientation), utilizes Christian doctrines of God and the Trinity so as to dismantle from within any theism of a transcendent paternal authority (with this type of authority epitomizing Lacan's unbarred big Other and subject supposed to know).

The point of Lacan's immanent-critical passage through theism is to dismantle and dispel its God using its own theological and doctrinal resources (in a way, to make this God lose faith in Himself and thereby vanish). Given that, as I underscore in my main-body contribution, Lacan identifies God as a paradigmatic instantiation of the structural function of *le sujet supposé savoir*, a God who did not know Himself due to self-deception or self-doubt would not be God properly speaking as a subject supposed to know. If the agnostic dimension of Lorenzo's position hinges on there possibly being a self-deceiving God in addition to the possibility of there being nothing but indifferent not-Oneness, then it is debatable whether para-ontological agnostic atheism can claim to be a position consistent with Lacan's own commitments. Additionally, even if Lorenzo's self-deceiving God amounts to nothing other than an oscillation or indistinction between One/A and not-One/$\bcancel{A}$, I see no reason to divinize this oscillation/indistinction.

Moreover, if Lacan's self-deceiving God is a self-negating One, then all that remains is indifferent not-Oneness or $\bcancel{A}$. The ground for any agnostic wavering between two-plus possibilities disappears. One is abandoned to unqualified atheism alone.

Before proceeding further, I should note some tensions between Lorenzo and me apropos what he characterizes as 'indifferent not-Oneness'. Succinctly stated, I construe Lorenzo as equivocating between two distinct meanings of 'indifferent'/'indifference'. On the one hand, indifference can mean just a lack of differences, a sort of flat homogeneity or monochromatic uniformity. Below, I will refer to this first sense as 'structural indifference'. On the other hand, indifference can also (and usually does) mean a lack of affection, attention, care, concern, etc. Unlike structural indifference as simple absence of difference (i.e. as homogeneity, uniformity and so on), this second, more typical sense of indifference is, by its own definition, tied up with reference to agents, minds or subjects capable of adopting attitudes, dispositions, outlooks, perspectives and the like in relation to other beings. In what follows, I will refer to this second sense as 'attitudinal indifference'.

As Lorenzo relies upon and as I would readily admit, my concept of weak nature advances a picture of pre/non-human natural realms as internally differentiated by antagonisms, clashes, conflicts, frictions, incompatibilities and oppositions (as variegated forms of Hegelian negativity) within and between its countless entities and events. This clearly is contrary to myriad images of nature past and present as a harmonious and homogeneous One-All, a balanced cosmic Totality or Whole. However, Lorenzo's conflating of the two distinct meanings of 'indifference', a conflation flagged in the preceding paragraph as one sandwiching together 'structural' and 'attitudinal' senses of indifference, leads him to charge me with dubiously (or even indefensibly) anthropomorphizing non-human nature, with illegitimately retrojecting the differences of human existence, including those expressive of non-indifference as affection, attention, care, concern and so on, back into pre-human nature. If my internally differentiated and self-differentiating weak nature is non-indifferent in the attitudinal sense of being not-coldly-indifferent dispositionally, then indeed I am guilty of a crude anthropomorphism or even an implausible panpsychism invalidly spiritualizing un-spiritual nature.

My response to the above is simple: For transcendental materialism, nature is not structurally indifferent – physicalist reductionisms and eliminativisms, with their two-dimensional ontologies of mathematizable matter-in-motion or particle fields, envision the natural Real as structurally indifferent *qua* monistically monochromatic – but is attitudinally indifferent. Looking at nature as a set of internally differentiated structures perturbed by various negativities, one still can join Hegel in shrugging one's shoulders with an '*Es ist so*' whose attitudinal indifference mirrors back to nature the attitudinal indifference it displays towards us. I am just as insistent on nature's attitudinal indifference as is Lorenzo. In fact, given my rejection of anything along the lines of panpsychism, this indifference is due to pre/non-human nature, as simultaneously objective and non-sapient, not containing, and being unable to contain, attitudes and the like. Phrased in Hegelese, natural substance is not (yet) spiritual subject (too). Prior to sentient and sapient life, it has neither attitudes nor even capacities for attitudes.

As for Lorenzo's closely related worries about me anachronistically retrojecting spiritual subject back into natural substance, I would refer readers to my replies to these worries (ones voiced by a number of others too in addition to Lorenzo) elaborated on prior occasions.[19] As I explain on those occasions, transcendental materialism, on the basis of epistemological and methodological considerations, moves from spiritual subject to natural substance within its order of reasons. It does so in a process of reverse-engineering an ontology of nature starting from the question of what pre-human nature must have been, and of what non-human nature must continue to be, such that this nature is responsible for giving rise to the irreducibly more-than-natural and self-denaturalizing existences that we are as human beings and socio-symbolic subjects. But, this movement in thought from subject to substance within transcendental materialism's order of reasons is, I insist, entirely distinct from what this materialism acknowledges to be the complementary inverse movement in reality from substance to subject within the order of being. Because of my insistence on an ontological trajectory from natural substance to denaturalized subject, as the reverse of a strictly epistemological and methodological trajectory from denaturalized subject back to natural substance, I am not at risk of lapsing into the sorts of anthropomorphism or even panpsychism whose serious problems understandably trouble Lorenzo.

These clarifications about epistemological and ontological orders aside, agnosticisms rightly are associated with treating modesty as a key virtue.

Religious agnosticism involves modestly accepting one's presumed inability to know anything about possible super-natures, afterlives, etc. Kantian critical epistemology is a general metaphysical modesty agnostic about claims regarding everything beyond the phenomenal realm within the limits of possible experience. The later Lacan's mockery of fundamental ontologies from the ancient Greeks through Heidegger suggests (at least to some such as Lorenzo) that agnosticism apropos being *qua* being continues to be, under Kant's long shadow, the only appropriate stance or attitude.

To bring up once again the Kant–Hegel rapport, one of Hegel's recurrent complaints about Kantian critical epistemology is that its ostensibly virtuous modesty is, in truth, false modesty. This complaint is bound up with one of Hegel's main objections to Kant's theoretical philosophy (as subjectivist transcendental idealism). According to this Hegelian objection, Kant cannot but repeatedly violate his own strictures on the supposed scope of the knowable. For Kant to know the limits of possible experience as limits, he must already be able to see beyond them – something he maintains is impossible. Likewise, Kant claims that things-in-themselves are unknowable, yet seems to know that there are a plurality of such noumenal things differing from, but consistent with, each other and affecting human minds so as somehow to generate corresponding phenomenal objects-as-appearances for an experiencing and knowing subject – with these things, moreover, untouched by the dialectical strife affecting thinking subjectivity. In short, Kant, while feigning modestly not to feign any ontological hypotheses, in reality immodestly presupposes a multifaceted ontology/metaphysics in the guise of subject-centric transcendental idealism – with this ontology/metaphysics transgressing the very limits purportedly enforced by Kant's own critical epistemology.[20]

One should remember at this juncture that Lorenzo appeals to the tradition of Kantian critique through his choice of the adjective 'critical' to qualify his own para-ontological position. And, an upshot of Hegel's just-mentioned (immanent) critique of Kant is that even perhaps the single most rigorous systematic effort in the entire history of Western philosophy to remain agnostic about ontological matters (i.e. Kantian critical epistemology) fails to remain so. What is more, the failed agnosticism of the author of the *Critique of Pure Reason* and related texts signals the unavoidability of a non-agnostic ontology and corresponding untenability of an agnostic para-ontology.[21] As per a Hegelian-style dialectical coincidence of (apparent) opposites, maybe the greatest metaphysical immodesty is the pretense of being agnostically modest about metaphysics.

As regards more directly religion-related agnosticism, Hegel, at one moment during his Berlin *Lectures on the History of Philosophy*, utters some barbed remarks about the supposedly virtuous modesty of rendering God both epistemologically and ontologically transcendent, an infinite Supreme Being withdrawn from the finitude of wretchedly limited human knowers. He states regarding the modesty (*die Bescheidenheit*) of Pascal, Jacobi and Kant alike:

> People of this kind say: We are good for nothing, and because we are good for nothing, we are good for nothing, and wish to be good for nothing. But it is a very false idea of Christian humility and modesty (*ein sehr falsche christliche Demut und Bescheidenheit*) to desire through one's abjectness (*Jämmerlickeit*) to attain to excellence; this confession of one's own nothingness is really inward pride and great self-conceit. But for the honour of true humility we must not remain in our misery (*Erbärmlichkeit*), but raise ourselves above it by laying hold of the Divine (*durch Ergreifung des Göttlichen*).[22]

Given my construal of Hegel as a proto-Feuerbachian (or Feuerbach as a faithful Hegelian), once one 'lays hold of the Divine' through dialectical-speculative thinking, one learns that the Divine is not so divine, not what it might previously have appeared to be. That said, Hegel's rejection of this kind of 'Christian humility and modesty' (including secularized permutations of it, some of which involve agnostic attitudes) has to do with considerations regarding infinity and absoluteness residing at the very core of the Hegelian philosophical apparatus.

Hegel, despite the severity of his critique of Spinoza's metaphysics,[23] nonetheless takes to heart an insight foundational for 1677's *Ethics*. Specifically, Spinoza, in identifying his *Deus sive natura* as infinite, fundamentally recasts the difference between the infinite and the finite.[24] With fitting reference in this context to the Hegelian distinction between the understanding (*Verstand*) and reason (*Vernunft*), Spinoza replaces a *Verstand*-type opposition of mutual exclusion between finite and infinite with a *Vernunft*-type relationship between these two terms. What does this mean?

For Spinoza, if the infinite and the finite are external to each other in being opposed to one another as contradictory poles – as per the understanding's fashion of drawing its categorial and conceptual distinctions, the infinite is the negation of the finite and vice versa – then the infinite is not really infinite (as Hegel might say, this would be a 'spurious' infinite). Why? If the infinite is meant to be all-encompassing, yet the finite is posited as being outside of the infinite as the latter's *Verstand*-style negation, then the infinite cannot be all-encompassing, since there is something (i.e. the finite) beyond or external to it. The understanding's cognitive *modus operandi* thereby renders the infinite finite, de-infinitizing infinity through excluding the finite from its domain.

Spinoza's alternative to this self-undermining misconception of the infinity-finitude relation anticipates a structural motif writ large across the expanse of Hegel's encyclopedic System and essential to dialectical speculation (a motif already discernible in the Hegelian-Schellingian slogan, coined by Hegel in 1801, about 'the Identity of Identity and Difference'[25]). Specifically, Spinoza insists (rightly, in Hegel's view) that, worded in a Hegelian style, the distinction between the finite and the infinite is a distinction internal to the infinite itself. This insistence not only avoids the just-described dead end of a spurious-*qua*-de-infinitized infinity – it illustrates one of the ways in which Hegelian Vernunft refashions differences and contrasts. In this instance, reason's way is to fold the terms of an opposition of the understanding (e.g. the finite versus the infinite) into one of the poles (here, the infinite) of the opposition itself.

What holds for the Spinozistic infinite also holds for the Hegelian Absolute. Just as the distinction between infinity and finitude must be internal to the former so that the former can be what it is, so too with absoluteness and non-absoluteness, respectively. In other words, the distinction between the Absolute and the non-Absolute has to be internal to the Absolute. This is so because nothing can exist separate from and external to the Absolute by the very definition of it in its proper absoluteness.

All of the immediately preceding leads both Spinoza and Hegel to highly heterodox depictions of the divine. These two philosophical giants agree that, if nothing else, a monotheistic God cannot be, as He traditionally is portrayed as being, simultaneously both transcendent and infinite/Absolute. Why not?

The very notion of transcendence entails a relationship of externality between Above (i.e. that which transcends) and Below (i.e. that which is transcended). But, if God is transcendent, then everything non-divine falls outside of Him, thereby de-infinitizing/de-absolutizing this divinity. Therefore, everything (apparently) finite must be immanent to *Deus sive natura* as the infinite and/or the Absolute. Only a radical monism, and not any sort of dualistic ontology of imagined heights and depths, can do justice to the divine. It is no accident that Spinoza gets expelled as a heretic by his Jewish community and branded as an atheist by much of popular opinion for a long while subsequently. It also is no accident that Hegel inspires Feuerbach and the irreligiosity of the Young/Left Hegelians as well as of Marxism thereafter.

Referring back to the preceding block quotation from Hegel's *Lectures on the History of Philosophy*, the 'Christian humility and modesty' Hegel denounces as 'very false' (*sehr falsche*) is bound up with a neither-dialectical-nor-speculative Verstand-level (rather than dialectical-speculative Vernunft-level) manner of distinguishing between ourselves (as finite, non-Absolute, immanent, Below, this-worldly, natural, etc.) and God (as infinite, Absolute, transcendent, Above, other-worldly, supernatural, etc.). The falsity of this modesty ultimately is due to its subtly arrogant false belief that we, supposedly wretched humans, have the power to be utterly and completely detached and separate from the omnipotent infinitude of *Deus sive natura* or the Absolute, an omnipotent infinitude which, as such, brooks no Outside or Other. Paraphrasing this same Berlin-era Hegel, one could say that 'the honour of true humility' comes from realizing that you simply cannot avoid 'laying hold of the Divine' (as the infinite or Absolute) because the

Divine always-already has laid hold of you. For the likes of Spinoza, Schelling and Hegel, it would be fair to say that not only are we monistically immanent to the infinite/Absolute – we are this infinity/absoluteness as pre- and non-subjective being subjectivizing itself in and through us, with us as this being's consciousness of itself. From this to Feuerbachianism or other strains of 'Christian atheism' is but a short step.

Related to the above, Schelling in particular nicely foregrounds what cannot but strike the eye as paradoxical features of the post-Kantian and post-Fichtean German idealist conception of the Absolute as per 'absolute idealism'. If my reconstruction of Hegel's doctrine of modal categories is correct,[26] he definitely shares with Schelling these same intuitions about absoluteness (and this despite some of the older Schelling's misguided criticisms of Hegel). Specifically, Schelling repeatedly associates the *Ur-Grund*, as what is most grounding and rational, with the *Un-Grund*, as what is groundless and irrational[27] – with the German '*Grund*' being translatable as both 'ground' and 'reason' (the latter in the sense of justification, explanation, etc.). The Schellingian–Hegelian infinite Absolute integrally involves this counterintuitive combination of groundedness and rationality (as the *Ur-Grund*) with groundlessness and irrationality (as the *Un-Grund*). How so?

For both Schelling and Hegel, the Absolute cannot but be self-grounding. Given its infinitude, there is nothing greater or more that could ground it in turn. Schellingian and Hegelian absolute idealisms insist that, phrased in a Lacanian fashion, there is no Absolute of the Absolute. In other words, there is no further *Grund* for this *Ur-Grund*, no *Ur-Ur-Grund* of the *Ur-Grund*; *Ur-Ur* would just equal the zero of *Un-*. Although the Absolute grounds itself along with everything else, the absence of anything else leaves the Absolute without further grounds beyond itself. As the point at which the giving of and asking for reasons driven by 'Why?'-type questions comes to a halt, as the desk where the explanatory buck stops, the ultimate Reason of reasons is itself *ohne Warum*. Hence, in a dialectical convergence of opposites, the *Ur-Grund* of the Absolute, as the peak of groundedness and rationality, is also an *Un-Grund*, as the abyss of groundlessness and irrationality.

With respect to Lorenzo and the agnostic aspects of his para-ontological position, these just-summarized Schellingian–Hegelian reflections on the strange status of the infinite Absolute indicate that Lacan's terminological pairs of One and not-One or A and $\cancel{A}$ ought not to be held apart as two separate poles, as alternatives between which one might agnostically waver. And, in line with Schelling's and Hegel's shared Spinoza-sparked tendencies, the oppositions expressed by these pairs should be folded into one of the terms of each pair. Classical German idealist sensibilities suggest that such a distinction between One/A and not-One/$\cancel{A}$ is a distinction internal to One/A (à la the distinction between the infinite Absolute and the finite non-Absolute allegedly being a distinction internal to the infinite Absolute itself).

By contrast, Lacanian thought suggests the reverse, namely, that the distinction between One/A and not-One/$A̸$ is a distinction internal to not-One/$A̸$. Consistent with this, and for my ontology *contra* Lorenzo's para-ontology, there is, as being in its most basic and elementary form, only pre/non-human nature as not-One/$A̸$ (i.e. what I refer to as 'weak nature'). Any gods, including self-deceiving ones, are Ones/As coming into existence as secondary by-products produced by humans who themselves are (by-)products of this same nature *qua* not-One/$A̸$. With even a self-deceiving God being such a secondary by-product, there is no basis for having faith that, at the most foundational of ontological/metaphysical levels, there are two (or more) actual possibilities allowing for agnostic vacillation between them. There really is only one atheistic option, namely, the uniquely ultimate not-One/$A̸$ – with any instances of One/A as merely subsequent inner inflections within this absolute groundlessness as *unhintergehbar* barred-ness.

As I demonstrate in my contribution to this book's main body, Lacan's 'God hypothesis' is, in Kantian terms, a sort of transcendental illusion inevitably generated and repeatedly succumbed to by speaking beings (*parlêtres*) made to be subjects in and through conflict-ridden symbolic orders. Although the Lacanian Real and Symbolic big Others of nature-writ-large and socio-linguistic systems, respectively, are both barred *qua* riddled with internal discrepancies and tensions, they still can and do congeal out of themselves semblances of what I might baptize 'un-barred-ness'. For the same Lacan of the early 1970s who speaks of the God hypothesis, there likewise is, as he puts it, something of the One (*y'a de l'Un*), if only as a non-epiphenomenal effect or residue, despite the ontological ultimacy of the not-One[28] (and this in line with the distinction between One/A and not-One/$A̸$ being internal to not-One/$A̸$ itself).

With German idealism, all of the above is about, at least in part, accepting groundlessness along with groundedness. With psychoanalysis, it is about accepting groundedness, the undead persistence of Ones, As, S_1s, and so on, along with groundlessness (as not-One, $A̸$, \$, etc.). Nevertheless, for both of these orientations, the coincidence of the opposites of groundedness and groundlessness means that, *pace* most traditional religious convictions, there is no pure and undiluted *Ur-Grund* transcending and untouched by the vortex of the *Un-Grund*. One could say that German idealism and Lacanianism alike propose '$A = A̸$', and not '$\forall x \, (x \wedge \sim x)$' and/or '$(\forall A \, [A \wedge A̸] \wedge \forall A̸ \, [A̸ \wedge A])$', as an ontological/metaphysical *Grundsatz* – with these orientations admittedly differing somewhat in exactly how they interpret and unpack this (un)grounding proposition (i.e. $A = A̸$).

Agnostics tend to accuse theists and atheists alike of clinging to certainty (of God's existence and non-existence, respectively) as a defence against uncertainty. Such agnostics, implicitly or explicitly maintaining a self-flattering intellectual criterion having it that epistemological modesty is always a virtue, overtly claim or at least strongly hint that accepting the uncertainty of non-knowledge is praiseworthy bravery while embracing certainty of whatever sort (theistic, atheistic, etc.) is blameworthy cowardice. All of this might even seem compatible with and congenial to psychoanalysis, with investments in certainties as libidinally and affectively motivated repressions of underlying uncertainties.

Yet, the psychoanalytic unconscious is a knowing that does not know that it knows, a thinking that does not think that it thinks. In the now-famous Rumsfeldian epistemological inventory of 'known knowns' (the things one knows that one knows), 'known unknowns' (the things one knows that one does not know) and 'unknown unknowns' (the things one does not know that one does not know), the analytic unconscious is the missing fourth category of 'unknown knowns' (the things one does not know that one knows). As such, repression (*Verdrängung*) in the strict psychoanalytic sense is more about maintaining ignorance regarding unconscious certainties (as unknown knowns) than using certainties to conceal deeper uncertainties.

I can utilize at this juncture mortality and accompanying questions of possible afterlives, topics at the very heart of religiosity in many of its guises, to flesh out what I have in mind in terms of turning the tables on the agnostic who accuses the atheist (along with the theist) of defending against or repressing uncertainty. In classical Aristotelian terms, one could say that death is when the combination of matter and form generative of a living substance comes undone. Perishing results from the right sorts of organic material entities losing, whether through age, disease or injury, enough of their anatomical and physiological configuration (i.e. their 'form' as structural and functional arrangements) so as also to lose their status as living substance, as being alive or supporting life.

In light of the Aristotelian matter–form–substance triad, the existence of life holds when the appropriate kind of matter is in the appropriate kind of form. Correlatively but conversely, the non-existence of death holds when this specific matter–form combination (yielding a living substance) is not in place. Additionally and importantly, the non-existence of the matter–form combination constitutive of a living substance is the case not only after the end of a life but before its beginning too. A living entity's non-being precedes as well as succeeds its lifespan. Or, in Saint Bonaventura's words as quoted by Maurice Blanchot, 'Life is but the belled cap worn by Nothingness'.[29]

And, everyone without exception is, whether they want to acknowledge it or not, intimately acquainted with this nothingness. How so? If one is asked to recall what anything whatsoever was like before one was born (or, really, before one's earliest recallable episodic memories), one draws a blank. However, this is a blank that, in order to be seen clearly on its own, demands diligently suspending one's habitual reliance on others' narratives (whether those older than oneself or any sort of reports about anything in the world predating one's birth) concerning everything prior to when one's actually remembered life history begins. This blank is nothing other than one's own non-existence. I am able to be acutely aware that I did not exist for the unimaginable expanse of time prior to my coming into the world as a living organism endowed with both sentience and sapience. Therefore, I could be said to be very well acquainted with my not being, to know what it is not to exist.

Yet, agnostics' views as regards mortality and the afterlife typically rest on the claim that finite human experiencers and knowers are not and, as alive, cannot be acquainted with their own non-existence following their deaths. But, as I have just argued, turning one's gaze from future (i.e. post-demise) to past (i.e. pre-conception) non-existence immediately problematizes this agnostic claim. I have no reason to believe that my future non-existence after death will be any different from my past non-existence before birth, since nothingness and zero do not permit differentiating between multiple individual instances of themselves.

Do we not live our lives already knowing, if only in the shadowy recesses of our minds, what it is not to be? If so, then the agnostic is using his/her uncertainty about immortality (as an inability not to be) to repress and defend against his/her certainty about mortality (as an ability not to be testified to by all-too-familiar pre-birth nothingness). This is so rather than it being the atheist who, along with the theist, uses certainty to repress and defend against uncertainty. The 'unknown known' of the agnostic's unconscious is the eternal past (as Schelling might put it) of his/her non-existence. An atheism untinged by uncertainties looks to be the more courageously honest stance.

To take back up the topic of agnosticism's essential characteristic modesty (including the secular sort of agnostic modesty epitomized by the likes of the critical Kant), Žižek eloquently advocates for reversing the standard tendency to dismiss Hegel's (not to mention Schelling's) talk of "the Absolute" as the height of immodesty, as deludedly grandiose intellectual-philosophical hubris. In 2012's *Less Than Nothing: Hegel and the Shadow of Dialectical Materialism*, Žižek explains why Hegel's distinctive brand of 'absolutism' is, in truth, significantly more modest than any scepticisms or relativisms[30] (or, for that matter, any agnosticisms too):

> It is a commonplace to oppose Hegel's 'ridiculous' Absolute Knowing to a modest skeptical approach which recognizes the excess of reality over every conceptualization. What if, however, it is Hegel who is much more modest? What if his Absolute Knowing is the assertion of a radical closure: there is no meta-language, we cannot climb on our own shoulders and see our own limitations, we cannot relativize or historicize ourselves? What really is arrogant, as Chesterton made clear, is precisely such self-relativization, the attitude of 'knowing one's limitations,' of not agreeing with oneself – as in the proverbial 'wise' insight according to which we can only approach reality

asymptotically. What Hegel's Absolute Knowing deprives us of is precisely this minimal self-distance, the ability to put ourselves at a 'safe distance' from our own location.[31]

What if part of Lacan's point when speaking of a self-deceiving or self-doubting God dovetails with Žižek's point about the modesty of the Hegelian Absolute? What if the ability to be radically sceptical, relativistic or agnostic is afforded only to the one who is omniscient and/or infinite (i.e. God)? Asked differently, what if, by attributing self-deception or self-doubt to God, Lacan means to place them beyond the reach of finite, mortal humans? What if the capacity to elevate oneself to one or more meta-levels over and above any initial first-order choice between theism and atheism, belief and unbelief – Lorenzo's para-ontology could be said to introduce agnosticism as a second-order qualifier of atheism – is reserved exclusively for a being that would be omnipotent and eternal? Just as Kantian epistemological critique could be deemed, despite its superficially apparent modesty, to be a surreptitiously arrogant assumption of a God's-eye view from nowhere – Kant purports to know that there is a difference-in-kind between phenomenal objects-as-appearances and noumenal things-in-themselves, despite this purported knowledge being ruled out as epistemologically indefensible due to Kant's recurrently invoked limits of possible experience – what if Chiesian 'meta-critical realism' inherits the same surreptitious arrogance from its critical ancestor residing in eighteenth-century Königsberg?

4. When the game is over: Cashing out for good at the last call

In the above block quotation from *Less Than Nothing*, Žižek alludes to an intimate link between his rendition of Hegel and particular Lacanian theses. Specifically, he reiterates Lacan's 'there is no meta-language', one of a set of several related one-liners regularly repeated by Lacan. This set also includes 'there is no Other of the Other' and 'there is no truth about the truth'. I deal with this family of *'il n'y a pas'* theses elsewhere.[32] So, in the present context, I will be highly selective in my glosses on and redeployments of these Lacanian assertions.

Moreover, having explored at length Lacan's sustained engagements with Pascal in my part of this book's preceding main body, I also, in what immediately follows, will be drawing upon a Lacanianized version of Pascal's wager. Specifically, I will be establishing a connection between the Pascalian 'but you must wager. There is no choice, you are already committed' (*mais il faut parier. Cela n'est pas volontaire: vous êtes embarqué*)[33] and the Lacanian triad of *'il n'y a pas'* theses (i.e. there is no meta-language, Other of the Other, or truth of the truth). Establishing this will further clarify and sharpen my reservations with respect to the agnostic dimension of Lorenzo's para-ontology and my corresponding preference for an atheism unqualified by agnostic (or sceptical or relativistic) reservations.

I cannot shake the impression that Lorenzo's agnosticism involves valorizing as an intellectual-philosophical ideal a movement of (potentially, theoretically) infinite oscillation between contradictory poles. For Lorenzo, the theist's affirmation of One/A can be negated by the atheist's contradictory affirmation of not-One/A̶. But, the latter affirmation in turn elevates not-One/A̶ to being a new One/A in the guise of a non-agnostic atheism whose fundamental ontology (as, for Lorenzo, inevitably onto-theology) treats barred-ness, conflict, difference, inconsistency and the like as the unique Being of beings (i.e. as another One/A). For instance, from the para-ontological perspective, Empedocles (as an ancient Greek proponent of not-One/A̶), despite the substantial differences in content between his and Parmenides's philosophies, shares with Parmenides (as an ancient Greek proponent of One/A) the onto-theological form of a unified metaphysical account of all reality.

As Lorenzo sees things, the allegedly inevitable onto-theologization of not-One/A̶, reducing it to yet another figure of One/A, must be negated in turn. But as with Hegelian bad/spurious infinity, the same onto-theologizing dynamic affects this next negation, which therefore requires yet another de-onto-theologizing negation, and so on and on presumably *ad infinitum*. For Chiesian para-ontology, the only true atheism is an agnostic sort tirelessly being carried along the indefinitely oscillating sequence forever restlessly moving from One/A → not-One/A̶ → One/A → not-One/A̶ . . .

In Kant's practical philosophy as per the *Critique of Practical Reason* and related texts, the in-principle infinite progress of the finite subject's asymptotic approach to a moral perfection unattainable in this time-limited life compels positing the immortality of the soul as a 'postulate of pure practical reason'.[34] Likewise, in Fichte's 'primacy-of-the-practical' systematization of Kantian transcendental idealism epitomized by his 1794 *Wissenschaftslehre*, acting subjectivity's 'striving' (*Streben*) to assert its total and complete dominance over all natural objectivities is an infinite task, a never-finished project kept going precisely by the goad of incompletion, by the provocative residue of subject-defying objectivity.[35] And these aspects of Kant's and Fichte's philosophies are, as is well known, Hegel's preferred examples of what he labels 'bad' or 'spurious' infinity (*schlechte Unendlichkeit*).[36]

Kant's doctrine of the immortal soul as a postulate of pure practical reason provides the most telling comparison here when placed side-by-side with the agnostic dimension of Lorenzo's position. Just as an infinite lifespan is necessary for the attainment of moral perfection as defined within the parameters of the deontological ethics of pure practical reason, so too with the agnosticism of para-ontology: The Chiesian agnostic likewise would need an infinite lifespan in order to sustain the endless toing and froing of One/A → not-One/A̶ → One/A → not-One/A̶ ... Minus a meta-level God's-eye view from nowhere and/or an immortal soul, one simply cannot, in one's inescapable finitude, keep wavering *ad infinitum* between One/A and not-One/A̶ (or between indifferent not-Oneness and the self-deceiving God). A vestige of religiosity, specifically the infinitude of an imperishable subject (as the eternal oscillator between ontological options in Chiesian para-ontology), clings to Lorenzo's agnosticism. This critical observation as regards Lorenzo brings me back to Pascal and his wager, as well as to a Lacanian rendition of Pascal's wager cross-resonating with Lacan's '*il n'y a pas*' theses.

To begin with, Pascal, in laying out his wager, insists that agnosticism strictly speaking is an impossible non-option due to it really being tantamount to atheism. Why? Pascal's wager is designed to confront its addressees with an inescapable choice between believing (say, A) or not believing (say, ~A) in the specifically Christian God. Within these parameters, anything and everything other than belief in the Christian God (A) is subsumable under the heading of non-belief (~A), including not only atheism but agnosticism as well as beliefs in non-Christian deities. From this Pascalian perspective, not choosing to believe in God due to epistemic reservations (i.e. agnosticism) ends up being equivalent to choosing not to believe in God (i.e. atheism). Avoiding A for whatever reasons automatically and unavoidably places one on the side of ~A.

By comparing Lorenzo with the Kant and Fichte featuring in Hegel's discussion of *schlechte Unendlichkeit* as I do above, I equate Lorenzo's agnosticism, not with atheism as would the just-summarized Pascal of the wager, but with theism instead. The infinite regression of negations posited by such agnosticism arguably requires postulating, however implicitly or unconsciously, an equally infinite agent to carry out these negations' never-ending succession of back-and-forth alternations between each other. The ghost of Christianity's immortal soul appears to haunt Chiesian para-ontology despite Lorenzo's admirable efforts along more atheistic lines.

Another facet of Pascal's wager is relevant and worthy of further consideration now. As seen, Pascal emphatically stresses that his wager is inescapable. I already linked this inescapability, in my contribution to the present book's main body, to the motif of what comes to be designated by Heidegger as 'thrownness' (*Geworfenheit*), a motif taken up by Lacan, among others. Of course, for the proto-existentialist Pascal and the existentialist Heidegger alike, what one is thrown into is nothing other than finite mortal life (or Heideggerian 'being-towards-death' [*Sein-zum-Tode*]).

The temporal limits (i.e. mortality and/as being-towards-death) entailed by such thrownness introduce a further inflection to the significance of the alleged inescapability of the Pascalian wager. At some point, Pascal's wagerer cannot take back a previous bet with an opposite bet or bet yet again. Eventually, the chips fall, the buck stops and the game ends. The wagerer is finite both as epistemically constrained and as mortal, with the death made inevitable by the latter bringing any wagering (and wavering) to a halt. For each and every perishable player, there inevitably will be a last bet never to be followed by any second-guessing.

To return to Lacan's '*il n'y a pas*' theses, especially his 'there is no metalanguage', perhaps these theses, in addition to their other meanings and implications, also reinforce the anti-agnostic argument I am making here using a proto-existential and Lacanianized Pascal. The set of Lacan's 'there is no . . .' claims suggests a rejection on his part of any perspective that would involve infinitely proliferating meta-levels (whether as meta-languages, Others of Others, truths about truths, etc.). Any such proliferations are rendered finite by eventually being stopped short somehow or other: The analysand exits the analyst's consulting room for the last time; the wagerer ceases placing bets on the gaming table; the person dies. This is the sole real sense in which there can be said to be any 'Last Judgment'.

To invoke another Lacanian notion-phrase, the 'time to conclude' (*le moment de conclure*) always arrives sooner or later. Or, with reference to Freud's 1937 paper 'Analysis Terminable and Interminable' (*Die endliche und die unendliche Analyse*), there ultimately is only terminable/finite analysis (*endliche Analyse*). Hence, as Pascal insists, 'you must wager'. To conclude, as one always is compelled to eventually, this is why I am a Lacanian non-agnostic atheist.

Notes

Introduction

1. R. Dawkins, 'A Scientist's Case against God', *The Independent*, 20 April 1992.
2. J. Baggini, *Atheism: A Very Short Introduction* (Oxford: Oxford University Press, 2003), 3.
3. A. Kojève, *Atheism* (New York: Columbia University Press, 2018), 123.
4. See M. Hägglund, *Radical Atheism: Derrida and the Time of Life* (Stanford: Stanford University Press, 2008), 4–11.
5. Ibid., 3.
6. See ibid., 8.
7. Ibid., 1.
8. Q. Meillassoux, *After Finitude* (London: Continuum, 2008), 46. 'Atheism is no longer an individual decision, but the stigma of the present time' (Q. Meillassoux, 'Nothingness against the Death of God – Mallarmé's Poetics after 1866', in *The Experience of Atheism*, ed. R. Horner and C. Romano (London: Bloomsbury, 2021), 48).
9. Q. Meillassoux, 'Appendix: Excerpts from *L'Inexistence divine*', in G. Harman, *Quentin Meillassoux. Philosophy on the Making* (Edinburgh: Edinburgh University Press, 2011), 226.
10. Q. Meillassoux, 'Spectral Dilemma', *Collapse*, 4 (2008): 268.
11. 'Interview with Quentin Meillassoux', in Harman, *Quentin Meillassoux. Philosophy on the Making*, 163.
12. Meillassoux, 'Appendix', 215.
13. L. Chiesa, 'Hyperstructuralism's Necessity of Contingency', *S*, 3 (2010): 159–77; A. Johnston, 'Hume's Revenge: À Dieu, Meillassoux?', in *The Speculative Turn: Continental Materialism and Realism*, ed. L. R. Bryant, N. Srnicek and G. Harman (Melbourne: re.press, 2011), 92–113; M. O. Burns and B. Smith, 'Materialism, Subjectivity and the Outcome of French Philosophy: Interview with Adrian Johnston', *Cosmos and History*, 7, no. 1: 167–81; A. Johnston, *Prolegomena to Any Future Materialism, Volume One: The Outcome of Contemporary French Philosophy* (Evanston: Northwestern University Press, 2013), 131–74; L. Chiesa, *The Not-Two: Logic and God in Lacan* (Cambridge, MA: MIT Press, 2016).
14. Hägglund, *Radical Atheism*, 11; see also 192–3.

15 See 'Interview with Quentin Meillassoux', 166.
16 See Chiesa, 'Hyperstructuralism's Necessity of Contingency', 177; Chiesa, *The Not-Two*, xiv–xv, 67, 74–5.
17 Meillassoux, 'Appendix', 233.
18 Ibid., 228.
19 Q. Meillassoux, *Métaphysique et fiction des mondes hors-science* (Paris: Aux forges de Vulcain, 2013), 25, 32, 41.
20 M. Hägglund, *This Life: Secular Faith and Spiritual Freedom* (New York: Anchor Books, 2020).
21 Ibid., 17.
22 Ibid., 5.
23 G. Harman, 'Author Q&A with Adrian Johnston', available at https://www.euppublishing.com/userimages/ContentEditor/1397840563624/Adventures%20in%20Transcendental%20Realism%20-%20Author%20Q%26A.pdf.
24 Hägglund, *Radical Atheism*, 38.
25 Ibid., 2–3.
26 See L. Chiesa, 'Exalted Obscenity and the Lawyer of God: Lacan and Deleuze on the Baroque', in *Lacan and Deleuze. A Disjunctive Synthesis*, ed. B. Nedoh and A. Zevnik (Edinburgh: Edinburgh University Press, 2017), 141–62.
27 But, in brief, Deleuze's allegedly *immanent* equation of Difference with univocal being is still not the self-deceiving God. The latter amounts to the equation of *indifference* with identity, which is an *equation* between immanence and transcendence, whereby these two terms become undistinguishable. It is only this move that enables us *not* to evoke a transcendence with respect to the equation of *Difference* with univocal being (in my view, Deleuze's mistake).
28 See 26–7 below.
29 See 30 below.
30 See 37, 40, 55 below.
31 See R. Sbriglia and S. Žižek, 'Introduction: Subject Matters', in *Subject Lessons: Hegel, Lacan, and the Future of Materialism*, ed. R. Sbriglia and S. Žižek (Evanston: Northwestern University Press, 2020), 19; see also N. L. Popow, 'To Dialectisize or Non-Dialectisize', available at https://cuny.academia.edu/NikolaiPopow.
32 Chiesa, *The Not-Two*, 185.
33 A. Johnston, 'Fear of Science: Transcendental Materialism and Its Discontents', in *Subject Lessons: Hegel, Lacan, and the Future of Materialism*, ed. Sbriglia and Žižek, 128–30.
34 S. Freud, 'The Question of a Weltanschauung', in *The Standard Edition of the Complete Works of Sigmund Freud*, Volume XXII (London: Vintage, 2001), 158.
35 Ibid., 182.
36 Ibid., 159.
37 See Chiesa, *The Not-Two,* 69–75.
38 A. Johnston, 'Confession of a Weak Reductionist: Responses to Some Recent Criticisms of My Materialism', in *Neuroscience and Critique. Exploring the Limits*

of the Neurological Turn, ed. J. De Vos and E. Pluth (Abingdon: Routledge, 2016), 154 (my emphasis). To the best of my understanding, in published form, the arguments I comment on are now split between 'Confession of a Weak Reductionist' and 'Fear of Science'. They were originally all contained in an initial draft of 'Confession'. The latter was the impetus for an excellent roundtable discussion between Adrian, Paul Livingston and me, entitled 'Lacan between the Formal and the Material', which took place at the University of New Mexico in March 2015. Adrian was responding to my criticism of his stance in the manuscript of *The Not-Two* (as yet unpublished at that point) and Paul's own criticism in 'Politics, Subjectivity, and Cosmological Antinomy' (*Crisis and Critique*, 1, no. 2 (2014): 23–50). We were responding to Adrian's critique of our criticisms in 'Confession'. I here rely and expand on extensive notes I took on that occasion.

39 Johnston, 'Fear of Science', 131.

40 Popow, 'To Dialectisize or Non-Dialectisize'.

41 Johnston, 'Fear of Science', 131.

42 Johnston, 'Confession of a Weak Reductionist' (unpublished version).

43 Sbriglia and Žižek, 'Introduction: Subject Matters' (phrase excised from published version).

44 S. J. Gould, *Life's Grandeur* (London: Vintage, 1997), 33.

45 Johnston, 'Fear of Science', 132.

46 This is one of Popow's main (Johnstonian?) mistaken assumptions in his reading of my para-ontology. Para-ontologically, speaking of the 'indifferent part of nature' does not make any sense. I never used this phrase, which he gives the impression of attributing to me by using quotation marks.

47 Private communication, 28 April 2022.

48 See S. Žižek, *Less Than Nothing* (London: Verso, 2013), esp. 4, 498, 596. On how Adrian still significantly differs from Žižek, see *The Not-Two*, 71ff.

49 Meillassoux, *After Finitude*, 116.

50 See 37, 40, 55 below.

51 A. Johnston, 'Naturalism or Anti-Naturalism?', *Revue Internationale de Philosophie*, 66, no. 261 (3) (2012): 321–46.

52 J. Lacan, 'Conférences et Entretiens dans des Universités Nord-Américaines: Yale University, 24 novembre 1975, Entretien avec des Étudiants, Réponses à leurs Questions', *Scilicet*, 6/7 (1976): 32.

53 J. Lacan, *The Seminar of Jacques Lacan, Book XI: The Four Fundamental Concepts of Psychoanalysis. 1964*, ed. Jacques-Alain Miller; trans. Alan Sheridan (New York: Norton, 1977), 59.

54 See 21 below.

55 See 21ff below.

56 See 22 below.

57 J. Lacan, *The Seminar of Jacques Lacan, Book XVII: The Other Side of Psychoanalysis. 1969-1970*, ed. Jacques-Alain Miller; trans. Russell Grigg (New York: Norton, 2007), 100.

58 T. Adorno, 'Freudian Theory and the Pattern of Fascist Propaganda', in *The Culture Industry: Selected Essays on Mass Culture* (London and New York: Routledge, 1991), 144.

59 Private communication, 21 February 2022.

60 See 21 below.

61 See 28 below.

62 See 27 below.

63 See 27 below.

64 See 54 below.

65 See 56 below.

66 J. Lacan, 'The Triumph of Religion', in *The Triumph of Religion Preceded by Discourse to Catholics* (Cambridge: Polity Press, 2013), 72.

67 J. Lacan, Seminar XXVII, lesson of 18 March 1980, unpublished.

68 On the latter, I recommend G. P. Cima's *Il seminario perpetuo: Il tardo e l'ultimo Lacan* (Napoli-Salerno: Orthotes, 2020) and his work on 'dark Lacanianism', available at https://www.sovrapposizioni.com/blog/note-per-un-lacanismo-nero-il-pessimismo-di-lacan.

69 E. Fachinelli, *On Freud* (Cambridge, MA: MIT Press, 2023), 67.

70 E. Fachinelli, *La mente estatica* (Milan: Adelphi, 1989), 16. See also G. P. Cima, 'Elvio Fachinelli: A Dissident Psychoanalyst', in Fachinelli, *On Freud*, esp. xlii–xlvi.

71 'The death of God [. . .] *in the form of* S(A) [the signifier of the barred Other] [. . .] signifies the *final response* to the *guarantee* asked of the Other [. . .] Christianity, through the drama of passion, gives a *full content* to [. . .] the death of God' (J. Lacan, *The Seminar of Jacques Lacan, Book VII: The Ethics of Psychoanalysis. 1959-1960*, ed. Jacques-Alain Miller; trans. Dennis Porter (New York: Norton, 1992), 193, my emphases).

72 J. Lacan, Seminar XXIV, lesson of 17 May 1977, unpublished. Lacan indeed speaks of a 'new signifier' yet to be 'invented' (ibid.). The latter would be meaningless, closely related to the real and, as such, 'fruitful', 'a good sign' (ibid.). Lacan does not provide any further explanation. He does instead, at the same time, far less optimistically, state that (a) 'the mental illness that is the unconscious does not wake up', and *this* is the final message of psychoanalysis (ibid.); (b) science is at best a 'suspect' awakening since 'everything that has so far been enunciated as science is suspended to the idea of God' (ibid.); (c) while the invention of a truly new signifier would be something 'extreme', the fact that we might access it through psychoanalysis would anyway soon return it to 'meaning' via interpretation (ibid.); (d) meaning is as such religious and 'psychoanalysis [is] the modern form of faith, of religious faith' (lesson of 14 December 1976). I do not see how this could be taken as a manifesto for the future of psychoanalysis (or science).

73 L. Chiesa, *Subjectivity and Otherness: A Philosophical Reading of Lacan* (Cambridge, MA: MIT Press, 2007), esp. 189–92.

74 See L. Chiesa, 'Supreme Being-in-Evil, Criminal Good, and Criminal Desire', in *Studying Lacan's Seminar VII*, ed. C. Owens (Abingdon: Routledge, 2023), 1–28.

75 One should revisit Lacan's early works on paranoia and 'the paranoic structure of the ego' (J. Lacan, 'Aggressiveness in Psychoanalysis', in *Écrits* (New York: Norton, 2002), 93). Their clear limit is, of course, that paranoia is here presented as inherent only to the human imaginary, not the symbolic, and, put simply, the latter would structurally supersede paranoia.

76 In this light, one should also reread two phenomenal texts by Derrida: 'Cogito and the History of Madness', in *Writing and Difference* (Chicago: University of Chicago Press, 1978), 31–63 and '"To Do Justice to Freud": The History of Madness in the Age of Psychoanalysis', *Critical Inquiry*, 20, no. 2 (Winter 1994): 227–66. Let us just recall that, for Derrida, (a) the threat of the Cartesian Evil Genius structurally remains '*perpetual*' (ibid., 241); (b) there is a re-emergence of the Evil Genius with psychoanalysis – 'a certain Evil Genius *of* Freud' (ibid., 240); (c) in his *History of Madness*, Foucault would unsuccessfully repress both.

77 Freud, 'The Question of a Weltanschauung', 166.

78 S. Freud, *Totem and Taboo*, in *The Standard Edition of the Complete Works of Sigmund Freud*, Volume XII, 24, 76–7, 92–3.

79 Ibid., 24.

80 S. Freud, *The Future of an Illusion* (London: Hogarth Press, 1934), 28–9.

81 Freud, 'The Question of a Weltanschauung', 165–6; S. Freud, *Civilisation and Its Discontents*, in *The Standard Edition of the Complete Works of Sigmund Freud*, Volume XXI, 120.

82 Freud, *Civilisation and Its Discontents*, 120; Freud, 'The Question of a Weltanschauung', 165–6.

83 S. Freud, 'A Seventeenth-Century Demonological Neurosis', in *The Standard Edition of the Complete Works of Sigmund Freud*, Volume XIX, 86.

84 See ibid., 105.

85 Ibid., 82ff.

86 Ibid., 72.

87 Ibid.

88 S. Freud, '"Some Dreams of Descartes". A Letter to Maxime Leroy', in *The Standard Edition of the Complete Works of Sigmund Freud*, Volume XXI, 203–4. See also James Strachey's 'Editor's Note' to the letter, ibid., 200–1.

89 C. G. Jung, 'On the Psychology of the Trickster Figure', in P. Radin, *The Trickster: A Study in American Indian Mythology* (New York: Schocken Books, 1972), 200.

90 'The Trickster Myth of the Winnebago Indians', in Radin, *The Trickster: A Study in American Indian Mythology*, 14, 18, 25.

91 Ibid., 18.

92 P. Radin, 'Prefatory Note', in *The Trickster: A Study in American Indian Mythology*, xxiii.

93 'The Trickster Myth of the Winnebago Indians', 19–20.

94 Jung, 'On the Psychology of the Trickster Figure', 201–7.

95 J. Lacan, *The Seminar of Jacques Lacan, Book II: The Ego in Freud's Theory and in the Technique of Psychoanalysis. 1954-1955*, ed. Jacques-Alain Miller; trans. Sylvana Tomaselli (New York: Norton, 1988), 224. I am here relying also on the

Staferla version since in the official edition the passage under examination has been abridged.

96 Private communication, 4 January 2022.

97 Ibid.

98 Lacan, *The Seminar of Jacques Lacan, Book XI*, 225 (transl. modified).

99 See, for instance, R. Descartes, *The Philosophical Writings of Descartes, Volume III* (Cambridge: Cambridge University Press, 1991), 25, 358–9.

100 However, I do concede that lack of knowledge remains central to my reading of Descartes. But, again, already in Descartes, knowledge is to begin with separated from truth. The self-deceiving God as the truth without knowledge of itself – instead of, more fundamentally, as the One that is not-One and the not-One that is One on the level of truth – is lacking knowledge only from the perspective of human knowledge.

101 Private communication, 20 March 2022.

102 Work yet to be done is more generally reflected by the length of the footnotes throughout my contribution. Readers may well decide to skip them, although they obviously both substantiate and open up my arguments.

103 Meillassoux, 'Appendix', 233. Meillassoux understands the position 'not believing in God because he exists' – which is not my 'not believing in God because he *might* exist as *self-deceiving*', but I fear could be grossly confused with it – as 'Luciferian' since it holds 'someone responsible for the evils of the world' (ibid., 238). This makes sense at face value. But, as I have explained, it is rather Meillassoux's own position that is, in a more complex manner, truly Luciferian and thus salvific. If the only necessity is contingency, namely, contingency cannot be contingent, then not only Meillassoux's own positing of this as excepted from absolute contingency is required to ensure that contingency cannot not be necessary but also, with the same move, the very possibility of immanent resurrection depends on the philosopher's transcendent responsibility for the current evils of the world. *It is necessary to believe in the God to come because Meillassoux exists now as the external guarantor of the fact that God currently does not exist.* Going one step further, and assuming that Meillassoux would find it hard to subscribe to this assessment, it is necessary to believe in God because Meillassoux self-deceives himself.

104 M. Ruti, *The Singularity of Being: Lacan and the Immortal Within* (New York: Fordham University Press, 2021), 153.

105 Han-yu Huang, 'The Crime of Indistinction? The Undead and the Politics of Redemption from an Agambenian Perspective', *Concentric: Literary and Cultural Studies,* March 2012: 171–94 (see esp. 179, 190).

106 F. Nietzsche, 'The Anti-Christ: A Curse on Christianity', in *The Anti-Christ, Ecce Homo, Twilight of Idols and Other Writings* (Cambridge: Cambridge University Press, 2005), 34.

107 L. Chiesa, 'Anthropie: Beside the Pleasure Principle', *Continental Thought and Theory,* 3, no. 2 (2021): 152.

108 A. Badiou, *Briefings on Existence: A Short Treatise on Transitory Ontology* (Albany: SUNY, 2006), 25, 22 (transl. modified).

Divine ignorance: Jacques Lacan and Christian atheism

1. Elisabeth Roudinesco, *Jacques Lacan & Co.: A History of Psychoanalysis in France, 1925-1985*, trans. Jeffrey Mehlman (Chicago: The University of Chicago Press, 1990), 104.
2. Paul Roazen, 'Lacan's First Disciple', *Journal of Religion and Health* 35, no. 4 (Winter 1996): 321–36.
3. Roudinesco, *Jacques Lacan & Co.*, 260–1; Elisabeth Roudinesco, *Jacques Lacan: Outline of a Life, History of a System of Thought*, trans. Barbara Bray (New York: Columbia University Press, 1997), 204–6.
4. Stanley A. Leavy, 'The Image and the Word: Further Reflections on Jacques Lacan', in *Interpreting Lacan*, ed. Joseph H. Smith and William Kerrigan (New Haven: Yale University Press, 1983), 13.
5. Sidi Askofaré, 'De l'inconscient au sinthome: Conjectures sur les usages et le renoncement possible au Nom-du- Père', *L'en-je lacanien*, no. 6 (2006): 30.
6. Jean-Louis Sous, *Pas très catholique, Lacan?* (Paris: EPEL, 2015), 15–16.
7. Louis Beirnaert, 'Introduction a la psychanalyse freudienne de la religion', in *Aux frontières de l'acte analytique: La Bible, saint Ignace, Freud et Lacan* (Paris: Editions du Seuil, 1987), 57–8.
8. Lacan, *The Seminar of Jacques Lacan, Book VII*, 170–1.
9. Jacques Lacan, 'Conférence de Bruxelles sur l'éthique de la psychanalyse', *Psychoanalyse: La Revue de l'École Belge de Psychanalyse*, no. 4 (1986): 170.
10. Ibid., 181.
11. Jacques Lacan, 'The Subversion of the Subject and the Dialectic of Desire in the Freudian Unconscious', in *Écrits: The First Complete Edition in English*, trans. Bruce Fink (New York: W.W. Norton and Company, 2006), 693.
12. Jean-Daniel Causse, *Lacan et le christianisme* (Paris: Campagne Premiere, 2018), 148.
13. Sous, *Pas très catholique, Lacan?*, 38.
14. Jacques Lacan, 'Science and Truth', in *Écrits*, 741.
15. Causse, *Lacan et le christianisme*, 201.
16. Lacan, 'Science and Truth', 744.
17. Ibid.,
18. Jacques Lacan, 'Mis en question du psychanalyste', in *Lacan Redivivus*, ed. Jacques-Alain Miller and Christiane Alberti, Ornicar?, hors-série (Paris: Navarin, 2021), 77.
19. Jacques Lacan, 'De la psychanalyse dans ses rapports avec la réalité', in *Autres Écrits*, ed. Jacques-Alain Miller (Paris: Éditions du Seuil, 2001), 352.
20. Lacan, 'The Triumph of Religion', 63.
21. Jacques Lacan, 'The Youth of Gide, or the Letter and Desire', in *Écrits*, 627.

22 Jacques Lacan, *Le Séminaire de Jacques Lacan, Livre XVI: D'un Autre à l'autre, 1968-1969,* ed. Jacques-Alain Miller (Paris: Éditions du Seuil, 2006), 280–1.

23 Jacques Lacan, 'La méprise du sujet supposé savoir', in *Autres Écrits*, 337.

24 Lacan, *Le Séminaire de Jacques Lacan, Livre XVI*, 280; Johnston, *Prolegomena to Any Future Materialism, Volume One*, 22–3.

25 Causse, *Lacan et le christianisme*, 45.

26 Jacques-Alain Miller, 'Religion, Psychoanalysis', trans. Barbara P. Fulks, *Lacanian Ink,* no. 23 (Spring 2004): 11–12.

27 Lacan, *Le Séminaire de Jacques Lacan, Livre XVI*, 176.

28 Lacan, 'Conferences et entretiens dans des universités nord-américaines', 32.

29 Lacan, *Le Séminaire de Jacques Lacan, Livre XVI*, 281.

30 Jacques Lacan, *Le Séminaire de Jacques Lacan, Livre XVII: L'envers de la psychanalyse, 1969-1970,* ed. Jacques-Alain Miller (Paris: Editions du Seuil, 1991), 139; Lacan, *The Seminar of Jacques Lacan, Book XVII*, 119.

31 Louis Beirnaert, 'Psychanalyse et vie de foi', in *Aux frontières de l'acte analytique*, 138.

32 Johnston, *Prolegomena to Any Future Materialism, Volume One*, 22–3.

33 Jacques Lacan, *Le Séminaire de Jacques Lacan, Livre X: L'angoisse, 1962-1963*, ed. Jacques-Alain Miller (Paris: Editions du Seuil, 2004), 357; Jacques Lacan, *The Seminar of Jacques Lacan, Book X: Anxiety, 1962-1963*, ed. Jacques-Alain Miller; trans. A. R. Price (Cambridge: Polity, 2014), 308.

34 Lacan, *Le Séminaire de Jacques Lacan, Livre X*, 357; Lacan, *The Seminar of Jacques Lacan, Book X*, 308.

35 Sigmund Freud, *Gesammelte Werke*, ed. E. Bibring, W. Hoffer, E. Kris and O. Isakower (Frankfurt: S. Fischer, 1952), (henceforth *GW*), 7: 139. Sigmund Freud, *The Standard Edition of the Complete Works of Sigmund Freud* (London: Vintage, 2001), (henceforth *SE*), 9: 126–7.

36 Jacques Lacan, 'Le triomphe de la religion', in *Le triomphe de la religion, precede de Discours aux catholiques,* ed. Jacques-Alain Miller (Paris: Editions du Seuil, 2005), 79. Lacan, 'The Triumph of Religion', 64.

37 Jacques Lacan, 'Freud pour toujours: Entretien avec J. Lacan', 21 November 1974, available at http://ecole-lacanienne.net/wp-content/uploads/2016/04/1974-11-21.pdf.

38 *SE* 12: 101, 106.

39 Lacan, 'Conférences et entretiens dans des universités nord-américaines', 32.

40 *SE* 12: 154.

41 *GW* 8: 478. *SE* 12: 143.

42 Lacan, *Le Séminaire de Jacques Lacan, Livre XVI*, 388–9.

43 François Balmès, *Dieu, le sexe et la vérité* (Ramonville Saint-Agne: Erès, 2007), 27–30; Askofaré, 'De l'inconscient au sinthome', 25.

44 Askofaré, 'De l'inconscient au sinthome', 34; Sous, *Pas très catholique, Lacan?*, 93.

45 Causse, *Lacan et le christianisme*, 162.

46 Jacques Lacan, *Le Séminaire de Jacques Lacan, Livre XIX: Le savoir du psychanalyste, 1971-1972* [unpublished typescript], session of 6 January 1972.
47 Askofaré, 'De l'inconscient au sinthome', 36.
48 Causse, *Lacan et le christianisme*, 240.
49 Ibid., 48.
50 Lacan, *The Seminar of Jacques Lacan, Book XI*, 59.
51 Balmes, *Dieu, le sexe et la vérité,* 13–15, 169–70; Adrian Johnston, *Adventures in Transcendental Materialism: Dialogues with Contemporary Thinkers* (Edinburgh: Edinburgh University Press, 2014), 219–21; Adrian Johnston, 'Lacan's Endgame: Philosophy, Science, and Religion in the Final Seminars', *Crisis and Critique,* special issue: 'Lacan: Psychoanalysis, Philosophy, Politics', ed. Agon Hamza and Frank Ruda, 6, no. 1 (2019): 156–87; Adrian Johnston, 'The Triumph of Theological Economics: God Goes Underground', *Philosophy Today*, special issue: 'Marxism and New Materialisms', 64, no. 1 (Winter 2020): 3–50.
52 Lacan, *The Seminar of Jacques Lacan, Book VII*, 14.
53 Johnston, 'Lacan's Endgame'.
54 Lacan, *The Seminar of Jacques Lacan, Book VII*, 192–3. François Balmès, *Le nom, la loi, la voix* (Ramonville Saint-Agne: Erès, 1997), 145. Causse, *Lacan et le christianisme*, 46–7.
55 Causse, *Lacan et le christianisme*, 20–1.
56 Lacan, *Le Séminaire de Jacques Lacan, Livre XIX: Le savoir du psychanalyste, 1971-1972*, session of 6 January 1972.
57 Jacques Lacan, *Le Séminaire de Jacques Lacan, Livre XII: Problèmes cruciaux pour la psychanalyse, 1964-1965* [unpublished typescript], session of 3 March 1965; Jacques Lacan, *The Seminar of Jacques Lacan, Book XX: Encore, 1972-1973,* ed. Jacques-Alain Miller; trans. Bruce Fink (New York: W.W. Norton and Company, 1998), 45, 108; Askofaré, 'De l'inconscient au sinthome', 34.
58 Lacan, *Le Séminaire de Jacques Lacan, Livre XII*, session of 3 March 1965.
59 Jacques Lacan, *Le Séminaire de Jacques Lacan, Livre XV: L'acte psychanalytique, 1967-1968* [unpublished typescript], session of 21 February 1968.
60 Jacques Lacan, 'On a Question Prior to Any Possible Treatment of Psychosis', in *Écrits,* 480.
61 Jacques Lacan, 'Du discours psychanalytique', in *Lacan in Italia, 1953–1978. En Italie Lacan* (Milan: La Salamandra, 1978), 45.
62 Lacan, *The Seminar of Jacques Lacan, Book II*, 48; Lacan, 'Conférence de Bruxelles sur l'éthique de la psychanalyse', 165; Lorenzo Chiesa and Alberto Toscano, 'Ethics and Capital, Ex Nihilo', in *Umbr(a): A Journal of the Unconscious – The Dark God*, ed. Andrew Skomra (Buffalo: Center for the Study of Psychoanalysis and Culture, State University of New York at Buffalo, 2005), 10; Lorenzo Chiesa, 'Psychoanalysis, Religion, Love', *Crisis & Critique,* special issue: 'Politics and Theology Today', ed. Frank Ruda and Agon Hamza, 2, no. 1 (2015): 63.
63 Lacan, 'Conférence de Bruxelles sur l'éthique de la psychanalyse', 166, 176; Beirnaert, 'Introduction a la psychanalyse freudienne de la religion', 53.

64. Lacan, 'Conférence de Bruxelles sur l'éthique de la psychanalyse', 181.
65. Lacan, 'The Triumph of Religion', 56, 64, 67, 71–2, 77–8; Jacques Lacan, *Le Séminaire de Jacques Lacan, Livre XXIV: L'insu que sait de l'une-bévue s'aile à mourre, 1976-1977* [unpublished typescript], session of 17 May 1977; Miller, 'Religion, Psychoanalysis', 16–19; Causse, *Lacan et le christianisme*, 47; Johnston, *Prolegomena to Any Future Materialism, Volume One*, xiii, 32–3, 37, 175–6; Johnston, *Adventures in Transcendental Materialism*, 187–8; Johnston, 'The Triumph of Theological Economics', 3–50.
66. Jacques Lacan, 'In Memory of Ernest Jones: On His Theory of Symbolism', in *Écrits*, 596.
67. Johnston, *Prolegomena to Any Future Materialism, Volume One*, 13–38.
68. Lacan, *The Seminar of Jacques Lacan, Book XVII*, 66.
69. Lacan, *The Seminar of Jacques Lacan, Book VII*, 261; Lacan, *The Seminar of Jacques Lacan, Book XX*, 41, 43; Chiesa and Toscano, 'Ethics and Capital, Ex Nihilo', 10–11; Lorenzo Chiesa and Alberto Toscano, '*Agape* and the Anonymous Religion of Atheism', *Angelaki: Journal of the Theoretical Humanities*, 12, no. 1 (April 2007): 118; Causse, *Lacan et le christianisme*, 35.
70. Jacques Lacan, *Le Séminaire de Jacques Lacan, Livre XX: Encore, 1972-1973*, ed. Jacques-Alain Miller (Paris: Editions du Seuil, 1975), 98; Lacan, *The Seminar of Jacques Lacan, Book XX*, 108.
71. Blaise Pascal, *Pensées*, trans. A. J. Krailsheimer (New York: Penguin, 1966), §142 (73), §190 (86).
72. Lacan, 'The Subversion of the Subject and the Dialectic of Desire in the Freudian Unconscious', 694.
73. Lacan, *Le Séminaire de Jacques Lacan, Livre XX*, 45; Lacan, *The Seminar of Jacques Lacan, Book XX*, 45.
74. Lacan, *Le Séminaire de Jacques Lacan, Livre XX*, 45; Lacan, *The Seminar of Jacques Lacan, Book XX*, 45.
75. Lacan, *The Seminar of Jacques Lacan, Book XX*, 45.
76. Causse, *Lacan et le christianisme*, 208.
77. Ludwig Feuerbach, *The Essence of Christianity*, trans. George Eliot (Amherst: Prometheus Books, 1989), xvii–xviii, xxiii, 17–18, 29–30, 336–9.
78. Lacan, *The Seminar of Jacques Lacan, Book XX*, 68.
79. Karl Marx, 'A Contribution to the Critique of Hegel's Philosophy of Right. Introduction', in *Early Writings*, trans. Rodney Livingstone and Gregor Benton (New York: Penguin, 1992), 244.
80. Roazen, 'Lacan's First Disciple', 331.
81. Immanuel Kant, *Kritik der reinen Vernunft, 1, Werkausgabe, Band III*, ed. Wilhelm Weischedel (Frankfurt am Main: Suhrkamp, 1968), A293/B349-A298/B355 (308–11); Immanuel Kant, *Critique of Pure Reason*, trans. Paul Guyer and Allen Wood (Cambridge: Cambridge University Press, 1998), A293/B349-A298/B355 (384–7); Marc De Kesel, 'Religion as Critique, Critique as Religion: Some Reflections on the Monotheistic Weakness of Contemporary Criticism', in *Umbr(a): A Journal of the Unconscious*, 121–2, 126–7.

82 Kant, *Kritik der reinen Vernunft, 1,* A293/B349-350 (308); Kant, *Critique of Pure Reason,* A293/B349-350 (384).

83 Kant, *Critique of Pure Reason,* A296-297/B353-354 (386).

84 Ibid., A298/B354-355 (386–7).

85 Karl Marx, *Critique of Hegel's Doctrine of the State, Early Writings*, trans. Rodney Livingstone and Gregor Benton (New York: Penguin, 1992), 161; Karl Marx, *Grundrisse: Foundations of the Critique of Political Economy (Rough Draft),* trans. Martin Nicolaus (New York: Penguin, 1973), 85, 88, 100–2, 104–5, 142–6, 157, 164, 331, 449–50, 831–2; Karl Marx, *Capital: A Critique of Political Economy, Volume I*, trans. Ben Fowkes (New York: Penguin, 1976), 739, 909; Karl Marx, *Capital: A Critique of Political Economy, Volume II*, trans. David Fernbach (New York: Penguin, 1978), 185; Karl Marx, *Capital: A Critique of Political Economy, Volume III*, trans. David Fernbach (New York: Penguin, 1981), 275, 596–7, 603.

86 Adrian Johnston, *Žižek's Ontology: A Transcendental Materialist Theory of Subjectivity* (Evanston: Northwestern University Press, 2008), 43–4, 281–3; Johnston, *Adventures in Transcendental Materialism*, 13–22.

87 Bruno Bauer, *The Trumpet of the Last Judgment over Hegel the Atheist and Antichrist: An Ultimatum*, trans. Michael Malloy, in *The Young Hegelians: An Anthology*, ed. Lawrence S. Stepelevich (Amherst: Humanity Books, 1999), 177–86.

88 Ernst Bloch, *Atheism in Christianity*, trans. J. T. Swann (New York: Herder and Herder, 1972), 65, 208–10, 268.

89 Ludwig Feuerbach, 'Letter to Hegel: November 22, 1828', in G. W. F. Hegel, *Hegel: The Letters,* trans. Clark Butler and Christiane Seiler (Bloomington: Indiana University Press, 1984), 547–50.

90 G. W. F. Hegel, 'Hegel to Creuzer [draft]: End of May 1821', in *Hegel: The Letters,* 467–8.

91 G. W. F. Hegel, *Grundlinien der Philosophie des Rechts oder Naturrecht und Staatswissenschaft im Grundrisse: Mit Hegels eigenhändigen Notizen und den mündlichen Zusätzen, Werke in zwanzig Bänden, 7*, ed. Eva Moldenhauer and Karl Markus Michel (Frankfurt am Main: Suhrkamp, 1970), §258 (403). G. W. F. Hegel, *Elements of the Philosophy of Right*, ed. Allen W. Wood; trans. H. B. Nisbet (Cambridge: Cambridge University Press, 1991), §258 (279).

92 Rudolf Haym, 'Preußen und die Rechtsphilosophie (1857): Hegel und seine Zeit', in *Materialien zu Hegels Rechtsphilosophie*, ed. Manfred Riedel (Frankfurt am Main: Suhrkamp, 1975), 365–94.

93 Adrian Johnston, *Prolegomena to Any Future Materialism, Volume Two: A Weak Nature Alone* (Evanston: Northwestern University Press, 2019), 15–69.

94 G. W. F. Hegel, *Jenaer Systementwürfe III: Naturphilosophie und Philosophie des Geistes*, ed. Rolf-Peter Horstmann (Hamburg: Felix Meiner, 1987), 256.

95 G. W. F. Hegel, 'The Spirit of Christianity and Its Fate', in *Early Theological Writings*, trans. T. M. Knox (Philadelphia: University of Pennsylvania Press, 1975), 266.

96 Ludwig Feuerbach, *Principles of the Philosophy of the Future*, trans. Manfred H. Vogel (Indianapolis: The Bobbs-Merrill Company, 1966), §7 (10).

97   G. W. F. Hegel, *System of Ethical Life, System of Ethical Life and First Philosophy of Spirit*, trans. H. S. Harris and T. M. Knox (Albany: State University of New York Press, 1979), 143–5.

98   Ibid., 144.

99   G. W. F. Hegel, *First Philosophy of Spirit (Part III of the System of Speculative Philosophy 1803/4)*, in *System of Ethical Life and First Philosophy of Spirit*, 211.

100 Lacan, 'Conférence de Bruxelles sur l'éthique de la psychanalyse', 165.

101 Feuerbach, *The Essence of Christianity*, 175; Ludwig Feuerbach, 'The Necessity of a Reform in Philosophy', in *The Fiery Brook: Selected Writings*, trans. Zawar Hanfi (London: Verso, 2012), 149–51. Feuerbach, *Principles of the Philosophy of the Future*, §60 (71).

102 G. W. F. Hegel, *The Philosophy of History*, trans. J. Sibree (New York: Dover, 1956), 422–3.

103 Ibid., 422.

104 G. W. F. Hegel, *Lectures on the Philosophy of Religion, Volume III: The Consummate Religion*, ed. Peter C. Hodgson; trans. R. F. Brown, P. C. Hodgson, J. M. Stewart and H. S. Harris (Berkeley: University of California Press, 1985), 373–4.

105 G. W. F. Hegel, 'The Relationship of Religion to the State', in *Political Writings*, ed. Laurence Dickey and H. B. Nibset; trans. H. B. Nisbet (Cambridge: Cambridge University Press, 1999), 226.

106 De Kesel, 'Religion as Critique, Critique as Religion', 125.

107 Feuerbach, *Principles of the Philosophy of the Future*, §1–2 (5).

108 Feuerbach, *The Essence of Christianity*, 32.

109 Ludwig Feuerbach, 'Vorläufige Thesen zur Reform der Philosophie', http://www.zeno.org/Philosophie/M/Feuerbach,+Ludwig/Vorläufige+Thesen+zur+Reform+der+Philosophie; Ludwig Feuerbach, 'Preliminary Theses on the Reform of Philosophy', in *The Fiery Brook,* 172–3.

110 Bloch, *Atheism in Christianity,* 210–12.

111 Louis Beirnaert, 'De l'athéisme', in *Aux frontières de l'acte analytique*, 128–9; Chiesa, 'Psychoanalysis, Religion, Love', 63; Causse, *Lacan et le christianisme*, 221, 245.

112 Jacques Lacan, *Le Séminaire de Jacques Lacan, Livre VII: L'ethique de la psychanalyse, 1959-1960*, ed. Jacques-Alain Miller (Paris: Editions du Seuil, 1986), 209; Lacan, *The Seminar of Jacques Lacan, Book VII*, 178.

113 Lacan, *The Seminar of Jacques Lacan, Book VII*, 192–3.

114 Causse, *Lacan et le christianisme,* 201–3.

115 Lacan, *Le Séminaire de Jacques Lacan, Livre VII*, 227; Lacan, *The Seminar of Jacques Lacan, Book VII*, 193.

116 Jacques Lacan, *The Seminar of Jacques Lacan, Book IV: The Object Relation, 1956-1957*, ed. Jacques-Alain Miller; trans. A. R. Price (Cambridge: Polity, 2020), 33–50; Johnston, *Prolegomena to Any Future Materialism, Volume One*, 59–77.

117 Kant, *Critique of Pure Reason,* Bxxx (117).

118 Lacan, 'The Triumph of Religion', 80–5.
119 Lacan, *Le Séminaire de Jacques Lacan, Livre XV,* session of 21 February 1968.
120 Bloch, *Atheism in Christianity,* 169–70.
121 Jacques Lacan, *Le Séminaire de Jacques Lacan, Livre XIII: L'objet de la psychanalyse, 1965-1966* [unpublished typescript], session of 25 May 1966; Lacan, *Le Séminaire de Jacques Lacan, Livre XVI*, 177; Lacan, *Le Séminaire de Jacques Lacan, Livre XIX: Le savoir du psychanalyste, 1971-1972*, session of 6 January 1972.
122 Jacques Lacan, *Le Séminaire de Jacques Lacan, Livre XXI: Les non-dupes errent, 1973-1974* [unpublished typescript], session of 21 May 1974.
123 Ibid.
124 Ibid.
125 Ibid.
126 Lacan, *Le Séminaire de Jacques Lacan, Livre XXI*, session of 19 February 1974.
127 Jacques Lacan, *Le Séminaire de Jacques Lacan, Livre XVIII: D 'un discours qui ne seraitpas du semblant, 1971*, ed. Jacques-Alain Miller (Paris: Éditions du Seuil, 2006), 14; Johnston, *Adventures in Transcendental Materialism*, 70–2.
128 Jacques Lacan, *Le Séminaire de Jacques Lacan, Livre III: Les Psychoses, 1955-1956*, ed. Jacques-Alain Miller (Paris: Éditions du Seuil, 1981), 324; Jacques Lacan, *The Seminar of Jacques Lacan, Book III: The Psychoses, 1955-1956*, ed. Jacques-Alain Miller; trans. Russell Grigg (New York: W.W. Norton and Company, 1993), 288.
129 Lacan, *The Seminar of Jacques Lacan, Book III*, 53; Lacan, *The Seminar of Jacques Lacan, Book IV*, 161; Jacques Lacan, *The Seminar of Jacques Lacan, Book V: The Formations of the Unconscious, 1957-1958*, ed. Jacques-Alain Miller; trans. Russell Grigg (Cambridge: Polity, 2017), 472–3; Jacques Lacan, *The Seminar of Jacques Lacan, Book VI: Desire and Its Interpretation, 1958-1959*, ed. Jacques- Alain Miller; trans. Bruce Fink (Cambridge: Polity, 2019), 307–12; Lacan, *Le Séminaire de Jacques Lacan, Livre XII*, session of 19 May 1965; Lacan, *Le Séminaire de Jacques Lacan, Livre XVI*, 224–5; Lacan, 'The Subversion of the Subject and the Dialectic of Desire in the Freudian Unconscious', 689–90. Adrian Johnston, 'Jacques Lacan (1901-1981)', in *Stanford Encyclopedia of Philosophy*, 2013, http:// plato.stanford.edu/entries/lacan/; Adrian Johnston, *Irrepressible Truth: On Lacan's 'The Freudian Thing'* (Basingstoke: Palgrave Macmillan, 2017), 164–5, 174–6.
130 *SE* 1: 318, 331; Lacan, *The Seminar of Jacques Lacan, Book VII*, 19–84.
131 Balmès, *Dieu, le sexe et la verite*, 184.
132 Ibid., 185.
133 Lacan, 'The Triumph of Religion', 66.
134 Chiesa and Toscano, *'Agape* and the Anonymous Religion of Atheism', 118.
135 Causse, *Lacan et le christianisme,* 199–201.
136 Lacan, *Le Séminaire de Jacques Lacan, Livre XX*, 98; Lacan, *The Seminar of Jacques Lacan, Book XX*, 107.
137 Lacan, *Le Séminaire de Jacques Lacan, Livre XX*, 10; Lacan, *The Seminar of Jacques Lacan, Book XX,* 114.

138 Jacques Lacan, 'Kant with Sade', in *Écrits,* 651.

139 De Kesel, 'Religion as Critique, Critique as Religion', 126–7.

140 Karl Marx, 'Theses on Feuerbach', in Karl Marx and Friedrich Engels, *The German Ideology* (Amherst: Prometheus Books, 1998), 570.

141 Lacan, 'Conférence de Bruxelles sur l'éthique de la psychanalyse', 172, 174; Jacques Lacan, 'Discourse to Catholics', in *The Triumph of Religion, Preceded by Discourse to Catholics*, 22–3. Askofaré, 'De l'inconscient au sinthome', 27.

142 Lacan, *Le Séminaire de Jacques Lacan, Livre XII*, session of 3 March 1965.

143 Balmès, *Le nom, la loi, la voix*, 35.

144 Miller, 'Religion, Psychoanalysis', 27–8, 34–5.

145 Lacan, 'The Subversion of the Subject and the Dialectic of Desire in the Freudian Unconscious', 688.

146 Causse, *Lacan et le christianisme,* 240–1.

147 Lacan, *The Seminar of Jacques Lacan, Book XVII*, 117, 137.

148 Ibid., 137; Russell Grigg, 'Beyond the Oedipus Complex', in *Jacques Lacan and the Other Side of Psychoanalysis: Reflections on Seminar XVII*, ed. Justin Clemens and Russell Grigg (Durham: Duke University Press, 2006), 51.

149 Lacan, *The Seminar of Jacques Lacan, Book III*, 214–15.

150 Lacan, *Le Séminaire de Jacques Lacan, Livre XVII*, 127; Lacan, *The Seminar of Jacques Lacan, Book XVII*, 111.

151 Jacques Lacan, *Le Séminaire de Jacques Lacan, Livre IX: L 'identification, 1961-1962* [unpublished typescript], session of 20 December 1961; Lacan, *Le Séminaire de Jacques Lacan, Livre XVI*, 190; Jacques Lacan, 'Overture to this Collection', in *Écrits,* 4; Jacques Lacan, 'Seminar on "The Purloined Letter"', in *Écrits,* 11; Jacques Lacan, 'Psychoanalysis and Its Teaching', in *Écrits,* 376; Lacan, 'The Youth of Gide, or the Letter and Desire', 625.

152 Grigg, 'Beyond the Oedipus Complex', 57.

153 Lacan, *Le Séminaire de Jacques Lacan, Livre XVII*, 114; Lacan, *The Seminar of Jacques Lacan, Book XVII*, 100;

154 Lacan, *Le Séminaire de Jacques Lacan, Livre XVII*, 114; Lacan, *The Seminar of Jacques Lacan, Book XVII*, 100–1.

155 Lacan, *Le Séminaire de Jacques Lacan, Livre XVII*, 114–15; Lacan, *The Seminar of Jacques Lacan, Book XVII*, 101.

156 Lacan, *The Seminar of Jacques Lacan, Book IV*, 202–3; acan, *The Seminar of Jacques Lacan, Book XVII*, 112–13; Jacques Lacan, *The Seminar of Jacques Lacan, Book XIX: . . . or Worse, 1971-1972*, ed. Jacques-Alain Miller; trans. R. Price (Cambridge: Polity, 2018), 25.

157 Lacan, *The Seminar of Jacques Lacan, Book XVII*, 124.

158 Ibid., 112–13.

159 Jacques Lacan, 'Les complexes familiaux dans la formation de l'individu: Essai d'analyse d'une fonction en psychologie', in *Autres Écrits,* 60–1.

160 G. W. F. Hegel, *Phenomenology of Spirit*, trans. A. V. Miller (Oxford: Oxford University Press, 1977), 111–19.

161 Lacan, *The Seminar of Jacques Lacan, Book XVII,* 20–2, 30, 79, 89, 170–1.

162 Ibid., 152; Lacan, *The Seminar of Jacques Lacan, Book XIX,* 30, 52, 62, 131–2, 160; Lacan, *The Seminar of Jacques Lacan, Book XX,* 17, 30, 54; Lacan, *Le Séminaire de Jacques Lacan, Livre XXI,* sessions of 11 December 1973, 15 January 1974, 9 April 1974, 21 May 1974; Johnston, *Adventures in Transcendental Materialism,* 68.

163 Lacan, *The Seminar of Jacques Lacan, Book XVII,* 20, 69, 102–3, 148–9, 152; Lacan, *Le Séminaire de Jacques Lacan, Livre XVIII,* 9; Jacques Lacan, 'Radiophonie', in *Autres Écrits,* 435–6; Bruce Fink, 'The Master Signifier and the Four Discourses', in *Key Concepts of Lacanian Psychoanalysis,* ed. Dany Nobus (New York: Other Press, 1998), 31; Slavoj Žižek, 'Four Discourses, Four Subjects', in *Cogito and the Unconscious*, ed. Slavoj Žižek (Durham: Duke University Press, 1998), 75; Slavoj Žižek, 'The Undergrowth of Enjoyment: How Popular Culture Can Serve as an Introduction to Lacan', in *The Žižek Reader,* ed. Elizabeth Wright and Edmond Wright (Oxford: Blackwell, 1999), 28; Slavoj Žižek, *Iraq: The Borrowed Kettle* (London: Verso, 2004), 133; Johnston, *Žižek's Ontology,* 251–68.

164 Lacan, *The Seminar of Jacques Lacan, Book XVII*, 89.

165 Paul Verhaeghe, 'Enjoyment and Impossibility: Lacan's Revision of the Oedipus Complex', in *Jacques Lacan and the Other Side of Psychoanalysis,* 42–3, 46.

166 Lacan, *The Seminar of Jacques Lacan, Book XVII*, 123.

167 Lacan, 'On a Question Prior to Any Possible Treatment of Psychosis', 464; Jacques Lacan, 'Introduction to the Names-of-the-Father Seminar', ed. Jacques-Alain Miller; trans. Jeffrey Mehlman, in *Television/A Challenge to the Psychoanalytic Establishment,* ed. Joan Copjec (New York: W.W. Norton and Company, 1990), 89.

168 Lacan, *Le Séminaire de Jacques Lacan, Livre XVII*, 142; Lacan, *The Seminar of Jacques Lacan, Book XVII,* 123.

169 Verhaeghe, 'Enjoyment and Impossibility', 40–1.

170 Lacan, *Le Séminaire de Jacques Lacan, Livre XVII*, 143; Lacan, *The Seminar of Jacques Lacan, Book XVII,* 123.

171 Lacan, *Le Séminaire de Jacques Lacan, Livre XVIII*, 68–9; Adrian Johnston, *Time Driven: Metapsychology and the Splitting of the Drive* (Evanston: Northwestern University Press, 2005), xix–xxiv, 283.

172 Jacques Lacan, 'A Theoretical Introduction to the Functions of Psychoanalysis in Criminology', in *Écrits,* 106–7; Lacan, *The Seminar of Jacques Lacan, Book V,* 470; Lacan, *The Seminar of Jacques Lacan, Book XVII,* 119–20; Lacan, 'Conférence de Bruxelles sur l'éthique de la psychanalyse', 173; Lacan, 'Discourse to Catholics', 25; Miller, 'Religion, Psychoanalysis', 36; Balmès, *Le nom, la loi, la voix,* 94; Johnston, *Time Driven,* 286; Johnston, *Adventures in Transcendental Materialism*, 219–20.

173 *SE* 13: 143.

174 *SE* 13: 147–9, 154.

175 Lacan, *The Seminar of Jacques Lacan, Book VII*, 176–7; Lacan, *Le Séminaire de Jacques Lacan, Livre XVI,* 151; Johnston, *Time Driven,* xxvii–xxxviii, 333–41.

176 Lacan, *The Seminar of Jacques Lacan, Book VI,* 342.

177 Lacan, *Le Séminaire de Jacques Lacan, Livre XVIII*, 141–61; Lacan, *The Seminar of Jacques Lacan, Book XIX*, 34–5, 179–80; Lacan, *Le Séminaire de Jacques Lacan, Livre XIX: Le savoir du psychanalyste, 1971-1972*, session of 1 June 1972; Jacques Lacan, 'L'etourdit', in *Autres Écrits,* 479; Jacques Lacan, 'Un homme et une femme', in *Bulletin de l'Association freudienne*, no. 54 (September 1993): 15.

178 Lacan, *The Seminar of Jacques Lacan, Book XVII*, 112.

179 Ibid., 113.

180 *GW* 9: 192; *SE* 13: 159–60.

181 *SE* 1: 259–60.

182 *SE* 13: 159–61.

183 *SE* 16: 406; *SE* 17: 247, 249, 262–3.

184 *SE* 13: 161.

185 *GW* 9: 194; *SE* 13: 161.

186 Sigmund Freud, 'Overview of the Transference Neuroses', in *A Phylogenetic Fantasy: Overview of the Transference Neuroses*, ed. Ilse Grubrich-Simitis; trans. Axel Hoffer and Peter T. Hoffer (Cambridge, MA: Harvard University Press, 1987), 20.

187 Lacan, *The Seminar of Jacques Lacan, Book XX*, 108–9.

188 Causse, *Lacan et le christianisme*, 248.

189 Miller, 'Religion, Psychoanalysis', 37.

190 Johnston, *Time Driven,* 283, 337.

191 Slavoj Žižek, *The Puppet and the Dwarf: The Perverse Core of Christianity* (Cambridge, MA: MIT Press, 2003), 171.

192 François Regnault, *Dieu est inconscient: Etudes lacaniennes autour de saint Thomas d'Aquin* (Paris: Navarin, 1985), 43.

193 G. K. Chesterton, *Orthodoxy* (San Francisco: Ignatius Press, 1995), 145.

194 Bloch, *Atheism in Christianity*, 233.

195 Chesterton, *Orthodoxy,* 145.

196 Ibid.

197 Ibid.

198 Bloch, *Atheism in Christianity,* 129, 169, 171, 257.

199 Žižek, *The Puppet and the Dwarf,* 91, 101–2, 138, 171; Slavoj Žižek, *The Parallax View* (Cambridge, MA: MIT Press, 2006), 352; Slavoj Žižek, 'The Fear of Four Words: A Modest Plea for the Hegelian Reading of Christianity', in *The Monstrosity of Christ: Paradox or Dialectic?* ed. Creston Davis (Cambridge, MA: MIT Press, 2009), 39–40, 48–9.

200 De Kesel, 'Religion as Critique, Critique as Religion', 135.

201 Lacan, *Le Séminaire de Jacques Lacan, Livre XVI*, 59–60.

202 Causse, *Lacan et le christianisme,* 245–6.

203 Jacques Lacan, *The Seminar of Jacques Lacan, Book XXIII: The Sinthome, 1975-1976*, ed. Jacques-Alain Miller; trans. A. R. Price (Cambridge: Polity, 2016), 116.

204 Verhaeghe, 'Enjoyment and Impossibility', 30, 44–5; Dominiek Hoens, 'Toward a New Perversion: Psychoanalysis', in *Jacques Lacan and the Other Side of Psychoanalysis*, 100.

205 De Kesel, 'Religion as Critique, Critique as Religion', 128–9.

206 Friedrich Nietzsche, *Beyond Good and Evil: Prelude to a Philosophy of the Future*, trans. Walter Kaufmann (New York: Vintage, 1989), §1 (9), §4 (11), §24 (35).

207 Friedrich Nietzsche, 'Attempt at a Self-Criticism', in *The Birth of Tragedy and The Case of Wagner*, trans. Walter Kaufmann (New York: Vintage, 1967), §5 (23); Nietzsche, *Beyond Good and Evil*, §46 (60); Friedrich Nietzsche, *Twilight of the Idols, Twilight of the Idols/The Anti-Christ*, trans. R. J. Hollingdale (New York: Penguin, 1990), 52–3, 55–6, 120.

208 Lacan, *Le Séminaire de Jacques Lacan, Livre XIII*, session of 25 May 1966.

209 Jacques Lacan, 'Introduction théorique aux fonctions de la psychanalyse en criminologie', in *Écrits* (Paris: Editions du Seuil, 1966), 130; Lacan, 'A Theoretical Introduction to the Functions of Psychoanalysis in Criminology', 106.

210 Lacan, *The Seminar of Jacques Lacan, Book VII*, 198.

211 Lacan, *The Seminar of Jacques Lacan, Book XI*, 27.

212 Lacan, *The Seminar of Jacques Lacan, Book XIX*, 148–9.

213 Jacques Lacan, 'Television', trans. Denis Hollier, Rosalind Krauss and Annette Michelson in *Television/A Challenge to the Psychoanalytic Establishment,* 30.

214 Lacan, *The Seminar of Jacques Lacan, Book X*, 49.

215 Lacan, *Le Séminaire de Jacques Lacan, Livre XII*, session of 16 June 1965; Jacques Lacan, *Le Séminaire de Jacques Lacan, Livre XIV: La logique du fantasme, 1966-1967* [unpublished typescript], sessions of 15 February 1967, 31 May 1967.

216 Lacan, *Le Séminaire de Jacques Lacan, Livre XVI*, 292, 382, 401.

217 Lacan, 'Introduction to the Names-of-the-Father Seminar', 89.

218 Lacan, *Le Séminaire de Jacques Lacan, Livre XXI,* session of 18 December 1973.

219 Lacan, *Le Séminaire de Jacques Lacan, Livre XVI*, 253.

220 Ibid., 302.

221 Ibid., 292.

222 Jacques Lacan, *Le Séminaire de Jacques Lacan, Livre XXIII: Le sinthome, 1975-1976,* ed. Jacques-Alain Miller (Paris: Editions du Seuil, 2005), 85; Lacan, *The Seminar of Jacques Lacan, Book XXIII*, 69.

223 Lacan*, The Seminar of Jacques Lacan, Book XX*, 108.

224 Octave Mannoni, 'Je sais bien, mais quand même . . .' in *Clefs pour l'Imaginaire ou l'Autre Scene* (Paris: Editions du Seuil, 1969)*,* 12–13, 32.

225 Jacques Lacan, *Le Séminaire de Jacques Lacan, Livre XXII: R.S.I., 1974-1975* [unpublished typescript], session of 21 January 1975.

226 Lacan, *The Seminar of Jacques Lacan, Book XXIII*, 11.

227 Lacan, *Le Séminaire de Jacques Lacan, Livre XXIII*, 85; Lacan, *The Seminar of Jacques Lacan, Book XXIII*, 69.

228 Lacan, *Le Séminaire de Jacques Lacan, Livre XXII*, session of 8 April 1975; Lacan, *The Seminar of Jacques Lacan, Book XXIII*, 130.

229 Lacan, *Le Séminaire de Jacques Lacan, Livre XXII*, session of 8 April 1975.

230 Jacques Lacan, 'Monsieur A.', *Ornicar?*, no. 21–22 (Summer 1980): 20.

231 Lacan, *The Seminar of Jacques Lacan, Book XXIII*, 132.

232 Lacan, *Le Séminaire de Jacques Lacan, Livre XXIII*, 153; Lacan, *The Seminar of Jacques Lacan, Book XXIII*, 132.

233 Lacan, *Le Séminaire de Jacques Lacan, Livre XXIV*, session of 17 May 1977; Johnston, 'Lacan's Endgame', 156–87.

234 Jacques Lacan, *Télévision* (Paris: Éditions du Seuil, 1973), 72; Lacan, 'Television', 46.

235 Blaise Pascal, 'Sur la casuistique et laprobabilite', in *Euvres completes*, ed. Jacques Chevalier (Paris: Gallimard, 1954), 1061–5.

236 Blaise Pascal, 'Memorial', in *Euvres completes*, 554; Blaise Pascal, 'Entretien de M. Pascal et de M. De Sacy sur la lecture d'Epictete et de Montaigne', in *De l'esprit geometrique, Entretien avec M. De Sacy, Écrits sur la grace, et autres textes*, ed. Andre Clair (Paris: Flammarion, 1985), 104; Pascal, *Pensées*, §142 (73), §190 (86), §449 (169); Lacan, *Le Séminaire de Jacques Lacan, Livre XIII*, session of 2 February 1966; Lacan, *Le Séminaire de Jacques Lacan, Livre XIV*, session of 1 February 1967; Lacan, *Le Séminaire de Jacques Lacan, Livre XVI*, 71.

237 Lacan, *The Seminar of Jacques Lacan, Book II*, 74, 296, 299.

238 Pascal, 'Memorial', 553–4.

239 Etienne Souriau, *L'ombre de Dieu* (Paris: Presses Universitaires de France, 1955), 49–50, 60; Georges Brunet, *Le pari de Pascal* (Paris: Desclee de Brouwer, 1956), 28, 63–4, 87, 121; Alexandre Koyre, 'Pascal Savant', in *Etudes d'historie de la pensee scientifique* (Paris: Gallimard, 1973), 371. Henri Gouthier, 'Le caur qui sent les trois dimensions: Analyse d'une pensee de Pascal', *La passion de la raison: Hommage a FerdinandAlquie* (Paris: Presses Universitaires de France, 1983), 203–15.

240 Pascal, *Pensées*, §100 (55), §143 (73), §423 (154), §530 (216), §709 (249), §821 (274).

241 Blaise Pascal, *Pensées*, ed. Leon Brunschvicg (Paris: Flammarion, 1976), §423 (127); Pascal, *Pensées*, §423 (154).

242 Blaise Pascal, *Écrits sur la grâce*, in *Euvres complètes*, 952.

243 Pascal, *Pensées*, §130 (161).

244 Pascal, *Pensées*, §124 (61), §129 (62), §130 (62), §354 (133), §616 (234); Lucien Goldmann, *The Hidden God: A Study of Tragic Vision in the Pensées of Pascal and the Tragedies of Racine*, trans. Philip Thody (London: Verso, 2016), 218–19.

245 Pascal, *Pensées*, §629 (161); Pascal, *Pensées*, §629 (236).

246 Pascal, *Pensées*, §112 (59), §406 (147).

247 Pascal, *Pensées*, §121 (60), §522 (214).

248 Pascal, *Pensées*, §128 (62).

249 Pascal, *Pensées*, §131 (64–6), §442 (166).

250 Pascal, *Pensées,* §131 (64–6), §149 (76), §442 (166).
251 Pascal, *Pensées,* §131 (64–6), §442 (166).
252 Pascal, *Pensées,* §410 (147), §621 (235).
253 Pascal, *Pensées,* §616 (234).
254 Pascal, *Écrits sur la grace,* 955; Pascal, *Pensées,* §241 (103).
255 Sara Vassallo, *Le desir et la grace: Saint Augustin, Lacan, Pascal* (Paris: EPEL, 2020), 22, 248.
256 Pascal, *Pensées,* §24 (85); Pascal, *Pensées,* §24 (36).
257 Pascal, *Pensées,* §78 (85); Pascal, *Pensées,* §78 (50).
258 Johnston, 'Jacques Lacan (1901-1981)'.
259 Pascal, *Pensées,* §47 (43), §148 (74–5), §427 (157), §639 (238), §641 (238).
260 Pascal, *Pensées,* §57 (45).
261 Jacques Lacan, 'The Signification of the Phallus', in *Écrits,* 579–80.
262 Pascal, *Pensées,* §73 (83); Pascal, *Pensées,* §73 (49).
263 Pascal, *Pensées,* §136 (69).
264 Pascal, *Pensées,* §133 (66), §134 (66–7, §136 (68–70-), §138 (72), §622 (235), §773 (261–2).
265 Jacques Lacan, *The Seminar of Jacques Lacan, Book I: Freud's Papers on Technique, 1953-1954,* ed. Jacques- Alain Miller; trans. John Forrester (New York: W.W. Norton and Company, 1988), 191; Lacan, *The Seminar of Jacques Lacan, Book III,* 46, 60; Lacan, *The Seminar of Jacques Lacan, Book V,* 426; Lacan, *Le Séminaire de Jacques Lacan, Livre XIV,* session of 14 December 1966; Johnston, *Irrepressible Truth,* 17, 26, 41, 43, 47, 104–5, 176.
266 Pascal, *Pensées,* §597 (229–30), §668 (242), §978 (347–9); Brunet, *Le pari de Pascal,* 105–6.
267 Pascal, *Pensées,* §655 (240), §803 (270), §978 (349–50); Blaise Pascal, 'Comparaison des chretiens des premiers temps avec ceux d'aujourd'hui', in *Euvres completes* (555–9).
268 Johnston, 'Lacan's Endgame', 156–87.
269 Pascal, *Pensées,* §412 (160); Pascal, *Pensées,* §412 (148).
270 Lacan, *The Seminar of Jacques Lacan, Book III,* 16; Jacques Lacan, 'The Function and Field of Speech and Language in Psychoanalysis', in *Écrits,* 234; Jacques Lacan, 'Discours de Rome', in *Autres Écrits,* 161.
271 Jacques Lacan, 'Propos sur la causalite psychique', in *Écrits,* 170; Jacques Lacan, 'Presentation on Psychical Causality', in *Écrits,* 139.
272 Lacan, 'On a Question Prior to Any Possible Treatment of Psychosis', 480.
273 Jacques Lacan, 'Le stade du miroir comme formateur de la fonction du Je telle qu'elle nous est révélée dans l'experience psychanalytique', in *Écrits,* 99; Lacan, 'The Mirror Stage as Formative of the I Function as Revealed in Psychoanalytic Experience', in *Écrits,* 80.
274 Lacan, *The Seminar of Jacques Lacan, Book VI,* 318; Lacan, 'Presentation on Psychical Causality', 153; Jacques Lacan, 'Le méprise du sujet suppos savoir', in *Autres Écrits,* 337.

275 Lacan, 'The Function and Field of Speech and Language in Psychoanalysis', 266.
276 Jean-Pierre Cléro, 'Lacan and Probability', *Electronic Journal for History of Probability and Statistics,* 4, no. 2 (December 2008), www.jehps.net.
277 Cormac Gallagher, 'What does Jacques Lacan see in Blaise Pascal?', Autumn 2001, http:// www.lacaninireland.com/web/wp-content/uploads/2010/06/Aut_2001-WHAT-D0ES-JACQUES-LACAN-SEE-IN- BLAISE-PASCAL-Cormac-Gallagher.pdf.
278 Dominiek Hoens, 'You never know Your Luck: Lacan Reads Pascal', *Continental Philosophy Review,* special issue: 'Reading *Seminar XIII: The Object of Psychoanalysis*', ed. Thomas Brockelman and Dominiek Hoens, 46, no. 2 (August 2013): 241–9; Dominiek Hoens, 'Is Life but a Pascalian Dream? A Commentary on Lacan's Louvain Lecture', *Psychoanalytische Perspectieven,* 36, no. 2 (2018): 169–85.
279 Lacan, *Le Séminaire de Jacques Lacan, Livre XII*, session of 20 January 1965.
280 Lacan, *Le Séminaire de Jacques Lacan, Livre IX*, session of 17 January 1962.
281 Pascal, *Pensées,* §68 (48), §201 (95), §427 (158); Lacan, *Le Séminaire de Jacques Lacan, Livre X,* 83; Lacan, *The Seminar of Jacques Lacan, Book X*, 67–8.
282 Lacan, *The Seminar of Jacques Lacan, Book II*, 239–40; Lacan, *Le Séminaire de Jacques Lacan Livre IX,* sessions of 17 January 1962, 16 May 1962; Jacques Lacan, 'Conferencia de Lacan en Londres', *Revista Argentina de Psicología,* 1975, 138, https://ecole-lacanienne.net/wp-content/uploads/2016/04/1975-02-03.pdf.
283 Lacan, *Le Séminaire de Jacques Lacan, Livre XII,* session of 20 January 1965; Lacan, *Le Séminaire de Jacques Lacan, Livre XIII*, sessions of 15 December 1965, 2 February 1966; Lacan, *Le Séminaire de Jacques Lacan, Livre XVI,* 337; Lacan, 'Introduction to the Names-of-the-Father Seminar', 90.
284 Lacan, *Le Séminaire de Jacques Lacan, Livre XII,* session of 20 January 1965; Lacan, *Le Séminaire de Jacques Lacan, Livre XIII*, session of 15 December 1965; Jean-Louis Chassing, 'Le songe et le réveil', *La célibataire: Revue de psychanalyse – clinique, logique, politique*, no. 13, *Lacan et Pascal* (Autumn 2006) (17).
285 Lacan, *Le Séminaire de Jacques Lacan, Livre XIII*, session of 1 June 1966.
286 Lacan, *Le Séminaire de Jacques Lacan, Livre XVI*, 165; Adrian Johnston, *Infinite Greed: Money, Marxism, Psychoanalysis* (New York: Columbia University Press, 2023 [under review]).
287 Pascal, *Pensées,* §199 (89).
288 Lacan, *Le Séminaire de Jacques Lacan, Livre IX,* session of 17 January 1962; Lacan, *Le Séminaire de Jacques Lacan, Livre XII*, session of 20 January 1965; Jacques Lacan, 'Massachusetts Institute of Technology, 2 decembre 1975', *Scilicet*, no. 6/7 (1976): 54.
289 Jacques Lacan, 'Introduction aux Noms-du-Père', in *Des Noms-du-Père*, ed. Jacques-Alain Miller (Paris: Editions du Seuil, 2005), 92; Lacan, 'Introduction to the Names-of-the-Father Seminar', 90.
290 Lacan, *Le Séminaire de Jacques Lacan, Livre XIII,* sessions of 2 February 1966, 9 February 1966.
291 Lacan, 'Introduction to the Names-of-the-Father Seminar', 90–4.

292 Lacan, *The Seminar of Jacques Lacan, Book X,* 76, 116, 160, 173, 218, 261, 297, 312.
293 Lacan, *The Seminar of Jacques Lacan, Book X*, 80–1.
294 Ibid., 211–18; Lacan, *The Seminar of Jacques Lacan, Book XI*, 215–16; Lacan, 'Science and Truth', 141; Richard Boothby, *Freud as Philosopher: Metapsychology After Lacan* (New York: Routledge, 2001), 241–8.
295 Brunet, *Le pari de Pascal,* 125.
296 Lacan, *Le Séminaire de Jacques Lacan, Livre XVI*, 109; Souriau, *L'ombre de Dieu,* 53.
297 Lacan, *Le Séminaire de Jacques Lacan, Livre XVI*, 18.
298 Ibid., 111; Alban Krailsheimer, *Pascal* (New York: Hill and Wang, 1980), 11.
299 Lacan, *Le Séminaire de Jacques Lacan, Livre XII*, session of 19 May 1965.
300 Ibid.
301 *SE* 18: 14–17.
302 Lacan, *Le Séminaire de Jacques Lacan, Livre XIII*, session of 2 February 1966.
303 G.-T. Guilbaud, *La cybernétique* (Paris: Presses Universitaires de France, 1954), 131.
304 Ibid., 124; Keith Devlin, *The Unfinished Game: Pascal, Fermat, and the Seventeenth-Century Letter that Made the World Modern* (New York: Basic Books, 2008), 6, 149.
305 Devlin, *The Unfinished Game*, 2, 52, 149.
306 Lacan, *Le Séminaire de Jacques Lacan, Livre XII*, session of 19 May 1965.
307 Hegel, *Phenomenology of Spirit*, 111–19.
308 Lacan, 'The Subversion of the Subject and the Dialectic of Desire in the Freudian Unconscious', 686.
309 Lacan, *Le Séminaire de Jacques Lacan, Livre XIII*, session of 2 February 1966; Lacan, *Le Séminaire de Jacques Lacan, Livre XVI*, 115–16, 178, 366.
310 Jacques Lacan, 'Allocution sur les psychoses de l'enfant', in *Autres Écrits*, 364.
311 Pascal, *Pensées,* §418 (153).
312 Pascal, *Pensées,* §418 (151).
313 Pascal, *Pensées,* §418 (115); Pascal, *Pensées,* §418 (151); Brunet, *Le pari de Pascal,* 66–8, 80, 127–8.
314 Lacan, *Le Séminaire de Jacques Lacan, Livre XIII*, session of 2 February 1966; Brunet, *Le pari de Pascal,* 81–2, 88–9, 118, 127–9.
315 Lacan, *Le Séminaire de Jacques Lacan, Livre X*, 83; Lacan, *The Seminar of Jacques Lacan, Book X*, 67.
316 Lacan, *Le Séminaire de Jacques Lacan, Livre X*, 83; Lacan, *The Seminar of Jacques Lacan, Book X*, 67–8.
317 Blaise Pascal, *Discours sur les passions de l'amour, &uvres completes*, 540–1.
318 Pascal, *Discours sur les passions de l'amour*, 544.
319 Lacan, *The Seminar of Jacques Lacan, Book VII*, 150, 152.
320 Ibid., 150, 152.

321   Lacan, *The Seminar of Jacques Lacan, Book X*, 81.

322   Ibid., 81–2.

323   Ibid., 82.

324   Jacques Lacan, *Le Séminaire de Jacques Lacan, Livre XI: Le quatre concepts fondamentaux de la psychanalyse, 1964*, ed. Jacques-Alain Miller (Paris: Editions du Seuil, 1973), 247; Lacan, *The Seminar of Jacques Lacan, Book XI*, 275.

325   Lacan, *The Seminar of Jacques Lacan, Book XI*, 275–6.

326   Ibid., 276.

327   Lacan, *Le Séminaire de Jacques Lacan, Livre XVI*, 171.

328   *GW* 14: 338–40, 352–3; *SE* 21: 17–19, 30.

329   Lacan, *Le Séminaire de Jacques Lacan, Livre XII*, sessions of 20 January 1965, 19 May 1965; Lacan, *Le Séminaire de Jacques Lacan, Livre XIII*, session of 9 February 1966.

330   *SE* 1: 318; *SE* 20: 154–5, 167.

331   *GW* 14: 338–40, 352–3; *SE* 21: 17–19, 30.

332   Lacan, 'Les complexes familiaux dans la formation de l'individu', 33–4.

333   Elizabeth Grosz, *Jacques Lacan: A Feminist Introduction* (New York: Routledge, 1990), 33.

334   Johnston, *Prolegomena to Any Future Materialism, Volume Two*, 187–255.

335   Lacan, 'The Mirror Stage as Formative of the I Function', 76.

336   Jacques Lacan, *Le Séminaire de Jacques Lacan, Livre IV: La relation d'objet, 1956-1957*, ed. Jacques-Alain Miller (Paris: Editions du Seuil, 1994), 168–9; Lacan, *The Seminar of Jacques Lacan, Book IV*, 161.

337   Lacan, *The Seminar of Jacques Lacan, Book V*, 473.

338   Lacan, *The Seminar of Jacques Lacan, Book VI*, 309–10; Lacan, 'The Subversion of the Subject and the Dialectic of Desire in the Freudian Unconscious', 690.

339   Slavoj Žižek, 'The Abyss of Freedom', in Slavoj Žižek and F. W. J. Schelling, *The Abyss of Freedom/Ages of the World* (Ann Arbor: University of Michigan Press, 1997), 79.

340   Joel Dor, *Introduction a la lecture de Lacan, Tome II: La structure du sujet* (Paris: Denoel, 1992), 32.

341   Sigmund Freud, *Entwurf einer Psychologie, Aus den Anfängen der Psychoanalyse, 1887-1902*, ed. Marie Bonaparte, Anna Freud and Ernst Kris (Frankfurt am Main: S. Fischer, 1975), 402–3; *SE* 1: 318.

342   Alphonse De Waelhens, *Schizophrenia: A Philosophical Reflection on Lacan's Structuralist Interpretation*, trans. Wilfried Ver Eecke (Pittsburgh: Duquesne University Press, 1978), 57.

343   Freud, *Entwurf einer Psychologie*, 416; *SE* 1: 331.

344   Lacan, *The Seminar of Jacques Lacan, Book VII*, 39, 51; Lacan, *Le Séminaire de Jacques Lacan, Livre XVI*, 224–5.

345 Adrian Johnston, 'Nothing is not always no-one: (a)Voiding Love', *Filozofski Vestnik*, special issue: 'The Nothing(ness)/Le *rien/Das Nichts*', ed. Alenka Zupancic, 26, no. 2 (2005): 67–81; Johnston, 'Jacques Lacan (1901-I981)'.

346 Slavoj Žižek, *Did Somebody Say Totalitarianism? Five Interventions in the (Mis)use of a Notion* (London: Verso, 2001), 165.

347 Slavoj Žižek, *The Ticklish Subject: The Absent Centre of Political Ontology* (London: Verso, 1999), 52–3.

348 *SE* 16: 329.

349 Alain Juranville, *Lacan et la philosophie* (Paris: Presses Universitaires de France, 1984), 201, 215. Jonathan Scott Lee, *Jacques Lacan* (Amherst: University of Massachusetts Press, 1990), 164; Boothby, *Freud as Philosopher*, 206–7.

350 Lacan, *The Seminar of Jacques Lacan, Book VII*, 67.

351 Jacques Lacan, *The Seminar of Jacques Lacan, Book VIII: Transference, 1960-1961*, ed. Jacques-Alain Miller; trans. Bruce Fink (Cambridge: Polity, 2015), 353–4; Bruce Fink, *A Clinical Introduction to Lacanian Psychoanalysis: Theory and Technique* (Cambridge, MA: Harvard University Press, 1997), 88.

352 Lacan, *Le Séminaire de Jacques Lacan, Livre XII,* session of 3 February 1965; Wilfried Ver Eecke, 'The Usefulness of the Theory of De Waelhens/Lacan as an Effective Approach to Schizophrenia, after the Decade of the Brain', in Alphonse De Waelhens and Wilfried Ver Eecke, *Phenomenology and Lacan on Schizophrenia, after the Decade of the Brain* (Leuven: Leuven University Press, 2001), 74–5.

353 Lacan, *The Seminar of Jacques Lacan, Book III*, 96.

354 Lacan, *The Seminar of Jacques Lacan, Book IV*, 370; Lacan, 'On a Question Prior to Any Possible Treatment of Psychosis', 464–5.

355 Bruce Fink, *The Lacanian Subject: Between Language and Jouissance* (Princeton: Princeton University Press, 1995), 57.

356 Roberto Harari, *Lacan's Seminar on 'Anxiety': An Introduction*, ed. Rico Franses; trans. Jane C. Lamb-Ruiz (New York: Other Press, 2001), 108.

357 Lacan, *The Seminar of Jacques Lacan, Book V*, 222–3; Anika Lemaire, *Jacques Lacan*, trans. David Macey (New York: Routledge, 1977), 86–7.

358 Lacan, 'On a Question Prior to Any Possible Treatment of Psychosis', 463.

359 Lacan, *The Seminar of Jacques Lacan, Book III*, 319.

360 Lacan, *The Seminar of Jacques Lacan, Book XVII,* 112.

361 Lacan, *Le Séminaire de Jacques Lacan, Livre XVII*, 129; Lacan, *The Seminar of Jacques Lacan, Book XVII*, 112.

362 Lacan, *The Seminar of Jacques Lacan, Book XVII*, 112.

363 Fink, *The Lacanian Subject,* 56–7; Žižek, *The Puppet and the Dwarf*, 71–2.

364 Charles Shepherdson, 'From *Oedipus Rex* to *Totem and Taboo*: Lacan's Revision of the Paternal Metaphor', in *Vital Signs: Nature, Culture, Psychoanalysis* (New York: Routledge, 2000), 127.

365 Boothby, *Freud as Philosopher,* 264.

366 Lacan, *Le Séminaire de Jacques Lacan, Livre XXI*, session of 19 March 1974.

367 Lacan, *Le Séminaire de Jacques Lacan, Livre XII,* session of 3 February 1965; Lacan, 'On a Question Prior to Any Possible Treatment of Psychosis', 485.

368 Lacan, *The Seminar of Jacques Lacan, Book III,* 96.

369 Lacan, *The Seminar of Jacques Lacan, Book VII,* 67–8; Lacan, *Le Séminaire de Jacques Lacan, Livre XXII,* session of 15 April 1975.

370 Lacan, *The Seminar of Jacques Lacan, Book V,* 186; Jean Laplanche, *Holderlin et la question du père* (Paris: Presses Universitaires de France, 1961), 36; Harari, *Lacan's Seminar on 'Anxiety',* 73.

371 Fink, *A Clinical Introduction to Lacanian Psychoanalysis,* 80.

372 Moustapha Safouan, *Lacaniana: Les Séminaires de Jacques Lacan, 1953-1963* (Paris: Librairie Artheme Fayard, 2001), 261–2.

373 Paul Verhaeghe, *Does the Woman Exist? From Freud's Hysteric to Lacan's Feminine,* trans. Marc du Ry (New York: Other Press, 1997), 197.

374 Safouan, *Lacaniana,* 235.

375 Ibid., 237.

376 Lacan, *The Seminar of Jacques Lacan, Book X,* 106; Jacques Lacan, 'On Freud's "Trieb" and the Psychoanalyst's Desire', in *Écrits,* 723.

377 Lacan, *Le Séminaire de Jacques Lacan, Livre XVI,* 277; Lacan, *The Seminar of Jacques Lacan, Book XVII,* 46; Lacan, *Le Séminaire de Jacques Lacan, Livre XVIII,* 20–1; Lacan, *Le Séminaire de Jacques Lacan, Livre XIX: Le savoir du psychanalyste, 1971-1972,* session of 4 November 1971.

378 Lacan, 'Allocution sur les psychoses de l'enfant', 364.

379 Jacques Lacan, 'Discours de cloture des journees sur les psychoses', *Recherches,* December 1968: 146.

380 Žižek, *The Puppet and the Dwarf,* 59.

381 Ibid., 59–60.

382 Lacan, *Le Séminaire de Jacques Lacan, Livre XVIII,* 68–9; Verhaeghe, *Does the Woman Exist?,* 192.

383 *SE* 13: 143.

384 Lacan, *Le Séminaire de Jacques Lacan, Livre XIV,* session of 26 April 1967.

385 Johnston, *Time Driven,* xix–xxiv, 333–41.

386 Lacan, *The Seminar of Jacques Lacan, Book XI,* 34.

387 Lacan, *Le Séminaire de Jacques Lacan, Livre XIII,* session of 27 April 1966.

388 Lacan, *Le Séminaire de Jacques Lacan, Livre XVI,* 225.

389 Lacan, *The Seminar of Jacques Lacan, Book V,* 438.

390 Pascal, *Pensées,* §418 (114); Pascal, *Pensées,* §418 (150).

391 Jean-Paul Sartre, *Being and Nothingness: A Phenomenological Essay on Ontology,* trans. Hazel E. Barnes (New York: Citadel Press, 2001), 460–2; Jean-Paul Sartre, *Existentialism and Humanism,* trans. Philip Mairet (London: Methuen, 1948), 34; Souriau, *L'ombre de Dieu,* 48.

392 Pascal, 'Entretien de M. Pascal et de M. De Sacy sur la lecture d'Epictete et de Montaigne', 110; Pascal, *Écrits sur la grace,* 977; Blaise Pascal, *The Provincial*

Letters, trans. A. J. Krailsheimer (New York: Penguin, 1967), Letter XV (218–19]); Pascal, *Pensées,* §131 (63–4); Goldmann, *The Hidden God,* 214, 243, 252, 283.

393   Pascal, *Pensées,* §418 (149).

394   Baruch Spinoza, 'Letter 50: Spinoza to Jelles, 2 June 1674', in *Spinoza: Complete Works*, ed. Michael L. Morgan; trans. Samuel Shirley (Indianapolis: Hackett, 2002), 892.

395   Lacan, *Le Séminaire de Jacques Lacan, Livre XIII,* sessions of 2 February 1966, 9 February 1966, 25 May 1966; Lacan, *Le Séminaire de Jacques Lacan, Livre XVI*, 147, 158–60, 165; Lacan, *The Seminar of Jacques Lacan, Book XVII*, 106; Pierre-Christophe Cathelineau, 'L'objet du Pari', *La celibataire: Revue de psychanalyse – clinique, logique, politique*, no. 13, *Lacan et Pascal* (Autumn 2006), 158.

396   Karl Marx, *The Eighteenth Brumaire of Louis Bonaparte*, trans. Ben Fowkes, in *Surveys from Exile: Political Writings, Volume 2*, ed. David Fernbach (Harmondsworth: Penguin, 1973), 146; Karl Marx, *A Contribution to the Critique of Political Economy*, ed. Maurice Dobb; trans. S. W. Ryazanskaya (New York: International, 1970), 20–1; Marx, *Grundrisse*, 496.

397   Pascal, *Pensées,* §78 (85); Pascal, *Pensées,* §78 (50).

398   Krailsheimer, *Pascal,* 50.

399   Lacan, *Le Séminaire de Jacques Lacan, Livre IX*, session of 19 May 1965; Lacan, *Le Séminaire de Jacques Lacan, Livre XIII,* sessions of 2 February 1966, 1 June 1966; Lacan, *Le Séminaire de Jacques Lacan, Livre XIV*, session of 21 December 1966; Lacan, *Le Séminaire de Jacques Lacan, Livre XVI*, 119–20, 136, 147, 364; Chassing, 'Le songe et le réveil', 9; Cathelineau, 'L'objet du Pari', 153.

400   Lacan, *Le Séminaire de Jacques Lacan, Livre XIII*, session of 2 February 1966.

401   Chassing, 'Le songe et le reveil', 17; Vassallo, *Le desir et la grace*, 192.

402   Lacan, *Le Séminaire de Jacques Lacan, Livre XVI*, 123; Jorge Cacho, 'Disgrace', *La celibataire: Revue depsychanalyse – clinique, logique, politique*, no. 13, *Lacan et Pascal* (Autumn 2006): 161; Vassallo, *Le desir et la grace*, 13.

403   Lacan, *Le Séminaire de Jacques Lacan, Livre XIII,* sessions of 2 February 1966, 9 February 1966; Lacan, *Le Séminaire de Jacques Lacan, Livre XVI*, 123, 47–8.

404   Lacan, 'Introduction to the Names-of-the-Father Seminar', 82.

405   Ibid.

406   Lacan, 'Mis en question du psychanalyste', 93.

407   Lacan, *Le Séminaire de Jacques Lacan, Livre XIII,* sessions of 26 January 1966, 2 February 1966, 9 February 1966, 1 June 1966; Lacan, *Le Séminaire de Jacques Lacan, Livre XVI*, 107, 119; Vassallo, *Le desir et la grace*, 22.

408   Lacan, *Le Séminaire de Jacques Lacan, Livre XXI*, session of 9 April 1974.

409   Brunet, *Le pari de Pascal*, 65.

410   Lacan, *Le Séminaire de Jacques Lacan, Livre XVI*, 155, 160; Lacan, *The Seminar of Jacques Lacan, Book XVII*, 100.

411   Lacan, *Le Séminaire de Jacques Lacan, Livre XVI*, 128, 133, 142, 146.

412   Cathelineau, 'L'objet du Pari', 157.

413   Chassing, 'Le songe et le réveil', 9.

414 Lacan, *Le Séminaire de Jacques Lacan, Livre XVI*, 128.

415 Ibid., 142.

416 Ibid., 133, 146.

417 Ibid., 133.

418 *SE* 2: 305.

419 Pascal, *Pensées,* §418 (115); Pascal, *Pensées,* §418 (151).

420 Lacan, *Le Séminaire de Jacques Lacan, Livre XIII*, session of 2 February 1966; Lacan, *Le Séminaire de Jacques Lacan, Livre XVI*, 149; Lacan, *The Seminar of Jacques Lacan, Book XVII*, 100; Cathelineau, 'L'objet du Pari', 158–60.

421 Lacan, *Le Séminaire de Jacques Lacan, Livre VII*, 368; Lacan, *The Seminar of Jacques Lacan, Book VII*, 319.

422 Adrian Johnston, 'The Vicious Circle of the Super-Ego: The Pathological Trap of Guilt and the Beginning of Ethics', *Psychoanalytic Studies,* 3, no. 3/4 (September–December 2001), 411–24.

423 *SE* 19: 159–70.

424 Johnston, 'The Vicious Circle of the Super-Ego', 411–24.

425 Lacan, *Le Séminaire de Jacques Lacan, Livre XVI*, 191.

426 Lacan, *The Seminar of Jacques Lacan, Book VII*, 72–3, 76–7; Lacan, 'Kant with Sade', 646–7.

427 Immanuel Kant, *Critique of Practical Reason, Practical Philosophy*, ed. and trans. Mary J. Gregor (Cambridge: Cambridge University Press, 1996), 239–46.

428 Kant, *Critique of Pure Reason,* A824-830/B852-858 (686–90); Goldmann, *The Hidden God*, 299.

429 Goldmann, *The Hidden God,* 233, 299.

430 Kant, *Critique of Pure Reason,* A592/B620-A642/B670 (563–89).

431 Goldmann, *The Hidden God,* 262, 266, 291.

432 Lacan, *The Seminar of Jacques Lacan, Book XX*, 45.

433 Immanuel Kant, 'Groundwork of The Metaphysics of Morals', in *Practical Philosophy*, 61–2.

434 Souriau, *L'ombre de Dieu*, 50–2.

435 Lacan, *The Seminar of Jacques Lacan, Book XX*, 108.

436 Jacques Lacan, 'La mort est du domaine de la foi', *Quarto*, no. 3 (1981): 8; Hoens, 'Is Life but a Pascalian Dream?', 169–85.

437 *Lacan, The Seminar of Jacques Lacan, Book XX*, 111–12; Johnston, *Time Driven,* xiv, xxxiv–xxxv, 239–41, 243, 248, 250, 282–3, 285–7, 297–8, 318, 324–5, 327, 329–30, 336–7, 339.

438 Lacan, 'La mort est du domaine de la foi', 8.

439 Pascal, *Pensées*, §418 (115); Pascal, *Pensées*, §418 (151).

440 Gilles Deleuze, *Qu'est-ce que l'acte de création?* ed. Charles J. Stivale, 17 March 1987, https://deleuze.cla.purdue.edu/sites/default/files/pdf/lectures/fr/1b%20 Deleuze%20What%20Is%20A%20Creative%20Act%20-%20French.pdf; Gilles Deleuze, 'What Is the Creative Act?', trans. Alison M. Gingeras, in *French Theory*

in America, ed. Sylvère Lotringer and Sande Cohen (New York: Routledge, 2001), 103.

441 Lacan, 'La mort est du domaine de la foi', 11.
442 Pascal, *Pensées,* §131 (173); Pascal, *Pensées,* §131 (65).
443 Pascal, *Pensées,* §56 (97); Pascal, *Pensées,* §56 (44).
444 Lacan, *Le Séminaire de Jacques Lacan, Livre XVI*, 22–3, 109, 119; Thierry Jean, 'C'est quoi un névrosé?', *La célibataire: Revue de psychanalyse – clinique, logique, politique, no. 13, Lacan et Pascal* (Autumn 2006), 184; Devlin, *The Unfinished Game*, 4, 33.
445 Lacan, *Le Séminaire de Jacques Lacan, Livre XVI*, 396.
446 Ibid., 119.
447 Johnston, *Infinite Greed*.
448 Karl Marx and Friedrich Engels, *Manifest der kommunistischen Partei*, 1848, https://www.marxists.org/deutsch/archiv/marx-engels/1848/manifest/index.htm; Karl Marx and Friedrich Engels, *The Communist Manifesto*, trans. Samuel Moore, in *Karl Marx: Selected Writings*, ed. David McLellan (Oxford: Oxford University Press, 1977), 223.
449 Marx and Engels, *Manifest der kommunistischen Partei;* Marx and Engels, *The Communist Manifesto*, 224.
450 Lacan, *Le Séminaire de Jacques Lacan, Livre XIII*, session of 2 February 1966; Goldmann, *The Hidden God*, 90–1, 93–5, 172, 258, 285, 300–2, 308–9.
451 Lacan, *Le Séminaire de Jacques Lacan, Livre XVI*, 174.
452 Ibid.
453 Johnston, *Adventures in Transcendental Materialism*, 65–107; Johnston, 'Lacan's Endgame', 156–87; Johnston, *Infinite Greed*.
454 Karl Marx, 'Thesen über Feuerbach', in Karl Marx and Friedrich Engels, *Die deutsche Ideologie* (Berlin: Dietz, 1953), 594; Marx, 'Theses on Feuerbach', 570.
455 Feuerbach, *The Essence of Christianity*, xvii–xviii xxiii, 17–18, 29–30, 336–9; Feuerbach, *Principles of the Philosophy of the Future,* §1 (5), §2 (5), §4 (5–6), §7 (8, 10), §8 (11), §13 (19).
456 Marx, 'Theses on Feuerbach', 571.
457 Jacques Lacan, 'Journees d'etude des cartels de L'École freudienne de Paris: Seance de cloture', *Lettres de l'École freudienne*, no. 18 (1976): 265.
458 Lacan, 'Mis en question du psychanalyste', 59.
459 Ibid.
460 Johnston, 'The Triumph of Theological Economics', 3–50; Johnston, *Infinite Greed*.
461 Roudinesco, *Jacques Lacan & Co.*, 1045; Roudinesco, *Jacques Lacan*, 7–8, 11.
462 Michel de Certeau, 'Lacan: An Ethics of Speech', trans. Marie-Rose Logan, in *Heterologies: Discourse on the Other*, trans. Brian Massumi (Minneapolis: University of Minnesota Press, 1986), 54, 58–62; Jacques Sédat, 'Préface', in Marc-François Lacan, *Dieu n'est pas un assureur* (Paris: Albin Michel, 2010), 7–25; Matthieu Vassal, 'Deux frères: Témoignage du père Matthieu Vassal, archiviste et moine beénédiction de Ganagobie', in Lacan, *Dieu n'est pas un assureur*, 138;

Jacques Sédat, 'Deux hommes à la recherche de la vérité: À propos d'une lettre de Marc-François Lacan', *Figures de la psychanalyse*, no. 34 (2017): 253–67; John Gale, 'Lacan and the Benedictines', *European Journal of Psychoanalysis,* no. 10 (2018), https://www.journal-psychoanalysis.eu/lacan-and-the-benedictines/; (Chase Padusniak, 'Jacques Lacan's Benedict Option', *Church Life Journal: A Journal of the McGrath Institute for Church Life*, 21 March 2022, https://churchlifejournal.nd.edu/articles/jacques-lacans-benedict-option/.

463 Roudinesco, *Jacques Lacan & Co.*, 104–5; Roudinesco, *Jacques Lacan,* 12–14; Vassal, 'Deux freres', 138.

464 Roudinesco, *Jacques Lacan*, 13.

465 Ibid., 14; Vassal, 'Deux freres', 139.

466 Roudinesco, *Jacques Lacan*, 78.

467 Ibid.; Vassal, 'Deux freres', 139.

468 Catherine Clement, *The Lives and Legends of Jacques Lacan*, trans. Arthur Goldhammer (New York: Columbia University Press, 1983), 30–2, 65.

469 Roudinesco, *Jacques Lacan*, 181.

470 Ibid.

471 Ibid., 182.

472 Roudinesco, *Jacques Lacan & Co.*, 104.

473 Ibid.

474 Clement, *The Lives and Legends of Jacques Lacan*, 30–2.

475 Jacques Lacan, 'Lettre de Jacques Lacan à son frère Marc-François, 1953: 5 septembre 1953', in *Lacan Redivivus*, 244; Vassal, 'Deux freres', 141–2.

476 Roudinesco, *Jacques Lacan & Co.*, 260–2; Roudinesco, *Jacques Lacan*, 205–6.

477 Catherine Millot, *Life with Lacan*, trans. Andrew Brown (Cambridge: Polity, 2018), 16.

478 Marc-François Lacan, 'Lettre de Marc François à son frère Jacques Lacan, 1953: 9 avril 1953', in *Lacan Redivivus*, 234.

479 Roudinesco, *Jacques Lacan,* 205.

480 Roazen, 'Lacan's First Disciple', 321–36.

481 Ibid., 327.

482 Roudinesco, *Jacques Lacan & Co.*, 260; Roudinesco, *Jacques Lacan*, 204–6; Elisabeth Roudinesco, in Alain Badiou and Elisabeth Roudinesco, *Jacques Lacan Past and Present: A Dialogue,* trans. Jason E. Smith (New York: Columbia University Press, 2014), 23.

483 Roudinesco, *Jacques Lacan & Co.*, 261.

484 Ibid., 262.

485 Roudinesco, in Badiou and Roudinesco, *Jacques Lacan Past and Present*, 23.

486 Roudinesco, *Jacques Lacan*, 408.

487 Vassal, 'Deux freres', 144.

488 Marcelle Marini, *Jacques Lacan: The French Context*, trans. Anne Tomiche (New Brunswick: Rutgers University Press, 1992), 97.

489 Jacques Lacan, 'Lettre de Jacques Lacan a son frere Marc Frangois, 1953: Ce mardi de Paques 53', in *Lacan Redivivus*, 220–7.
490 Millot, *Life with Lacan,* 25.
491 Lacan, 'Lettre de Jacques Lacan a son frere Marc Frangois, 1953: Ce mardi de Paques 53', 222.
492 Ibid., 224.
493 Ibid.
494 Ibid., 224, 226.
495 Lacan, 'Lettre de Jacques Lacan a son frere Marc Frangois, 1953: 5 septembre 1953', 246.
496 Lacan, 'Lettre de Jacques Lacan a son frere Marc Frangois, 1953: Ce mardi de Paques 53', 226.
497 Ibid.
498 Lacan, 'Lettre de Jacques Lacan à son frère Marc Frangois, 1953: 5 septembre 1953', 244.
499 Ibid.
500 Roudinesco, *Jacques Lacan & Co.*, 104; Roudinesco, *Jacques Lacan*, 8.
501 Jacques Lacan, 'Lettre de Jacques Lacan a son frere Marc Frangois, 1962: 3 janvier 1962', in *Lacan Redivivus*, 248.
502 Marc-François Lacan, 'Lettre de Marc-François Lacan a Jacques Sedat: 3 decembre 1982', in *Dieu n'est pas un assureur*, 195–6.
503 Lacan, 'Lettre de Jacques Lacan a son frere Marc Frangois, 1962: 3janvier 1962', 248.

Psychoanalysis and agnostic atheism

1 S. Freud, *The Future of an Illusion* (London: Hogarth Press, 1928), 53. I rely on the first English edition as I find its translation of some crucial phrases more convincing than that provided by *The Standard Edition of the Complete Works of Sigmund Freud*.
2 Ibid., 54.
3 Ibid.
4 Ibid.
5 Ibid.
6 Ibid.
7 See S. Freud, *Moses and Monotheism*, in *The Standard Edition of the Complete Works of Sigmund Freud*, Volume XXIII, 85ff.
8 Freud, *The Future of an Illusion*, 55.
9 Ibid., 56.
10 Ibid.

11 Ibid., 49.
12 Ibid.
13 Ibid.
14 Ibid., 57 (my emphasis).
15 O. Pfister, 'The Illusion of a Future', *International Journal of Psychoanalysis*, 74, no. 3 (1993): 557–79; H. Meng and E. L. Freud (eds), *The Letters of Sigmund Freud & Oskar Pfister* (New York: Basic Books, 1963). In trying to persuade Freud that 'he battles against religion out of religious feeling', Pfister goes as far as claiming that 'Jesus overcame the collective neurosis of his people according to good psychoanalytic practice' ('The Illusion of a Future', 559, 561). For a Christian, and specifically Catholic, approach that is far more nuanced, see H. Küng, 'Freud and the Problem of God', *The Wilson Quarterly*, 3, no. 4 (Autumn 1979): 162–71. See also the Jesuit psychoanalyst L. Beirnaert, *Aux frontières de l'acte analytique: La Bible, Saint Ignace, Freud et Lacan* (Paris: Seuil, 1987), esp. 47–8, 119–31.
16 C. Hitchens, *God Is Not Great. How Religion Poisons Everything* (Toronto: McClelland & Stewart, 2007).
17 Freud, *The Future of an Illusion*, 50 (my emphasis).
18 Ibid., 49.
19 Ibid., 90.
20 Ibid., 67 (my emphasis).
21 Ibid., 50.
22 Ibid., 51.
23 'In analysis we never discover a "no" in the unconscious' (S. Freud, 'Negation', in *The Standard Edition of the Complete Psychological Works of Sigmund Freud*, Volume XIX, 239).
24 Lacan, *The Seminar of Jacques Lacan, Book XI*, 59.
25 O. Mannoni, *Clefs pour l'Imaginaire ou l'Autre Scène* (Paris: Seuil, 1969), 12–13, 32.
26 'A negative judgement' – such as, in our case, 'God is not' – 'is the intellectual substitute for repression; its "no" is the hallmark of repression. [. . .] Thinking frees itself from the restrictions of repression and enriches itself with material that is indispensable for its proper functioning'. *Yet*, at the same time, 'with the help of negation only one consequence of the process of repression is undone' and '*what is essential to the repression persists*' (Freud, 'Negation', 236, my emphasis).
27 Freud, *The Future of an Illusion*, 65.
28 Ibid., 67.
29 Ibid., 61–2.
30 Ibid., 62.
31 Ibid., 83 (my emphasis).
32 Ibid., 84.
33 S. Freud, 'Obsessive Action and Religious Practices', in *The Standard Edition of the Complete Psychological Works of Sigmund Freud*, Volume IX, 126.
34 Ibid., 125.

35 Ibid., 126–7.
36 Although, for Freud, 'repression' (*Verdrängung*) is a specific case of 'suppression' (*Unterdrückung*), in that the former is an unconscious suppression that is otherwise conscious, here he does not seem to give much importance to this distinction. Also, 'suppression' and 'renunciation' (*Verzicht*) are treated as synonymous (ibid., 125).
37 Ibid., 124.
38 Ibid., 126.
39 Freud, *The Future of an Illusion*, 24.
40 Ibid., 26, 32 (my emphasis).
41 Ibid. (my emphasis).
42 Ibid., 14–15 (my emphasis).
43 Ibid., 12.
44 Ibid., 25–6.
45 Ibid., 42.
46 Ibid., 25.
47 Ibid., 28 (my emphasis).
48 Ibid., 29.
49 Ibid., 31.
50 Ibid., 32.
51 Ibid., 78.
52 'No one is under the illusion that nature has so far been vanquished'. Today, 'the great common task [is still] the preservation of mankind against the supremacy of nature' (ibid., 26–7).
53 Ibid., 22.
54 Ibid., 85.
55 Ibid., 57.
56 Ibid., 15.
57 Ibid., 84.
58 Ibid., 15. Six years later, in 1933, Freud's assessment of the USSR becomes harsher: 'Theoretical Marxism, as realized in Russian Bolshevism, has acquired the energy and self-contained and exclusive character of a Weltanschauung [. . .] it has created a prohibition of thought which is just as ruthless as was that of religion in the past'. Having said that: 'The future will tell us; perhaps it will show that the experiment was undertaken prematurely' (S. Freud, 'The Question of a Weltanschauung', in *The Standard Edition of the Complete Psychological Works of Sigmund Freud*, Volume XXII, 179–81). Any residual hope in Soviet Russia's dealing with religion – which 'withdraw[s] the "opium" of the people' only at the cost of robbing them of 'freedom of thought' – is dismissed in the first 'Prefatory Note' to the third chapter of *Moses and Monotheism*, written in early 1938 (Freud, *Moses and Monotheism*, 54).
59 Freud, *The Future of an Illusion*, 10. This nascent doubt concerning a possible religious involution of science resurfaces in the strange status of science vis-

à-vis religion as treated, and not fully acknowledged, in 'The Question of a Weltanschauung'. First, religion is an Ur-Weltanschauung as 'an intellectual construction which solves all the problems of our existence uniformly on the basis of one overriding hypothesis', and thus as an illusory wish-fulfilment. Second, there is nonetheless a scientific Weltanschauung. But, third, the latter 'departs noticeably' from the definition of Weltanschauung in that the overriding hypothesis about the uniformity of the universe is only a 'programme [. . .] relegated to the future'. Still, fourth, despite its 'present incompleteness', due to its unheard-of advancements, in comparison to religion, the scientific Weltanschauung is already 'complete in all essential respects'. Thus, fifth, 'our best hope for the future is that [. . .] scientific spirit may [. . .] establish a dictatorship in the mental life of man'. However, sixth, 'a Weltanschauung erected upon science has [. . .] mainly negative traits' (Freud, 'The Question of a Weltanschauung', 155–82).

60 Freud, *The Future of an Illusion*, 34.
61 Ibid., 47.
62 See ibid., 76.
63 Ibid., 65.
64 See ibid., 67–8.
65 Ibid., 83.
66 Ibid., 84.
67 Ibid., 92.
68 Ibid.
69 Ibid., 95.
70 Ibid.
71 See ibid., 12.
72 Ibid., 18.
73 Ibid., 73.
74 Ibid., 76.
75 Ibid., 69.
76 Ibid., 20, 68.
77 Ibid., 69.
78 Ibid., 96–7.
79 Ibid., 87.
80 Ibid., 97–8 (my emphasis).
81 Interestingly, Freud's stance here seems to clash, at least in part, with his vitriolic attack against the negative Weltanschauung of the 'intellectual nihilists' whose alleged epistemological anarchism would derive from the 'relativity theory of modern physics [that has] gone to their head' (see 'The Question of a Weltanschauung', 175–6). The problem for Freud is that, insofar as the intellectual nihilists refuse any ultimate criterion of truth as correspondence with the external world and 'scientific truth is only the product of our own needs as they are bound to find utterance under changing external conditions', they would nominally be scientific only in order to force science into 'suicide' – and thereby replace it with

'some kind of mysticism'. Predictably, Freud accuses them of being too 'abstract' and inept with regard to 'practical life'. Yet, in opposition to *The Future of an Illusion*, in this case excessive abstraction stems precisely from a limitation of scientific truth to the world-for-us.

82 In *Moses and Monotheism*, Freud instead clearly opts for atheism. In this later context, and with specific regard to the origins of monotheism, he distinguishes between 'historical truth' and 'material truth'. The historical truth here corresponds to the fact that 'in primaeval times there was a single person who was bound to appear huge at that time and who afterwards returned in men's memory elevated to divinity'. But the material truth is simply that 'there is [not] a single great god'. Hence, religious belief in the distorted historical truth as material truth is a sheer 'delusion' – not an illusion (Freud, *Moses and Monotheism*, 129–30).

83 Lacan, 'Discourse to Catholics', 26 (transl. modified).

84 Ibid., 43, 21.

85 Ibid., 29.

86 Ibid., 31.

87 See ibid., 29.

88 Ibid., 28.

89 Ibid., 25.

90 Ibid., 24–5.

91 See S. J. Gould, 'Non-overlapping Magisteria', in *The Richness of Life* (New York: Norton, 2006), 590–603.

92 Lacan, 'Discourse to Catholics', 17. See also Lacan, *The Seminar of Jacques Lacan, Book VII*, 170: 'Whether from personal conviction or in the name of a methodological point of view, the so-called scientific point of view [. . .] there is a paradox involved in practically excluding from the debate and from analysis things, terms, and doctrines that have been articulated in the field of faith, on the pretext that they belong to a domain that is reserved to believers'. In the same lesson, delivered one week after 'Discourse to Catholics', Lacan then mildly and in passing reproaches Freud on this point, only to immediately praise him again for his atheistic investigation of religion and, specifically, the function of the Father: 'Freud took an unequivocal position on the subject of religious experience. He said that everything of that kind [. . .] was literally a dead letter for him. *Yet* [. . .] *that doesn't solve a thing*; however dead it might be, that letter was nevertheless definitely articulated'. Still, 'Freud has what it takes' in these matters (ibid., 171, transl. modified, my emphasis).

93 Lacan, 'Discourse to Catholics', 18.

94 'What they [believers] believe in [. . .] they believe they know. The knowledge in question is like any other, and for this reason it falls into the field of inquiry that we should conduct on all forms of knowledge; and such is the case, because as analysts we believe that there is no knowledge which doesn't emerge against a background of ignorance' (Lacan, *The Seminar of Jacques Lacan, Book VII*, 171).

95 Lacan, 'Discourse to Catholics', 19.

96 See ibid., 41.

97 J. Lacan, 'Introduction to the Names-of-the-Father', in *On the Names-of-the-Father* (Cambridge: Polity, 2013), 62.

98 'In the fashion of his times, *which is that of an alibi*, he [Freud] called it [illusion] religion' (ibid., 63, transl. modified, my emphasis).

99 Lacan, 'Discourse to Catholics', 20.

100 Lacan, *The Seminar of Jacques Lacan, Book II*, 70.

101 Lacan, *The Seminar of Jacques Lacan, Book XVII*, 100.

102 Lacan, *The Seminar of Jacques Lacan, Book XIX*, 108, 136.

103 Lacan, 'Discourse to Catholics', 31 (transl. modified, my emphases).

104 Lacan, *The Seminar of Jacques Lacan, Book II*, 69.

105 Ibid. (transl. modified).

106 Ibid.

107 Ibid.

108 Ibid.

109 Lacan, *The Seminar of Jacques Lacan, Book XIX*, 136. Lacan also specifies that if one abides by such a – again – 'coarse' (*grossier*) take on Eros, then Thanatos (the Freudian death instinct) becomes itself a misleading cosmological notion, namely, a destructive force of death (ibid.). The dyad Eros/Thanatos makes sense only when understood linguistically as 'the figure in which the sexual relationship fails, namely the figure of the One and the not-One, or zero' (ibid., 108, transl. modified) – which also better explains, structurally, what Hyppolite referred to as 'a knowledge of an entirely different depth' in Seminar II. 'Exorcising' Eros as a principle of union equally means having it done with a mistaken approach to the death instinct 'made out of thin air' with which post-Freudians 'have been pissing us off for a long time' (ibid., 136, 108, transl. modified).

110 Lacan, *The Seminar of Jacques Lacan, Book XVII*, 100.

111 Ibid., 101.

112 On Freud's underestimated proximity to some aspects of Christianity, see already 'Discourse to Catholics', 32 and *The Seminar of Jacques Lacan, Book VII*, 174, although here Lacan's tone is not yet critical.

113 Lacan, *The Seminar of Jacques Lacan, Book XVII*, 101.

114 Lacan, *The Seminar of Jacques Lacan, Book XIX*, 184 (transl. modified). This passage from Seminar XIX has been transcribed and interpreted in very different ways. The official French edition opts for a basic 'the nonsensical story of *Totem and Taboo*' ('*histoire à dormir debout de* Totem et Tabou'). The Staferla version prefers 'the nonsensical story of *Totem and . . . Standing Up*' ('*histoire à dormir debout de* Totem et . . . Debout'). Given the theoretical context, and the fact that the audio recording is not clear, I propose to read it as '*histoire à dormir debout de* Totem et . . . Début'. I fail to understand the rationale behind the English translation: 'the cock-and-bull story of *Totem and Total Bull*'.

115 Lacan, *The Seminar of Jacques Lacan, Book XVII*, 101.

116 See ibid., 119.

117 Ibid., 100.

118 Ibid., 66.
119 *The Letters of Sigmund Freud & Oskar Pfister*, 137, 116 (transl. modified). See also Pfister, 'The Illusion of a Future', 572–3 (my emphasis): 'Natural science without metaphysics doesn't exist, has never existed, and will never exist. [. . .] How can the religious problem be taken care of if basic epistemological questions are left out of account? Isn't it simply a *negative dogmatism* to declare [. . .] that a world-will and a world-meaning do not exist?'.
120 *The Letters of Sigmund Freud & Oskar Pfister*, 116. The Devil's island should be understood here in the sense that our *forever* helpless world (not-One) is the island *delimited* by a diabolical ocean (One). The, on close inspection, *non*-interventionist evil Will stands as our ultimate horizon and not as the prince of *this* world with whom we wrestle and whom we finally defeat through redemption and subsume under the subset of Hell. As Lacan puts it in a 1975 conversation with Yale University students, from this standpoint, atheists 'believe sufficiently in God to believe that God has nothing to do with it when they are sick' ('Conférences et Entretiens dans des Universités Nord-Américaines', 32).
121 See Lacan, 'The Triumph of Religion', 72, 64–5. For Lacan, in its mainstream IPA version, psychoanalysis is *already* a dogmatic and intolerant Church. However, the question as to what makes the psychoanalytic community 'so reminiscent of religious practice' remains an important one. See, for instance, *The Seminar of Jacques Lacan, Book XI*, 4, 7. In this regard, Lacan comes close – from an opposite perspective and with an antithetical agenda – to liberal-conservative archenemies of psychoanalysis such as Ernest Gellner, for whom psychoanalysis is a 'secular religion, capable of [. . .] offering a kind of secular salvation, comparable in its totality to that which had previously been offered in the literal sense' (E. Gellner, *The Psychoanalytic Movement* (Evanston: Northwestern University Press, 1993), xiii).
122 Lacan, 'The Triumph of Religion', 60–1.
123 Ibid., 61, 64.
124 Ibid., 72, 67.
125 See ibid., 62–3, 72.
126 Ibid., 77.
127 Ibid., 71–2, 61.
128 Ibid., 61 (my emphases).
129 Ibid., 71–2, 64.
130 Ibid., 64–5, 66.
131 Lacan, 'Discourse to Catholics', 35–6.
132 Ibid., 36.
133 Ibid.
134 Ibid. (transl. modified).
135 Lacan, 'The Triumph of Religion', 64 (my emphasis).
136 Ibid., 65.
137 Ibid., 56.
138 See ibid., 59.

139 See ibid., 61.
140 Ibid., 63, 72. 'Confession? Certainly not! You don't confess a damn thing to the psychoanalyst. You just go there and simply tell him everything that is in your head' (J. Lacan and E. Granzotto, 'Freud per sempre. Intervista con Jacques Lacan', *Panorama*, 21 November 1974).
141 Lacan, 'The Triumph of Religion', 77.
142 Ibid. At one point, Lacan somewhat misleadingly speaks of science's not 'producing results' (ibid., 61). This should be understood in the sense that science cannot obtain a (lasting) *Weltanschauung*. But, for him, it is precisely this structural deadlock that fuels the effectiveness of science.
143 Ibid., 77.
144 Ibid., 77, 79.
145 Ibid., 78.
146 Ibid., 79.
147 See ibid., 81.
148 To sum up, Freud is contradictorily both weakly agnostic – the not-One is the world *for us*; we must not venture into metaphysics – and weakly atheistic – the not-One is the world *in itself for itself*; there is absolutely no God. Lacan's strong agnosticism refuses these options: the not-One is the world *in itself* for us (which liquidates weak agnosticism) and it *might* be but not necessarily is the world *in itself for itself*, or better, in itself for us *and* for itself (which challenges weak atheism's tacit theism). Bluntly put, what Freud misses is the level of the in-itself-for-us.
149 See J. Lacan, 'Journées des cartels de l'École freudienne de Paris', *Lettre de l'École freudienne*, no. 18 (1976): 268; 'Discourse to Catholics', 17.
150 See J. Lacan, 'Entretien avec Gilles Lapouge', *Le Figaro Littéraire*, no. 1076 (1 December 1966): 2.
151 Lacan, *The Seminar of Jacques Lacan, Book XIX*, 178.
152 See J. Lacan, Seminar XIII, lesson of 23 March 1966, unpublished.
153 Ibid.
154 J. Lacan, 'Conférence de presse du docteur Jacques Lacan au Centre Culturel Français, Rome, le 29 octobre 1974', *Lettres de l'École freudienne*, no. 16 (1975): 7. It remains important to cite blunt passages like these since, unfortunately, there is still no shortage of naively religious interpretations of Lacan's teaching, even where textual evidence frankly proves unassailable. For instance, Dunlap reads 'The Triumph of Religion' as Lacan's late 'turn to religion' whereby he would endorse religious meaning as the only viable 'answer' to our contemporary predicament (A. Dunlap, *Lacan and Religion* (Abingdon: Routledge, 2014), 160–1).
155 'The pinnacle of psychoanalysis is well and truly atheism, provided one gives this term another sense than that of "God is dead"' (Lacan, *The Seminar of Jacques Lacan, Book XVII*, 138).
156 See J. Lacan, 'Alla "Scuola Freudiana"', in *Lacan in Italia. 1953-1978*, 108.
157 Lacan, *The Seminar of Jacques Lacan, Book X*, 308.
158 Ibid.

159 Lacan, 'Conférences et Entretiens dans des Universités Nord-Américaines', 32.
160 Lacan, *The Seminar of Jacques Lacan, Book XIX,* 178 (transl. modified).
161 Lacan, 'Conférences et Entretiens dans des Universités Nord-Américaines', 32.
162 See Lacan, *The Seminar of Jacques Lacan, Book X*, 308.
163 J. Lacan, Seminar XII, lesson of 3 March 1965, unpublished.
164 We should of course not forget his close personal relations and intellectual dialogues with several clergy people, such as first and foremost his brother Marc-Marie, a Benedictine monk and his 'first disciple' according to Paul Roazen ('Lacan's First Disciple', 321–36), and Father Beirnaert, who remained a practising member of Lacan's École Freudienne de Paris until the latter's death. Lacan's intense correspondence with Sister Marie de la Trinité (see 'Lettre de Jacques Lacan à Soeur Marie de la Trinité', *Le Nouvel Âne*, no. 9 (September 2008)), an erudite and severely depressed Dominican mystic who came close to being lobotomised, underwent psychoanalysis with him, developed a strong transference, and then became a therapist, is yet to be appropriately investigated. Allegedly, during treatment, Sister Marie lent her unpublished spiritual notebooks to Lacan, one of which he never returned in spite of legal intervention. See C. Schmitt, 'Marie de la Trinité et Jacques Lacan. Une relation à l'épreuve de la foi', available at http://www.mariedelatrinite.org/IMG/pdf/2014_marie_de_la_trinite_et_jacques_lacan_christiane_schmitt-2.pdf.
165 J. Lacan, 'Petit discours à l'ORTF', in *Autres Écrits*, 222. See also Chiesa and Toscano, 'Ethics and Capital: Ex Nihilo'; Chiesa, 'Psychoanalysis, Religion, Love'; Chiesa, *The Not-Two*; Chiesa, 'Supreme Being-in-Evil, Criminal Good, and Criminal Desire'.
166 See, for instance, J. Lacan, *The Seminar of Jacques Lacan, Book VII*, 178 and *The Seminar of Jacques Lacan, Book VIII*, 44.
167 See Chiesa, 'Psychoanalysis, Religion, Love'; L. Chiesa, 'Exalted Obscenity and the Lawyer of God', in *Deleuze and Lacan. A Disjunctive Synthesis*, ed. B. Nedoh and A. Zevnik (Edinburgh: Edinburg University Press, 2018).
168 Lacan, *The Seminar of Jacques Lacan, Book XX*, 109, 107.
169 Ibid., 56.
170 Ibid., 107.
171 Ibid., 113.
172 Ibid., 107.
173 John 1:14.
174 Lacan, 'The Triumph of Religion', 74.
175 Ibid., 77.
176 'The Christian Logos as incarnated Logos gives *a precise solution to the mystery of the relations between man and speech*, and it's not for nothing that God incarnate was called the Word' (Lacan, *The Seminar of Jacques Lacan, Book V*, 477 (transl. modified; my emphases)). Here I follow the Staferla version; the official one instead speaks of 'the system of the relations between man and speech'.

177 J. Lacan, Seminar XXI, lesson of 11 December 1973, unpublished. 'That it is the true religion, as it claims, is not an excessive claim, all the more so in that, *when the true is examined closely, it's the worst that can be said about it*' (Lacan, *The Seminar of Jacques Lacan, Book XX*, 107, my emphasis).

178 Ibid., 116.

179 See ibid., 109–13. For Lacan's critique of Aristotelian animism, see also Chiesa, *The Not-Two*, 39–40.

180 Lacan, *The Seminar of Jacques Lacan, Book XX*, 113.

181 Ibid., 108.

182 Ibid. (transl. modified). Similarly, in 'Science and Truth' Lacan characterises 'the notion of a Three and One God' as 'untenable' and argues that here Christianity 'discourage[s] thought' (Lacan, 'Science and Truth', 741).

183 Lacan, *The Seminar of Jacques Lacan, Book XIX*, 20 (transl. modified).

184 Lacan, *The Seminar of Jacques Lacan, Book XX*, 108 (transl. modified).

185 Ibid. (transl. modified).

186 Ibid.

187 Lacan, *The Seminar of Jacques Lacan, Book XX*, 45 (transl. modified).

188 R. Boothby, 'The No-Thing of God: Psychoanalysis of Religion After Lacan', in *The Oxford Handbook of Philosophy and Psychoanalysis*, ed. R. G. T. Gipps and M. Lacewing (Oxford: Oxford University Press, 2018), 574.

189 Even Kristeva seems to lend herself to such an identification when she equates Lacan's 'God is unconscious' with 'God is language'. See J. Kristeva, 'The Forces of Monotheism Confronting the Need to Believe', available at http://www.kristeva.fr/theforces.html.

190 J. Lacan, Seminar XXII, lesson of 17 December 1974, unpublished.

191 Ibid.

192 Simply stating, without further specifications, that, unlike for Freud, 'for [Lacan] God exists', as Leupin does, is therefore highly misleading (A. Leupin, *Lacan Today. Psychoanalysis, Science, Religion* (New York: Other Press, 2004), 106) and facilitates untenable religious appropriations of his work. On the other hand, I agree with Kenneth Reinhard's point that, differing from Badiou, 'Lacan's exploration of the question of One also passes through theology' and that 'it is only by bringing the One into explicit relationship with [. . .] monotheistic issues that we can fully understand its implications for analytic discourse and political life' (K. Reinhard, 'There Is Something of One (God). Lacan and Political Theology', in C. Davis, M. Pound and C. Crockett, *Theology After Lacan* (Eugene: Cascade Books, 2014), 151).

193 Lacan, *The Seminar of Jacques Lacan, Book II*, 48.

194 Davis, Pound, and Crockett ignore, and in a way reverse, this argument when they claim that 'it is precisely by *rejecting* the idol of God's necessity (*deus ex machina*) that theology can only make sense in and through the wild untameable flux and fury of an uncontrollable contingency'. Indeed, such a move is consistent with their religious agenda, namely, grounding 'the truth of an infinite *faith*' in 'radical

contingency' (*Theology After Lacan*, 1, my emphases), which is however radically anti-Lacanian.

195 See Lacan, *The Seminar of Jacques Lacan, Book II*, 47.
196 Ibid., 48.
197 Ibid.
198 Ibid.
199 Ibid.
200 See J. Lacan, Seminar IX, lesson of 9 May 1962, unpublished.
201 Ibid.
202 Ibid.
203 Ibid.
204 See ibid.
205 Ibid.
206 Ibid.
207 J. Lacan, Seminar XIV, lesson of 18 January 1967, unpublished.
208 Ibid.
209 Ibid.
210 Ibid.
211 Ibid., lesson of 25 January 1967.
212 Ibid.
213 Ibid.
214 Lacan, *The Seminar of Jacques Lacan, Book XX*, 28.
215 See Lacan, *Le Séminaire livre XVIII*, 42–3.
216 Ibid. See also Chiesa, *The Not-Two*, 87, 93–4.
217 See Lacan, *The Seminar of Jacques Lacan, Book XX*, 77.
218 It is indeed a hardly disputable matter of fact that historically mysticism has flourished *within* monotheism, and more often than not in a non-heretical manner. With specific regard to Christianity, Richardson (a Jesuit priest and psychoanalyst) has convincingly recovered from a Lacanian perspective a considerable mystical element and a 'God of the real' even in Thomas Aquinas, the theologian that has most thoroughly influenced the official doctrines of the Catholic Church. This element does not contradict Aquinas's paradigmatic 'God of philosophers'. See W. J. Richardson, '"Like Straw": Religion and Psychoanalysis', *Budhi. A Journal of Ideas and Culture*, 2, no. 1 (1998): 51–64.
219 Lacan, Seminar XIV, lesson of 26 April 1967. Lacan, 'De la psychanalyse dans ses rapports avec la réalité', 352 (my emphases).
220 See Lacan, Seminar IX, lesson of 20 June 1962. Lacan, 'De James Joyce comme symptôme', *Le croquant*, no. 28 (November 2000).
221 See especially Chiesa, *The Not-Two*, Chapter 1.
222 Lacan, *The Seminar of Jacques Lacan, Book XX*, 83.

223 This equation is instead normally taken for granted by most Lacanians. See, for instance, Causse, *Lacan et le christianisme*, 120: 'Lacan interprets mysticism as a feminine enjoyment'.

224 Lacan, *The Seminar of Jacques Lacan*, Book XIX, 124 (transl. modified). In my use of Lacan's onto-numerical jargon, this means that the not-One *pole* of the oscillation corresponds to the in-existence of the *zero*, while the *not-One* of incompleteness corresponds to the *ex*-sistence of the impossibility of numbering. Throughout the present work, for the sake of simplicity, I refrain from thematising the (various figures of the) zero in Lacan's logic of sexuation – which I have extensively covered in *The Not-Two*, especially the Conclusion.

225 Lacan, 'L'étourdit', 485 (my emphasis).

226 See Chiesa, *The Not-Two*, Chapter 1.

227 Lacan, *Le Séminaire de Jacques Lacan, Livre XVI*, 136.

228 In *The Not-Two* I already insisted on the *non*-transcendent status of feminine non-phallic enjoyment ('[it] should by no means be seen as a transcendence') but I still refer to it as 'mystical' (ibid., 1, 4). This should now be amended since mysticism cannot but entail transcendence. On the one hand, it is indeed the case that 'feminine [non-phallic] *jouissance* constitutes the *basis* of one face of God' (ibid., 1). On the other, it is imperative to specify that it is only mysticism's attempted isolation of feminine non-phallic enjoyment that institutes the not-One pole of the God *hypothesis* as one face of *God*, or unity of substance. This specification is already partly anticipated in the Conclusion of *The Not-Two*, where I claim that 'drifting into an illusory transcendence [. . .] is a possible outcome of the [. . .] mystical' (ibid., 177), but there remained an unsolved tension in my argument.

229 For an approach that somehow synthetises the two, see T. Dalzell, 'On the Death of God in Lacan: A Nuanced Atheism', *The Heythrope Journal*, March 2021: 1–8.

230 Lacan, 'De James Joyce comme symptôme'; Lacan, *The Seminar of Jacques Lacan*, Book VII, 124. For other clear warnings against associating psychoanalysis with mysticism, see for instance: Lacan, Seminar IX, lesson of 20 June 1962; Lacan, *The Seminar of Jacques Lacan*, Book XI, 9; Lacan, Seminar XIII, lesson of 27 April 1966; Lacan, Seminar XIV, lesson of 21 December 1966; J. Lacan, Seminar XV, lesson of 21 February 1968, unpublished; J. Lacan, *Je parle aux murs* (Paris: Seuil, 2011), 16; J. Lacan, 'Réponse à une question de Catherine Millot', *L'Âne*, no. 3 (1981): 3.

231 Lacan, 'Introduction to the Names-of-the-Father', 77 (my emphasis).

232 J. Lacan, Seminar XXV, lesson of 11 April 1978, unpublished.

233 Ibid. This poses the tricky question of mystical *men*, which Lacan only hints at. What is beyond doubt is that, for him, biological males symbolically sexuated as women can be mystical women (this is for instance the case of John of the Cross – see *The Seminar of Jacques Lacan*, Book XX, 76). But we are left with the problem of how mystical men (Lacan's recurrent example is Angelus Silesius ibid.) differ from mystical women and their not-One *as One*. My very tentative solution would be to say that mystical men share with mystical women what they both take as an experience of *transcendence*-in-immanence, yet for men the latter is centred on the *One* pole of the God hypothesis. Better said, mystical men *identify* the symbolic existence of the One with the One Being tout-court. In short, what

is at stake is the One *as One*. I think Lacan points at something along these lines when he claims that for mystics 'the symbolic is Nature that begins to sing', due to the fact that the symbolic, imaginary, and real are for them no longer distinguished (P. Caruso (ed.), *Conversaciones con Lévi-Strauss, Foucault y Lacan* (Barcelona: Anagrama, 1969), 111). Or also, we could suggest that while for mystical men the *symbolic* is the confusion of symbolic, imaginary, and real, for mystical women the *real* is the confusion of real, symbolic, and imaginary.

234 Lacan, 'Introduction to the Names-of-the-Father', 64–5.
235 Ibid., 80 (transl. modified). 'Ego sum qui sum' is usually rendered in English as 'I am who I am'. I opt for a literal translation of the French 'Je suis *celui* qui suis' since it better suits Lacan's overall argument.
236 Ibid., 80.
237 Lacan, *The Seminar of Jacques Lacan*, *Book XX*, 76 (transl. modified).
238 Given these coordinates, the desire of the *Other* thus lies at the antipodes of the desire for the One Being (which in Seminar XX Lacan equates with love) I mentioned at the end of the previous section.
239 Moving very quickly, one could argue that the question of the Abrahamic God as the *real*-of-the-symbolic then coalesces in (Christian) *theodicy* as an attempted answer to the question: If there is One God why is there evil?
240 Lacan, 'Introduction to the Names-of-the-Father', 76.
241 Ibid.
242 Ibid., 80. Dominiek Hoens is right in pointing out that, elsewhere in his work, Lacan provides other interpretations of the Biblical '*Ehyeh Asher Ehyeh*' (private communication, 4 January 2022); a comparative analysis of these variations falls beyond the remit of my present investigation. I agree with Moritz Herrmann (private communication, 28 April 2022) that I here perhaps slightly force Lacan's point by translating '*Je suis l'Étant*', with which Lacan renders the Greek '*Ego heimi ho on*', as 'I am the *Existent*', as Fink also does – but this is in line with Lacan's own more general argument about Moses's God *and* what follows in *this* specific passage. As Herrmann observes, Lacan goes on to say that this Greek rendition of the Biblical formula is still 'not correct' (only in Miller's official edition of the text . . .), although 'it makes sense' (ibid.), whereas Augustine's Christian rendition of it is meaningless. Yet, unlike what Herrmann claims, Lacan does not argue that the Greeks already turned '*Ehyeh Asher Ehyeh*' into a (proto-Christian) 'supreme Being' – which would contradict my reading – considering it instead as a 'supreme *Existent*' (*l'Étant supreme*) (ibid.) – which is what I aim at highlighting in the Mosaic God. Are we here, for Lacan, not dealing with our best possible understanding of the Mosaic God as grasped retrospectively from our Greek-Christian standpoint and yet as *irreducible* to the Christian God as One *Being*?
243 Lacan, 'Introduction to the Names-of-the-Father', 78.
244 Lacan, Seminar XV, lesson of 19 June 1968.
245 Lacan, *The Seminar of Jacques Lacan, Book XVII*, 136.
246 Ibid., 116. Schematically, we could thus render the God of Abraham as based on $\bar{A} \rightarrow S$, the oscillation from the barred Other to the signifier One, and that of Moses as based on $S \rightarrow \bar{A}$, the oscillation from the signifier One to the barred Other. Using the same algebra, the God of Christian philosophers and theologians is s(A), the

signified of the Other, the Other as One Being, and that of women mystics Ⱥ=A, the barred Other *as* the Other as One Being.

247 Lacan, *The Seminar of Jacques Lacan, Book XIX*, 179.

248 Ibid., 176, 114 (transl. modified).

249 For a more detailed discussion of these issues, see Chiesa, *The Not-Two*, especially the Conclusion.

250 Balmès, *Dieu, le sexe et la vérité*, 15.

251 Ibid., 23–4.

252 Ibid., 136 (my emphasis).

253 Lacan, *The Seminar of Jacques Lacan, Book XX*, 83.

254 See especially Balmès, *Dieu, le sexe et la vérité*, 14, 16, 26.

255 See Lacan, 'Introduction to the Names-of-the-Father', 78–85. Lacan refers to Moses's God as *Shem*. I agree with Fink that this should be corrected to read *Hashem*. I leave aside the question of whether Lacan's etymological and scriptural disquisitions are sound. What matters here is his separation of Moses's God from Abraham's. We should recall that the distinction between the Mosaic God and the Jewish God that preceded him lies also at the basis of Freud's however different arguments in *Moses and Monotheism*: to begin with 'the god Yahweh certainly bore no resemblance to the Mosaic god. [. . .] In the course of time the god Yahweh lost his own characteristics and grew more and more to resemble the god of Moses' (ibid., 63).

256 See Lacan, 'Introduction to the Names-of-the-Father', 80–1.

257 See ibid., 80–1, 85.

258 Balmès, *Dieu, le sexe et la vérité*, 21.

259 Ibid., 20.

260 Lacan, 'Introduction to the Names-of-the-Father', 78 (my emphasis).

261 Ibid., 88 (transl. modified).

262 See J.-A. Miller, 'La nature des semblants', lesson of 4 December 1991, unpublished.

263 Lacan, 'La méprise du sujet supposé savoir', 337.

264 Lacan, *The Seminar of Jacques Lacan, Book XXIII*, 4.

265 Lacan, 'La méprise du sujet supposé savoir', 337.

266 Miller, 'La nature des semblants', lesson of 4 December 1991.

267 This short and relatively unknown passage has curiously caught the attention of both Michel de Certeau and Jean-Luc Nancy and Philippe Lacoue-Labarthe, but they hurriedly take for granted that dio-logy is synonymous with mysticism (M. de Certeau and M. Cifali, 'Entretien, mystique et psychanalyse', *Espaces Temps*, no. 80–81 (2002): 166; Ph. Lacoue-Labarthe and J.-L. Nancy, *The Title of the Letter: A Reading of Lacan* (Albany: SUNY Press, 1992), 132). At first sight, this interpretation finds support in the fact that the list of dio-logists proposed by Lacan also includes Meister Eckhart – problematically for my own reading. Yet, given what I have argued so far, it remains extremely difficult to substantiate how, according to Lacan, Moses could be regarded as a mystic. As for Joyce, in

the past, I was myself tempted to juxtapose Lacan's understanding of him as a *saint homme* with mysticism (see Chiesa, *Subjectivity and Otherness*, 234). For reasons that would need to be further articulated elsewhere, I now attune Joyce's *symbolic* that does not imaginarily 'encircle' the real (Miller, 'Préface', in *Joyce avec Lacan*, 12) – as such nonetheless still *discrete* and thus distant from the mystical confusion of the three orders – to Moses's prefiguration of the One as real.

268 See Lacan, *The Seminar of Jacques Lacan*, *Book XVII*, 137. 'The legends of the patriarchs of the people – Abraham, Isaac and Jacob – were introduced. Yahweh asserted that he was already the god of these forefathers' (Freud, *Moses and Monotheism*, 44).

269 See, for instance, Lacan, Seminar XV, lesson of 7 February 1968.

270 Lacan, *The Seminar of Jacques Lacan, Book XX,* 129; Lacan, *The Seminar of Jacques Lacan, Book XIX*, 116. The bifidity of the One is therefore also the 'gap [. . .] of the two' (J. Lacan, *Le Séminaire, Livre XIX: . . . ou pire. 1971-1972* (Paris: Seuil, 2011), 106).

271 We could thus schematise the passage from polytheism to Judeo-Christian monotheism as R→S (first account) as opposed to I→R-S→I/R-S (second account).

272 Lacan, *The Seminar of Jacques Lacan, Book VIII*, 44, 385, 82; Lacan, *The Seminar of Jacques Lacan, Book X*, 307. See also Lacan, *The Seminar of Jacques Lacan*, *Book VII*, 172; Lacan, Seminar IX, lessons of 21 February 1962 and of 13 June 1962.

273 Lacan, *The Seminar of Jacques Lacan, Book VIII*, 44; Lacan, *The Seminar of Jacques Lacan, Book VII*, 172.

274 Lacan, *The Seminar of Jacques Lacan, Book III*, 266; Lacan, *The Seminar of Jacques Lacan, Book VII*, 172.

275 Lacan, *The Seminar of Jacques Lacan, Book VII*, 314 (my emphasis).

276 Ibid., 172.

277 Ibid. (my emphasis). This is in line with Lacan's stance when he disputes Hyppolite's critique of Freud's atheism in Seminar II.

278 Ibid., 173 (my emphasis).

279 Ibid., 174, 68–9 (my emphasis).

280 Ibid., 173.

281 Ibid., 173–4.

282 Ibid., 259, 172.

283 Ibid., 81, 181.

284 Lacan, *The Seminar of Jacques Lacan, Book VIII*, 44.

285 Ibid., 52.

286 Ibid., 51–2.

287 Lacan, *The Seminar of Jacques Lacan, Book II*, 100 (my emphasis).

288 Lacan, *The Seminar of Jacques Lacan, Book XX*, 115–16 (my emphasis).

289 Ibid.

290 See Lacan, *The Seminar of Jacques Lacan, Book III*, 125–6, 288 (my emphases).

291 Lacan, *The Seminar of Jacques Lacan, Book VII*, 172 (my emphases). For Lacan, a 'trace' lies at the border between the imaginary and the symbolic.
292 Ibid. (my emphasis).
293 Ibid. (my emphases)
294 Lacan, *The Seminar of Jacques Lacan, Book XVII*, 136. The further question to be investigated on another occasion is how polytheism as an immanent imaginarisation of the real both comes very close to Lacan's understanding of psychosis and nonetheless structurally differs from it. For Lacan, on the one hand, Schreber's God is indeed an 'imaginary-real'. Yet, on the other hand, polytheism is symbolically effective whereas psychosis forecloses the symbolic order.
295 Ibid., 116.
296 See ibid., 136.
297 See ibid., 139–40.
298 See ibid., 136.
299 See Paul, 1 Corinthians Chapters 5 and 6.
300 See Lacan, *The Seminar of Jacques Lacan, Book XVII*, 76.
301 Lacan, *The Seminar of Jacques Lacan, Book V*, 477 (transl. modified; my emphasis).
302 Lacan, *The Seminar of Jacques Lacan, Book XVII*, 31.
303 Ibid.
304 Ibid., 33 (transl. modified).
305 Lacan, *The Seminar of Jacques Lacan, Book XX*, 113.
306 Ibid., 116 (my emphasis). Despite Lacan's almost complete silence on Islam, save for some rather facile clinical considerations on the Islamic subject's particular relation with a 'totalitarian' Law (Lacan, *The Seminar of Jacques Lacan, Book I*, 197) and a couple of other isolated passages, we could position the third monotheism in the historical-dialectical matrix I am delineating as a further radicalisation of both the real of the symbolic *and* of its imaginarisation. Parting ways with Freud's simplistic take, for which at bottom Islam remains an 'abbreviated repetition' and 'imitation' of Judaism (*Moses and Monotheism*, 92), on the one hand, Allah epitomises an iconoclastic One-all-alone under the auspices of whom, still today, the caducity of earthly life not only persists in being very vividly marked by the absence of the sexual relationship (the missing of the missing partner is reinforced by restrictions on interactions between men and women) but also continues to be on the verge of reducing the sexual liaisons made possible by this very impossibility to sheer 'prostitution' (the condemnation of Western, neo-pagan, permissive hedonism). Yet, on the other hand, we should at the same time single out the Islamic, or at least Islamist, *sexualisation* of the life-to-come – centred on polygamous men and virginal monogamous women (as inferred, for example, from Quran 56:35-37; 55:56). As Nadia Tazi succinctly puts it, 'the Islamist doxa – true to the dogma – promises to the righteous, sex, sex, and more sex, *ad infinitum*' (N. Tazi, 'Jannah', *S. Journal of the Jan van Eyck Circle for Lacanian Ideology Critique*, no. 2 (2009): 29). Let us recall that the Christian resurrected body is instead similar to an angelical body (Matthew 22:30) that, convolutedly, preserves sexual difference but *not* the sexual act. This view

can be traced back to as early as second-century Fathers of the Church such as Athenagoras and Irenaeus and finds its systematisation in Thomas Aquinas: 'And though there be difference of sex there will be no shame in seeing one another, since there will be no lust to invite them to shameful deeds which are the cause of shame' (*Summa Theologiae*, Supplement to the Third Part, Question 81, Article 3). It is perhaps against this background that we should read Lacan's otherwise misleading remark for which, like all other religions, but with the exception of (Judeo-)Christianity, Islam would still promote a 'knowledge of jouissance' (Lacan, *The Seminar of Jacques Lacan, Book XIX*, 148). Needless to say, these considerations would need further elaboration.

307 F. Récanati, untitled presentation of 10 April 1973, available at http://staferla.free.fr/S20/S20.htm; Lacan, *The Seminar of Jacques Lacan, Book XX*, 77 (transl. modified).

308 Lacan, *The Seminar of Jacques Lacan, Book VII*, 93.

309 Lacan, *The Seminar of Jacques Lacan, Book VIII*, 44 (my emphasis); J. Lacan, 'Réponses de Jacques Lacan à des questions sur les noeuds et l'inconscient', *Lettres de l'École*, no. 21 (1977): 473.

310 See for instance Lacan, Seminar IX, lesson of 22 November 1962; Lacan, *Le Séminaire de Jacques Lacan, Llivre XVI*, 176.

311 That is to say, due to the structural precariousness already inherent to the Christian solution, One (not-One) → *One*, modern philosophy does not fully manage to move from the One (*not-One*) to the *One*, and thus prepares the advent of contemporary philosophies and scientific theories of alleged not-Oneness, as implicitly resting on the *One* (not-One).

312 Lacan, *The Seminar of Jacques Lacan, Book XX*, 43 (my emphases).

313 See A. Koyré, *From the Closed World to the Infinite Universe* (Baltimore: The John Hopkins University Press, 1968); A. Kojève, *L'origine chrétienne de la science moderne* (Paris: Hermann, 2021).

314 Lacan, *The Seminar of Jacques Lacan, Book XX*, 36 (my emphasis).

315 Lacan, *The Seminar of Jacques Lacan, Book XVII*, 159.

316 Ibid., 158.

317 Ibid., 47.

318 Ibid., 159.

319 Ibid.

320 Ibid.

321 Of course, the latter can also bluntly be grasped as the in-substantial realm of today's paradigmatic oscillation between One and not-One, the bit or binary digit, along with its inherent impasses, malware and bugs.

322 Ibid.

323 Ibid.; Lacan, *Le Séminaire de Jacques Lacan, Livre XVI*, 67.

324 Lacan, *The Seminar of Jacques Lacan, Book XVII*, 163 (transl. modified). See also Chiesa, *The Not-Two*, esp. 153 ff.

325 'Why, in fact, wouldn't laws evolve when we conceive of the world as having evolved?' (Lacan, 'The Triumph of Religion', 81).

326 Lacan, *The Seminar of Jacques Lacan*, *Book XVII*, 162. I here read 'para-ousie' instead of 'parousie'. Given the context – Lacan has just referred to 'insubstance' – what is most likely at stake is not Parousia, namely, the second coming of Christ, the final revelation of Being and recuperation of beings in Being, but, on the contrary, the delineation of an anti-religious ontological discourse on *para*-being, on 'being *beside*' theo-philosophical ontology (see Lacan, *The Seminar of Jacques Lacan*, *Book XX*, 44, my emphasis), as such focused on the contingency and materiality of the signifier. On para-ontology, see also Chiesa, *The Not-Two*, especially the Preface.

327 Lacan, *The Seminar of Jacques Lacan, Book XVII*, 160 (transl. modified).

328 'At the level of the operated-on [. . .] the truth is not at all unveiled' (ibid., 161).

329 Ibid. (my emphasis).

330 Ibid., 110, 149.

331 See Lacan, 'The Triumph of Religion', 78–9; J. Lacan, 'La troisième', *Lettres de l'École freudienne*, no. 16 (1975): 202–3; Lacan and Granzotto, 'Freud per sempre'; J. Lacan, 'Le phénomène lacanien', *Les Cahiers Cliniques de Nice*, no. 1 (June 1998): 12.

332 Lacan, *The Seminar of Jacques Lacan*, *Book XX*, 82 (transl. modified).

333 Lacan, 'La troisième', 203.

334 Ibid., 202.

335 Already in 1936, Lacan spoke of 'the correspondences that unite the *I* with [. . .] the automaton with which the world of [the subject's] own making tends to achieve fruition in an ambiguous relation' (Lacan, 'The Mirror Stage as Formative of the *I* Function', 76–7).

336 On the question of sex-bots from a psychoanalytic perspective, see I. Millar, *The Psychoanalysis of Artificial Intelligence* (London: Palgrave, 2021).

337 Lacan, 'La troisième', 203.

338 See, for instance, Lacan, *Le Séminaire de Jacques Lacan, Livre XVIII*, 66; Lacan, *The Seminar of Jacques Lacan, Book XIX*, 81.

339 Lacan, *The Seminar of Jacques Lacan*, *Book XVII*, 73, 159, 162; Lacan and Granzotto, 'Freud per sempre'. In his interview with Granzotto, Lacan also speaks, in very Marcusean-Pasolinian terms, of a 'false liberalisation that is awarded to us, as a good agreed from above, by so-called permissive society'. The fact that sex is today omnipresent does not bring any psychoanalytic 'benefit' and should rather be taken as an 'advertising phenomenon' (ibid.).

340 In relation to this, see, for example, J.-C. Milner, *A Search for Clarity* (Evanston: Northwestern University Press, 2021), 35–6. See also Lacan, *The Seminar of Jacques Lacan*, *Book VII*, 131.

341 Lacan, *The Seminar of Jacques Lacan*, *Book XVII*, 104 (transl. modified). Such a loss of hesitation amounts at bottom to the loss of the Cartesian doubt with which modern science is initiated.

342 See ibid., 151.

343 J. Lacan, 'La psychanalyse en ce temps', *La Cause du Désir*, no. 100 (2018): 38. 'Science is replacing religion, with the same amount of despotism, dullness, and

obscurantism. There is an atom-God, a space-God, etc. If science wins, or religion wins, psychoanalysis is over' (Lacan and Granzotto, 'Freud per sempre').

344 Lacan, 'La psychanalyse en ce temps', 38 (my emphasis).
345 Lacan, 'Radiophonie', 422; Lacan, Seminar XXI, lessons of 9 and 23 April 1974.
346 J. Lacan, Seminar XXIV, lesson of 17 May 1977, unpublished.
347 S. Žižek, 'Preface to the New Edition', in *The Sublime Object of Ideology* (London: Verso, 2008), vii–viii; C. Rovelli, *Reality Is Not What It Seems. The Journey to Quantum Gravity* (New York: Penguin, 2016).
348 J. Lacan, 'Des religions et du réel', *La Cause du Désir*, no. 90 (2015): 11.
349 Ibid.
350 Ibid.
351 For a reading that, first, alerts us to the current proximity of science to religion; second, senses the danger of equating woman's enjoyment with mysticism; but, third, hastily identifies the real not-all with All and presents it as psychoanalysis' 'relative atheism', see J. Adam, 'Ouverture: Lacan, un athéisme du Pas-tout', *Champ lacanien*, 8, no. 1 (2010): 13–21.
352 Lacan, 'Des religions et du réel', 11–12.
353 Meillassoux, *After Finitude*, 7, 26, 63.
354 See, for instance, Lacan, *The Seminar of Jacques Lacan, Book III*, esp. 64–5. On Einstein's assumption of a non-deceiving God, see also Lacan, *Le Séminaire de Jacques Lacan, Livre XVI*, 280–1.
355 Lacan, 'The Triumph of Religion', 81 (my emphasis).
356 See, for example, Lacan, 'Aggressiveness in Psychoanalysis', esp. 98–101.
357 I have recently offered a new reading of the Thing as evil in Seminar VII in Chiesa, 'Supreme Being-in-Evil, Criminal Good, and Criminal Desire'.
358 See also Chiesa, 'Anthropie: Beside the Pleasure Principle', esp. 145–8.
359 'Perhaps what they [scientists] are doing could be very dangerous. I don't believe so. [. . .] Bacteria won't get rid of all of that' (Lacan, 'The Triumph of Religion', 60). 'And if it's too late? They call them biologists, or physicists or chemists. For me they are morons. Only now, when they are already wrecking the universe, they begin to wonder whether perhaps it might be dangerous. What if everything is blown up? What if the bacteria they so lovingly culture in their white labs were to turn into mortal enemies? [. . .] I am not a pessimist. Nothing will happen. For the simple fact that man is a good-for-nothing, not even capable of destroying himself' (Lacan and Granzotto, 'Freud per sempre'). On the equally remote, but not impossible, prospect of a positive totalisation, see Chiesa, *The Not-Two*, 92–3. Let me point out in passing that both negative and positive totalisations, the two versions of a real-isation of the symbolic, would obviously entail the elimination of every *Weltanschauung*, positive and negative.
360 See, for example, D. J. Linden, *The Accidental Mind* (Cambridge, MA: Harvard University Press, 2007), 221–34. For an overview, see J. L. Barrett and E. Reed Burdett, 'The Cognitive Science of Religion', *The Psychologist*, 24 (April 2011): 252–5.

361 I borrow the notion of 'crisis of presence' from the great anthropologist and historian of religions Ernesto de Martino (see, for instance, 'Crisis of Presence and Religious Reintegration', *HAU. Journal of Ethnographic Theory*, 2, no. 2 (2012): 431–50). Throughout his works, de Martino also extensively investigated instances in which smooth religious reintegration – or also the 'de-historicization of the negative' – fails and leads to what he names 'cultural apocalypse' and the potential collapse of a given civilization (see especially E. de Martino, *La fine del mondo. Contributo all'analisi delle apocalissi culturali* (Turin: Einaudi, 1977)). Lacan problematically appears to rule out an apocalyptic dimension inherent to polytheistic religions when, on a few occasions, he gives the impression of considering them as static and quasi-animalic/Edenic formations in which there simply *is* a sexual relationship (see Lacan, *The Seminar of Jacques Lacan, Book XIX*, 56–7). The prevalence and effectiveness of the imaginary in polytheism turns out to be instead far from incompatible with end-of-the-world symbolic scenarios aimed at moderating irruptions of the real that cannot easily be contained (criticising Miller, Žižek makes a similar point with regard to the radical fragility of the Aztec Weltanschauung and its recourse to human sacrifices to maintain the status quo; see S. Žižek, *Incontinence of the Void* (Cambridge, MA: MIT Press, 2017), 14–15). It is also unclear how Lacan situates polytheism vis-à-vis *magic*, which in his seminal 'Science and Truth' he considers as an independent kind of discourse, structurally different from religion – in that context questionably equated with Christianity (see Lacan, 'Science and Truth', 739–42). If magic basically amounts to 'signifiers [in nature] answer[ing] as such to [incantatory] signifiers', whereby the shaman is 'part of nature' (ibid., 739), how does this immanent symbolisation relate to the symbolic imaginarisation of the real operated by polytheism? Should we perhaps schematise the two through the same theoretical matrix? If not, in what way is the discourse of magic different from that of *polytheistic* religions?

362 Or One (S $\rightleftarrows$ A̸).

363 Given that both polytheism and mysticism in the end revolve around variations on the One (One plus One equals two-as-*one*, in the case of the former; not-One *as One*, in the case of the latter), and given what I argued about the irreducibility of woman's *non*-phallic enjoyment to the mystical position, this cannot but be some form of *phallic* enjoyment. I therefore think we should pay far more attention to Lacan's underestimated association of Christian 'feminine' mystics with 'puerile' sadomasochism in Seminar VII. See Lacan, *The Seminar of Jacques Lacan, Book VII*, 187–8, 261–2. See also Chiesa, 'Supreme Being-in-Evil, Criminal Good, and Criminal Desire'.

364 This specification justifies Lacan's passing remark that while 'in every tradition', including Judeo-Christianity, mysticism is a 'headlong plunge into the jouissance of God', Judeo-Christian mystics are 'uncomfortable' with it, precisely because of the centrality of the God of desire and then love (Lacan, 'Introduction to the Names of the Father', 77). I think his decision not to side Sufism with Judeo-Christian mysticism is unwarranted (see Lacan, *The Seminar of Jacques Lacan, Book XIX*, 148).

365 Although Lacan's genealogy of divinity has a distinct Western focus, he also applies it more widely to Eastern religions. For instance, Taoism is often presented as a paradigmatic form of polytheism and a quasi-optimal sexual knowledge, which nonetheless has at bottom a profound awareness of castration (see, for example, Lacan, *The Seminar of Jacques Lacan, Book XX*, 115, 108). The same roughly goes with Hinduism, in spite of the fact that it presents a certain (sexualised) metaphysics (Lacan, *Le Séminaire de Jacques Lacan, Livre XVI*, 205). Lacan's take on Chen and Zen Buddhism is far more sophisticated and would require a separate inquiry. Very schematically, what is at stake in Buddhism is, in my jargon, the One *as not-One*, or better the One *as the immanent-in-transcendence not-One*. I am thus tempted to roughly label it as an *inverted mysticism*, with the important specification that we are dealing with an immanent One of 'infinite *multiplicity*' ('A One that is not *pan* but *poly*') which is as such identified with a transcendent not-One (Nirvana as a 'zero-point' and a salvific 'renunciation of thought'). Or also, the immanent One of infinite multiplicity 'converg[es] towards a centre that, by essence, is nowhere a centre' (Lacan, *The Seminar of Jacques Lacan, Book X*, 224, 242, 226; transl. modified, my emphasis. Lacan, *The Seminar of Jacques Lacan, Book XX*, 115). Unlike Eastern polytheisms and their stress on enjoyment, Buddhism is thus in this sense a religion of desire, but it organises it in a way that is very different from that of Judeo-Christianity. More precisely, Buddhism short-circuits 'all the variations of desire' (as poly-desire, we might add), which appear in it 'in a most incarnate fashion', with the 'ultimate apprehension of the radically illusory character of all desire' (Lacan, *The Seminar of Jacques Lacan, Book X*, 226). The latter is the case since desire 'does not have any support [or] outlet' in a One-All-Being – the religious aim of Buddhism is 'avoiding the *One* Other' (Lacan, *Le Séminaire de Jacques Lacan, Livre XVI*, 364, my emphasis) – which, Lacan adds, is not the same as naively claiming that Nirvana amounts to a 'sheer reduction to nothingness' and 'all is nothing' (Lacan, *The Seminar of Jacques Lacan, Book X*, 222, 231). For these reasons, Buddhism equally suspends 'the monotheism/polytheism opposition' (ibid., 224).

366 Lacan, Seminar XXII, lesson of 21 January 1975.

367 Luis Izcovich is surprisingly the only author I have come across who singles out this passage *and* relates the half-God (*mi-Dieu*) to half-saying (*mi-dire*) the truth. However, he develops his reading in a very different and clinical direction. See L. Izcovich, 'Du Dieure au Dire', *Champ lacanien*, 8, no. 1 (2010): 85–91.

368 The tortuous idea Lacan appears to be sketching out here is, more precisely, the following: *within* the half-saying the truth of incompleteness that does not assume half-saying God, there would be a renewed reification of either the not-One (here as no-two-as-One) into a deceiving God or of the One (pole of the God hypothesis) into the salvific God. Or better, we would sooner or later end up concluding that the truth of incompleteness cannot fully be said either because (a) our *saying* it is structurally limited but the truth of incompleteness conclusively is, which makes us again unwillingly fall back into the deceiving God, or because (b) there is finally *no* truth of incompleteness and instead the salvific God is, as attested by the fact that we always return to the One pole when we try to say it. It would elsewhere be interesting to develop the phenomenology of these two subjective positions. Very roughly speaking, the latter could be associated with the figure of the born-again believer.

369 Lacan, Seminar XXII, lesson of 21 January 1975.

370 Ibid.

371 '*There is no sexual relationship.* [. . .] move outside it and you will say only worse. *There is no sexual relationship* is proposed, therefore, as truth' (Lacan, *The Seminar of Jacques Lacan, Book XIX*, 4–5; transl. modified).

372 'A congruous truth – not the truth that claims to be whole, but that of the *half*-saying, the truth that is borne out by guarding against going as far as *confession*, which would be *the worst*' (Lacan, *The Seminar of Jacques Lacan, Book XX*, 93; transl. modified, my emphases).

373 Lacan, *The Seminar of Jacques Lacan, Book XIX*, 114 (transl. modified).

374 Or also, from slightly different (epistemological and existential, rather than ontological) perspectives, and to put it in an even more down-to-earth manner: 'This is not what I mean, I mean, this is not what I mean, I mean . . .'; or 'I don't recognise myself, but it's me, but I don't recognise myself, but it's me . . .'.

375 One could justifiably argue that much of the late and the last Lacan is precisely just that – a mimicking of the unconscious – but this does not solve the issue I am raising. However, conversely, one could argue in an equally and even more convincing manner that much of Lacan's conscious mimicking of the unconscious (not in this case) was actually a *pantomime* aimed precisely at showing how the unconscious can never be replicated not to mention drained. This is the case in the specific sense that the *panto*-mime, as an exaggerated, literally, *all*-mimicking, always entails meta-linguistic statements that betray the incompleteness of the unconscious.

376 Lacan, *The Seminar of Jacques Lacan, Book XVII*, 152; Lacan, *The Seminar of Jacques Lacan, Book XX*, 5.

377 See Chiesa, *Subjectivity and Otherness*, 141–67; L. Chiesa, 'Author, Subject, Structure', in *Lacan contra Foucault*, ed. N. Bou Ali and R. Goel (London: Bloomsbury, 2018), 61–2.

378 'One must resolve to speak of truth as a *fundamental position, even if* not all is known about this truth, since I define it by the fact that it cannot more than half-say itself' (Lacan, *The Seminar of Jacques Lacan, Book XIX*, 152; transl. modified, my emphasis).

379 'It is not possible for me not to do *this* worse' – the worst – 'just like everyone else' (ibid., 5, my emphasis), since otherwise the '". . . *or worse*," then, *that* sighs and or-worsens itself' (Lacan, *The Seminar of Jacques Lacan, Book XX*, 2; transl. modified, my emphasis).

380 Lacan, 'The Triumph of Religion', 81 (my emphases).

381 Lacan, 'Des religions et du réel', 11.

382 'J'essaye d'articuler quelque chose qui *ose* pour la première fois avancer [. . .]' (ibid., my emphasis).

383 To be honest, Lacan's statements in 'Des religions et du réel' are – deliberately? – quite ambiguous, as often happens when he ventures into this territory. He also appears to argue that 'it is not certain that the real makes *a whole*' (ibid., my emphasis), that is to say, it is not necessarily the case that there is a deceiving God. What seems to me incontrovertible, however we interpret his overall stance, is the *dubitative* mode he is employing throughout this passage ('je ne suis pas sûr'; 'il n'est pas sûr'; 'hypothèse'; 'peut-être'). Whether we claim that it is not necessarily the case that the not-One is everything there is or that it is not

necessarily the case that the not-One turns into a One, we are here firmly in the field of *agnosticism*. Miller's decision to title the most crucial section of this article 'The Real Is Not Everything' is therefore slightly misleading.

384 See 'A Short Manifesto for Agnostic Atheism' below .

385 Or also, in Lacan's jargon, the identity between language and the absence of the sexual relationship.

386 'Regarding this analytical discourse [. . .] this is neither ontological nor philosophical' (Lacan, *The Seminar of Jacques Lacan, Book XIX*, 199); 'What is annoying is that whenever [. . .] you aim, in a discourse, at what holds the function of the One [. . .] given what I have been articulating, anyone could turn it into an ontology, in keeping with what he presupposes beyond [. . .] the horizons of the signifier' (ibid., 132, transl. modified); 'To say that I practice ontology is all the same fairly odd' (ibid., 198); 'Ontology is a disgrace that haunts us [*l'ontologie est une honte*]' (ibid., 100, transl. modified).

387 Freud, *The Future of an Illusion*, 97–8 (my emphasis).

388 Lacan, *The Seminar of Jacques Lacan, Book XIX*, 25.

389 Ibid.

390 Ibid.

391 See ibid., 38.

392 Ibid., 40. This passage confirms that Lacan's creationism, as presented especially in Seminar VII, should not at all be understood in a religious sense. On how what is at stake in his – provocative – apology of the *ex nihilo* rather revolves around a thematization of the *cum nihilo* of the signifier, see Chiesa, 'Supreme Being-in-Evil, Criminal Good, and Criminal Desire'.

393 Lacan, *The Seminar of Jacques Lacan, Book XIX*, 40.

394 Ibid., 43.

395 See ibid., 43, 177–8.

396 See R. Thom, 'Entretien sur les catastrophes, le langage et la métaphysique extrême', *Ornicar?*, 16 (January 1978): 73–110. This debate between Thomians and Lacanians includes interventions by Miller, Milner, and Culioli among others. Lacan was in attendance but limited his contribution to a short remark on the status of negation in Freud.

397 On the primacy of number over logic in Lacan, Hoens is right in exegetically specifying that Lacan at times hesitates in this regard (private communication, 4 January 2022). But in what are for me his most advanced pronouncements on the topic, logic (including Frege's) is basically an 'error of counting' and as such 'abusive'. See Chiesa, *The Not-Two*, esp. 161–2, 179.

398 Thom, 'Entretien sur les catastrophes, le langage et la métaphysique extrême', 101.

399 See Lacan, *The Seminar of Jacques Lacan, Book XIX*, 61, 79 and Thom, 'Entretien sur les catastrophes, le langage et la métaphysique extrême', esp. 84, 87–8, 100, 103.

400 Lacan, *The Seminar of Jacques Lacan, Book XIX*, 61–2.

401 Ibid., 61.

402 Ibid.
403 Ibid.
404 Ibid., 60 (transl. modified; my emphases).
405 Ibid., 60–1 (transl. modified).
406 Ibid., 61.
407 Thom, 'Entretien sur les catastrophes, le langage et la métaphysique extrême', 109.
408 Lacan, *The Seminar of Jacques Lacan, Book XIX,* 124 (transl. modified). This brings us back, from a different perspective, to the question of woman's enjoyment, as treated earlier.
409 Ibid., 62 (my emphases).
410 Ibid., 77.
411 Ibid., 77.
412 Ibid., 101. 'Language is thereby reduced to the outcome of the intrusion in the microcosm, through a sort of simplifying filter-mirror, of the most habitual conflicts that are developed in the macrocosm' (R. Thom, *Paraboles et catastrophes. Entretiens sur les mathématiques, la science et la philosophie* (Paris: Flammarion, 1983), 140).
413 Lacan, *The Seminar of Jacques Lacan, Book XIX*, 61–2 (transl. modified; my emphasis).
414 Ibid., 63. (transl. modified).
415 Thom, 'Entretien sur les catastrophes, le langage et la métaphysique extrême', 100, 102–3.
416 Bear in mind that *directly* choosing this option would still leave us exposed to the paradoxes of incompleteness and the deceiving God. On other potential forms of difference and number (and thus of terrestrial or extra-terrestrial rationality) from this meta-critical stance, see also Chiesa, *The Not-Two*, 46–7.
417 Notwithstanding his speaking of 'plans' in the plural, Thom at times comes very close to endorsing Intelligent Design: 'Shall we conclude that there exists a general plan of nature? *A* plan, not *the* plan. Today, the idea of a general plan of organisation preserves all its validity, but we need to abandon the idea of the unicity of such a plan' (Thom, *Paraboles et catastrophes*, 135).
418 Thom, 'Entretien sur les catastrophes, le langage et la métaphysique extrême', 73–4.
419 L. Mottron, 'Recouvrements et incompatibilités entre René Thom et Jacques Lacan', *Littoral*, no. 18 (January 1986): 149. However, Thom remains very sceptical about modern biology, which he considers as a 'paranoia of DNA' (Thom, *Paraboles et catastrophes*, 158). In terms that closely echo Lacan's own critique of biology's anthropocentric 'animism', 'the formal mechanisms attributed to DNA are correct and acceptable on an epistemological level. But we could attribute to DNA its central role in biology [. . .] only by bestowing upon it almost magical powers, embodied in words such as genetic information, genetic control, etc.' (ibid., 158–9). Thom's proximity to Lacan's views is also evidenced not only by his extensive use of psychoanalytic notions (fantasy, complex, personal myths,

censorship mechanisms, the ego as other, etcetera – ibid., 129, 154, 157) but also, more specifically, by his theory of the origins of language as a 'process that enables the defusing of the external forms' power of fascination thanks to the construction of concepts' (ibid., 154).

420 See Thom, 'Entretien sur les catastrophes, le langage et la métaphysique extrême', 88.
421 See Lacan, *The Seminar of Jacques Lacan, Book XIX*, 63.
422 Option 'a' above.
423 Ibid., 64.
424 Ibid. (transl. modified).
425 Ibid., 100 (transl. modified).
426 Ibid., 99–100 (transl. modified).
427 'If [God] were deceitful, what he would think to deceive us [. . .] that would be the truth' (Lacan, 'Alla "Scuola Freudiana"', 146).
428 Lacan, *The Seminar of Jacques Lacan, Book XIX*, 100. There is equally no psychoanalysis if 'what thinks is not thinkable' (ibid., 99, transl. modified).
429 Lacan, *The Seminar of Jacques Lacan, Book II*, 224. I am here relying also on the Staferla version since in the official edition the passage under examination has been abridged.
430 Lacan, *The Seminar of Jacques Lacan, Book III*, 186.
431 Lacan, Seminar IX, lesson of 17 January 1962, unpublished.
432 Lacan, *The Seminar of Jacques Lacan, Book VII*, 121.
433 Lacan, Seminar XXII, lesson of 10 December 1974, unpublished.
434 Lacan, Seminar XXVII, lesson of 10 June 1980, unpublished. Similarly, 'it is strictly impossible to think that this knowledge would be the knowledge for the best, I think none of you doubt that, if only for the scourge of [. . .] language' (Lacan, 'Le phénomène lacanien', 21).
435 Lacan, *The Seminar of Jacques Lacan, Book XXIII*, 50.
436 Lacan, *The Seminar of Jacques Lacan, Book III*, 64–5, transl. modified.
437 On the dimension of resentment associated with the assumption of a vicious God, see F. Ensslin, 'Accesses to the Real', in *Lacan and Philosophy. The New Generation*, ed. L. Chiesa (Melbourne: Repress, 2014), 36–62. Obviously, the idea of the deceiving God is closely related to the clinic of paranoia, of the evil Other. On the latter, see, for instance, *L'Autre méchant: Six cas cliniques commentés*, ed. J.-A. Miller (Paris: Navarin, 2010). For what we have said, the clinic of paranoia calls for a meta-critical revisitation. Perhaps its main focus should be shifted from the domain of the epistemological – bluntly put, the paranoid might after all be right! – to that of the ethical – the overcoming of the comforting aspect of resentment; the facing and constructive use of anxiety as the only affect that does not deceive (Lacan, *The Seminar of Jacques Lacan, Book X*, 116, 160, 173, 261), which still stands even and especially if there were a deceiving God . . .
438 '[. . .] the impasse, or the impossible of the "I think, therefore I am". It is precisely this impossible that gives it its value' (Lacan, Seminar IX, lesson of 22 November 1961). Descartes is arguably the philosopher Lacan deals with most extensively

in his oeuvre. Here I will limit myself to those aspects of his reading that are most pertinent to my delineation of agnostic atheism. There is a vast and solid literature on Lacan's more general reassessment and appropriation of the Cartesian *cogito*. See, for instance, B. Baas and A. Zaloszyc, *Descartes et les fondements de la psychanalyse* (Paris: Navarin, 1988); M. Dolar, 'Cogito as the Subject of the Unconscious', *Cogito and the Unconscious*, 11–40; F. Pellion, *Ce qui Lacan doit à Descartes* (Paris: Éditions du Champ lacanien, 2014).

439 Lacan, *The Seminar of Jacques Lacan, Book XI*, 222–4.

440 Ibid., 224; see also Lacan, Seminar XIV, lessons of 14 December 1966 and of 10 May 1967. 'You know that you exist [. . .] just because you are doubting' (R. Descartes, *The Search for Truth*, in *The Philosophical Writings of Descartes, Volume II* (Cambridge: Cambridge University Press, 2008), 410).

441 See, for instance, J. Lacan, 'Réponses à des étudiants en philosophie sur l'objet de la psychanalyse', *Cahiers pour l'Analyse*, no. 3 (1966): 5–6; J. Lacan, 'Problèmes cruciaux pour la psychanalyse. Compte rendu du Séminaire 1964-1965', in *Autres Écrits*, 199; and especially J. Lacan, 'Interview du 14 décembre 1966 à la RTB (III)', *Quarto*, no. 7 (1982): 8–9. In other words, the thinking subject is (primarily) not the 'I' of the consequent clause in 'If I think, therefore I am'.

442 Lacan, Seminar IX, lesson of 22 November 1961.

443 Ibid.

444 Lacan, 'Interview du 14 décembre 1966 à la RTB (III)', 9.

445 J. Lacan, 'The Instance of the Letter in the Unconscious', in *Écrits*, 430 (transl. modified).

446 Lacan, Seminar IX, lesson of 22 November 1961.

447 Ibid. In the First Meditation, Descartes does indeed raise the question, in passing, as to whether a good God could still 'occasionally' deceive me. His answer is in my view ambiguous and changes significantly between the Latin original and the French translation (supervised by Descartes). The latter reads: 'It would seem equally foreign to his goodness to allow me to be deceived even occasionally; *yet I cannot doubt that he does allow this*', which could be read in opposite ways. Does the 'yet' reinforce or oppose the previous sentence? The former reads: 'It would seem equally foreign to his goodness to allow me to be deceived even occasionally; *yet this last assertion cannot be made* [quod ultimum tamen non potest dici]', which more clearly lends itself to a positive answer. He does occasionally deceive me (R. Descartes, *Meditations on First Philosophy*, in *The Philosophical Writings of Descartes. Volume II*, 14). One might justifiably argue that Descartes's argument entails three stages: (a) that of the good God who occasionally deceives me; (b) that of a nonetheless ultimately good God who, in *this* world, deceives me all the time; (c) that of the 'malicious demon' who absolutely deceives me all the time. There is no consensus in the specialised literature on Descartes as to whether (b) is only the initial part of the argument that leads to (c) or a separate argument. Lacan always treats them as the same argument and uses 'deceiving God' (*Dieu trompeur*) and 'malicious demon' (*génie malin*) as synonyms. It is thus misleading to simply claim that Lacan 'confuses the malicious demon with the deceiving God' (É. Pelletier, 'Lacan, le *cogito* et le

sujet de l'inconscient', available at https://www.academia.edu/21698566/Lacan le cogito et le sujet de linconscient).
448 Lacan, Seminar IX, lesson of 22 November 1961.
449 Ibid. On Descartes's distance from scepticism, see also Lacan, *The Seminar of Jacques Lacan, Book XI*, 223–4.
450 Lacan, Seminar IX, lesson of 22 November 1961.
451 Ibid.
452 Ibid. See also Lacan, *The Seminar of Jacques Lacan, Book XI*, 36.
453 Lacan, Seminar IX, lesson of 22 November 1961.
454 Descartes, *Meditations on First Philosophy*, 35.
455 Lacan, 'The Instance of the Letter in the Unconscious', 430 (my emphasis). In Seminar XI, Lacan thus speaks of a 'certitude in the flaw' with regard to Descartes. This passage has been omitted in the official edition of Seminar XI.
456 Descartes's deceiving God has to do with an 'ectopy, a rejection of what should instead be reintegrated. At the end of the day, starting from the moment when we approach this notion of the ego, we cannot avoid at the same time to put into question that there is somewhere some sort of misdeal' (Lacan, *The Seminar of Jacques Lacan, Book II*, 9; transl. modified) (I rely on the Staferla version, which is here significantly different from the official one).
457 Lacan, *The Seminar of Jacques Lacan, Book III*, 64.
458 Ibid., 65. Even more broadly, Lacan speaks of this supposition as constituting modern people's 'mentality' (ibid., 66).
459 Lacan, *The Seminar of Jacques Lacan, Book II*, 224. See also Lacan, Seminar XIII, lesson of 2 February 1966.
460 'The cogito is untenable if it is not completed with a *sum, ergo Deus est*' (Lacan, Seminar XIV, lessons of 11 and 18 January 1967; see also J. Nassif, 'Pour une logique du fantasme', *Scilicet*, 2/3 (1970): 237 and R. Descartes, *Rules for the Direction of the Mind*, in *The Philosophical Writings of Descartes. Volume I*, 46). The ego thus remains 'dependent on the God of religion' (Lacan, Seminar XIII, lesson of 1 December 1965).
461 See Lacan, Seminar IX, lesson of 22 November 1961.
462 Ibid.
463 See ibid.
464 Lacan, *The Seminar of Jacques Lacan, Book XI*, 224–5. Lacan's interpretation of Descartes's doctrine of God's will and of eternal truths – and my expansion and radicalization of it in what follows – is far from mainstream but not short of authoritative allies. For instance, Harry Frankfurt contends that Descartes's God can do what is logically impossible, and hence deems this notion of deity as incoherent (H. Frankfurt, 'Descartes on the Creation of Eternal Truths', *Philosophical Review*, 86, no. 1 (1977): 36–57; see esp. 43–4). Frankfurt argues that, for Descartes, God created the eternal truths and that he was thus not determined in his creation of the law of contradiction, which is supported by many scholars and based on strong textual evidence (especially Descartes's letter to Mesland of 2 May 1644). But his argument also implies that, at different moments,

Descartes seems to suggest that God: (a) could have chosen to actualise the negation of the law of contradiction; (b) can repeal the law of contradiction and replace it with its negation; and (c) can violate the law of contradiction. Here textual evidence is weaker, and relies on a few selected extracts, but I would not go as far as claiming, as La Croix does, that Frankfurt's reading is fully unsubstantiated (R. R. La Croix, 'Descartes on God's Ability to Do the Logically Impossible', *Canadian Journal of Philosophy*, 14, no. 3 (1984): 455–75). In line with what I am arguing, Frankfurt also senses how a thus understood doctrine of eternal truths *complicates* the question of the deceiving God: 'According to the standard interpretation of Descartes's theory of knowledge, this coincidence of harmony between the principles of human reason and the eternal truths God has created is precisely what Descartes intends his proof that God is not a deceiver to establish. In my view, the standard interpretation is untenable. [. . .] The proof that God is not a deceiver, like any rational demonstration, can establish for Descartes nothing more than that its conclusion is required by the principles of human reason' (Frankfurt, 'Descartes on the Creation of Eternal Truths', 52). Let me also note in passing that: (a) Descartes's positing of eternal truth as *both* eternal and created is for Badiou's own project what Descartes has best to offer to contemporary irreligious philosophy (see A. Badiou, *Logics of Worlds* (London: Continuum, 2009), esp. 512–13; I owe this observation to Frank Ruda); and (b) surprisingly given Lacan's significant indebtedness to Koyré, the latter considered the doctrine of eternal truths as an – anti-scientific – abomination in Descartes's system (see A. Koyré, *Essai sur l'idée de Dieu et les preuves de son existence chez Descartes* (Paris: Leroux, 1922)).

465 See Lacan, *The Seminar of Jacques Lacan*, *Book XI*, 227. Lacan, Seminar XII, lessons of 9 and 16 June 1965.

466 See Lacan, Seminar XII, lesson of 16 June 1965.

467 See Lacan, *The Seminar of Jacques Lacan*, *Book XI*, 226. Thom is thus not only anti-Galilean but also, in this sense, anti-Cartesian.

468 See Lacan, Seminar IX, lesson of 17 January 1962; Lacan, Seminar XII, lesson of 16 June 1965.

469 See Lacan, Seminar IX, lesson of 17 January 1962; Lacan, *The Seminar of Jacques Lacan*, *Book XI*, 36, 226.

470 See Lacan, Seminar XII, lesson of 16 June 1965.

471 This stance on the Cartesian impossible also enables Lacan to constructively read the *cogito ergo sum* as an innovative 'refusal of the hard path of thinking *Being* and the knowledge that has to take this path' (Lacan, Seminar XIV, lesson of 11 January 1967). The speaking being's being the one who thinks – or better, the 'therefore I am' of 'I think "therefore I am"' – amounts in this sense to a 'shortcut' in comparison to traditional ontologies (ibid.). The ego is thus located outside of the reach of a Being that would embrace thinking. But, precisely because of that, as a 'I am only to the extent that your question about Being is elided, I am done with Being, I . . . *am not*, save for where I necessarily am insofar as I can say it', the ego turns into an 'empty set' ('"Am not" means that there is no element in this set that exists under the term "I"' – ibid.). The very structure of the *cogito* shows that the 'being of man' is a detritus, or better, a '*d(être)itus*' (ibid.).

472 Lacan, Seminar IX, lesson of 17 January 1962.

473 Ibid.

474 This equation between Being and the creative will to truth should also be extended to understanding (and knowledge): 'In God, willing, understanding and creating are all the same thing without one being prior to the other even conceptually' (R. Descartes, Letter to Mersenne of 27 May 1630, in *The Philosophical Writings of Descartes. Volume III*, 25–6). So, to put it simply, and this is important for the further development of my argument below, for Descartes himself, God does not know anything prior to wanting it as true.

475 Lacan, *The Seminar of Jacques Lacan, Book XI*, 36 (my emphasis; transl. modified). By rendering '*bascule dans*' as 'lurches into' instead of 'topples into', the English translation obscures the crucial fact that, again, this real is such as the impossible – and the 'I am' is real only as that which does not work.

476 Lacan, Seminar IX, lesson of 17 January 1962.

477 Lacan, *The Seminar of Jacques Lacan, Book XI*, 224.

478 Miller comes close to acknowledging this, albeit only in passing: 'Descartes re-establishes a God about whom it would be too much to say that he is veracious. [. . .] God is re-established as the creator of eternal truths [. . .]: it is true because God made it. There is thus only a very slim difference from the deceiving God' (J.-A. Miller, 'Des réponses du réel', lesson of 23 November 1983, available at https://jonathanleroy.be/wp-content/uploads/2016/01/1983-1984-Des-réponses-du-Réel-JA-Miller.pdf).

479 See Lacan, *The Seminar of Jacques Lacan, Book III*, 65.

480 Lacan, Seminar XII, lesson of 3 March 1965; Lacan, *The Seminar of Jacques Lacan, Book III*, 65.

481 See Lacan, *The Seminar of Jacques Lacan, Book XI*, 225–6.

482 R. Descartes, *Discourse on the Method*, in *The Philosophical Writings of Descartes. Volume I*, 120, 127; Descartes, *Meditations on First Philosophy*, 15.

483 Lacan, Seminar XII, lesson of 3 February 1965.

484 See Lacan, Seminar XIII, lesson of 9 February 1966. See also lesson of 11 May 1966.

485 Lacan, Seminar XXI, lesson of 23 April 1974.

486 Ibid.

487 See Lacan, *The Seminar of Jacques Lacan, Book XI*, 225.

488 Lacan, Seminar XII, lesson of 3 March 1965 (my emphasis).

489 Ibid.

490 See Lacan, *Je parle aux murs,* 82; Lacan, Seminar XXI, lesson of 21 May 1974; Lacan, 'Alla "Scuola Freudiana"', 145; Lacan, Seminar XXVII, lesson of 10 June 1980.

491 With regard to the first option, on one occasion, Lacan argues that a thus conceived real not-One could still be regarded as 'all' in a different sense: 'The real [. . .] is not universal, which means that it is all [*tout*] only in the strict sense that each of its elements is identical with itself but without the possibility of them being said to be "all" [*tous*]. There is no "all the elements"; in each case there are only sets to be determined' (Lacan, 'La troisième', 184). He does not develop

this point any further. Instead, sensing again the deceiving God lurking beneath 'There is no "all the elements"', he admits: 'It is not worth adding, "that's all"' (ibid.).
492 See J.-A. Miller, 'Ce qui fait insigne', lesson of 5 November 1985, available at https://jonathanleroy.be/wp-content/uploads/2016/01/1986-1987-Ce-qui-fait-insigne-JA-Miller.pdf.
493 Lacan, *Le Séminaire de Jacques Lacan*, *Livre XVI*, 219 (my emphases).
494 Lacan, Seminar XXI, lesson of 21 May 1974.
495 Lacan, Seminar XXVII, lesson of 10 June 1980.
496 Lacan, Seminar XXI, lesson of 13 November 1973.
497 Ibid.
498 Ibid., lesson of 21 May 1974.
499 See Lacan, Seminar XXII, lesson of 8 April 1975; Lacan, *The Seminar of Jacques Lacan, Book XXIII*, 116.
500 Lacan, Seminar XXII, lesson of 18 March 1975; Lacan, 'Alla "Scuola Freudiana"', 121.
501 Lacan, Seminar XXVII, lesson of 10 June 1980.
502 Lacan, 'Alla "Scuola Freudiana"', 145.
503 Lacan, 'La troisième', 181.
504 Lacan, Seminar XV, lesson of 19 June 1968.
505 Lacan, *The Seminar of Jacques Lacan, Book XXIII*, 116.
506 Lacan, *The Seminar of Jacques Lacan, Book X*, 309 (my emphasis; transl. modified).
507 Lacan, *Le Séminaire de Jacques Lacan, Livre XVI*, 253, 256, 292.
508 Lacan, *The Seminar of Jacques Lacan, Book XXIII*, 47.
509 Lacan, Seminar XXI, lesson of 13 November 1973.

Conclusion

1 Johnston, *Adventures in Transcendental Materialism*, 219–21.
2 Karl Marx, *The Civil War in France, The First International and After: Political Writings*, Volume 3, ed. David Fernbach (Harmondsworth: Penguin, 1974), 212–14.
3 *SE* 23: 221–3.
4 Marx, *The Civil War in France*, 213.
5 Lacan, *The Seminar of Jacques Lacan, Book XI*, 29–30, 134; Lacan, *The Seminar of Jacques Lacan, Book XVII*, 180; Lacan, *The Seminar of Jacques Lacan, Book XIX*, 100, 198–9; Lacan, *The Seminar of Jacques Lacan, Book XX*, 30–1; Lacan, 'Radiophonie', 426; Adrian Johnston, 'Misfelt Feelings: Unconscious Affect Between Psychoanalysis, Neuroscience, and Philosophy', in Adrian Johnston and Catherine Malabou, *Self and Emotional Life: Philosophy, Psychoanalysis, and Neuroscience* (New York: Columbia University Press, 2013), 82, 153–62; Johnston, *Adventures*

in Transcendental Materialism, 81–3, 209–10; Johnston, *Irrepressible Truth*, 230–1; Johnston, *Infinite Greed*.

6 Johnston, *Adventures in Transcendental Materialism*, 65–107.
7 Lacan, *The Seminar of Jacques Lacan, Book XI*, 72; Johnston, *Adventures in Transcendental Materialism*, 82–3.
8 Lacan, *The Seminar of Jacques Lacan, Book XIX*, 163; Johnston, *Prolegomena to Any Future Materialism, Book One*, 3.
9 Jacques Lacan, 'Le Séminaire de Caracas', in *Almanack de la dissolution*, ed. Nicolas Francion (Paris: Navarin, 1986), 82.
10 *SE* 6: 259.
11 Johnston, *Adventures in Transcendental Materialism*, 65–107, 248–73; Adrian Johnston, 'Philosophy and Psychoanalysis', in *The Routledge Handbook of Psychoanalysis in the Social Sciences and Humanities,* ed. Anthony Elliott and Jeffrey Prager (New York: Routledge, 2016), 278–99; Johnston, 'Lacan's Endgame', 156–87.
12 *SE* 6: 239–79.
13 *SE* 19: 52.
14 Hegel, *Phenomenology of Spirit*, 88–9, 101–3; G. W. F. Hegel, *Science of Logic*, trans. A. V. Miller (London: George Allen & Unwin, 1969), 121; G. W. F. Hegel, *The Encyclopedia Logic: Part I of the Encyclopedia of the Philosophical Sciences with the* Zusätze, trans. T. F. Geraets, W. A. Suchting and H. S. Harris (Indianapolis: Hackett, 1991), §44 (87); Johnston, *Žižek's Ontology*, 137–8.
15 Johnston, *Infinite Greed*.
16 Adrian Johnston, 'On Deep History and Lacan', *Journal of European Psychoanalysis,* special issue: 'Lacan and Philosophy: The New Generation', ed. Lorenzo Chiesa, no. 32 (2012): 91–121.
17 Johnston, *Prolegomena to Any Future Materialism, Book One*, 59–77.
18 Lacan, *The Seminar of Jacques Lacan, Book IV*, 33–50; Johnston, *Prolegomena to Any Future Materialism, Book One*, 59–77; Adrian Johnston, 'History', in *The Marx Through Lacan Vocabulary: A Compass for Libidinal and Political Economies*, ed. Christina Soto van der Plas, Edgar Miguel Juarez-Salazar, Carlos Gomez Camarena and David Pavon-Cuellar (New York: Routledge, 2022), 85–95.
19 Adrian Johnston, 'Confession of a Weak Reductionist: Responses to Some Recent Criticisms of My Materialism', in *Neuroscience and Critique: Exploring the Limits of the Neurological Turn*, ed. Jan De Vos and Ed Pluth (New York: Routledge, 2015), 141–70; Johnston, 'Fear of Science', 125–41.
20 Hegel, *Science of Logic,* 132, 134–5; Hegel, *The Encyclopedia Logic,* §60 (105–6), §92 (148); G. W. F. Hegel, *Lectures on Logic: Berlin, 1831*, trans. Clark Butler (Bloomington: Indiana University Press, 2008), §93 (104); G. W. F. Hegel, *Philosophy of Mind: Part Three of the Encyclopedia of the Philosophical Sciences with the Zusatze*, trans. William Wallace and A. V. Miller (Oxford: Oxford University Press, 1971), §386 (23–4).
21 Adrian Johnston, 'Repeating Engels: Renewing the Cause of the Materialist Wager for the Twenty-First Century', *Theory @ Buffalo,* special issue: 'animal.machine. sovereign', no. 15 (2011): 155–6; Adrian Johnston, *A New German Idealism: Hegel,*

Žižek, and Dialectical Materialism (New York: Columbia University Press, 2018), 11–37.
22 G. W. F. Hegel, *Vorlesungen überdie Geschichte der Philosophie III, Werke in zwanzig Bänden, 20, Werke in zwanzig* Bänden, ed. Eva Moldenhauer and Karl Markus Michel (Frankfurt am Main: Suhrkamp, 1971), 362; G. W. F. Hegel, *Lectures on the History of Philosophy: Volume Three*, trans. E. S. Haldane and Frances H. Simson (New York: The Humanities Press, 1955), 454–5.
23 Johnston, *Adventures in Transcendental Materialism*, 23–64.
24 Baruch Spinoza, *Ethics, Spinoza: Complete Works*, ed. Michael L. Morgan; trans. Samuel Shirley (Indianapolis: Hackett, 2002), Part I, Proposition 8 (219–21), Propositions 13–16 (224–7), Proposition 18 (229), Proposition 25 (232), Proposition 28 (233).
25 G. W. F. Hegel, 'Fragment of a System', trans. Richard Kroner, in *Miscellaneous Writings of G.W.F. Hegel*, ed. Jon Stewart (Evanston: Northwestern University Press, 2002), 154; G. W. F. Hegel, *The Difference Between Fichte's and Schelling's System of Philosophy*, trans. H. S. Harris and Walter Cerf (Albany: State University of New York Press, 1977), 112; G. W. F. Hegel, *Faith and Knowledge*, trans. Walter Cerf and H. S. Harris (Albany: State University of New York Press, 1977), 59–60, 113; F. W. J. Schelling, *Bruno, or, On the Natural and the Divine Principle of Things*, trans. Michael G. Vater (Albany: State University of New York Press, 1984), 136, 143; F. W. J. Schelling, *System der Weltalter: Munchener Vorlesung 1927/28 in einer Nachschrift von Ernst von Lasaulx*, ed. Siegbert Peetz (Frankfurt am Main: Klostermann, 1990), 142.
26 Johnston, *A New German Idealism*, 74–128.
27 F. W. J. Schelling, 'On Construction in Philosophy', trans. Andrew A. Davis and Alexi I. Kukeljevic, *Epoche*, no. 12 (2008): 283; F. W. J. Schelling, *Philosophical Investigations into the Essence of Human Freedom*, trans. Jeff Love and Johannes Schmidt (Albany: State University of New York Press, 2006), 68–9, 87, 92–3; F. W. J. Schelling, *The Ages of the World: Third Version (c. 1815)*, trans. Jason M. Wirth (Albany: State University of New York Press, 2000), 23, 25–8.
28 Lacan, *The Seminar of Jacques Lacan, Book XIX*, 118–27; Lacan, *The Seminar of Jacques Lacan, Book XX*, 143; Lacan, *The Seminar of Jacques Lacan, Book XXIII*, 50; Jacques Lacan, *Le Séminaire de Jacques Lacan, Livre XXIV: L'insu que sait de l'une-bévue, s'aile à mourre, 1976-1977* (unpublished typescript), session of 10 May 1977.
29 Saint Bonaventura, in Maurice Blanchot, *The Writing of the Disaster*, trans. Ann Smock (Lincoln: University of Nebraska Press, 1986), 31.
30 Slavoj Žižek, *Less Than Nothing: Hegel and the Shadow of Dialectical Materialism* (London: Verso, 2012), 388–93.
31 Ibid., 390.
32 Johnston, *Adventures in Transcendental Materialism*, 70–6.
33 Pascal, *Pensées*, §418 (114); Pascal, *Pensées*, §418 (150).
34 Kant, *Critique of Practical Reason*, 238–9.

35 J. G. Fichte, *The Science of Knowledge*, ed. and trans. Peter Heath and John Lachs (Cambridge: Cambridge University Press, 1982), 230–1, 237–8, 242, 247, 253.

36 G. W. F. Hegel, *Wissenschaft der Logik I, Werke in zwanzig Bänden, 5, Werke in zwanzig Bänden*, ed. Eva Moldenhauer and Karl Markus Michel (Frankfurt am Main: Suhrkamp, 1969), 142–56; Hegel, *Science of Logic,* 131–43; G. W. F. Hegel, *Die Wissenschaft der Logik: Enzyklopädie der philosophischen Wissenschaften I, Werke in zwanzig Banden, 8, Werke in zwanzig Banden*, ed. Eva Moldenhauer and Karl Markus Michel (Frankfurt am Main: Suhrkamp, 1970), §93–4 (198–200); Hegel, *The Encyclopedia Logic,* §93–4 (149–50).

Bibliography

Adam, Jacques. 'Ouverture: Lacan, un athéisme du Pas-tout'. *Champ lacanien*, 8, no. 1 (2010): 13–21.
Adorno, Theodor W. 'Freudian Theory and the Pattern of Fascist Propaganda'. In Theodor W. Adorno, *The Culture Industry: Selected Essays on Mass Culture*, 132–57. London: Routledge, 1991.
Askofaré, Sidi. 'De l'inconscient au sinthome: Conjectures sur les usages et le renoncement possible au Nom-du-Père'. *L'en-je lacanien*, no. 6 (2006): 23–36.
Baas, Bernard and Armand Zaloszyc. *Descartes et les fondements de la psychanalyse*. Paris: Navarin, 1988.
Badiou, Alain and Élisabeth Roudinesco. *Jacques Lacan Past and Present: A Dialogue*. Translated by Jason E. Smith. New York: Columbia University Press, 2014.
Badiou, Alain. *Briefings on Existence. A Short Treatise on Transitory Ontology*. Translated by Norman Madarasz. Albany: SUNY, 2006.
Badiou, Alain. *Logics of Worlds*. Translated by Alberto Toscano. London: Continuum, 2009.
Baggini, Julian. *Atheism. A Very Short Introduction*. Oxford: Oxford University Press, 2003.
Balmès, François. *Dieu, le sexe et la vérité*. Ramonville Saint-Agne: Érès, 2007.
Balmès, François. *Le nom, la loi, la voix*. Ramonville Saint-Agne: Érès, 1997.
Barrett, Justin and Emily Reed Burdett. 'The Cognitive Science of Religion'. *The Psychologist*, 24 (April 2011): 252–5.
Bauer, Bruno. *The Trumpet of the Last Judgment over Hegel the Atheist and Antichrist: An Ultimatum*, translated by Michael Malloy. In *The Young Hegelians: An Anthology*, edited by Lawrence S. Stepelevich, 177–86. Amherst: Humanity Books, 1999.
Beirnaert, Louis. *Aux frontières de l'acte analytique: La Bible, Saint Ignace, Freud et Lacan*. Paris: Seuil, 1987.
Blanchot, Maurice. *The Writing of the Disaster*. Translated by Ann Smock. Lincoln: University of Nebraska Press, 1986.
Bloch, Ernst. *Atheism in Christianity*. Translated by J. T. Swann. New York: Herder and Herder, 1972.
Boothby, Richard. *Freud as Philosopher: Metapsychology After Lacan*. New York: Routledge, 2001.
Boothby, Richard. 'The No-Thing of God: Psychoanalysis of Religion After Lacan'. In *The Oxford Handbook of Philosophy and Psychoanalysis*, edited by Richard G. T. Gipps and Michael Lacewing, 571–88. Oxford: Oxford University Press, 2018.
Brunet, Georges. *Le pari de Pascal*. Paris: Desclée de Brouwer, 1956.

Burns, Michael O. and Brian Smith. 'Materialism, Subjectivity and the Outcome of French Philosophy: Interview with Adrian Johnston'. *Cosmos and History*, 7, no. 1 (2011): 167–81.
Cacho, Jorge. 'Disgrâce'. *La célibataire: Revue de psychanalyse—clinique, logique, politique*, no. 13, *Lacan et Pascal* (Autumn 2006): 161–7.
Caruso, Paolo, ed. *Conversaciones con Lévi-Strauss, Foucault y Lacan*. Barcelona: Anagrama, 1969.
Cathelineau, Pierre-Christophe. 'L'objet du Pari'. *La célibataire: Revue de psychanalyse—clinique, logique, politique*, no. 13, *Lacan et Pascal* (Autumn 2006): 153–60.
Causse, Jean-Daniel. *Lacan et le christianisme*. Paris: Éditions Campagne Première, 2018.
Chassing, Jean-Louis. 'Le songe et le réveil'. *La célibataire: Revue de psychanalyse—clinique, logique, politique*, no. 13, *Lacan et Pascal* (Autumn 2006): 9–21.
Chesterton, G. K. *Orthodoxy*. San Francisco: Ignatius Press, 1995.
Chiesa, Lorenzo. 'Anthropie: Beside the Pleasure Principle'. *Continental Thought and Theory*, 3, Issue 2 (2021): 189–205.
Chiesa, Lorenzo. 'Author, Subject, Structure. Lacan Contra Foucault'. In *Lacan contra Foucault*, edited by Nadia Bou Ali and Rohit Goel, 55–80. London: Bloomsbury, 2018.
Chiesa, Lorenzo. 'Exalted Obscenity and the Lawyer of God: Lacan and Deleuze on the Baroque'. In *Lacan and Deleuze. A Disjunctive Synthesis*, edited by Boštjan Nedoh and Andreja Zevnik, 141–62. Edinburgh: Edinburgh University Press, 2017.
Chiesa, Lorenzo. 'Hyperstructuralism's Necessity of Contingency'. *S. Journal of the Jan van Eyck Circle for Lacanian Ideology Critique*, 3 (2010): 159–77.
Chiesa, Lorenzo. 'Psychoanalysis, Religion, Love'. *Crisis and Critique*, special issue: 'Politics and Theology Today', edited by Frank Ruda and Agon Hamza, 2, no. 1 (2015): 56–71.
Chiesa, Lorenzo. *The Not-Two. Logic and God in Lacan*. Cambridge, MA: MIT Press, 2016.
Chiesa, Lorenzo. *Subjectivity and Otherness. A Philosophical Reading of Lacan*. Cambridge, MA: MIT Press, 2007.
Chiesa, Lorenzo. 'Supreme Being-in-Evil, Criminal Good, and Criminal Desire'. In *Studying Lacan's Seminar VII*, edited by Carol Owens, 1–28. Abingdon: Routledge, 2023.
Chiesa, Lorenzo and Alberto Toscano. '*Agape* and the Anonymous Religion of Atheism'. *Angelaki: Journal of the Theoretical Humanities*, 12, no. 1 (April 2007): 113–26.
Chiesa, Lorenzo and Alberto Toscano. 'Ethics and Capital, *Ex Nihilo*'. In *Umbr(a): A Journal of the Unconscious—The Dark God*, edited by Andrew Skomra, 9–25. Buffalo: Center for the Study of Psychoanalysis and Culture, State University of New York at Buffalo, 2005.
Cima, Gioele P. 'Elvio Fachinelli: A Dissident Psychoanalyst'. In Elvio Fachinelli, *On Freud*, xi–xlvi. Cambridge, MA: MIT Press, 2023.
Cima, Gioele P. *Il seminario perpetuo. Il tardo e l'ultimo Lacan*. Napoli-Salerno: Orthotes, 2020.
Clément, Catherine. *The Lives and Legends of Jacques Lacan*. Translated by Arthur Goldhammer. New York: Columbia University Press, 1983.

Clero, Jean-Pierre. 'Lacan and Probability'. *Electronic Journ@l for History of Probability and Statistics*, 4, no. 2 (December 2008). www.jehps.net.

Dalzell, Tom. 'On the Death of God in Lacan – A Nuanced Atheism'. *The Heythrope Journal*, 63, no. 1 (2021): 1–8.

Davis, Creston, Marcus Pound and Clayton Crockett. 'Introduction'. In *Theology After Lacan*, edited by Creston Davis, Marcus Pound and Clayton Crockett, 1–15. Eugene: Cascade Books, 2014.

Dawkins, Richard. 'A Scientist's Case against God'. *The Independent*, 20 April 1992.

de Certeau, Michel. 'Lacan: An Ethics of Speech', translated by Marie-Rose Logan. In *Heterologies: Discourse on the Other*, translated by Brian Massumi, 47–64. Minneapolis: University of Minnesota Press, 1986.

de Certeau, Michel and Mireille Cifali. 'Entretien, mystique et psychanalyse'. *Espaces Temps*, no. 80–1 (2002): 156–75.

De Kesel, Marc. 'Religion as Critique, Critique as Religion: Some Reflections on the Monotheistic Weakness of Contemporary Criticism'. In *Umbr(a): A Journal of the Unconscious—The Dark God*, edited by Andrew Skomra, 119–37. Buffalo: Center for the Study of Psychoanalysis and Culture, State University of New York at Buffalo, 2005.

de Martino, Ernesto. 'Crisis of Presence and Religious Reintegration'. *HAU. Journal of Ethnographic Theory*, 2, no. 2 (2012): 431–50.

de Martino, Ernesto. *La fine del mondo. Contributo all'analisi delle apocalissi culturali*. Turin: Einaudi, 1977.

De Waelhens, Alphonse. *Schizophrenia: A Philosophical Reflection on Lacan's Structuralist Interpretation*. Translated by Wilfried Ver Eecke. Pittsburgh: Duquesne University Press, 1978.

Deleuze, Gilles. 'Qu'est-ce que l'acte de création?'. Edited by Charles J. Stivale, March 17, 1987, https://deleuze.cla.purdue.edu/sites/default/files/pdf/lectures/fr/1b%20 Deleuze%20What%20Is%20A%20Creative%20Act%20-%20French.pdf.

Deleuze, Gilles. 'What Is the Creative Act?', translated by Alison M. Gingeras. In *French Theory in America*, edited by Sylvère Lotringer and Sande Cohen, 99–107. New York: Routledge, 2001.

Derrida, Jacques. 'Cogito and the History of Madness', translated by Alan Bass. In Jacques Derrida, *Writing and Difference*, 31–63. Chicago: University of Chicago Press, 1978.

Derrida, Jacques. '"To Do Justice to Freud": The History of Madness in the Age of Psychoanalysis', translated by Pascale-Anne Brault and Michael Naas. *Critical Inquiry*, 20, no. 2 (1994): 227–66.

Descartes, René. *The Philosophical Writings of Descartes. Volume I*. Translated by John Cottingham, Robert Stoothoff, Dugald Murdoch. Cambridge: Cambridge University Press, 2008.

Descartes, René. *The Philosophical Writings of Descartes. Volume II*. Translated by John Cottingham, Robert Stoothoff, Dugald Murdoch. Cambridge: Cambridge University Press, 2008.

Descartes, René. *The Philosophical Writings of Descartes. Volume III*. Translated by John Cottingham, Dugald Murdoch, Robert Stoothoff, Anthony Kenny. Cambridge: Cambridge University Press, 2008.

Devlin, Keith. *The Unfinished Game: Pascal, Fermat, and the Seventeenth-Century Letter that Made the World Modern*. New York: Basic Books, 2008.

Dolar, Mladen. 'Cogito as the Subject of the Unconscious'. In *Cogito and the Unconscious*, edited by Slavoj Žižek, 11–40. Durham: Duke University Press, 1998.

Dor, Joël. *Introduction à la lecture de Lacan, Tome II: La structure du sujet*. Paris: Denoël, 1992.
Dunlap, Aron. *Lacan and Religion*. Abingdon: Routledge, 2014.
Ensslin, Felix. 'Accesses to the Real'. In *Lacan and Philosophy. The New Generation*, edited by Lorenzo Chiesa, 35–62. Melbourne: Re.press, 2014.
Fachinelli, Elvio. *La mente estatica*. Milan: Adelphi, 1989.
Fachinelli, Elvio. *On Freud*. Translated by Christina Chalmers. Cambridge, MA: MIT Press, 2023.
Feuerbach, Ludwig. *The Essence of Christianity*. Translated by George Eliot. Amherst: Prometheus Books, 1989.
Feuerbach, Ludwig. 'Letter to Hegel: November 22, 1828'. In G. W. F. Hegel, *Hegel: The Letters*, translated by Clark Butler and Christiane Seiler, 547–50. Bloomington: Indiana University Press, 1984.
Feuerbach, Ludwig. 'The Necessity of a Reform in Philosophy'. In *The Fiery Brook: Selected Writings*, translated by Zawar Hanfi, 145–52. London: Verso, 2012.
Feuerbach, Ludwig. 'Preliminary Theses on the Reform of Philosophy'. In *The Fiery Brook: Selected Writings*, translated by Zawar Hanfi, 153–73. London: Verso, 2012.
Feuerbach, Ludwig. *Principles of the Philosophy of the Future*. Translated by Manfred H. Vogel. Indianapolis: The Bobbs-Merrill Company, 1966.
Feuerbach, Ludwig. 'Vorläufige Thesen zur Reform der Philosophie', 1842, http://www.zeno.org/Philosophie/M/Feuerbach,+Ludwig/Vorläufige+Thesen+zur+Reform+der+Philosophie.
Fichte, J. G. *The Science of Knowledge*. Edited by and translated by Peter Heath and John Lachs. Cambridge: Cambridge University Press, 1982.
Fink, Bruce. *A Clinical Introduction to Lacanian Psychoanalysis: Theory and Technique*. Cambridge, MA: Harvard University Press, 1997.
Fink, Bruce. *The Lacanian Subject: Between Language and Jouissance*. Princeton: Princeton University Press, 1995.
Fink, Bruce. 'The Master Signifier and the Four Discourses'. In *Key Concepts of Lacanian Psychoanalysis*, edited by Dany Nobus, 29–47. New York: Other Press, 1998.
Frankfurt, Harry. 'Descartes on the Creation of Eternal Truths'. *Philosophical Review*, 86, no. 1 (1977): 36–57.
Freud, Sigmund. *Entwurf einer Psychologie*, Aus den Anfängen der Psychoanalyse, 1887–1902. Edited by Marie Bonaparte, Anna Freud and Ernst Kris, 371–466. Frankfurt am Main: S. Fischer, 1975.
Freud, Sigmund. *The Future of an Illusion*. London: Hogarth Press, 1934.
Freud, Sigmund. *Gesammelte Werke*. Edited by E. Bibring, W. Hoffer, E. Kris and O. Isakower. Frankfurt: S. Fischer, 1952.
Freud, Sigmund. 'Overview of the Transference Neuroses'. In *A Phylogenetic Fantasy: Overview of the Transference Neuroses*, edited by Ilse Grubrich-Simitis, translated by Axel Hoffer and Peter T. Hoffer, 1–20. Cambridge, MA: Harvard University Press, 1987.
Freud, Sigmund. *The Standard Edition of the Complete Psychological Works of Sigmund Freud*, 24 vols. Edited by and translated by James Strachey, in collaboration with Anna Freud, assisted by Alix Strachey and Alan Tyson. London: Vintage, Hogarth Press and the Institute of Psycho-Analysis, 2001.
Gale, John. 'Lacan and the Benedictines'. *European Journal of Psychoanalysis*, no. 10 (2018). https://www.journal-psychoanalysis.eu/lacan-and-the-benedictines/.
Gallagher, Cormac. 'What does Jacques Lacan see in Blaise Pascal?', Autumn 2001. http://www.lacaninireland.com/web/wp-content/uploads/2010/06/Aut_2001-WHAT-DOES-JACQUES-LACAN-SEE-IN-BLAISE-PASCAL-Cormac-Gallagher.pdf.

Gellner, Ernest. *The Psychoanalytic Movement*. Evanston: Northwestern University Press, 1993.

Goldmann, Lucien. *The Hidden God: A Study of Tragic Vision in the Pensées of Pascal and the Tragedies of Racine*. Translated by Philip Thody. London: Verso, 2016.

Gould, Stephen Jay. *Life's Grandeur*. London: Vintage, 1997.

Gould, Stephen Jay. 'Non-overlapping Magisteria'. In Stephen Jay Gould, *The Richness of Life*, 584–97. New York: Norton, 2006.

Gouthier, Henri. 'Le cœur qui sent les trois dimensions: Analyse d'une pensée de Pascal'. In Henri Gouthier, *La passion de la raison: Hommage à Ferdinand Alquié*, 203–15. Paris: Presses Universitaires de France, 1983.

Grigg, Russell. 'Beyond the Oedipus Complex'. In *Jacques Lacan and the Other Side of Psychoanalysis: Reflections on Seminar XVII*, edited by Justin Clemens and Russell Grigg, 50–68. Durham: Duke University Press, 2006.

Grosz, Elizabeth. *Jacques Lacan: A Feminist Introduction*. New York: Routledge, 1990.

Guilbaud, G.-T. *La cybernétique*. Paris: Presses Universitaires de France, 1954.

Hägglund, Martin. *Radical Atheism. Derrida and the Time of Life*. Stanford: Stanford University Press, 2008.

Hägglund, Martin. *This Life. Secular Faith and Spiritual Freedom*. New York: Anchor Books, 2020.

Harari, Roberto. *Lacan's Seminar on 'Anxiety': An Introduction*. Edited by Rico Franses, translated by Jane C. Lamb-Ruiz. New York: Other Press, 2001.

Harman, Graham. 'Author Q&A with Adrian Johnston'. https://www.euppublishing.com/userimages/ContentEditor/1397840563624/Adventures%20in%20Transcendental%20Realism%20-%20Author%20Q%26A.pdf.

Harman, Graham. 'Interview with Quentin Meillassoux'. In Graham Harman, *Quentin Meillassoux. Philosophy on the Making*, 159–74. Edinburgh: Edinburgh University Press, 2011.

Haym, Rudolf. 'Preußen und die Rechtsphilosophie (1857): Hegel und seine Zeit'. In *Materialien zu Hegels Rechtsphilosophie*, edited by Manfred Riedel, 365–94. Frankfurt am Main: Suhrkamp, 1975.

Hegel, G. W. F. *Die Wissenschaft der Logik: Enzyklopädie der philosophischen Wissenschaften I, Werke in zwanzig Bänden, 8*. Edited by Eva Moldenhauer and Karl Markus Michel. Frankfurt am Main: Suhrkamp, 1970.

Hegel, G. W. F. *The Difference Between Fichte's and Schelling's System of Philosophy*. Translated by H. S. Harris and Walter Cerf. Albany: State University of New York Press, 1977.

Hegel, G. W. F. *The Encyclopedia Logic: Part I of the Encyclopedia of the Philosophical Sciences with the Zusätze*. Translated by T. F. Geraets, W. A. Suchting and H. S. Harris. Indianapolis: Hackett, 1991.

Hegel, G. W. F. *Elements of the Philosophy of Right*. Edited by Allen W. Wood, translated by H. B. Nisbet. Cambridge: Cambridge University Press, 1991.

Hegel, G. W. F. *Faith and Knowledge*. Translated by Walter Cerf and H. S. Harris. Albany: State University of New York Press, 1977.

Hegel, G. W. F. *First Philosophy of Spirit (Part III of the System of Speculative Philosophy 1803/4), System of Ethical Life and First Philosophy of Spirit*. Translated by H. S. Harris and T. M. Knox, 187–250. Albany: State University of New York Press, 1979.

Hegel, G. W. F. 'Fragment of a System', translated by Richard Kroner. In *Miscellaneous Writings of G.W.F. Hegel*, edited by Jon Stewart, 151–60. Evanston: Northwestern University Press, 2002.

Hegel, G. W. F. *Grundlinien der Philosophie des Rechts oder Naturrecht und Staatswissenschaft im Grundrisse: Mit Hegels eigenhändigen Notizen und den mündlichen Zusätzen, Werke in zwanzig Bänden, 7*. Edited by Eva Moldenhauer and Karl Markus Michel. Frankfurt am Main: Suhrkamp, 1970.

Hegel, G. W. F. 'Hegel to Creuzer [draft]: End of May 1821'. In *Hegel: The Letters*, translated by Clark Butler and Christiane Seiler, 466–8. Bloomington: Indiana University Press, 1984.

Hegel, G. W. F. *Jenaer Systementwürfe III: Naturphilosophie und Philosophie des Geistes*. Edited by Rolf-Peter Horstmann. Hamburg: Felix Meiner, 1987.

Hegel, G. W. F. *Lectures on the History of Philosophy: Volume Three*. Translated by E. S. Haldane and Frances H. Simson. New York: The Humanities Press, 1955.

Hegel, G. W. F. *Lectures on Logic: Berlin, 1831*. Translated by Clark Butler. Bloomington: Indiana University Press, 2008.

Hegel, G. W. F. *Lectures on the Philosophy of Religion, Volume III: The Consummate Religion*. Edited by Peter C. Hodgson, translated by R. F. Brown, P. C. Hodgson, J. M. Stewart and H. S. Harris. Berkeley: University of California Press, 1985.

Hegel, G. W. F. *Phenomenology of Spirit*. Translated by A. V. Miller. Oxford: Oxford University Press, 1977.

Hegel, G. W. F. *The Philosophy of History*. Translated by J. Sibree. New York: Dover, 1956.

Hegel, G. W. F. *Philosophy of Mind: Part Three of the Encyclopedia of the Philosophical Sciences with the Zusätze*. Translated by William Wallace and A. V. Miller. Oxford: Oxford University Press, 1971.

Hegel, G. W. F. 'The Relationship of Religion to the State'. In *Political Writings*, edited by Laurence Dickey and H. B. Nibset, translated by H. B. Nisbet, 225–33. Cambridge: Cambridge University Press, 1999.

Hegel, G. W. F. *Science of Logic*. Translated by A.V. Miller. London: George Allen & Unwin, 1969.

Hegel, G. W. F. *The Spirit of Christianity and Its Fate*, *Early Theological Writings*. Translated by T. M. Knox, 182–301. Philadelphia: University of Pennsylvania Press, 1975.

Hegel, G. W. F. *System of Ethical Life*, *System of Ethical Life and First Philosophy of Spirit*. Translated by H. S. Harris and T. M. Knox, 97–177. Albany: State University of New York Press, 1979.

Hegel, G. W. F. *Vorlesungen über die Geschichte der Philosophie III, Werke in zwanzig Bänden, 20*. Edited by Eva Moldenhauer and Karl Markus Michel. Frankfurt am Main: Suhrkamp, 1971.

Hegel, G. W. F. *Wissenschaft der Logik I, Werke in zwanzig Bänden, 5*. Edited by Eva Moldenhauer and Karl Markus Michel. Frankfurt am Main: Suhrkamp, 1969.

Hitchens, Christopher. *God Is Not Great. How Religion Poisons Everything*. Toronto: McClelland & Stewart, 2007.

Hoens, Dominiek. 'Is Life but a Pascalian Dream? A Commentary on Lacan's Louvain Lecture'. *Psychoanalytische Perspectieven*, 36, no. 2 (2018): 169–85.

Hoens, Dominiek. 'Toward a New Perversion: Psychoanalysis'. In *Jacques Lacan and the Other Side of Psychoanalysis: Reflections on Seminar XVII*, edited by Justin Clemens and Russell Grigg, 88–103. Durham: Duke University Press, 2006.

Hoens, Dominiek. 'You never know Your Luck: Lacan Reads Pascal'. *Continental Philosophy Review*, special issue: 'Reading *Seminar XIII: The Object of Psychoanalysis*', edited by Thomas Brockelman and Dominiek Hoens, 46, no. 2 (August 2013): 241–9.

Huang, Han-yu. 'The Crime of Indistinction? The Undead and the Politics of Redemption from an Agambenian Perspective'. *Concentric: Literary and Cultural Studies*, March 2012: 171–94.

Izcovich, Luis. 'Du Dieure au Dire'. *Champ lacanien*, 8, no. 1 (2010): 85–91.

Jean, Thierry. 'C'est quoi un névrosé?'. *La célibataire: Revue de psychanalyse—clinique, logique, politique*, no. 13, *Lacan et Pascal* (Autumn 2006): 183–7.

Johnston, Adrian. *Adventures in Transcendental Materialism: Dialogues with Contemporary Thinkers*. Edinburgh: Edinburgh University Press, 2014.

Johnston, Adrian. 'Confession of a Weak Reductionist: Responses to Some Recent Criticisms of My Materialism'. In *Neuroscience and Critique: Exploring the Limits of the Neurological Turn*, edited by Jan De Vos and Ed Pluth, 141–70. New York: Routledge, 2015.

Johnston, Adrian. 'Fear of Science: Transcendental Materialism and Its Discontents'. In *Subject Lessons: Hegel, Lacan, and the Future of Materialism*, edited by Russell Sbriglia and Slavoj Žižek, 125–41. Evanston: Northwestern University Press, 2020.

Johnston, Adrian. 'History'. In *The Marx Through Lacan Vocabulary: A Compass for Libidinal and Political Economies*, edited by Christina Soto van der Plas, Edgar Miguel Juárez-Salazar, Carlos Gómez Camarena and David Pavón-Cuéllar, 85–95. New York: Routledge, 2022.

Johnston, Adrian. 'Hume's Revenge: À Dieu, Meillassoux?'. In *The Speculative Turn: Continental Materialism and Realism*, edited by Levi R. Bryant, Nick Srnicek and Graham Harman, 92–113. Melbourne: Re.press, 2011.

Johnston, Adrian. *Infinite Greed: The Inhuman Selfishness of Capital*. New York: Columbia University Press, 2024.

Johnston, Adrian. *Irrepressible Truth: On Lacan's 'The Freudian Thing'*. Basingstoke: Palgrave Macmillan, 2017.

Johnston, Adrian. 'Jacques Lacan (1901–1981)'. *Stanford Encyclopedia of Philosophy*, 2013, http://plato.stanford.edu/entries/lacan/.

Johnston, Adrian. 'Lacan's Endgame: Philosophy, Science, and Religion in the Final Seminars'. *Crisis and Critique*, special issue: 'Lacan: Psychoanalysis, Philosophy, Politics', edited by Agon Hamza and Frank Ruda, 6, no. 1 (2019): 156–87.

Johnston, Adrian. 'Misfelt Feelings: Unconscious Affect between Psychoanalysis, Neuroscience, and Philosophy'. In Adrian Johnston and Catherine Malabou, *Self and Emotional Life: Philosophy, Psychoanalysis, and Neuroscience*, 73–210. New York: Columbia University Press, 2013.

Johnston, Adrian. 'Naturalism or Anti-Naturalism?'. *Revue Internationale de Philosophie*, 66, no. 261 (3) (2012): 321–46.

Johnston, Adrian. *A New German Idealism: Hegel, Žižek, and Dialectical Materialism*. New York: Columbia University Press, 2018.

Johnston, Adrian. 'Nothing is not always no-one: (a)Voiding Love'. *Filozofski Vestnik*, special issue: 'The Nothing(ness)/Le rien/Das Nichts', edited by Alenka Zupančič, 26, no. 2 (2005): 67–81.

Johnston, Adrian. 'On Deep History and Lacan'. *Journal of European Psychoanalysis*, special issue: 'Lacan and Philosophy: The New Generation', edited by Lorenzo Chiesa, no. 32 (2012): 91–121.

Johnston, Adrian. 'Philosophy and Psychoanalysis'. In *The Routledge Handbook of Psychoanalysis in the Social Sciences and Humanities*, edited by Anthony Elliott and Jeffrey Prager, 278–99. New York: Routledge, 2016.

Johnston, Adrian. *Prolegomena to Any Future Materialism, Volume One: The Outcome of Contemporary French Philosophy*. Evanston: Northwestern University Press, 2013.

Johnston, Adrian. *Prolegomena to Any Future Materialism, Volume Two: A Weak Nature Alone*. Evanston: Northwestern University Press, 2019.
Johnston, Adrian. 'Repeating Engels: Renewing the Cause of the Materialist Wager for the Twenty-First Century'. *Theory @ Buffalo*, special issue: 'animal.machine. sovereign', no. 15 (2011): 141–82.
Johnston, Adrian. *Time Driven: Metapsychology and the Splitting of the Drive*. Evanston: Northwestern University Press, 2005.
Johnston, Adrian. 'The Triumph of Theological Economics: God Goes Underground'. *Philosophy Today*, special issue: 'Marxism and New Materialisms', 64, no. 1 (Winter 2020): 3–50.
Johnston, Adrian. 'The Vicious Circle of the Super-Ego: The Pathological Trap of Guilt and the Beginning of Ethics'. *Psychoanalytic Studies*, 3, no. 3/4 (September–December, 2001): 411–24.
Johnston, Adrian. *Žižek's Ontology: A Transcendental Materialist Theory of Subjectivity*. Evanston: Northwestern University Press, 2008.
Jung, Carl Gustav. 'On the Psychology of the Trickster Figure'. In Paul Radin, *The Trickster. A Study in American Indian Mythology*, 194–211. New York: Schocken Books, 1972.
Juranville, Alain. *Lacan et la philosophie*. Paris: Presses Universitaires de France, 1984.
Kant, Immanuel. *Critique of Practical Reason*, *Practical Philosophy*. Edited by and translated by Mary J. Gregor, 133–271. Cambridge: Cambridge University Press, 1996.
Kant, Immanuel. *Critique of Pure Reason*. Translated by Paul Guyer and Allen Wood. Cambridge: Cambridge University Press, 1998.
Kant, Immanuel. *Groundwork of The Metaphysics of Morals*, *Practical Philosophy*. Edited by and translated by Mary J. Gregor, 41–108. Cambridge: Cambridge University Press, 1996.
Kant, Immanuel. *Kritik der reinen Vernunft, 1, Werkausgabe, Band III*. Edited by Wilhelm Weischedel. Frankfurt am Main: Suhrkamp, 1968.
Kojève, Alexandre. *Atheism*. Translated by Jeff Love. New York: Columbia University Press, 2018.
Kojève, Alexandre. *L'origine chrétienne de la science moderne*. Paris: Hermann, 2021.
Koyré, Alexandre. *Essai sur l'idée de Dieu et les preuves de son existence chez Descartes*. Paris: Leroux, 1922.
Koyré, Alexandre. *From the Closed World to the Infinite Universe*. Baltimore: The John Hopkins University Press, 1968.
Koyré, Alexandre. 'Pascal Savant'. In Alexandre Koyré, *Études d'historie de la pensée scientifique*, 362–89. Paris: Gallimard, 1973.
Krailsheimer, Alban. *Pascal*. New York: Hill and Wang, 1980.
Kristeva, Julia. 'The Forces of Monotheism Confronting the Need to Believe'. http://www.kristeva.fr/the_forces.html.
Küng, Hans. 'Freud and the Problem of God'. *The Wilson Quarterly*, 3, no. 4 (Autumn 1979): 162–71.
La Croix, Richard R. 'Descartes on God's Ability to Do the Logically Impossible'. *Canadian Journal of Philosophy*, 14, no. 3 (1984): 455–75.
Lacan, Jacques. 'Aggressiveness in Psychoanalysis'. In Jacques Lacan, *Écrits: The First Complete Edition in English*, translated by Bruce Fink, 82–101. New York: Norton, 2006.
Lacan, Jacques. 'Alla "Scuola Freudiana"'. In Jacques Lacan, *Lacan in Italia. 1953–1978. En Italie Lacan*, 104–25. Milan: La Salamandra, 1978.

Lacan, Jacques. 'Allocution sur les psychoses de l'enfant'. In Jacques Lacan, *Autres écrits*, edited by Jacques-Alain Miller, 361–71. Paris: Éditions du Seuil, 2001.

Lacan, Jacques. 'Conférence de Bruxelles sur l'éthique de la psychanalyse'. *Psychoanalyse: La Revue de l'École Belge de Psychanalyse*, no. 4 (1986): 163–87.

Lacan, Jacques. 'Conférence de presse du docteur Jacques Lacan au Centre Culturel Français, Rome, le 29 octobre 1974'. *Lettres de l'École freudienne*, no. 16 (1975): 6–26.

Lacan, Jacques. 'Conférences et Entretiens dans des Universités Nord-Américaines: Yale University, 24 novembre 1975, Entretien avec des Étudiants, Réponses à leurs Questions'. *Scilicet*, no. 6/7 (1976): 7–31.

Lacan, Jacques. 'Conferencia de Lacan en Londres'. *Revista Argentina de Psicología* (1975): 137–41.

Lacan, Jacques. 'De James Joyce comme symptôme'. *Le croquant*, no. 28, November 2000.

Lacan, Jacques. 'De la psychanalyse dans ses rapports avec la réalité'. In Jacques Lacan, *Autres écrits*, edited by Jacques-Alain Miller, 351–9. Paris: Éditions du Seuil, 2001.

Lacan, Jacques. 'Des religions et du réel'. *La Cause du Désir*, no. 90 (2015): 9–14.

Lacan, Jacques. 'Discours de clôture des journées sur les psychoses'. *Recherches* (December 1968): 143–50.

Lacan, Jacques. 'Discours de Rome'. In Jacques Lacan, *Autres écrits*, edited by Jacques-Alain Miller, 133–64. Paris: Éditions du Seuil, 2001.

Lacan, Jacques. 'Discourse to Catholics'. In Jacques Lacan, *The Triumph of Religion, Preceded by Discourse to Catholics*, translated by Bruce Fink, 1–52. Cambridge: Polity, 2013.

Lacan, Jacques. 'Du discours psychanalytique'. In Jacques Lacan, *Lacan in Italia. 1953–1978. En Italie Lacan*, 32–55. Milan: La Salamandra, 1978.

Lacan, Jacques. 'Entretien avec Gilles Lapouge'. *Le Figaro Littéraire*, 1 December 1966.

Lacan, Jacques. 'Freud pour toujours: Entretien avec J. Lacan', 21 November 1974. http://ecole-lacanienne.net/wp-content/uploads/2016/04/1974-11-21.pdf.

Lacan, Jacques. 'The Function and Field of Speech and Language in Psychoanalysis'. In Jacques Lacan, *Écrits: The First Complete Edition in English*, translated by Bruce Fink, 197–268. New York: W.W. Norton and Company, 2006.

Lacan, Jacques. 'The Instance of the Letter in the Unconscious, or Reason Since Freud'. In Jacques Lacan, *Écrits: The First Complete Edition in English*, translated by Bruce Fink, 412–41. New York: Norton, 2006.

Lacan, Jacques. 'In Memory of Ernest Jones: On His Theory of Symbolism'. In Jacques Lacan, *Écrits: The First Complete Edition in English*, translated by Bruce Fink, 585–601. New York: W.W. Norton and Company, 2006.

Lacan, Jacques. '*Interview* du 14 décembre 1966 à la *RTB* (III)'. *Quarto*, no. 7 (1982): 7–11.

Lacan, Jacques. 'Introduction aux Noms-du-Père'. In Jacques Lacan, *Des Noms-du-Père*, edited by Jacques-Alain Miller, 65–104. Paris: Éditions du Seuil, 2005.

Lacan, Jacques. 'Introduction théorique aux fonctions de la psychanalyse en criminologie'. In Jacques Lacan, *Écrits*, 125–49. Paris: Éditions du Seuil, 1966.

Lacan, Jacques. 'Introduction to the Names-of-the-Father'. In Jacques Lacan, *On the Names-of-the-Father*, edited by Jacques-Alain Miller, 53–91. Cambridge: Polity, 2013.

Lacan, Jacques. 'Introduction to the Names-of-the-Father Seminar', edited by Jacques-Alain Miller, translated by Jeffrey Mehlman. In *Television/A Challenge to* the *Psychoanalytic Establishment*, edited by Joan Copjec, 81–95. New York: W.W. Norton and Company, 1990.

Lacan, Jacques. *Je parle aux murs*. Paris: Seuil, 2011.

Lacan, Jacques. 'Journées des cartels de l'École freudienne de Paris'. *Lettre de l'École freudienne*, no. 18 (1976): 263–70.

Lacan, Jacques. 'Kant with Sade'. In Jacques Lacan, *Écrits: The First Complete Edition in English*, translated by Bruce Fink, 645–68. New York: W.W. Norton and Company, 2006.

Lacan, Jacques. 'La méprise du sujet supposé savoir'. In Jacques Lacan, *Autres écrits*, 329–39, edited by Jacques-Alain Miller. Paris: Éditions du Seuil, 2001.

Lacan, Jacques. 'La mort est du domaine de la foi'. *Quarto*, no. 3 (1981): 5–20.

Lacan, Jacques. 'La psychanalyse en ce temps'. *La Cause du Désir*, no. 100 (2018): 35–40.

Lacan, Jacques. 'La troisième'. *Lettres de l'École freudienne*, no. 16 (1975): 177–203.

Lacan, Jacques. 'L'étourdit'. In Jacques Lacan, *Autres écrits*, edited by Jacques-Alain Miller, 449–95. Paris: Éditions du Seuil, 2001.

Lacan, Jacques. 'Le phénomène lacanien'. *Les Cahiers Cliniques de Nice*, no. 1 (June 1998): 9–25.

Lacan, Jacques. 'Le Séminaire de Caracas'. In *Almanach de la dissolution*, edited by Nicolas Francion, 79–87. Paris: Navarin, 1986.

Lacan, Jacques. 'Le stade du miroir comme formateur de la fonction du Je telle qu'elle nous est révélée dans l'expérience psychanalytique'. In Jacques Lacan, *Écrits*, 93–100. Paris: Éditions du Seuil, 1966.

Lacan, Jacques. 'Le triomphe de la religion'. In Jacques Lacan, *Le triomphe de la religion, précédé de Discours aux catholiques*, edited by Jacques-Alain Miller, 67–102. Paris: Éditions du Seuil, 2005.

Lacan, Jacques. 'Les complexes familiaux dans la formation de l'individu: Essai d'analyse d'une fonction en psychologie'. In Jacques Lacan, *Autres écrits*, edited by Jacques-Alain Miller, 23–84. Paris: Éditions du Seuil, 2001.

Lacan, Jacques. 'Lettre de Jacques Lacan à Sœur Marie de la Trinité'. *Le Nouvel Âne*, no. 9 (September 2008).

Lacan, Jacques. 'Lettre de Jacques Lacan à son frère Marc François, 1962: 3 janvier 1962'. In *Lacan Redivivus*, edited by Jacques-Alain Miller and Christiane Alberti. *Ornicar?*, hors-série, 248–51. Paris: Navarin, 2021.

Lacan, Jacques. 'Lettre de Jacques Lacan à son frère Marc François, 1953: 5 septembre 1953'. In *Lacan Redivivus*, edited by Jacques-Alain Miller and Christiane Alberti. *Ornicar?*, hors-série, 244–7. Paris: Navarin, 2021.

Lacan, Jacques. 'Lettre de Jacques Lacan à son frère Marc François, 1953: Ce mardi de Pâques 53'. In *Lacan Redivivus*, edited by Jacques-Alain Miller and Christiane Alberti. *Ornicar?*, hors-série, 220–7. Paris: Navarin, 2021.

Lacan, Jacques. 'Massachusetts Institute of Technology, 2 décembre 1975'. *Scilicet*, no. 6/7 (1976): 53–63.

Lacan, Jacques. 'The Mirror Stage as Formative of the I Function as Revealed in Psychoanalytic Experience'. In Jacques Lacan, *Écrits: The First Complete Edition in English*, translated by Bruce Fink, 75–81. New York: W.W. Norton and Company, 2006.

Lacan, Jacques. 'Mis en question du psychanalyste'. In *Lacan Redivivus*, edited by Jacques-Alain Miller and Christiane Alberti. *Ornicar?*, hors-série, 36–102. Paris: Navarin, 2021.

Lacan, Jacques. 'Monsieur A.'. *Ornicar?*, no. 21–22 (Summer 1980): 17–20.

Lacan, Jacques. 'On Freud's "Trieb" and the Psychoanalyst's Desire'. In Jacques Lacan, *Écrits: The First Complete Edition in English*, translated by Bruce Fink, 722–5. New York: W.W. Norton and Company, 2006.

Lacan, Jacques. 'On a Question Prior to Any Possible Treatment of Psychosis'. In Jacques Lacan, *Écrits: The First Complete Edition in English*, translated by Bruce Fink, 445–88. New York: W.W. Norton and Company, 2006.

Lacan, Jacques. 'Overture to this Collection'. In Jacques Lacan, *Écrits: The First Complete Edition in English*, translated by Bruce Fink, 3–5. New York: W.W. Norton and Company, 2006.

Lacan, Jacques. 'Petit discours à l'ORTF'. In Jacques Lacan, *Autres écrits*, edited by Jacques-Alain Miller, 221–6. Paris: Éditions du Seuil, 2001.

Lacan, Jacques. 'Presentation on Psychical Causality'. In Jacques Lacan, *Écrits: The First Complete Edition in English*, translated by Bruce Fink, 123–58. New York: W.W. Norton and Company, 2006.

Lacan, Jacques. 'Problèmes cruciaux pour la psychanalyse. Compte rendu du séminaire 1964–1965'. In Jacques Lacan, *Autres écrits*, edited by Jacques-Alain Miller, 199–202. Paris: Éditions du Seuil, 2001.

Lacan, Jacques. 'Propos sur la causalité psychique'. In Jacques Lacan, *Écrits*, 151–93. Paris: Éditions du Seuil, 1966.

Lacan, Jacques. 'Psychoanalysis and Its Teaching'. In Jacques Lacan, *Écrits: The First Complete Edition in English*, translated by Bruce Fink, 364–83. New York: W.W. Norton and Company, 2006.

Lacan, Jacques. 'Radiophonie'. In Jacques Lacan, *Autres écrits*, edited by Jacques-Alain Miller, 403–47. Paris: Éditions du Seuil, 2001.

Lacan, Jacques. 'Réponse à une question de Catherine Millot'. *L'Âne*, no. 3 (1981): 3–4.

Lacan, Jacques. 'Réponses à des étudiants en philosophie sur l'objet de la psychanalyse'. *Cahiers pour l'Analyse*, no. 3 (1966): 5–13.

Lacan, Jacques. 'Réponses de Jacques Lacan à des questions sur les nœuds et l'inconscient'. *Lettres de l'École*, no. 21 (1977): 471–5.

Lacan, Jacques. 'Science and Truth'. In Jacques Lacan, *Écrits: The First Complete Edition in English*, translated by Bruce Fink, 726–45. New York: W.W. Norton and Company, 2006.

Lacan, Jacques. 'Seminar on "The Purloined Letter"'. In Jacques Lacan, *Écrits: The First Complete Edition in English*, translated by Bruce Fink. 6–48. New York: W.W. Norton and Company, 2006.

Lacan, Jacques. *The Seminar of Jacques Lacan, Book I: Freud's Papers on Technique, 1953–1954*. Edited by Jacques-Alain Miller, translated by John Forrester. New York: W.W. Norton and Company, 1988.

Lacan, Jacques. *The Seminar of Jacques Lacan, Book II: The Ego in Freud's Theory and in the Technique of Psychoanalysis, 1954–1955*. Edited by Jacques-Alain Miller, translated by Sylvana Tomaselli. New York: W.W. Norton and Company, 1988.

Lacan, Jacques. *The Seminar of Jacques Lacan, Book III: The Psychoses, 1955–1956*. Edited by Jacques-Alain Miller, translated by Russell Grigg. New York: W.W. Norton and Company, 1993.

Lacan, Jacques. *Le Séminaire de Jacques Lacan, Livre III: Les psychoses, 1955–1956*. Edited by Jacques-Alain Miller. Paris: Éditions du Seuil, 1981.

Lacan, Jacques. *The Seminar of Jacques Lacan, Book IV: The Object Relation, 1956–1957*. Edited by Jacques-Alain Miller, translated by A. R. Price. Cambridge: Polity, 2020.

Lacan, Jacques. *Le Séminaire de Jacques Lacan, Livre IV: La relation d'objet, 1956–1957*. Edited by Jacques-Alain Miller. Paris: Éditions du Seuil, 1994.

Lacan, Jacques. *The Seminar of Jacques Lacan, Book V: The Formations of the Unconscious, 1957–1958*. Edited by Jacques-Alain Miller, translated by Russell Grigg. Cambridge: Polity, 2017.

Lacan, Jacques. *The Seminar of Jacques Lacan, Book VI: Desire and Its Interpretation, 1958–1959*. Edited by Jacques-Alain Miller, translated by Bruce Fink. Cambridge: Polity, 2019.

Lacan, Jacques. *The Seminar of Jacques Lacan, Book VII: The Ethics of Psychoanalysis, 1959–1960*. Edited by Jacques-Alain Miller, translated by Dennis Porter. New York: W.W. Norton and Company, 1992.

Lacan, Jacques. *Le Séminaire de Jacques Lacan, Livre VII: L'éthique de la psychanalyse, 1959–1960*. Edited by Jacques-Alain Miller. Paris: Éditions du Seuil, 1986.

Lacan, Jacques. *The Seminar of Jacques Lacan, Book VIII: Transference, 1960–1961*. Edited by Jacques-Alain Miller, translated by Bruce Fink. Cambridge: Polity, 2015.

Lacan, Jacques. *Le Séminaire de Jacques Lacan, Livre IX: L'identification, 1961–1962* (unpublished typescript).

Lacan, Jacques. *The Seminar of Jacques Lacan, Book X: Anxiety, 1962–1963*. Edited by Jacques-Alain Miller, translated by A. R. Price. Cambridge: Polity, 2014.

Lacan, Jacques. *Le Séminaire de Jacques Lacan, Livre X: L'angoisse, 1962–1963*. Edited by Jacques-Alain Miller. Paris: Éditions du Seuil, 2004.

Lacan, Jacques. *The Seminar of Jacques Lacan, Book XI: The Four Fundamental Concepts of Psychoanalysis, 1964*. Edited by Jacques-Alain Miller, translated by Alan Sheridan. New York: W.W. Norton and Company, 1977.

Lacan, Jacques. *Le Séminaire de Jacques Lacan, Livre XI: Le quatre concepts fondamentaux de la psychanalyse, 1964*. Edited by Jacques-Alain Miller. Paris: Éditions du Seuil, 1973.

Lacan, Jacques. *Le Séminaire de Jacques Lacan, Livre XII: Problèmes cruciaux pour la psychanalyse, 1964–1965* (unpublished typescript).

Lacan, Jacques. *Le Séminaire de Jacques Lacan, Livre XIII: L'objet de la psychanalyse, 1965–1966* (unpublished typescript).

Lacan, Jacques. *Le Séminaire de Jacques Lacan, Livre XIV: La logique du fantasme, 1966–1967* (unpublished typescript).

Lacan, Jacques. *Le Séminaire de Jacques Lacan, Livre XV: L'acte psychanalytique, 1967–1968* (unpublished transcript).

Lacan, Jacques. *Le Séminaire de Jacques Lacan, Livre XVI: D'un Autre à l'autre, 1968–1969*. Edited by Jacques-Alain Miller. Paris: Éditions du Seuil, 2006.

Lacan, Jacques. *The Seminar of Jacques Lacan, Book XVII: The Other Side of Psychoanalysis, 1969–1970*. Edited by Jacques-Alain Miller, translated by Russell Grigg. New York: W.W. Norton and Company, 2007.

Lacan, Jacques. *Le Séminaire de Jacques Lacan, Livre XVII: L'envers de la psychanalyse, 1969–1970*. Edited by Jacques-Alain Miller. Paris: Éditions du Seuil, 1991.

Lacan, Jacques. *Le Séminaire de Jacques Lacan, Livre XVIII: D'un discours qui ne serait pas du semblant, 1971*. Edited by Jacques-Alain Miller. Paris: Éditions du Seuil, 2006.

Lacan, Jacques. *The Seminar of Jacques Lacan, Book XIX: . . . or Worse, 1971–1972*. Edited by Jacques-Alain Miller, translated by A. R. Price. Cambridge: Polity, 2018.

Lacan, Jacques. *Le Séminaire de Jacques Lacan, Livre XIX: . . . ou pire, 1971–1972*. Edited by Jacques-Alain Miller. Paris: Éditions du Seuil, 2011.

Lacan, Jacques. *The Seminar of Jacques Lacan, Book XX: Encore, 1972–1973*. Edited by Jacques-Alain Miller, translated by Bruce Fink. New York: W.W. Norton and Company, 1998.
Lacan, Jacques. *Le Séminaire de Jacques Lacan, Livre XX: Encore, 1972–1973*. Edited by Jacques-Alain Miller. Paris: Éditions du Seuil, 1975.
Lacan, Jacques. *Le Séminaire de Jacques Lacan, Livre XXI: Les non-dupes errent, 1973–1974* (unpublished typescript).
Lacan, Jacques. *Le Séminaire de Jacques Lacan, Livre XXII: R.S.I., 1974–1975* (unpublished typescript).
Lacan, Jacques. *The Seminar of Jacques Lacan, Book XXIII: The Sinthome, 1975–1976*. Edited by Jacques-Alain Miller, translated by A. R. Price. Cambridge: Polity, 2016.
Lacan, Jacques. *Le Séminaire de Jacques Lacan, Livre XXIII: Le sinthome, 1975–1976*. Edited by Jacques-Alain Miller. Paris: Éditions du Seuil, 2005.
Lacan, Jacques. *Le Séminaire de Jacques Lacan, Livre XXIV: L'insu que sait de l'une-bévue s'aile à mourre, 1976–1977* (unpublished typescript).
Lacan, Jacques. *Le Séminaire de Jacques Lacan, Livre XXV: Le moment de conclure, 1977–1978* (unpublished typescript).
Lacan, Jacques. *Le Séminaire de Jacques Lacan, Livre XXVII: Dissolution, 1979–1980* (unpublished transcript).
Lacan, Jacques. 'The Signification of the Phallus'. In Jacques Lacan, *Écrits: The First Complete Edition in English*, translated by Bruce Fink, 575–84. New York: W.W. Norton and Company, 2006.
Lacan, Jacques. 'The Subversion of the Subject and the Dialectic of Desire in the Freudian Unconscious'. In Jacques Lacan, *Écrits: The First Complete Edition in English*, translated by Bruce Fink, 671–702. New York: W.W. Norton and Company, 2006.
Lacan, Jacques. *Télévision*. Paris: Éditions du Seuil, 1974.
Lacan, Jacques. 'Television'. In *Television/A Challenge to the Psychoanalytic Establishment*, edited by Joan Copjec, translated by Denis Hollier, Rosalind Krauss and Annette Michelson, 1–46. New York: W.W. Norton and Company, 1990.
Lacan, Jacques. 'A Theoretical Introduction to the Functions of Psychoanalysis in Criminology'. In Jacques Lacan, *Écrits: The First Complete Edition in English*, translated by Bruce Fink, 102–22. New York: W.W. Norton and Company, 2006.
Lacan, Jacques. 'The Triumph of Religion'. In Jacques Lacan, *The Triumph of Religion, Preceded by Discourse to Catholics*, translated by Bruce Fink, 53–85. Cambridge: Polity, 2013.
Lacan, Jacques. 'Un homme et une femme'. *Bulletin de l'Association freudienne*, no. 54 (September 1993): 13–21.
Lacan, Jacques. 'The Youth of Gide, or the Letter and Desire'. In Jacques Lacan, *Écrits: The First Complete Edition in English*, translated by Bruce Fink, 623–44. New York: W.W. Norton and Company, 2006.
Lacan, Jacques and Emilia Granzotto. 'Freud per sempre. Intervista con Jacques Lacan'. *Panorama*, 21 November 1974.
Lacan, Marc-François. 'Lettre de Marc François à son frère Jacques Lacan, 1953: 9 avril 1953'. In *Lacan Redivivus*, edited by Jacques-Alain Miller and Christiane Alberti, *Ornicar?*, hors-série, 228–43. Paris: Navarin, 2021.
Lacan, Marc-François. 'Lettre de Marc-François Lacan à Jacques Sédat: 3 décembre 1982'. In Marc-François Lacan, *Dieu n'est pas un assureur*, 193–200. Paris: Albin Michel, 2010.

Lacoue-Labarthe, Philippe and Jean-Luc Nancy. *The Title of the Letter: A Reading of Lacan*. Translated by François Raffoul and David Pettigrew. Albany: SUNY Press, 1992.

Laplanche, Jean. *Hölderlin et la question du père*. Paris: Presses Universitaires de France, 1961.

Leavy, Stanley A. 'The Image and the Word: Further Reflections on Jacques Lacan'. In *Interpreting Lacan*, edited by Joseph H. Smith and William Kerrigan, 3–20. New Haven: Yale University Press, 1983.

Lee, Jonathan Scott. *Jacques Lacan*. Amherst: University of Massachusetts Press, 1990.

Lemaire, Anika. *Jacques Lacan*. Translated by David Macey. New York: Routledge, 1977.

Leupin, Alexandre. *Lacan Today. Psychoanalysis, Science, Religion*. New York: Other Press, 2004.

Linden, David J. *The Accidental Mind*. Cambridge, MA: Harvard University Press, 2007.

Livingston, Paul. 'Politics, Subjectivity, and Cosmological Antinomy'. *Crisis and Critique*, 1, no. 2 (2014): 23–50.

Mannoni, Octave. *Clefs pour l'Imaginaire ou l'Autre Scène*. Paris: Seuil, 1969.

Marini, Marcelle. *Jacques Lacan: The French Context*. Translated by Anne Tomiche. New Brunswick: Rutgers University Press, 1992.

Marx, Karl. *Capital: A Critique of Political Economy, Volume I*. Translated by Ben Fowkes. New York: Penguin, 1976.

Marx, Karl. *Capital: A Critique of Political Economy, Volume II*. Translated by David Fernbach. New York: Penguin, 1978.

Marx, Karl. *Capital: A Critique of Political Economy, Volume III*. Translated by David Fernbach. New York: Penguin, 1981.

Marx, Karl. *The Civil War in France*, The First International and After: Political Writings, Volume 3. Edited by David Fernbach, 187–236. Harmondsworth: Penguin, 1974.

Marx, Karl. 'A Contribution to the Critique of Hegel's Philosophy of Right. Introduction'. In *Early Writings*, translated by Rodney Livingstone and Gregor Benton, 243–57. New York: Penguin, 1992.

Marx, Karl. *A Contribution to the Critique of Political Economy*. Edited by Maurice Dobb, translated by S. W. Ryazanskaya. New York: International, 1970.

Marx, Karl. *Critique of Hegel's Doctrine of the State*, Early Writings. Translated by Rodney Livingstone and Gregor Benton, 57–198. New York: Penguin, 1992.

Marx, Karl. *The Eighteenth Brumaire of Louis Bonaparte*, translated by Ben Fowkes. In *Surveys from Exile: Political Writings, Volume 2*, edited by David Fernbach, 143–249. Harmondsworth: Penguin, 1973.

Marx, Karl. *Grundrisse: Foundations of the Critique of Political Economy (Rough Draft)*. Translated by Martin Nicolaus. New York: Penguin, 1973.

Marx, Karl. 'Thesen über Feuerbach'. In Karl Marx and Friedrich Engels, *Die deutsche Ideologie*, 593–5. Berlin: Dietz, 1953.

Marx, Karl. 'Theses on Feuerbach'. In Karl Marx and Friedrich Engels, *The German Ideology*, 569–71. Amherst: Prometheus Books, 1998.

Marx, Karl and Friedrich Engels. *The Communist Manifesto*, translated by Samuel Moore. In *Karl Marx: Selected Writings*, edited by David McLellan, 221–47. Oxford: Oxford University Press, 1977.

Marx, Karl and Friedrich Engels. 'Manifest der kommunistischen Partei', 1848. https://www.marxists.org/deutsch/archiv/marx-engels/1848/manifest/index.htm.

Meillassoux, Quentin. *After Finitude*. Translated by Ray Brassier. London: Continuum, 2008.
Meillassoux, Quentin. 'Appendix: Excerpts from *L'Inexistence divine*'. In Graham Harman, *Quentin Meillassoux. Philosophy on the Making*, 175–238. Edinburgh: Edinburgh University Press, 2011.
Meillassoux, Quentin. *Métaphysique et fiction des mondes hors-science*. Paris: Aux forges de Vulcain, 2013.
Meillassoux, Quentin. 'Nothingness against the Death of God – Mallarmé's Poetics after 1866'. In *The Experience of Atheism*, edited by Robyn Horner and Claude Romano, 43–60. London: Bloomsbury, 2021.
Meillassoux, Quentin. 'Spectral Dilemma'. *Collapse*, 4 (2008): 261–75.
Meng, Heinrich and Ernst L. Freud, eds. *Psychoanalysis and Faith. The Letters of Sigmund Freud & Oskar Pfister*. New York: Basic Books, 1963.
Millar, Isabel. *The Psychoanalysis of Artificial Intelligence*. London: Palgrave, 2021.
Miller, Jacques-Alain, ed. *L'Autre méchant: Six cas cliniques commentés*. Paris: Navarin, 2010.
Miller, Jacques-Alain. 'Préface'. In *Joyce avec Lacan*, edited by Jacques Aubert, 10–12. Paris: Navarin, 1987.
Miller, Jacques-Alain. 'Religion, Psychoanalysis', translated by Barbara P. Fulks. *Lacanian Ink*, no. 23 (Spring 2004): 8–39.
Millot, Catherine. *Life with Lacan*. Translated by Andrew Brown. Cambridge: Polity, 2018.
Milner, Jean-Claude. *A Search for Clarity*. Translated by Ed Pluth. Evanston: Northwestern University Press, 2021.
Mottron, Laurent. 'Recouvrements et incompatibilités entre René Thom et Jacques Lacan'. *Littoral*, no. 18 (January 1986): 135–55.
Nassif, Jacques. 'Pour une logique du fantasme'. *Scilicet*, no. 2/3 (1970): 223–73.
Nietzsche, Friedrich. 'The Anti-Christ: A Curse on Christianity'. In Friedrich Nietzsche, *The Anti-Christ, Ecce Homo, Twilight of Idols and Other Writings*, translated by Judith Norman, 1–67. Cambridge: Cambridge University Press, 2005.
Nietzsche, Friedrich. 'Attempt at a Self-Criticism'. In Friedrich Nietzsche, *The Birth of Tragedy and The Case of Wagner*, translated by Walter Kaufmann, 17–27. New York: Vintage, 1967.
Nietzsche, Friedrich. *Beyond Good and Evil: Prelude to a Philosophy of the Future*. Translated by Walter Kaufmann. New York: Vintage, 1989.
Nietzsche, Friedrich. *Twilight of the Idols, or How to Philosophize with a Hammer*, *Twilight of the Idols/The Anti-Christ*. Translated by R. J. Hollingdale, 29–122. New York: Penguin, 1990.
Padusniak, Chase. 'Jacques Lacan's Benedict Option'. *Church Life Journal: A Journal of the McGrath Institute for Church Life*, 21 March 2022. https://churchlifejournal.nd.edu/articles/jacques-lacans-benedict-option/.
Pascal, Blaise. 'Comparaison des chrétiens des premiers temps avec ceux d'aujourd'hui'. In *Œuvres complètes*, edited by Jacques Chevalier, 555–9. Paris: Gallimard, 1954.
Pascal, Blaise. 'Entretien de M. Pascal et de M. De Sacy sur la lecture d'Épictète et de Montaigne'. In *De l'esprit géométrique, Entretien avec M. De Sacy, Écrits sur la grâce, et autres textes*, edited by André Clair, 97–114. Paris: Flammarion, 1985.
Pascal, Blaise. *Discours sur les passions de l'amour, Œuvres complètes*. Edited by Jacques Chevalier, 536–47. Paris: Gallimard, 1954.
Pascal, Blaise. *Écrits sur la grâce, Œuvres complètes*. Edited by Jacques Chevalier, 947–1044. Paris: Gallimard, 1954.

Pascal, Blaise. 'Mémorial'. In *Œuvres complètes*, edited by Jacques Chevalier, 553–4. Paris: Gallimard, 1954.
Pascal, Blaise. *Pensées*. Edited by Léon Brunschvicg. Paris: Flammarion, 1976.
Pascal, Blaise. *Pensées*. Translated by A. J. Krailsheimer. New York: Penguin, 1966.
Pascal, Blaise. *The Provincial Letters*. Translated by A. J. Krailsheimer. New York: Penguin, 1967.
Pascal, Blaise. 'Sur la casuistique et la probabilité'. In *Œuvres complètes*, edited by Jacques Chevalier, 1061–3. Paris: Gallimard, 1954.
Paul, 1 Corinthians.
Pelletier, Étienne. 'Lacan, le *cogito* et le sujet de l'inconscient'. https://www.academia.edu/21698566/Lacan_le_cogito_et_le_sujet_de_linconscient.
Pellion, Frédéric. *Ce qui Lacan doit à Descartes*. Paris: Éditions du Champ lacanien, 2014.
Pfister, Oskar. 'The Illusion of a Future'. *International Journal of Psychoanalysis*, 74, no. 3: (1993): 557–79.
Popow, Nikolai. 'To Dialectisize or Non Dialectisize'. https://www.academia.edu/66727893/To_Dialectisize_or_Non_Dialectisize.
Radin, Paul. 'Prefatory Note'. In Paul Radin, *The Trickster. A Study in American Indian Mythology*, xxiii–xxv. New York: Schocken Books, 1972.
Regnault, François. *Dieu est inconscient: Études lacaniennes autour de saint Thomas d'Aquin*. Paris: Navarin, 1985.
Reinhard, Kenneth. 'There Is Something of One (God). Lacan and Political Theology'. In *Theology After Lacan*, edited by Creston Davis, Marcus Pound and Clayton Crockett, 150–65. Eugene: Cascade Books, 2014.
Richardson, William J. '"Like Straw": Religion and Psychoanalysis'. *Budhi. A Journal of Ideas and Culture*, 2, no. 1 (1998): 51–64.
Roazen, Paul. 'Lacan's First Disciple'. *Journal of Religion and Health*, 35, no. 4 (Winter 1996): 321–36.
Roudinesco, Élisabeth. *Jacques Lacan: Outline of a Life, History of a System of Thought*. Translated by Barbara Bray. New York: Columbia University Press, 1997.
Roudinesco, Élisabeth. *Jacques Lacan & Co.: A History of Psychoanalysis in France, 1925–1985*. Translated by Jeffrey Mehlman. Chicago: The University of Chicago Press, 1990.
Rovelli, Carlo. *Reality Is Not What It Seems. The Journey to Quantum Gravity*. Translated by Erica Segre and Simon Carnell. New York: Penguin, 2016.
Ruti, Mari. *The Singularity of Being. Lacan and the Immortal Within*. New York: Fordham University Press, 2021.
Safouan, Moustapha. *Lacaniana: Les séminaires de Jacques Lacan, 1953–1963*. Paris: Librairie Arthème Fayard, 2001.
Sartre, Jean-Paul. *Being and Nothingness: A Phenomenological Essay on Ontology*. Translated by Hazel E. Barnes. New York: Citadel Press, 2001.
Sartre, Jean-Paul. *Existentialism and Humanism*. Translated by Philip Mairet. London: Methuen, 1948.
Sbriglia, Russell and Slavoj Žižek. 'Introduction: Subject Matters'. In *Subject Lessons. Hegel, Lacan, and the Future of Materialism*, edited by Russel Sbriglia and Slavoj Žižek, 3–28. Evanston: Northwestern University Press, 2020.
Schelling, F. W. J. *The Ages of the World: Third Version (c. 1815)*. Translated by Jason M. Wirth. Albany: State University of New York Press, 2000.
Schelling, F. W. J. *Bruno, or, On the Natural and the Divine Principle of Things*. Translated by Michael G. Vater. Albany: State University of New York Press, 1984.

Schelling, F. W. J. 'On Construction in Philosophy', translated by Andrew A. Davis and Alexi I. Kukuljevic. *Epoché*, no. 12 (2008): 260–88.

Schelling, F. W. J. *Philosophical Investigations into the Essence of Human Freedom*. Translated by Jeff Love and Johannes Schmidt. Albany: State University of New York Press, 2006.

Schelling, F. W. J. *System der Weltalter: Münchener Vorlesung 1927/28 in einer Nachschrift von Ernst von Lasaulx*. Edited by Siegbert Peetz. Frankfurt am Main: Klostermann, 1990.

Schmitt, Christiane. 'Marie de la Trinité et Jacques Lacan. Une relation à l'épreuve de la foi'. http://www.mariedelatrinite.org/IMG/pdf/2014_marie_de_la_trinite_et_jacques_lacan_christiane_schmitt-2.pdf.

Sédat, Jacques. 'Deux hommes à la recherche de la vérité: À propos d'une lettre de Marc-François Lacan'. *Figures de la psychanalyse*, no. 34 (2017): 253–67.

Sédat, Jacques. 'Préface'. In Marc-François Lacan, *Dieu n'est pas un assureur*, 7–25. Paris: Albin Michel, 2010.

Shepherdson, Charles. 'From *Oedipus Rex* to *Totem and Taboo*: Lacan's Revision of the Paternal Metaphor'. In Charles Shepherdson, *Vital Signs: Nature, Culture, Psychoanalysis*, 115–51. New York: Routledge, 2000.

Souriau, Étienne. *L'ombre de Dieu*. Paris: Presses Universitaires de France, 1955.

Sous, Jean-Louis. *Pas très catholique, Lacan?*. Paris: EPEL, 2015.

Spinoza, Baruch. 'Ethics'. In Baruch Spinoza, *Complete Works*, edited by Michael L. Morgan, translated by Samuel Shirley, 213–382. Indianapolis: Hackett, 2002.

Spinoza, Baruch. 'Letter 50: Spinoza to Jelles, 2 June 1674'. In Spinoza, *Complete Works*, edited by Michael L. Morgan, translated by Samuel Shirley, 891–2. Indianapolis: Hackett, 2002.

Tazi, Nadia. 'Jannah'. *S. Journal of the Jan van Eyck Circle for Lacanian Ideology Critique*, 2 (2009): 28–43.

Thom, René. 'Entretien sur les catastrophes, le langage et la métaphysique extrême'. *Ornicar?*, 16 (January 1978): 73–110.

Thom, René. *Paraboles et catastrophes. Entretiens sur les mathématiques, la science et la philosophie*. Paris: Flammarion, 1983.

Vassal, Matthieu. 'Deux frères: Témoignage du père Matthieu Vassal, archiviste et moine bénédiction de Ganagobie'. In Marc-François Lacan, *Dieu n'est pas un assureur*, 137–45. Paris: Albin Michel, 2010.

Vassallo, Sara. *Le désir et la grâce: Saint Augustin, Lacan, Pascal*. Paris: EPEL, 2020.

Ver Eecke, Wilfried. 'The Usefulness of the Theory of De Waelhens/Lacan as an Effective Approach to Schizophrenia, after the Decade of the Brain'. In Alphonse De Waelhens and Wilfried Ver Eecke, *Phenomenology and Lacan on Schizophrenia, after the Decade of the Brain*, 37–69. Leuven: Leuven University Press, 2001.

Verhaeghe, Paul. *Does the Woman Exist? From Freud's Hysteric to Lacan's Feminine*. Translated by Marc du Ry. New York: Other Press, 1997.

Verhaeghe, Paul. 'Enjoyment and Impossibility: Lacan's Revision of the Oedipus Complex'. In *Jacques Lacan and the Other Side of Psychoanalysis: Reflections on Seminar XVII*, edited by Justin Clemens and Russell Grigg, 29–49. Durham: Duke University Press, 2006.

Žižek, Slavoj. 'The Abyss of Freedom'. In Slavoj Žižek and F. W. J. Schelling, *The Abyss of Freedom/Ages of the World*, 1–104. Ann Arbor: University of Michigan Press, 1997.

Žižek, Slavoj. *Did Somebody Say Totalitarianism? Five Interventions in the (Mis)use of a Notion*. London: Verso, 2001.

Žižek, Slavoj. 'The Fear of Four Words: A Modest Plea for the Hegelian Reading of Christianity'. In *The Monstrosity of Christ: Paradox or Dialectic?*, edited by Creston Davis, 24–109. Cambridge, MA: MIT Press, 2009.

Žižek, Slavoj. 'Four Discourses, Four Subjects'. In *Cogito and the Unconscious*, edited by Slavoj Žižek, 74–113. Durham: Duke University Press, 1998.

Žižek, Slavoj. *Incontinence of the Void*. Cambridge, MA: MIT Press, 2017.

Žižek, Slavoj. *Iraq: The Borrowed Kettle*. London: Verso, 2004.

Žižek, Slavoj. *Less Than Nothing: Hegel and the Shadow of Dialectical Materialism*. London: Verso, 2012.

Žižek, Slavoj. *The Parallax View*. Cambridge, MA: MIT Press, 2006.

Žižek, Slavoj. 'Preface to the New Edition'. In Slavoj Žižek, *The Sublime Object of Ideology*, vii–xxii. London: Verso, 2008.

Žižek, Slavoj. *The Puppet and the Dwarf: The Perverse Core of Christianity*. Cambridge, MA: MIT Press, 2003.

Žižek, Slavoj. *The Ticklish Subject: The Absent Centre of Political Ontology*. London: Verso, 1999.

Žižek, Slavoj. 'The Undergrowth of Enjoyment: How Popular Culture Can Serve as an Introduction to Lacan'. In *The Žižek Reader*, edited by Elizabeth Wright and Edmond Wright, 11–36. Oxford: Blackwell, 1999.

Index

abjection   135–6, 141–2, 151–3, 205
Abrahamic God   57, 63–4, 143–7, 255 n.239, 256 n.246, 256 n.255
absoluteness, absolutism and   5, 128, 205–8, 210–11
   knowledge and   24–5, 28, 53, 153, 184
   negation and   49–56
abstraction   33–4, 123
achoses ('*no-things*')   153–7
acquired knowledge   71, 176
addiction   59
Adorno, Theodor   12
After Finitude (Meillassoux)   2, 4
afterlife, afterlives and   66–7, 82–3, 92, 119, 209–10
agency   72, 87, 90–1, 125
agnosticism   80, 208–9, 212–13, 268 n.438
   atheist   7, 11–12, 17, 123, 159–87, 197–8, 201–2, 211
   critical-epistemological   200–1, 204
   of Freud   111–24, 250 n.148
   of Lacan, J.   193–4, 250 n.148, 265 n.383
   metaphysical   199
   strong   11–12, 17, 132, 137, 166–8, 183–4, 186
   theoretical   114
   the unconscious and   210
   weak   12, 17, 125, 127, 166–7, 184, 250 n.148
alienation   98, 200
Allah   258 n.306

the Almighty (*Tout-Puissant*)   25–6, 146
alter-ego   40, 72, 81, 122
ambivalence   15–16, 51, 97, 116–17, 119, 130, 153
'Analysis Terminable and Interminable' (Freud)   192, 214
analytic atheism   26–7, 31, 36, 39
animism   14–16, 135, 156
animus (evil genius)   15, 158
Anselm (of Canterbury)   96, 139–40
anthropocentrism   6, 8, 10
anthropogenesis   10, 134–5, 190
anthropology   30–1, 35–6, 41, 97–8
anthropomorphism   35–6, 128, 131, 138, 156, 203
anti-Christianity   51–3, 101
anti-climax   59
anti-religion, anti-religiosity and   126–7, 131–2, 166, 198, 260 n.326
   of Freud   12–13, 22, 124
   of Meillassoux   4
anti-social instincts   116–18, 121
antitheism   113
anti-totalitarianism   187
anti-zombie, 19
anxiety   62–7, 74, 76–7, 84–5, 119, 131, 144
Aquinas, Thomas   253 n.218, 258 n.306
Aristotle   67–8, 112, 135, 143, 209
ascetic atheism   137, 162–6
'as if'   11, 18, 65, 90, 113–15, 183, 186
Askofaré, Sidi   26
atheism   6, 107, 199–210, 261 n.351, 268 n.438

agnostic 7, 11–12, 17, 123,
    159–87, 197–8, 201–2, 211
analytic 26–7, 31, 36, 39
ascetic 137, 162–6
Christian 1–4, 36–7, 49–56, 134,
    150, 207
conscious 29–30, 191
conservative 114–16, 120, 122
drowsy 28, 31
Feuerbach on 35–6, 41
Freud and 8, 12, 21–2, 29, 41,
    123, 127–8, 149, 247 n.82
God of 123–4, 133, 158, 184
of Hegel 33–5
Lacan, J., and 3, 12, 21–8, 52,
    56–7, 94, 101–10, 133–4,
    190–2, 211, 249 n.120
Meillassoux on 2–3
messianic 13, 56
naturalistic 13, 28
non-agnostic 12, 212, 214
practical 17, 166
scientific 138, 193
strong 17, 159–83, 186
true 13, 24–6, 28–30, 91
true religion and 132–5
weak 4, 12, 17, 123, 125, 132,
    136–8, 140, 161, 164–6,
    179–80, 183–4
attitudinal indifference 202–3
Aufhebung (sublation) 36, 50, 109,
    120
automatons 138, 260 n.335

bacteria 10, 129, 159
bad infinity (*schlechte
    Unendlichkeit*) 212–13
Badiou, Alain 19, 252 n.192
Balmès, François 26, 40–2, 145–7
barred big Other 36, 50
'barred' God 7, 11, 19. See also self-
    deceiving God
barred Other 27–8, 54–5
Bauer, Bruno 33
Beirnaert, Louis 103
belief 1–3, 18, 37, 137, 170
    atheism and 24
    disbelief and 13, 51, 133
    knowledge and 125–6

materialism and 29
in non-Christian Gods 80
benevolent God 120
besoin-demande-désir (need-demand-
    desire) 58–9
Beyond the Pleasure Principle
    (Freud) 77, 128
the Bible 111
    Old Testament God 64, 69, 98
big Other 31, 48, 80, 91, 192–3, 208
    barred 36, 50
    unbarred 24, 27–8, 39, 56
binary systems 73–4, 260 n.321
biology 70, 104, 267 n.419
birth 80–2, 134–5
Blanchot, Maurice 209
blind faith 121
Bloch, Ernst 29, 49
Blondin, Marie-Louise (Malou) 101–2,
    106
Bonaventura (Saint) 209
boredom 59
The Brothers Karamazov
    (Dostoyevsky) 51–2
Buddhism 18, 263 n.365

cannibalism 118, 122
capitalism 18, 94–100, 156, 186–7
Caravaggio 64
Cartesian doubt 106, 179, 261 n.341
castration 44–6, 48, 53, 78, 128,
    263 n.365
Catholicism 6, 21–3, 95, 100–10,
    134, 253 n.218
Causse, Jean-Daniel 22, 26, 40
Certeau, Michel de 257 n.267
chemistry 112
Chesterton, G. K. 29, 49–50, 54, 210
Chiesa, Lorenzo 40, 189–90, 197–8,
    201–3, 211–13
La chose freudienne 69–70, 81, 92,
    98
Christianity 14–15, 121, 202,
    213, 253 n.218, 258 n.306,
    259 n.311. See also Jesus Christ
    atheist 1–4, 36–7, 49–56, 134,
        150, 207
    capitalism and 94–100
    Chesterton on 49–50

divinity and 89–90, 135–6
Feuerbach on 35–6, 97
grace in 83
Hegel on 34–5
Holy Spirit and 36–7, 53, 98, 201
humility and 205–6
Kant and 89–90
Lacan, J., on 21–2, 36, 40–1, 53–7, 61–2, 83–4, 98, 134–6, 151–5, 160–1, 252 n.182
Pascal and 57–8, 61, 65–6, 68–9, 79–80, 83–4, 88
paternalism and 47–8, 201–2
science and 153–7
theology and 135–6, 143
as a true religion 134–5
truth and 35–6, 40–1, 134
Civilisation and Its Discontents (Freud) 15
civilization 123, 125, 127
religion and 14, 113, 115–19, 121–2, 124, 128
Civil War in France (Marx) 191
clavis universalis (Leibnizian concept) 153
Clero, Jean-Pierre 61
cogito (Cartesian concept) 172–3, 268 n.438, 269 n.460, 271 n.471
cogito ergo sum (Cartesian concept) 153, 172–3, 271 n.471
communism 95, 103–4, 107, 191
Communist Manifesto (Marx, Engels) 95
comrades in unbelief (*Unglaubensgenossen*) 122–4
conditional tense 25–6
'Confession of a Weak Reductionist' (Johnston) 216 n.38
conscious atheism 29–30, 191
consciousness 16, 28, 138, 163
conservative atheism 114–16, 120, 122
Covid-19 pandemic 190–1
creation *ex nihilo* 29, 134
creationism 265 n.392
'crisis of presence' 160, 262 n.361

critical-epistemological agnosticism, Kantian 200–1, 204
Critique of Practical Reason (Kant) 212
Critique of Pure Reason (Kant) 204
crocodile imagery 75–6
crucifixion 48–9, 91, 135, 151
cybernetics 57

Dark God (*le Dieu obscur*) 69
Darwinism 28
death 67, 92–3, 209–10. *See also* 'God is dead'
of Christ 37, 48–9, 53, 134–6
of God 19, 36, 40, 52, 125, 184, 218 n.71
Hegel on 94
helplessness and 119
instinct 127
of Lacan, J. 105
living 82
mortality and 5, 14–15, 119, 209–10, 213–14
paternal 45–7, 52, 78, 125, 128–9
resurrection and 3, 135–6
second 81
deceiving God 265 n.383, 267 n.427, 268 n.447, 269 n.456, 270 n.464, 272 n.491. *See also* self-deceiving God
Christianity and 158
Descartes on 16–18, 171–83
Lacan on 139, 161, 165, 171–2, 179–80
Meillassoux on 4
defensive risk 65–6
Deleuze, Gilles 6, 93, 216 n.27
delusions 111–13, 121
demons 14–15, 172, 178
denaturalized subject 9, 203
Derrida, Jacques 2, 6, 219 n.76
Descartes, René 220 n.100, 268 n.447, 269 nn.455–56
cogito concept by 172–3, 268 n.438, 269 n.460, 271 n.471
cogito ergo sum concept by 153, 172–3, 271 n.471
on the divine 57

on divinity   57
doubt and   106, 179, 261 n.341
on eternal truths   17–18, 270 n.464, 271 n.478
on existence of God   30, 96, 175–83
Freud on   15
'I think, therefore I am' concept by   173, 268 n.438, 268 n.441, 271 n.471
on knowledge   14, 220 n.100, 270 n.464
mathematics and   62, 96
Pascal on   30, 96
on self-deceiving God   16–18, 171–83
on will of God   175–8, 180, 270 n.464, 271 n.474
desire   45, 56, 58–60, 67–71, 86–94, 107
of desire   27
of God   83–5, 146
jouissance and   76–8
maternal   73–6, 78–9, 84–5, 98
of the Other   75, 82–4, 144, 255
sacrificial practices and   64–5, 93
science and   130
sexuality and   126
untruth and   51–2
determinate negation   49–56
Deus ex machina (God extracted from the machine)   138, 253 n.194
Deus sive natura (Spinozan concept)   18, 205–6
the Devil   15, 249 n.120
Diana (goddess)   69
Le Dieu caché (Goldmann)   97
difference   5–6, 9–11, 130, 170, 183, 187
between human and the divine   64
pure   184, 186
das Ding an sich (thing-in-itself) (Kantian concept)   6, 199–200, 204, 211
dio-logy   145–8, 257 n.267
'*le dire ça fait Dieu*'   30–1
disbelief   13, 26–8, 51, 133
'Discourse to Catholics' (Lacan)   124–7, 130–1

Discours sur les passions de l'amour (Pascal)   68
dissolution of transference   13, 26, 39, 51, 192
divertissement   59–60
divine ignorance   12, 149, 153–4
divine inexistence   3–4
Divine Inexistence (Meillassoux)   2, 4
divine Other   31, 69, 83–4
divinity   3–5, 18–19, 30–1, 119, 205–7, 263 n.365
atheism and   133
Christian   89–90, 135–6
Descartes on   57
Freud addressing   15
Hegel on   34–5
Lacan on   45–6, 50–1, 69–70, 92, 145–6, 159–60, 175–6
Pascal on   63–4, 66–7, 91–2
self-identity and   170
Dostoyevsky, Fyodor   45, 51–2, 139
double negation   112
double personality   16
doubt, hyperbolic   153, 172–5, 177–9
dreams   15, 42, 92–4
drowsy atheism   28, 31
dualism   58, 206

education, non-religious pedagogy and   116, 120–3, 125
ego   127, 174, 196, 269 n.456, 269 n.460
alter-ego   40, 71, 81, 122
Lacan on   27, 54, 60
super-ego   87–9, 93, 104, 122, 196
The Ego and the Id (Freud)   196
'*Ego sum qui sum*'   255 n.235
Einstein, Albert   16–17, 157–8, 172
either/or, 4, 11, 18, 171, 181, 184–6
Elements of the Philosophy of Right (Hegel)   33–4
Empedocles   28–9, 212
Engels, Friedrich   95
the enlightenment   1, 21–2
ennui   59, 66–7
entissimum (super-Being)   175
Eros   128, 248 n.109

The Essence of Christianity
(Feuerbach) 33–4, 97
eternal truth 17–18, 175–6, 179–80, 182, 270 n.464, 271 n.478
ethical agency 90–1
Ethics (Hegel) 205
The Ethics of Psychoanalysis (Lacan) 41, 65–6, 71, 86–7
l'Être suprême (Supreme Being) 24
eudaimonism 89–90
evil 14–16, 53, 179, 186
evil genius (*animus*) 15, 158, 219 n.76
'evil Will' 14–15, 119–20, 129, 249 n.120
evolution 28, 112, 134, 138, 260 n.325
existence of God 82
　Descartes on 30, 96, 175–83
　Freud on 114, 122–3
　Lacan on 50, 139, 149, 166, 175, 179–83
existentialism 67, 80, 213

Fachinelli, Elvio 13
faith 1, 3, 5, 101, 114, 179
　blind 121
　Christian 95–6
　God of 146–8
　irrational 185
　loss of 26, 48, 91, 99
　in science 112
　unconscious 25, 137
faitheism 192–3
fallenness 58, 83, 88, 136
false modesty 205–6
Faust (Goethe) 47
'Fear of Science' (Johnston) 216 n.38
feminine non-phallic enjoyment 142–3, 252 n.228, 262 n.363
Fermat, Pierre 65
fetishization 54, 155–6
Feuerbach, Ludwig 27, 29–31, 33, 200, 207. *See also specific works*
　on atheism 35–6, 41
　Freud and 41–9
　Marx and 41, 97–8
Fichte, J. G. 82, 212–13

filthy truth (*vérité d'immondice*) 134–6, 151
finite 5–6, 93, 205–8, 213–14
Fink, Bruce 76, 255 n.242, 256 n.255
first order 27
first-person 82, 173
First Philosophy of Spirit (Hegel) 34
formalistic reasoning 95–6
France 97, 100–5, 191
Franco-Prussian War 191
Frankfurt, Harry 270 n.464
free association 196–7
free-will 62
French Communist Party (Parti communiste français) (PCF) 103–4, 107
Freud, Sigmund 244 n.15, 245 n.52, 247 n.81, 258 n.306. *See also specific works*
　agnosticism of 111–24, 250 n.148
　atheism and 8, 12, 21–2, 29, 41, 123, 127–8, 149, 247 n.82
　on dissolution of the transference 192
　on the 'Evil Spirit' 14–16
　on existence of God 114, 122–3
　Feuerbachianism of 41–9
　on helplessness 116–21, 123–4, 127–9, 131
　Hilflosigkeit concept by 58, 70, 81
　on human sexuality 55, 124, 126
　irreligiosity of 21–2, 190
　Lacan, J., on 25–6, 28–9, 41–2, 46–7, 57–8, 124–31, 149–50
　on metaphysics 195–6
　on moral masochists 87–9
　on negation 115, 244 n.26
　on the not-One and 118, 123
　on Oedipus complex 41–5, 47, 69–70, 98
　on paternalism 116, 118–19, 128–9
　on psychoanalysis 86, 113, 123, 212
　on religion 21–2, 47–8, 111–31
　on repression 15, 46, 78, 117, 244 n.26, 245 n.36
　on the unconscious 15–16, 57–8, 78, 115, 244 n.23

Urvater concept of 44–8, 52–3, 78
  on USSR 120, 246 n.58
Freudo-Marxism 6
The Future of an Illusion (Freud) 14–15, 21–2, 70, 111–19, 121–3, 125, 127–8, 166

Gallagher, Cormac 61, 63
game theory 57, 65, 86, 88–9
Geist 37
Gellner, Ernest 249 n.121
German idealism 8, 82, 207–8
Geworfenheit ('thrownness') 80–2, 213–14
God 80, 138, 146, 152. *See also* deceiving God; existence of God; self-deceiving God; *specific religions*
  Abrahamic 56, 63–4, 143–7, 255 n.239, 256 n.246, 256 n.255
  of atheists 123–4, 133, 158, 184
  'barred' 7, 11, 19
  Dark 69
  death of 19, 36, 40, 125, 184
  desire of 83–5, 146
  of faith 146–8
  good 172, 177–83, 268 n.447
  good old 174–8
  knowledge of 172, 181–2
  Mosaic 143–8, 256 n.255
  mystical 141–4, 147
  non-deceiving 17, 171–2, 175, 178–9
  Old Testament 64, 69, 98
  of reason 146–8
  salvific 163, 185, 263 n.368
  will of 175–8, 180, 270 n.464, 271 n.474
'God does not believe in God' (Lacanian concept) 37–40, 181–3, 201
God extracted from the machine (*Deus ex machina*) 138, 253 n.194
God hypothesis 3, 30–2, 137–48, 208, 254 n.228, 255 n.233. *See also* the not-One; the One
  of Kant 90–1
oscillation of the 144–5, 160–3, 166–70, 183
paternalism and 45–6
'God is created through being spoken about' 7, 30
'God is dead' (Nietzschean concept) 56, 115, 125, 129, 139, 190–1
  Dostoyevsky augmenting 45, 51–2
  le sujet supposé savoir and 24
'God is unconscious' (Lacanian concept) 4, 12, 37–9, 115, 252 n.189
  atheists and 24, 27, 29–30, 32, 191
  libidinal economy and 52
  Miller on 181
Goethe, Johann Wolfgang von 47
Goldmann, Lucien 97, 99–100
good God 172, 177–83, 268 n.447
good old God 174–8
good will 90
Gould, Stephen Jay 10, 125
grace 82–4
le grand Autre 31, 54, 72, 80, 192. *See also* big Other
Grosz, Elizabeth 70
guilt 86–9, 93–4

Hägglund, Martin 1–3, 5–6
half-God 159–66
half-saying, 136, 138, 141, 161–67, 263 n.367, 263–4 n.368, 264 n.372
Hashem 146, 256 n.255
Haym, Rudolf 34
hedonism 52–3, 59, 61, 67
Hegel, Georg Wilhelm Friedrich 29, 32, 150, 199–201, 204–7. *See also specific works*
  on Absolute Knowing 210–11
  atheism of 33–5
  Lacan, J., and 33–41
  master–slave scenario 66
  on paternalism 44
Heidegger, Martin 80, 204, 213
Hell 67, 82, 86
helplessness 14–15, 58, 70–1, 81–2, 85

Freud on   116–21, 123–4, 127–9, 131
Herrmann, Moritz   10, 255 n.242
The Hidden God (Goldmann)   97, 99
Hilflosigkeit (Freudian concept)   58, 70, 81
Hinduism   263 n.365
historical truth   119, 123, 247 n.82
Hitchens, Christopher   113
Hoens, Dominiek   17, 61, 255 n.242, 266 n.397
d'Holbach, Baron   35
Holy Spirit, Christianity and   36–7, 53, 98, 201
Homo sapiens   134–5, 159, 165, 167, 186
hope   3, 121
horror vacui   62, 67–8
'The Human Animal in Politics, Science, and Psychoanalysis,' KW Institute for Contemporary Art   189
humanism   124, 129, 138
human knowledge   14–15, 182, 220 n.100
human nature   16, 58–60, 70, 98
humility   205–7
hyperbolic doubt   153, 172–5, 177–9
Hyppolite, Jean   126–8

idealism   7, 24, 29
    absolute   207
    German   8, 82, 207–8
    transcendental   36, 199, 204, 212
idolatry   152, 155–6
ignorance   37, 53, 113, 145, 149, 153–4, 209
'I know full well, but nonetheless' (*Je sais bien, mais quand même*)   54, 101, 115
illusions   73, 111–12, 115–16, 118–19, 121, 128
    religious   104, 113, 120, 124–5, 133
    salvation and   135
    science and   123
'*il n'y a pas*' theses   211–14
imaginarization of the real, symbolic   150

immanence   2–6, 39, 108, 216 n.27
    transcendence in   141–2, 160–1, 255 n.233
immortality   3, 19, 119, 210, 212
incarnation   83–4
incest   76, 118
incompleteness   5, 115, 127, 135, 142, 151
    truth of   136–9, 152, 155, 162, 165–6, 169, 173, 179, 184–5, 187
incorreligionnible   26
indifference   5–6, 9–11, 18–19, 159, 170, 185–7, 202–3, 216 n.27, 217n46
indifferent not-Oneness   198, 201–2
infinite finitude   2, 5
infinity, infinite and   63, 86, 92–3, 184, 205–8, 211–13
'In Memory of Ernest Jones' (Lacan, J.)   29
instinct   38–9
    anti-social   116–18, 121
    death   127
in-substances, 154–56, 260n321
intellectual nihilists   247 n.81
Intelligent Design   170, 266 n.417
International Psychoanalytic Association (IPA)   23
intersubjectivity   72–3, 81, 88, 138
'Introduction to the Names-of-the-Father' (Lacan, J.)   126
IPA. *See* International Psychoanalytic Association
irrationality   1, 185, 207
irreligiosity   6, 31, 36, 116, 120, 128–9
    of Freud   21–2, 190
    of Hegel   35
    historical truth and   123
    knowledge and   126
    Lacan and   21–3, 101–10, 126–7, 132, 180, 190
    non-agnostic   200
Islam   258 n.306
'I think, therefore I am' (Cartesian concept)   173, 268 n.438, 268 n.441, 271 n.471
Izcovich, Luis   263 n.267

Jansenism   56–61, 67, 80, 82–3, 85, 88, 95
Jenseits des Lustprinzips (Freud)   89, 91–2
Je sais bien, mais quand même ('I know full well, but nonetheless')   54, 101, 115
Jesus Christ   47, 244 n.15, 260 n.326
  crucifixion of   48–9, 91, 135, 151
  death of   37, 48–9, 53, 134–6
  Lacan, J., on   83–4
Johnston, Adrian   6–14, 18–19, 43, 216 n.38
jouissance   41, 45–6, 52–3, 76–9, 254 n.228, 263 n.364
  of God   146
  renunciation of   65
Joyce, James   147, 257 n.267
Judaism   15, 21–2, 149, 151–4, 160, 206, 257 n.306
Judeo-Christian monotheism   41–2, 50–4, 70, 147–8
Jung, Carl Gustav   15–17

Kant, Immanuel   91, 212–13. *See also specific works*
  Christianity and   89–90
  thing-in-itself concept of   6, 199–200, 204, 211
  transcendental idealism of   36
  on transcendental illusions   31–2
'Kant with Sade' (Lacan, J.)   41
Kesel, Marc De   49, 51
knowability   28
knowledge   123, 135, 147, 171, 267 n.434
  absolute   24–5, 28, 53, 153, 184
  acquired   71, 176
  belief and   125–6
  Descartes on   14, 220 n.100, 270 n.464
  Freud on   212
  of God   172, 181–2
  human   14–15, 182, 220 n.100
  Lacan, J., on   25, 37–9, 169, 248 n.94
  science and   130–1, 154
  truth and   17–18, 175–81

The Knowledge of the Psychoanalyst (Lacan, J.)   28
'known knowns,' 'known unknowns' and   209
Kojève, Alexandre   2, 153
Koyré, Alexandre   153
Krailsheimer, Alban   81
Kristeva, Julia   252 n.189

Lacan, Émile   107
Lacan, Jacques   218 n.71–72, 247 n.92, 248 n.109, 249 n.114, 250 n.154, 263 n.365. *See also specific works*
  agnosticism of   193–4, 250 n.148, 265 n.383
  atheism and   3, 12, 21–8, 52, 56–7, 94, 101–10, 133–4, 190–2, 211, 249 n.120
  on automatons   260 n.335
  on Buddhism   263 n.365
  on Christianity   21–2, 36, 40–1, 53–7, 61–2, 83–4, 98, 134–6, 151–5, 160–1, 252 n.182
  clergy people and   100–10, 251 n.164
  creationism of   265 n.392
  on deceiving God   139, 161, 165, 171–2, 179–80
  on dio-logists   257 n.267
  on divinity   45–6, 50–1, 69–70, 92, 159–60, 175–6
  ethics of   86–94
  on evil   14
  on evolution of laws   260 n.325
  on existence of God   50, 139, 149, 166, 175, 179–83
  on Freud   25–6, 28–9, 41–2, 46–7, 57–8, 124–31, 149–50
  'God does not believe in God' concept by   37–40, 181–3, 201
  'God is unconscious' concept by   4, 12, 24, 27, 29–30, 38–9, 52, 115, 181, 191, 252 n.189
  Hoens on   255 n.242
  irreligiosity and   21–3, 101–10, 126–7, 132, 180, 190
  on Islam   258 n.306
  on Jesus Christ   83–4

on knowledge   25, 37–9, 169, 248 n.94
on language   137, 164–70, 200–1
on libidinal economy   124–5
Marxism of   41–9
on materialism   29, 73, 154–5
on metaphysics   143, 180
on monotheism   48, 53, 160
on mystics   255 n.233
on the not-One   137–48, 151, 156, 159–65, 167–70, 179–81, 183–7
on Oedipus complex   41–5, 52, 69–79, 81–3, 97
on the One   137–48, 151, 159–62, 166–70, 179–81, 183–7, 252 n.192
on paranoia   219 n.75
on polytheism   160, 262 n.361
on possibility of a 'barred' God   7
on psychoanalysis   13, 23–4, 55, 61, 82–3, 129–33, 194–6, 249 n.121, 250 n.140, 260 n.339, 261 n.343, 267 n.428
on psychosis   258 n.294, 260 n.339
on religion   13, 21–3, 26–30, 40–1, 101–10
on science   28–9, 126–31, 153–9, 161, 176, 250 n.142, 261 n.343, 261 n.359, 267 n.419
on sexual relationships   264 n.371
sinthome concept of   13, 26–7, 54–7, 100
on subjectivity   50, 53, 78, 142
on transcendence   83, 107–8, 130–2, 160–1, 166, 180
on true religion   252 n.177
on truth   42, 264 n.374, 264 n.378
on the truth of incompleteness   263 n.368
on the unconscious   27, 32, 37–9, 54, 59–60, 115, 139, 181
Lacan, Marc François   21, 100–10, 251 n.164
Lacan et le christianisme (Causse)   22
Lacoue-Labarthe, Philippe   257 n.267
language   6, 266 n.412, 267 n.419, 267 n.434

Lacan, J., on   137, 164–70, 200–1
meta-language   115, 123–4, 128–9, 136–8, 161, 210–12, 214
Laplanche, Jean   181
law of contradiction   18, 270 n.464
Leclaire, Serge   181
Lectures on the History of Philosophy (Hegel)   204–6
Lectures on the Philosophy of Religion (Hegel)   35
Less Than Nothing (Žižek)   210–11
Leupin, Alexandre   252 n.192
Lévi-Strauss, Claude   45, 76
liberal politics   187
libido, libidinal economy and   56, 73, 84, 118, 120–2, 124–5
Oedipus complex and   76–9
Pascalian Christianity on   69
of the unconscious   52
living death   82
Livingston, Paul   18, 217 n.38
living substances   209–10
logos   30, 107, 121, 123–4, 135, 149
Christian   137, 151–2, 252 n.176
lordship, bondage and   66, 94
love   81, 128, 149–50, 160
maternal   71, 73–4, 78
Pascal on   68
paternal   43, 47
Luciferianism   220 n.103
Lucretius   149

madness   60–1
magic   262 n.361
malicious demon   268 n.448
Mannoni, Octave   54, 115
Marini, Marcelle   105
marriage   101–2, 106–7
Martino, Ernesto de   262 n.361
Marx, Karl   29, 31, 33, 191–2, 198, 200. *See also specific works*
on birth   80
on communism   95
on Feuerbach   41, 97–8
Marxism   8, 41–9, 97, 100, 246 n.58
masochism   87–9, 93
master–slave scenario   44, 66, 94
materialism   7, 10, 16, 35, 99, 126–8, 134

Lacan on   29, 73, 154–5
  signifiers and   23
  transcendental   6, 8–9, 11, 203
maternalism, Mother-the-Thing
    and   69–72, 77, 81–3, 92
  desire and   73–6, 78–9, 84–5, 98
mathematics   62, 86, 108, 154–7,
    167–71, 175–8
  probabilities and   5, 57, 65, 85,
    88–9, 91, 94–7
matter–form–substance triad   209
May 1968 (France)   97
meaninglessness   119, 121, 129, 131,
    144, 168–71
medieval era   16
Meillassoux, Quentin   2–5, 11, 18,
    220 n.103
mental illness   190, 218 n.72
mental objects   71–2
'*La méprise du sujet supposé savoir*'
    (Lacan, J.)   146–7
messianic atheism   13, 56
meta-critical realism   4, 6–7, 19, 165–
    67, 170–71, 174–75, 181–82,
    184, 186, 211
meta-language   115, 123–4, 128–9,
    136–8, 161, 210–12, 214
metaphysics   9, 28, 212, 249 n.119,
    250 n.148, 263 n.365
  agnostic   199
  Freud on   195–6
  Lacan on   143, 180
  mathematics and   62
  monotheism and   197
  of Pascal   63
  self-deceiving God and   5
  of Spinoza   205
  of Thom   167–8
metapsychology   5–6, 23, 47, 58,
    108, 195–6
Miller, Jacques-Alain   41–2, 44, 48,
    147, 169, 191, 271 n.478
Milner, Jean-Claude   156
mirror stage   73
'*Mis en question du psychanalyste*'
    (Lacan)   83, 99
misère (wretchedness)   81, 85, 94
misery   93, 205
mode of production, capitalist   95, 97

modernity   19, 57, 63
  capitalist   99
  Freud on   125
  Lacan on   44
  science and   16–17, 28, 61, 68,
    95, 138
modesty   203–5, 210–11
moi-Gestalt   73–4
monogamy   106, 196
monotheism   33, 98, 206, 252 n.192,
    257 n.271, 263 n.265
  dio-logy and   147–8
  divinity and   119
  Hegel on   34
  Judeo-Christian   41–2, 50–4, 70,
    147–8
  De Kesel on   49
  Lacan on   48, 53, 160
  metaphysics and   197
  mysticism and   253 n.219
  paternalism and   47
  polytheism and   148–53
morality   52, 71, 87–9, 114, 124–5,
    139, 196
mortality   5, 14–15, 119, 209–10,
    213–14
Mosaic God   143–8, 256 n.255
Moses and Monotheism (Freud)   22,
    149, 247 n.82
mystical women   255 n.233,
    256 n.246, 262 n.363
mysticism   253 n.219, 254 n.228,
    255 n.233, 257 n.267,
    261 n.351, 262 n.363,
    263 n.364
  mystical God   141–4, 147
  polytheism and   161

Name-of-the-Father (*le Nom-du-
    Père*)   21, 26, 56, 64, 83, 144
  God as   50–2
  paternalism and   74–6, 78–9, 107
'The Names of the Father' (Lacan, J.)
    64, 83, 143–4, 146–7
Nancy, Jean-Luc   257 n.267
narcissism   60, 70, 73, 96, 120
naturalism   28, 39, 190, 193
  atheist   13, 28
nature   62–3, 124, 127, 245 n.52

helplessness of humankind before 116–17
human 16, 58–60, 70, 98
humanization of 14–15, 119
non-human 9–11, 68, 202–3, 208
weak 11, 201–3, 208
Nature 39, 193
Nebenmensch als Ding (neighbor as Thing) 40, 69, 71–3, 92, 98
need-demand-desire (*besoin-demande-désir*) triad 58–9
negation 80, 151, 200, 205, 212–13, 270 n.464
determinate and absolute 49–56
double 112
Freud on 115, 244 n.26
neighbor as Thing (*Nebenmensch als Ding*) 40, 69, 71–3, 92, 98
neuroscience 7, 59
neuroses 24, 26, 46–7, 55, 62–3, 86, 93–4
obsessional 25, 117
neurotic pathos 79–86
new religion 35–6, 120–1, 126, 151
new signifiers 14, 56, 218 n.72
Nietzsche, Friedrich 19
'God is dead' concept by 24, 45, 51–2, 56, 115, 125, 129, 139, 190–1
NOMA. *See* non-overlapping magisteria
le Nom-du-Père. *See* Name-of-the-Father
non-absoluteness 206–8
non-agnostic atheism 12, 212, 214
non-being 209
non-Christian Gods 80
non-deceiving God 17, 171–2, 175, 178–9
non-dupes err ('*les non-dupes errent*') 60–1
'*les non-dupes errent*' (the non-dupes err) 60–1
non-existence 92, 102, 210
non-human nature 9–11, 68, 202–3, 208
non-living matter 190
non-overlapping magisteria (NOMA) 125

non-religious education 116, 120–3, 125
nothingness 167, 205, 209–10
'*no-things*' (achoses) 153–7
the not-One 207–8, 250 n.148, 254 n.228, 270 n.321, 272 n.491
Freud and 118, 123
indifference and 19
Johnston and 8–9, 18
Lacan on 137–48, 151, 156, 159–65, 167–70, 179–81, 183–7
strong atheism and 17
transcendence and 11
The Not-Two (Chiesa) 8–9, 189–90
no-two-as-One 130, 138–9, 142, 161–2, 165–70, 184, 263 n.368

objectivity 200, 212
objects-as-appearances, phenomenal 204, 211
obsession 25–6, 55, 117
'Obsessive Actions and Religious Practices' (Freud) 21–2, 25, 116, 119
Oedipus complex 41–5, 47, 52, 69–79, 81–2, 97–8
Oedipus Rex (Sophocles) 78
Old Testament God 64, 69, 98
omnipotence 25, 48–9, 63, 70
omniscience 25, 37, 39, 48, 80, 87, 211
the One 197, 207–8, 252 n.192, 254 n.224, 255 n.233, 260 n.321, 262 n.363
Freud promoting 128
Lacan on 137–48, 151, 159–62, 166–70, 179–81, 183–7
transcendental materialism and 11
weak agnosticism and 17
One-all-alone 151, 258 n.306
One-All-Being 147, 152–3, 160–1, 263 n.365
One Being 143–6, 171, 255 n.233, 255 n.238, 256 n.246
One (not-One), 11, 13, 17, 127–9, 131–32, 136, 160–61, 166, 170–71, 184–87

One = not-One, 4–5, 11, 17, 166, 181–83, 185–86
One/not-One oscillation 144–5, 160–3, 166–70, 183
One of existence 144
'On the Psychology of the Trickster Figure' (Jung) 15–16
ontology 9–11, 19, 196, 203, 265 n.386
 para-ontology 6, 193–5, 197–9, 202, 204, 207–8, 211–13, 217 n.46
onto-theologies 197–8, 212
optical illusions 32
optimism 12–13, 121–2, 127
ordinary suffering 79–86, 89, 94
Orthodoxy (Chesterton) 49
the Other 67, 69, 71, 140–1, 177, 211–12, 218 n.71. *See also* big Other; not-One
 barred 27–8, 54–5
 the desire of the 75, 82–4, 93–4, 255
 polytheism and 150
 Real 40, 72–3, 76, 79, 81–5, 92
 unbarred 13–14, 25, 53, 56
Otherness 31, 40, 64, 71–2, 76, 81
ousia 155–6, 158, 260 n.326

paganism 18, 52, 148–51, 154
panpsychism 203
pan-theistic bi-theism 152
paranoia 14, 219 n.75, 268 n.437
para-ontology 6, 195, 199, 208, 211–13, 217 n.46, 260 n.326
 agnosticism of 193–4, 197, 202, 204, 207
para-ousia 155
Paris Commune (1871) 191–2
parlêtres (speaking beings) 27, 31, 137, 183, 200–1, 208
Parmenides 212
Pascal, Blaise 18, 56, 59–60, 70–8, 81–2, 211, 213–14. *See also* specific works
 Christian capitalism and 94–100
 Christianity and 57–8, 61, 65–6, 68–9, 79–80, 83–4, 88
 on Descartes 30

 on divinity 63–4, 66–7, 91–2
 ethics of 86–94
 mathematics and 85–6
 on rationality 57–8, 61–4, 96
Pas très catholique, Lacan? (Sous) 22
paternalism 1, 15, 48–55, 83, 85, 107, 201–2
 death and 45–7, 52, 78, 125, 128–9
 Freud on 116, 118–19, 128–9
 Lacan on 149–50
 Oedipus complex and 41–5, 47, 52, 69–79, 81–2, 97–8
Paul (Saint) 22
PCF. *See* French Communist Party
pedagogy, non-religious 116, 120–3
penance 117
Pensées (Pascal) 57–63, 80–1, 88–90, 92, 95–6
 on fear of the vacuum 68
 gambling and 65
 Lacan, J., on 85
père-version 54–6
perfect Being 139–41
persistence 31, 190–1
personalization of God 152
perversion 52–5, 100, 115
pessimism 49, 55, 98, 121
Pfister, Oskar 113, 129, 244 n.15
phallus 74–5, 142–3, 262 n.363
phenomeno-logical 130, 141–4, 147, 165–7, 172–7, 179, 181–5
phenomenology 5–6, 113, 142, 160–1
Phenomenology of Spirit (Hegel) 44, 66
Philosophy of Spirit (Hegel) 34
physics 68, 157, 175
Pius XII (Pope) 102–3, 107
pleasure principle 89–91
plenism 67–8
polytheism 257 n.271, 258 n.294, 262 n.363, 263 n.365
 Lacan, J., on 160, 262 n.361
 monotheism and 148–53
Popow, Nikolai 217 n.46
positivism 104
posthuman 159
practical atheism 17, 166

'Preliminary Theses on the Reform of Philosophy' (Feuerbach)   25
'Presentation on Psychical Causality' (Lacan, J.)   60
probabilities   5, 57, 65, 85, 88–9, 91, 94–7
Project for a Scientific Psychology (Freud)   71–2
Prolegomena to Any Future Materialism (Johnston)   200
Proslogion (Anselm of Canterbury)   96
Protestantism   33–5, 129
psychoanalysis. *See specific topics*
psychopathology   192
The Psychopathology of Everyday Life (Freud)   195
psychosis   60, 77, 258 n.294
punishment   66–7, 88, 90–1, 117
pure difference   184, 186
pure reason   31–2, 204
Puy de Dôme experiments   67–8
Pyrrhic victories   78–9, 93
'The Question of a Weltanschauung' (Freud)   8, 15

Rabelais, François   67
Racine, Jean-Baptiste   97
Radical Atheism (Hägglund)   2
Radin, Paul   16
rationalist-humanism   127, 129, 131
rationalization   148–9, 151, 153
real   137, 141–5, 148–53
　abstractions   33
　God   144
　in-itself-for-itself   170–1
　real   131–2
realism   6–7, 10, 211
real-of-the-symbolic   144–5, 148–54, 255 n.239
Real Other, Real Otherness and   40, 72–3, 76, 79, 81–5, 92
reason, rationality and   42, 112, 121–4, 126, 205–7
　God of   146–8
　human   30, 32, 62, 96, 270 n.464
　Mosaic God and   149
　Pascal and   57–8, 61–4, 96
Récanati, François   152
reconversion   31, 95–6

redemption   53
Regnault, François   48
reintegration, religious   262 n.361
'The Relationship of Religion to the State' (Hegel)   34
religion, religiosity and   1–3, 66, 197–8, 213. *See also specific religions*
　Adorno on   12
　afterlives and   209
　belief and   126
　civilization and   14, 113, 115–19, 121–2, 124, 128
　Descartes on   14, 17
　'Evil Spirits' and   14–15
　Freud and   21–2, 47–8, 111–31
　Hegel and   33–5
　illusions and   104, 113, 120, 124–5, 133
　invincibility of   26, 29, 129–31
　Lacan, J., on   13, 21–3, 26–30, 40–1, 101–10
　new   35–6, 120–1, 126, 151
　against religion   126–9
　sacrificial practices and   64
　science and   120–1, 130–2, 157, 246 n.59, 261 n.343, 261 n.351
　true   35, 40, 132–5, 252 n.177
　truth and   22–3, 114–15, 122–3
'*Des religions et du réel*' (Lacan, J.)   111, 157–8, 166
renunciation   65, 88, 116, 121, 245 n.36
repression   53, 59–60, 79, 87–8, 98, 115, 174–5
　of the deceiving God   16–17, 179
　Freud on   15, 46, 78, 117, 244 n.26, 245 n.36
resurrection   3–5, 52, 135–6, 151–2, 179–80
risk, risk management and   65–79, 85, 88–9
Roazen, Paul   103
Roudinesco, Élisabeth   100–5, 107
Rovelli, Carlo   157
Ruda, Frank   8, 12

sacredness   106
sacrificial practices   64–5, 84–5, 92–3, 122

sadomasochism 55
Safouan, Moustapha 76
salvation 82–3, 135
salvific God 163, 185, 263 n.368
Sartre, Jean-Paul 80
Satan 129
Schelling, F. W. J. 207
schlechte Unendlichkeit (bad infinity) 212–13
science 7–8, 112–13, 122–4, 179, 261 n.341
   atheism and 138, 193
   capitalism and 187
   Christian 153–7
   illusions and 123
   knowledge and 130–1, 154
   Lacan, J., on 28–9, 126–31, 153–9, 161, 176, 250 n.142, 261 n.343, 261 n.359, 267 n.419
   mathematics and 57, 62, 65, 85–6, 95–6, 108, 154–7
   modernity and 16–17, 28, 61, 68, 95, 138
   religion and 120–1, 130–2, 157, 246 n.59, 261 n.343, 261 n.351
   technology and 155–6, 159, 187
   theism of 28–9
'Science and Truth' (Lacan, J.) 23, 69–70
second birth 82
second death 81
second-order 27
secular humanism 35, 36
secularism 1, 5, 19, 22, 99, 249 n.121
   big Other and 192
   of Christian abjection 161
   Hegel and 34–5
   mathematics and 96
self-consciousnesses 38, 54, 163, 173
self-deceiving God 4–7, 14, 179–87, 198, 201–2, 216 n.27, 220 n.100
   atheism and 208
   trickster figure and 16
   truth and 17
self-denaturalization 9–10, 203

self-destruction 100, 118, 125, 187
selfhood 27, 60
self-relativization 210–11
self-renunciation 88
Seminar II (Lacan, J.) 62, 127, 139, 172
Seminar III (Lacan, J.) 39–40, 60, 63
Seminar IV (Lacan, J.) 36
Seminar VII (Lacan, J.) 22, 27–8, 36, 40, 149, 172
Seminar IX (Lacan, J.) 62, 139, 140, 172
Seminar X (Lacan, J.) 62, 64, 67, 69, 133, 183
   on beliefs of atheists 24
   on perversion 52–3
Seminar XI (Lacan, J.) 29–30, 52, 63–4, 69, 194
Seminar XII (Lacan, J.) 41, 71, 86–9, 126, 137, 179
   on the Cartesian God 176
   on Pascal 65–6
Seminar XIII (Lacan, J.) 69–70, 97, 179
Seminar XIV (Lacan, J.) 139–41
Seminar XV (Lacan, J.) 36–7, 183
Seminar XVI (Lacan, J.) 61, 70, 93, 97
   on belief in Supreme Beings 24
   on Pascal 83, 85
   perversion linked to monotheism in 53
Seminar XVII (Lacan, J.) 24, 29, 43–7, 52, 73–4, 154, 157
   on atheism 133
   on ignorant Gods 145
   Miller on 42
   on monotheism 147
Seminar XIX (Lacan, J.) 126, 166, 171–2, 195
Seminar XX (Lacan, J.) 30–1, 45, 137, 140–4, 152–3
   on atheism 91
   on Christianity 40–1, 134
   on pagan gods 150
   on the symbolic 146
Seminar XXI (Lacan, J.) 37–8, 53, 60–1, 179, 181
Seminar XXII (Lacan, J.) 54–5, 161
Seminar XXIII (Lacan, J.) 55

Seminar XXIV (Lacan, J.) 56
Seminar XXV (Lacan, J.) 143
sensus 154–5
'A Seventeenth-Century Demonological Neurosis' (Freud) 15
sexuality 55, 104, 112, 124, 126–7, 131–2, 156, 184, 258 n.306
sexual relationships 130, 134, 150, 264 n.371
  absence of 10, 132, 135, 151–2, 159–60
Shepherdson, Charles 75
signifiers, signification and 13, 19, 27–8, 53, 140, 166
  master 51
  materiality of the 23
  mathematical 168–9
  new 14, 56, 218 n.72
  of the phallus 75
  unconscious and 181
sin 82–3, 88, 103
sinthome (Lacanian concept) 13, 26–7, 54–7, 100
socialism 117, 191
social psychosis 60
socio-linguistics 201, 208
Sophocles 78
soul 82
Sous, Jean-Louis 22–3, 26
Soviet Union (USSR) 120, 246 n.58
speaking beings (*parlêtres*) 27, 31, 137, 183, 200–1, 208
spheres 63, 152
Spinoza, Baruch 21, 80, 107, 207
  Deus sive natura concept of 18, 205–6
'The Spirit of Christianity and Its Fate' (Hegel) 34
strong agnosticism 11–12, 17, 132, 137, 166–8, 183–4, 186
strong atheism 17, 159–83, 186
structural helplessness 120, 128
structural indifference 202–3
structuralism 45
subjectivity 26, 31, 91, 200, 204, 207, 212
  denaturalized 9
  intersubjectivity 72–3, 81, 88, 138
  Lacan on 50, 53, 78, 142

Subjectivity and Otherness (Chiesa) 189
the subject supposed to know (*le sujet supposé savoir*) 24–8, 32, 36–9, 180, 192–3, 202
  faith in 147
  theology of science and 157
  transference and 51
sublation (*Aufhebung*) 36, 50, 109, 120
'The Subversion of the Subject and the Dialectic of Desire in the Freudian Unconscious' (Lacan, J.) 22, 30, 42
suffering 58–9, 67, 100, 124
  ordinary 79–86, 89, 94
le sujet supposé savoir (the subject supposed to know). See the subject supposed to know
super-Being (*entissimum*) 175
super-ego 87–9, 93, 104, 122, 196
supernaturalism 34, 36
super-Truth (*verissimum*) 175
suppression 52, 116–17, 122, 245 n.36
Supreme Being (*l'Être suprême*) 24
the symbolic 10, 31–2, 45–6, 72, 151
symbolic imaginarization of the real 150
symbolic order 37, 45–6, 60, 70, 72–3, 127
Symbolic Otherness 81, 85, 93
System (Hegel) 205–6
System of Ethical Life (Hegel) 34

Taoism 263 n.365
Tazi, Nadia 258 n.306
technology 155–6, 159, 187
teleology 28
telos 50–1
temptation 119
Thanatos 248 n.109
theism 1–2, 7, 13, 24–31, 35, 39, 47. See also religion, religiosity and
theodicy 28, 255 n.239
theogony 150
theology 1–2, 24, 28–31, 35–6, 41, 97–8. See also religion, religiosity and
  Christian 135–6, 143
  of science 157

theoretical agnosticism   114
'A Theoretical Introduction to the Functions of Psychoanalysis in Criminology' (Lacan)   52
theós   30, 51
'Theses on Feuerbach' (Marx)   97
thing-in-itself (*das Ding an sich*) (Kantian concept)   6, 199–200, 204, 211
Thom, René   167–71, 267 n.419
thoughtlessness   28, 31
Three Essays on the Theory of Sexuality (Freud)   55
'thrownness' (*Geworfenheit*)   80–2, 213–14
topology   108
Torricelli, Evangelista   68
Toscano, Alberto   40
total knowledge   25
Totem and Taboo (Freud)   14, 21–2, 43–8, 78, 118, 125, 128
Tout-Puissant (the Almighty)   25–6, 146
tragedy   56
transcendence   2–6, 14, 129, 206, 216 n.27, 254 n.228
  Freud on   115
  of God-the-Father   48, 53, 91
  Lacan, J., on   83, 107–8, 130–2, 160–1, 166, 180
  not-oneness and   11
  unknowable   57
transcendence-in-immanence   141–2, 160–1, 255 n.233
transcendental idealism   36, 199, 204, 212
transcendental illusions   31–3, 208
transcendental materialism   6, 8–9, 11, 203
transference   24–5, 27, 71–3
  dissolution of   13, 26, 39, 51, 192
translations, English   83, 249 n.114, 271 n.475
trickster figure   15–17
'The Triumph of Religion' (Lacan, J.)   13, 23, 25–6, 28–9, 40, 129, 131–4, 157
'True' atheism   13, 24–6, 28–30, 91
true religion   35, 40, 132–5, 252 n.177

truth   13, 199, 211–12, 220 n.100, 247 n.81
  of Christianity   35–6, 40–1, 134
  divine   176–7
  eternal   17–18, 175–6, 179–80, 182, 270 n.464, 271 n.478
  filthy   134–6, 151
  historical   119, 123, 247 n.82
  illusions and   112
  of incompleteness   136–9, 152, 155, 162, 165–6, 169, 173, 179, 184–5, 187, 263 n.368
  knowledge and   17–18, 175–81
  Lacan, J., on   42, 264 n.374, 264 n.378
  religious   22–3, 114–15, 122–3
  about truth   137–8, 141, 165, 175, 184, 187
  ultimate   22, 123, 161, 171, 177, 198
  unconscious   39
truth without knowledge of itself   181, 220 n.100
two-as-One   138–9, 145, 152, 160–2, 165, 184, 262 n.363
two God   152

ultimate truth   22, 123, 161, 171, 177, 198
ultra-transcendental   2, 6
unbarred big Other   24, 27–8, 39, 56
unbarred Other   13–14, 25, 27–8, 53, 56
uncertainty   74, 209
the unconscious   163, 196–7, 209, 218 n.72, 264 n.375
  agnostic   210
  faith and   25, 137
  Freud on   15–16, 57–8, 78, 115, 244 n.23
  Lacan on   27, 32, 37–9, 54, 59–60, 115, 139, 181
  super-ego and   87
the undead   19, 190–1
undecidability   114, 122–3
understanding   71, 205
Unglaubensgenossen (comrades in unbelief)   122–4
universality   33

University of New Mexico   189
unknowability   45, 50, 57, 63–4, 71–2, 199–200
'unknown unknowns,' 'unknown knowns' and   209–10
unthinkability   171–2, 180
untruth   51–2
Ur-Grund   207–8
Urvater (Freudian concept)   44–8, 52–3, 78
USSR. *See* Soviet Union

vacuum (*le vide*)   62, 67–8
vanity   60
Vasse, Denis   103
the Vatican   21, 102–4, 106–7
Verhaeghe, Paul   76
verissimum (super-Truth)   175
vérité d'immondice (filthy truth)   134–6, 151
le vide (vacuum)   62, 67–8
viruses   10, 159, 190

Waelhens, Alphonse De   71
weak agnosticism   12, 17, 125, 127, 166–7, 184, 250 n.148
weak atheism   4, 123, 125, 136, 140, 164–7, 183–4
　dio-logy and   148
　of Freud   12, 132
　Lacan, J., on   137–8
　oscillation of the God hypothesis and   161
　of science   179–80
　strong agnosticism countering   17
Weltanschauung   8, 17, 27–33, 156, 246 n.59, 250 n.142
　negative   157–9, 175, 179–80, 247 n.81
　scientific   12–13, 21–2, 158
W-hole   153
Wilde, Oscar   56
Wilhelm III, Friedrich (King)   34
will to truth   175–8, 180, 270 n.464, 271 n.474
Winnebago mythology   16
wish-fulfillment   121–2, 126, 246 n.59
Wissenschaftslehre (Fichte)   212
women, mystical   255 n.233, 256 n.246, 262 n.363
the Word   134–5, 149, 151–2
world-in-itself-for-us, world-in-itself-for-itself and   12, 250 n.148
World War II   102
wretchedness (*misère*)   81, 85, 94

Yahweh   145, 149, 256 n.255
'The Youth of Gide, or the Letter and Desire' (Lacan, J.)   24

zero   183–4, 210, 254 n.224
Žižek, Slavoj   6, 11, 29, 48–9, 71–2, 94, 210–11
　on Oedipus complex   77
　on science   157
zombies   19, 190